THE

Conscious Mind

PHILOSOPHY OF MIND SERIES

Series Editor: Owen Flanagan, Duke University

SELF EXPRESSIONS
Mind, Morals, and the Meaning of Life
Owen Flanagan

DECONSTRUCTING THE MIND
Stephen P. Stich

THE CONSCIOUS MIND
In Search of a Fundamental Theory
David J. Chalmers

THE

Conscious
Mind

IN SEARCH OF
A FUNDAMENTAL THEORY

David J. Chalmers

OXFORD UNIVERSITY PRESS
New York   Oxford

Oxford University Press

Oxford   New York
Athens   Auckland   Bangkok   Bogotá
Bombay   Buenos Aires   Calcutta   Cape Town
Dar es Salaam   Delhi   Florence   Hong Kong   Istanbul
Karachi   Kuala Lumpur   Madras   Madrid   Melbourne
Mexico City   Nairobi   Paris   Singapore
Taipei   Tokyo   Toronto   Warsaw

and associated companies in
Berlin   Ibadan

Copyright © 1996 by David J. Chalmers

First published by Oxford University Press, Inc., 1996
First issued as an Oxford University Press paperback, 1997

Oxford is a registered trademark of Oxford University Press

Library of Congress Cataloging-in-Publication Data
Chalmers, David John
The conscious mind : in search of a fundamental theory
p. cm. (Philosophy of mind series)
Includes bibliographical references and index.
ISBN 0-19-510553-2
ISBN 0-19-511789-1 (Pbk.)
1. Philosophy of mind.   2. Consciousness.   3. Mind and body.
4. Dualism.   I. Title.   II. Series.
BD418.3.C43   1996
128'.2—dc20   95-36036

1 3 5 7 9 10 8 6 4 2
Printed in the United States of America
on acid-free paper.

Acknowledgments

I first became excited by consciousness and the mind–body problem as an undergraduate studying mathematics at the University of Adelaide. Conversations with a number of people, especially Paul Barter, Jon Baxter, Ben Hambly, and Paul McCann, helped form my ideas. Even then, the subject seemed about as fascinating a problem as there could be. It seemed faintly unreasonable that somebody could be occupied full-time thinking about something that was so much fun.

Later, as a graduate student at Oxford, I found that the mind was always occupying my thoughts where mathematics should have been, and I decided to switch fields and eventually to switch continents. Many people were patient and supportive during this difficult time, especially Michael Atiyah, Michael Dummett, and Robin Fletcher. Thanks also to all those who were subjected to hearing about whatever my latest theory of consciousness happened to be; the ideas in this book are a distant descendant.

My decision to move to Indiana University to gain a grounding in philosophy, cognitive science, and artificial intelligence was one of the best that I have made. I owe special thanks to Doug Hofstadter; it was his writing that first introduced me to the mysteries of the mind when I was young, and it was the stimulating and comfortable environment of his research lab, the Center for Research on Concepts and Cognition, that allowed these ideas to develop. Although he disagrees with many of the ideas in this book, I would like to think that at some level what I have written remains true to the intellectual spirit of his work.

I wrote the first version of this work (then known as *Toward a Theory of Consciousness*) in a heady six-month period in 1992 and 1993. I had useful discussions with a number of people at Indiana around this time: everybody at CRCC, especially Bob French and Liane Gabora, and many in other departments, including Mike Dunn, Rob Goldstone, Anil Gupta, Jim Hettmer, Jerry Seligman, and Tim van Gelder. Thanks also to members of the consciousness discussion group in the back room at Nick's for many enjoyable Monday afternoon conversations.

A two-year McDonnell fellowship in philosophy, neuroscience, and psychology at Washington University has provided another stimulating environment, as well as a chance to experience Zeno's paradox in finishing this book. I am grateful to the James S. McDonnell Foundation for their support, to all the participants in my graduate seminar on consciousness for discussions that helped to refine the book, and to a number of people for conversation and comments, including Morten Christiansen, Andy Clark, Jason Clevenger, Peggy DesAutels, Pepa Toribio, and Tad Zawidzki.

In the last couple of years, I have had an enormous amount of helpful conversation and correspondence about the material in this book. Among many others, thanks are due to Jon Baxter, Ned Block, Alex Byrne, Francis Crick, Dan Dennett, Eric Dietrich, Avi Elitzur, Matthew Elton, Owen Flanagan, Stan Franklin, Liane Gabora, Güven Güzeldere, Chris Hill, Terry Horgan, Steve Horst, Frank Jackson, Jaegwon Kim, Christof Koch, Martin Leckey, Dave Leising, Kerry Levenberg, Joe Levine, David Lewis, Barry Loewer, Bill Lycan, Paul McCann, Daryl McCullough, Brian McLaughlin, Thomas Metzinger, Robert Miller, Andrew Milne, John O'Leary-Hawthorne, Joseph O'Rourke, Calvin Ostrum, Rhett Savage, Aaron Sloman, Leopold Stubenberg, and Red Watson. I am grateful to too many others to mention for interesting conversations about consciousness in general. A special note of thanks to Norton Nelkin, who returned his copy of the manuscript covered with many helpful comments not long before he died of lymphoma. He will be missed.

My broader philosophical debts are many. I developed my initial views on consciousness largely on my own, but these have been greatly enriched by my reading on the subject. One discovers quickly that any given idea has likely been expressed already by someone else. Among recent thinkers, Thomas Nagel, Frank Jackson, and Joseph Levine have done much to emphasize the perplexities of consciousness; their work covers much of the same territory as my early chapters. My work also overlaps with work by Ned Block, Robert Kirk, and Michael Lockwood at a number of points. The metaphysical framework that I develop in Chapter 2 owes much to the work of Terry Horgan, Saul Kripke, and David Lewis, among others, and Frank Jackson has independently developed a similar framework, presented in his marvelous 1995 John Locke lectures. The ideas of Daniel Dennett, Colin McGinn, John Searle, and Sydney Shoemaker have provided stimulating challenges throughout.

My greatest debts are to Gregg Rosenberg, for memorable conversations and valuable feedback; to Lisa Thomas, for a book on zombies and moral support; to Sharon Wahl, for expert editing and warm friendship; and above all, to all three of my parents, for their support and encouragement. And thanks to all my qualia, and to the environment responsible for producing them, for constant inspiration.

As I was finishing this book, I received a fortune cookie in a restaurant, saying "Your life will be full of delightful mysteries." So far it has been, and I am very grateful.

Contents

Introduction

Taking Consciousness Seriously

Consciousness is the biggest mystery. It may be the largest outstanding obstacle in our quest for a scientific understanding of the universe. The science of physics is not yet complete, but it is well understood; the science of biology has removed many ancient mysteries surrounding the nature of life. There are gaps in our understanding of these fields, but they do not seem intractable. We have a sense of what a solution to these problems might look like; we just need to get the details right.

Even in the science of the mind, much progress has been made. Recent work in cognitive science and neuroscience is leading us to a better understanding of human behavior and of the processes that drive it. We do not have many detailed theories of cognition, to be sure, but the details cannot be too far off.

Consciousness, however, is as perplexing as it ever was. It still seems utterly mysterious that the causation of behavior should be accompanied by a subjective inner life. We have good reason to believe that consciousness arises from physical systems such as brains, but we have little idea how it arises, or why it exists at all. How could a physical system such as a brain also be an *experiencer*? Why should there be *something it is like* to be such a system? Present-day scientific theories hardly touch the really difficult questions about consciousness. We do not just lack a detailed theory; we are entirely in the dark about how consicousness fits into the natural order.

Many books and articles on consciousness have appeared in the past few years, and one might think that we are making progress. But on a closer look, most of this work leaves the hardest problems about consciousness untouched. Often, such work addresses what might be called the "easy" problems of consciousness: How does the brain process environmental stimulation? How does it integrate information? How do we produce reports on internal states? These are important questions, but to answer them is not to solve the hard problem: Why is all this processing accompanied by an experienced inner life? Sometimes this question is ignored entirely; sometimes it is put off until another day; and sometimes it is simply declared answered. But in each case, one is left with the feeling that the central problem remains as puzzling as ever.

This puzzlement is not a cause for despair; rather, it makes the problem of consciousness one of the most exciting intellectual challenges of our time. Because consciousness is both so fundamental and so ill understood, a solution to the problem may profoundly affect our conception of the universe and of ourselves.

I am an optimist about consciousness: I think that we will eventually have a theory of it, and in this book I look for one. But consciousness is not just business as usual; if we are to make progress, the first thing we must do is face up to the things that make the problem so difficult. Then we can move forward toward a theory, without blinkers and with a good idea of the task at hand.

In this book, I do not solve the problem of consciousness once and for all, but I try to rein it in. I try to get clear about what the problems are, I argue that the standard methods of neuroscience and cognitive science do not work in addressing them, and then I try to move forward.

In developing my account of consciousness, I have tried to obey a number of constraints. The first and most important is to *take consciousness seriously*. The easiest way to develop a "theory" of consciousness is to deny its existence, or to redefine the phenomenon in need of explanation as something it is not. This usually leads to an elegant theory, but the problem does not go away. Throughout this book, I have assumed that consciousness exists, and that to redefine the problem as that of explaining how certain cognitive or behavioral functions are performed is unacceptable. This is what I mean by taking consciousness seriously.

Some say that consciousness is an "illusion," but I have little idea what this could even mean. It seems to me that we are surer of the existence of conscious experience than we are of anything else in the world. I have tried hard at times to convince myself that there is really nothing there, that conscious experience is empty, an illusion. There is something seductive about this notion, which philosophers throughout the ages have exploited, but in the end it is utterly unsatisfying. I find myself absorbed in an orange sensation, and *something is going on*. There is something that needs explaining, even after we have explained the processes of discrimination and action: there is the *experience*.

True, I cannot *prove* that there is a further problem, precisely because I cannot prove that consciousness exists. We know about consciousness more directly than we know about anything else, so "proof" is inappropriate. The best I can do is provide arguments wherever possible, while rebutting arguments from the other side. There is no denying that this involves an appeal to intuition at some point; but all arguments involve intuition somewhere, and I have tried to be clear about the intuitions involved in mine.

This might be seen as a Great Divide in the study of consciousness. If you hold that an answer to the "easy" problems explains everything that needs to be explained, then you get one sort of theory; if you hold that there is a further "hard" problem, then you get another. After a point, it is difficult to *argue* across this divide, and discussions are often reduced to table pounding. To me, it seems obvious that there is something further that needs explaining here; to others, it seems acceptable that there is not. (Informal surveys suggest that the numbers run two or three to one in favor of the former view, with the ratio fairly constant across academics and students in a variety of fields.) We may simply have to learn to live with this basic division.

This book may be of intellectual interest to those who think there is not much of a problem, but it is really intended for those who feel the problem in their bones. By now, we have a fairly good idea of the sort of theory we get if we assume there is no problem. In this work, I have tried to explore what follows given that there *is* a problem. The real argument of the book is that *if* one takes consciousness seriously, the position I lay out is where one should end up.

The second constraint I have followed is to *take science seriously.* I have not tried to dispute current scientific theories in domains where they have authority. At the same time, I have not been afraid to go out on a limb in areas where scientists' opinions are as ungrounded as everyone else's. For example, I have not disputed that the physical world is causally closed or that behavior can be explained in physical terms; but if a physicist or a cognitive scientist suggests that consciousness can be explained in physical terms, this is merely a hope ungrounded in current theory, and the question remains open. So I have tried to keep my ideas *compatible* with contemporary science, but I have not restricted my ideas to what contemporary scientists find fashionable.

The third constraint is that I take consciousness to be a natural phenomenon, falling under the sway of natural laws. If so, then there should be *some* correct scientific theory of consciousness, whether or not we can arrive at such a theory. That consciousness is a natural phenomenon seems hard to dispute: it is an extraordinarily salient part of nature, arising throughout the human species and very likely in many others. And we have every reason to believe that natural phenomena are subject to fundamental natural laws; it would be very strange if consciousness were not. This is not to say that the natural laws concerning consciousness will be just like laws in other domains, or even that they will be *physical* laws. They may be quite different in kind.

The problem of consciousness lies uneasily at the border of science and philosophy. I would say that it is properly a scientific subject matter: it is a natural phenomenon like motion, life, and cognition, and calls out for explanation in the way that these do. But it is not open to investigation by the usual scientific methods. Everyday scientific methodology has trouble getting a grip on it, not least because of the difficulties in observing the phenomenon. Outside the first-person case, data are hard to come by. This is not to say that no external data can be relevant, but we first have to arrive at a coherent philosophical understanding before we can justify the data's relevance. So the problem of consciousness may be a scientific problem that requires philosophical methods of understanding before we can get off the ground.

In this book I reach conclusions that some people may think of as "antiscientific": I argue that reductive explanation of consciousness is impossible, and I even argue for a form of dualism. But this is just part of the scientific process. Certain sorts of explanation turn out not to work, so we need to embrace other sorts of explanation instead. Everything I say here is compatible with the results of contemporary science; our picture of the natural world is broadened, not overturned. And this broadening allows the possibility of a naturalistic theory of consciousness that might have been impossible without it. It seems to me that to *ignore* the problems of consciousness would be antiscientific; it is in the scientific spirit to face up to them directly. To those who suspect that science requires materialism, I ask that you wait and see.

I should note that the conclusions of this work are *conclusions,* in the strongest sense. Temperamentally, I am strongly inclined toward materialist reductive explanation, and I have no strong spiritual or religious inclinations. For a number of years, I hoped for a materialist theory; when I gave up on this hope, it was quite reluctantly. It eventually seemed plain to me that these conclusions were forced on anyone who wants to take consciousness seriously. Materialism is a beautiful and compelling view of the world, but to account for consciousness, we have to go beyond the resources it provides.

By now, I have grown almost happy with these conclusions. They do not seem to have any fearsome consequences, and they allow a way of thinking and theorizing about consciousness that seems more satisfactory in almost every way. And the expansion in the scientific worldview has had a positive effect, at least for me: it has made the universe seem a more interesting place.

This book has four parts. In the first, I lay out the problems, and set up a framework within which they can be addressed. Chapter 1 is an introduction to consciousness, teasing apart a number of different concepts in the vicinity, drawing out the sense in which consciousness is really interesting, and giving a preliminary account of its subtle relation to the rest of the mind. Chapter

2 develops a metaphysical and explanatory framework within which much of the rest of the discussion is cast. What is it for a phenomenon to be reductively explained, or to be physical? This chapter gives an account of these things, centering on the notion of supervenience. I argue that there is good reason to believe that *almost* everything in the world can be reductively explained; but consciousness may be an exception.

With these preliminaries out of the way, the second part focuses on the irreducibility of consciousness. Chapter 3 argues that standard methods of reductive explanation cannot account for consciousness. I also give a critique of various reductive accounts that have been put forward by researchers in neuroscience, cognitive science, and elsewhere. This is not just a negative conclusion: it follows that a satisfactory theory of consciousness must be a new sort of *nonreductive* theory instead. Chapter 4 takes things a step further by arguing that materialism is false and that a form of dualism is true, and outlines the general shape that a nonreductive theory of consciousness might take. Chapter 5 is largely defensive: it considers some apparent problems for my view, involving the relationship between consciousness and our *judgments* about consciousness, and argues that they pose no fatal difficulties.

In the third part, I move toward a positive theory of consciousness. Each of the three chapters here develops a component of a positive theory. Chapter 6 focuses on the "coherence" between consciousness and cognitive processes, drawing a number of systematic links between the two. I use these links to analyze and ground the central role that neuroscience and cognitive science play in explaining human consciousness. Chapter 7 discusses the relation between consciousness and functional organization, using thought experiments to argue that consciousness is an "organizational invariant": that is, that every system with the right functional organization will have the same sort of conscious experience, no matter what it is made of. Chapter 8 considers what a *fundamental* theory of consciousness might look like, and suggests that it may involve a close relation between consciousness and information. This is by far the most speculative chapter, but at this point some speculation is probably needed if we are to make progress.

The last two chapters are dessert. Here, I apply what has gone before to central questions in the foundations of artificial intelligence and quantum mechanics. Chapter 9 argues for the thesis of "strong artificial intelligence": that the implementation of an appropriate computer program will give rise to a conscious mind. Chapter 10 considers the baffling question of how quantum mechanics should be interpreted, and uses the ideas about consciousness developed in previous chapters to lend support to a "no-collapse" interpretation of the theory.

Perhaps the negative material will provoke the most reaction, but my real goal is positive: I want to see a *theory* of consciousness that works. When I first came into philosophy, I was surprised to find that most of the debate over consciousness focused on whether there was a problem or not, or on whether it was physical or not, and that the business of building theories seemed to be left to one side. The only "theories" seemed to be put forward by those who (by my lights) did not take consciousness seriously. By now, I have come to enjoy the intricacies of the ontological debate as much as anyone, but a detailed theory is still my major goal. If some of the ideas in this book are useful to others in constructing a better theory, the attempt will have been worthwhile.

This book is intended as a serious work of philosophy, but I have tried to make it accessible to nonphilosophers. In my notional audience at all times has been my undergraduate self of ten years ago: I hope I have written a book that he would have appreciated. There are a few sections that are philosophically technical. These are marked with an asterisk (*), and readers should feel free to skip them. The most technical material is in Chapter 2 and Chapter 4. Section 4 of the former and sections 2 and 3 of the latter involve intricate issues in philosophical semantics, as does the final section of Chapter 5. Other asterisked sections might be worth at least skimming, to get an idea of what is going on. Often, I have put especially technical material and comments on the philosophical literature in the endnotes. The one technical concept that is crucial to the book is that of supervenience, introduced at the start of Chapter 2. This concept has an intimidating name but it expresses a very natural idea, and a good understanding of it will help central issues fall into place. Much of the material later in this chapter can be skipped on a first reading, although one might want to return to it later to clarify questions as they arise.

For a short tour that avoids technicalities, read Chapter 1, skim the early parts of Chapter 2 as background material, then read all of Chapter 3 (skimming section 1 where necessary) for the central arguments against reductive explanation, and the first and last sections of Chapter 4 for the central considerations about dualism. The beginning of Chapter 6 is worth reading for the basic shape of the positive approach. Of the positive material, Chapter 7 is perhaps the most self-contained chapter as well as the most fun, with easy-to-understand thought experiments involving silicon brains; and those who like wild and woolly speculation might enjoy Chapter 8. Finally, Chapters 9 and 10 should make sense to anyone with an interest in the issues involved.

A couple of philosophical notes. The philosophical literature on consciousness is quite unsystematic, with seemingly independent strands talking about related issues without making contact with each other. I have attempted to impose some structure on the sprawl by providing a unifying framework in which the various metaphysical and explanatory issues become clear. Much of the discussion in the literature can be translated into this framework without loss, and I hope the structure brings out the deep relationships between a number of different issues.

This work is perhaps unusual in largely eschewing the philosophical notion of identity (between mental and physical states, say) in favor of the notion of supervenience. I find that discussions framed in terms of identity generally throw more confusion than light onto the key issues, and often allow the central difficulties to be evaded. By contrast, supervenience seems to provide an ideal framework within which the key issues can be addressed. To avoid loose philosophy, however, we need to focus on the *strength* of the supervenience connection: Is it underwritten by logical necessity, natural necessity, or something else? It is widely agreed that consciousness supervenes on the physical in some sense; the real question is how tight the connection is. Discussions that ignore these modal issues generally avoid the hardest questions about consciousness. Those skeptical of modal notions will be skeptical of my entire discussion, but I think there is no other satisfactory way to frame the issues.

One of the delights of working on this book, for me, has come from the way the problem of consciousness has reached out to make contact with deep issues in many other areas of science and philosophy. But the scope and depth of the problem also make it humbling. I am acutely aware that at almost every point in this book there is more that could be said, and that in many places I have only scratched the surface. But I hope, minimally, to have suggested that it is possible to make progress on the problem of consciousness without denying its existence or reducing it to something it is not. The problem is fascinating, and the future is exciting.

No. Xia stopped, twirling toward him in slow motion. Her icy mint eyes grew wide. *You're in danger here.* Panic whitened her face as she stared toward the house. *Go home now. Before it's too late. And find me the antidote.*

What kind *of antidote?*

Xia disappeared beyond the junipers, yet her final message burst into Joey's mind like the pop of a firecracker: *The antidote for zombie poison.*

Dian Curtis Regan, My Zombie Valentine

PART I

Foundations

1

Two Concepts of Mind

1. What Is Consciousness?

Conscious experience is at once the most familiar thing in the world and the most mysterious. There is nothing we know about more directly than consciousness, but it is far from clear how to reconcile it with everything else we know. Why does it exist? What does it do? How could it possibly arise from lumpy gray matter? We know consciousness far more intimately than we know the rest of the world, but we understand the rest of the world far better than we understand consciousness.

Consciousness can be startlingly intense. It is the most vivid of phenomena; nothing is more real to us. But it can be frustratingly diaphanous: in talking about conscious experience, it is notoriously difficult to pin down the subject matter. *The International Dictionary of Psychology* does not even try to give a straightforward characterization:

> *Consciousness*: The having of perceptions, thoughts, and feelings; awareness. The term is impossible to define except in terms that are unintelligible without a grasp of what consciousness means. Many fall into the trap of confusing consciousness with self-consciousness—to be conscious it is only necessary to be aware of the external world. Consciousness is a fascinating but elusive phenomenon: it is impossible to specify what it is, what it does, or why it evolved. Nothing worth reading has been written about it. (Sutherland 1989)

Almost anyone who has thought hard about consciousness will have some sympathy with these sentiments. Consciousness is so intangible that even this limited attempt at a definition could be disputed: there can arguably perception and thought that is not conscious, as witnessed by the notions subliminal perception and unconscious thought. What is central to consci ness, at least in the most interesting sense, is *experience*. But this is not definition. At best, it is clarification.

Trying to define conscious experience in terms of more primitive notions is fruitless. One might as well try to define *matter* or *space* in terms of something more fundamental. The best we can do is to give illustrations and characterizations that lie at the same level. These characterizations cannot qualify as true definitions, due to their implicitly circular nature, but they can help to pin down what is being talked about. I presume that every reader has conscious experiences of his or her own. If all goes well, these characterizations will help establish that it is just *those* that we are talking about.

The subject matter is perhaps best characterized as "the subjective quality of experience." When we perceive, think, and act, there is a whir of causation and information processing, but this processing does not usually go on in the dark. There is also an internal aspect; there is something it feels like to be a cognitive agent. This internal aspect is conscious experience. Conscious experiences range from vivid color sensations to experiences of the faintest background aromas; from hard-edged pains to the elusive experience of thoughts on the tip of one's tongue; from mundane sounds and smells to the encompassing grandeur of musical experience; from the triviality of a nagging itch to the weight of a deep existential angst; from the specificity of the taste of peppermint to the generality of one's experience of selfhood. All these have a distinct experienced quality. All are prominent parts of the inner life of the mind.

We can say that a being is conscious if there is *something it is like* to be that being, to use a phrase made famous by Thomas Nagel.[1] Similarly, a mental state is conscious if there is something it is like to be in that mental state. To put it another way, we can say that a mental state is conscious if it has a *qualitative feel*—an associated quality of experience. These qualitative feels are also known as phenomenal qualities, or *qualia* for short.[2] The problem of explaining these phenomenal qualities is just the problem of explaining consciousness. This is the really hard part of the mind–body problem.

Why should there be conscious experience at all? It is central to a subjective viewpoint, but from an objective viewpoint it is utterly unexpected. Taking the objective view, we can tell a story about how fields, waves, and particles in the spatiotemporal manifold interact in subtle ways, leading to the development of complex systems such as brains. In principle, there is no deep philosophical mystery in the fact that these systems can process information in complex ways, react to stimuli with sophisticated behavior, and even exhibit such complex capacities as learning, memory, and language. All this is impressive, but it is not metaphysically baffling. In contrast, the existence of conscious experience seems to be a *new* feature from this viewpoint. It is not something that one would have predicted from the other ~~feat~~ures alone.

That is, consciousness is *surprising*. If all we knew about were the facts of physics, and even the facts about dynamics and information processing in complex systems, there would be no compelling reason to postulate the existence of conscious experience. If it were not for our direct evidence in the first-person case, the hypothesis would seem unwarranted; almost mystical, perhaps. Yet we know, directly, that there is conscious experience.The question is, how do we reconcile it with everything else we know?

Conscious experience is part of the natural world, and like other natural phenomena it cries out for explanation. There are at least two major targets of explanation here. The first and most central is the very *existence* of consciousness. Why does conscious experience exist? If it arises from physical systems, as seems likely, how does it arise? This leads to some more specific questions. Is consciousness itself physical, or is it merely a concomitant of physical systems? How widespread is consciousness? Do mice, for example, have conscious experience?

A second target is the specific *character* of conscious experiences. Given that conscious experience exists, why do individual experiences have their particular nature? When I open my eyes and look around my office, why do I have *this* sort of complex experience? At a more basic level, why is seeing red like *this*, rather than like *that*? It seems conceivable that when looking at red things, such as roses, one might have had the sort of color experiences that one in fact has when looking at blue things. Why is the experience one way rather than the other? Why, for that matter, do we experience the reddish sensation[3] that we do, rather than some entirely different kind of sensation, like the sound of a trumpet?

When someone strikes middle C on the piano, a complex chain of events is set into place. Sound vibrates in the air and a wave travels to my ear. The wave is processed and analyzed into frequencies inside the ear, and a signal is sent to the auditory cortex. Further processing takes place here: isolation of certain aspects of the signal, categorization, and ultimately reaction. All this is not so hard to understand in principle. But why should this be accompanied by an *experience*? And why, in particular, should it be accompanied by *that* experience, with its characteristic rich tone and timbre? These are the central questions that we would like a theory of consciousness to answer.

Ultimately one would like a theory of consciousness to do at least the following: it should give the conditions under which physical processes give rise to consciousness, and for those processes that give rise to consciousness, it should specify just what sort of experience is associated. And we would like the theory to explain *how* it arises, so that the emergence of consciousness seems intelligible rather than magical. In the end, we would like the theory to enable us to see consciousness as an integral part of the natural world. Currently it may be hard to see what such a theory would be like, but without such a theory we could not be said to fully understand consciousness.

Before proceeding, a note on terminology. The term "consciousness" is ambiguous, referring to a number of phenomena. Sometimes it is used to refer to a cognitive capacity, such as the ability to introspect or to report one's mental states. Sometimes it is used synonymously with "awakeness." Sometimes it is closely tied to our ability to focus attention, or to voluntarily control our behavior. Sometimes "to be conscious of something" comes to the same thing as "to know about something." All of these are accepted uses of the term, but all pick out phenomena distinct from the subject I am discussing, and phenomena that are significantly less difficult to explain. I will say more about these alternative notions of consciousness later, but for now, when I talk about consciousness, I am talking only about the subjective quality of experience: what it is like to be a cognitive agent.

A number of alternative terms and phrases pick out approximately the same class of phenomena as "consciousness" in its central sense. These include "experience," "qualia," "phenomenology," "phenomenal," "subjective experience," and "what it is like." Apart from grammatical differences, the differences among these terms are mostly subtle matters of connotation. "To be conscious" in this sense is roughly synonymous with "to have qualia," "to have subjective experience," and so on. Any differences in the class of phenomena picked out are insignificant. Like "consciousness," many of these terms are somewhat ambiguous, but I will never use these terms in the alternative senses. I will use all these phrases in talking about the central phenomenon of this book, but "consciousness" and "experience" are the most straightforward terms, and it is these terms that will recur.

A catalog of conscious experiences

Conscious experience can be fascinating to attend to. Experience comes in an enormous number of varieties, each with its own character. A far-from-complete catalog of the aspects of conscious experience is given in the following pretheoretical, impressionistic list. Nothing here should be taken too seriously as philosophy, but it should help focus attention on the subject matter at hand.

ual experiences.   Among the many varieties of visual experience, color sensations stand out as the paradigm examples of conscious experience, due to their pure, seemingly ineffable qualitative nature. Some color experiences can seem particularly striking, and so can be particularly good at focusing our attention on the mystery of consciousness. In my environment now, there is a particularly rich shade of deep purple from a book on my shelf; an almost surreal shade of green in a photograph of ferns on my wall; and a sparkling array of bright red, green, orange, and blue lights on a Christmas tree that I can see through my window. But any color can be awe-provoking if we attend to it, and reflect upon its nature. Why should it feel like *that*? Why should it feel like anything at all? How could I possibly convey the nature of this color experience to someone who has not had such an experience?

Other aspects of visual experience include the experience of shape, of size, of brightness, and of darkness. A particularly subtle aspect is the experience of depth. As a child, one of my eyes had excellent vision, but the other was very poor. Because of my one good eye, the world looked crisp and sharp, and it certainly seemed three-dimensional. One day, I was fitted with glasses, and the change was remarkable. The world was not much sharper than before, but it suddenly looked *more* three-dimensional: things that had depth before somehow got deeper, and the world seemed a richer place. If you cover one eye and then uncover it, you can get an idea of the change. In my previous state, I would have said that there was no way for the depth of my vision to improve; the world already seemed as three-dimensional as it could be. The change was subtle, almost ineffable, but extremely striking. Certainly there is an intellectual story one can tell about how binocular vision allows information from each eye to be consolidated into information about distances, thus enabling more sophisticated control of action, but somehow this causal story does not reveal the way the experience *felt*. Why that change in processing should be accompanied by such a remaking of my experience was mysterious to me as a ten-year-old, and is still a source of wonder today.

Auditory experiences. In some ways, sounds are even stranger than visual images. The structure of images usually corresponds to the structure of the world in a straightforward way, but sounds can seem quite independent. My telephone receives an incoming call, an internal device vibrates, a complex wave is set up in the air and eventually reaches my eardrum, and some almost magically, I hear a *ring*. Nothing about the quality of the ring se to correspond directly to any structure in the world, although I certainly know that it originated with the speaker, and that it is determined by a waveform. But why should that waveform, or even these neural firings, have given rise to a sound quality like *that*?

Musical experience is perhaps the richest aspect of auditory experience, although the experience of speech must be close. Music is capable of washing over and completely absorbing us, surrounding us in a way that a visual field can surround us but in which auditory experiences usually do not. One can analyze aspects of musical experience by breaking the sounds we perceive into notes and tones with complex interrelationships, but the experience of music somehow goes beyond this. A unified qualitative experience arises

Calvin and Hobbes   by Bill Watterson

Figure 1.1. Effability and ineffability in olfactory experience. (Calvin and Hobbes © Watterson. Distributed by Universal Press Syndicate. Reprinted with permission. All rights reserved)

from a chord, but not from randomly selected notes. An old piano and a far-off oboe can combine to produce an unexpectedly haunting experience. As always, when we reflect, we ask the question: why should *that* feel like *this*?

Tactile experiences.   Textures provide another of the richest quality spaces that we experience: think of the feel of velvet, and contrast it to the texture of cold metal, or a clammy hand, or a stubbly chin. All of these have their own unique quality. The tactile experiences of water, of cotton candy, or of another person's lips are different again.

Olfactory experiences.   Think of the musty smell of an old wardrobe, the stench of rotting garbage, the whiff of newly mown grass, the warm aroma of freshly baked bread. Smell is in some ways the most mysterious of all the es, due to the rich, intangible, indescribable nature of smell sensations. ermann (1990) calls it "the mute sense; the one without words." While there is something ineffable about any sensation, the other senses have properties that facilitate some description. Visual and auditory experiences have a complex combinatorial structure that can be described. Tactile and taste experiences generally arise from direct contact with some object, and a rich descriptive vocabulary has been built up by reference to these objects. Smell has little in the way of apparent structure and often floats free of any apparent object, remaining a primitive presence in our sensory manifold. (Perhaps animals might do better [Figure 1.1].) The primitiveness is perhaps partly due to the slot-and-key process by which our olfactory receptors are sensitive to various kinds of molecules. It seems arbitrary that a given sort of molecule should give rise to *this* sort of sensation, but give rise it does.

Taste experiences.   Psychophysical investigations tell us that there are only four independent dimensions of taste perception: sweet, sour, bitter, and salt. But this four-dimensional space combines with our sense of smell to produce a great variety of possible experiences: the taste of Turkish Delight, of curried black-eyed pea salad,[4] of a peppermint Lifesaver, of a ripe peach.

Experiences of hot and cold.   An oppressively hot, humid day and a frosty winter's day produce strikingly different qualitative experiences. Think also of the heat sensations on one's skin from being close to a fire, and the hot-cold sensation that one gets from touching ultracold ice.

Pain.   Pain is a paradigm example of conscious experience, beloved by philosophers. Perhaps this is because pains form a very distinctive class of qualitative experiences, and are difficult to map directly onto any structure in the world or in the body, although they are usually associated with some part of the body. Because of this, pains can seem even more subjective than most sensory experiences. There are a great variety of pain experiences, from shooting pains and fierce burns through sharp pricks to dull aches.

Other bodily sensations.   Pains are only the most salient kind of sensations associated with particular parts of the body. Others include headaches (which are perhaps a class of pain), hunger pangs, itches, tickles, and the experience associated with the need to urinate. Many bodily sensations have an entirely unique quality, different in kind from anything else in our experience: think of orgasms, or the feeling of hitting one's funny bone. There are also experiences associated with proprioception, the sense of where one's body is in space.

Mental imagery.   Moving ever inward, toward experiences that are not associated with particular objects in the environment or the body but that are in some sense generated internally, we come to mental images. There is often a rich phenomenology associated with visual images conjured up in one's imagination, though not nearly as detailed as those derived from direct visual perception. There are also the interesting colored patterns that one gets when one closes one's eyes and squints, and the strong after-images that one gets after looking at something bright. One can have similar kinds of auditory "images" conjured up by one's imagination, and even tactile, olfactory, and gustatory images, although these are harder to pin down and their associated qualitative feel is usually fainter.

Conscious thought.   Some of the things we think and believe do not have any particular qualitative feel associated with them, but many do. This applies particularly to explicit, occurrent thoughts that one thinks to oneself, and to various thoughts that affect one's stream of consciousness. It is often hard to pin down just what the qualitative feel of an occurrent thought is, but it is certainly there. There is *something* it is like to be having such thoughts.

When I think of a lion, for instance, there seems to be a whiff of leonine quality to my phenomenology: what it is like to think of a lion is subtly different from what it is like to think of the Eiffel tower. More obviously, cognitive attitudes such as desire often have a strong phenomenal flavor. Desire seems to exert a phenomenological "tug," and memory often has a qualitative component, as with the experience of nostalgia or regret.

Emotions.   Emotions often have distinctive experiences associated with them. The sparkle of a happy mood, the weariness of a deep depression, the red-hot glow of a rush of anger, the melancholy of regret: all of these can affect conscious experience profoundly, although in a much less specific way than localized experiences such as sensations. These emotions pervade and color all of our conscious experiences while they last.

Other more transient feelings lie partway between emotions and the more obviously cognitive aspects of mind. Think of the rush of pleasure one feels when one gets a joke. Another example is the feeling of tension one gets when watching a suspense movie, or when waiting for an important event. The butterflies in one's stomach that can accompany nervousness also fall into this class.

The sense of self.   One sometimes feels that there is something to conscious experience that transcends all these specific elements: a kind of background hum, for instance, that is somehow fundamental to consciousness and that there even when the other components are not. This phenomenology of f is so deep and intangible that it sometimes seems illusory, consisting in thing over and above specific elements such as those listed above. Still, there seems to be *something* to the phenomenology of self, even if it is very hard to pin down.

This catalog covers a number of bases, but leaves out as much as it puts in. I have said nothing, for instance, about dreams, arousal and fatigue, intoxication, or the novel character of other drug-induced experiences. There are also rich experiences that derive their character from the combination of two or many of the components described above. I have mentioned the combined effects of smell and taste, but an equally salient example is the combined experience of music and emotion, which interact in a subtle, difficult-to-separate way. I have also left aside the unity of conscious experience—the way that all of these experiences seem to be tied together as the experience of a single experiencer. Like the sense of self, this unity sometimes seems illusory—it is certainly harder to pin down than any specific experiences—but there is a strong intuition that unity is there.

Sad to say, we will not again be involved this closely with the rich varieties of conscious experience. In addressing the philosophical mysteries associated with conscious experience, a simple color sensation raises the problems as deeply as one's experience of a Bach chorale. The deep issues cut across these varieties in a way that renders consideration of the nature of specific experiences not especially relevant. Still, this brief look at the rich varieties of conscious experience should help focus attention on just what it is that is under discussion, and provides a stock of examples that can be kept in mind during more abstract discussion.[5]

2. The Phenomenal and the Psychological Concepts of Mind

Conscious experience is not all there is to the mind. To see this, observe that although modern cognitive science has had almost nothing to say about consciousness, it has had much to say about mind in general. The aspects of mind with which it is concerned are different. Cognitive science deals largely in the explanation of behavior, and insofar as it is concerned with mind at all, it is with mind construed as the internal basis of behavior, and with mental states construed as those states relevant to the causation and explanation of behavior. Such states may or may not be conscious. From the point of view of cognitive science, an internal state responsible for the causation of behavior is equally mental whether it is conscious or not.

At the root of all this lie two quite distinct concepts of mind. The first is the *phenomenal* concept of mind. This is the concept of mind as conscious experience, and of a mental state as a consciously experienced mental state. This is the most perplexing aspect of mind and the aspect on which I will concentrate, but it does not exhaust the mental. The second is the *psychological* concept of mind. This is the concept of mind as the causal or explanatory basis for behavior. A state is mental in this sense if it plays the right sort of causal role in the production of behavior, or at least plays an appropriate role in the explanation of behavior. According to the psychological concept, it matters little whether a mental state has a conscious quality or not. What matters is the role it plays in a cognitive economy.

On the phenomenal concept, mind is characterized by the way it *feels*; on the psychological concept, mind is characterized by what it *does*. There should be no question of competition between these two notions of mind. Neither of them is *the* correct analysis of mind. They cover different phenomena, both of which are quite real.

I will sometimes speak of the phenomenal and psychological "aspects" of mind, and sometimes of the "phenomenal mind" and the "psychological mind." At this early stage, I do not wish to beg any questions about whether the phenomenal and the psychological will turn out to be the same thing. Perhaps every phenomenal state is a psychological state, in that it plays a significant role in the causation and explanation of behavior, and perhaps every psychological state has an intimate relation to the phenomenal. For now, all that counts is the conceptual distinction between the two notions: what it *means* for a state to be phenomenal is for it to feel a certain way, and what it means for a state to be psychological is for it to play an appropriate causal role. These distinct notions should not be conflated, at least at the outset.

A specific mental concept can usually be analyzed as a phenomenal concept, a psychological concept, or as a combination of the two. For instance, sensation, in its central sense, is best taken as a phenomenal concept: to have a sensation is to have a state with a certain sort of feel. On the other hand, the concepts of learning and memory might best be taken as psychological. For something to learn, at a first approximation, is for it to adapt its behavioral capacities appropriately in response to certain kinds of environmental stimulation. In general, a phenomenal feature of the mind is characterized by what it is like for a subject to have that feature, while a psychological feature is characterized by an associated role in the causation and/or explanation of behavior.

Of course, this usage of the term "psychological" is a stipulation: it arises from identifying psychology with cognitive science as described above. The everyday concept of a "psychological state" is probably broader than this, and may well include elements of the phenomenal. But nothing will rest on my use of the term.

A potted history

The phenomenal and the psychological aspects of mind have a long history of being conflated. René Descartes may have been partly responsible for this. With his notorious doctrine that the mind is transparent to itself, he came close to identifying the mental with the phenomenal. Descartes held that every event in the mind is a *cogitatio,* or a content of experience. To this class he assimilated volitions, intentions, and every type of thought. In his reply to the Fourth Set of Objections, he wrote:

> As to the fact that there can be nothing in the mind, in so far as it is a thinking thing, of which it is not aware, this seems to me to be self-evident. For there is nothing that we can understand to be in the mind, regarded in this way, that is not a thought or dependent on a thought. If it were not a thought nor

dependent on a thought it would not belong to the mind *qua* thinking thing; and we cannot have any thought of which we are not aware at the very moment it is in us.

If Descartes did not actually identify the psychological with the phenomenal, he at least assumed that everything psychological that is worthy of being called mental has a conscious aspect.[6] To Descartes, the notion of an unconscious mental state was a contradiction.

Progress in psychological theory rather than in philosophy was responsible for drawing the two aspects of mind apart. As recently as a century ago, psychologists such as Wilhelm Wundt and William James were recognizably Cartesian in that they used introspection to investigate the causes of behavior, and developed psychological theories on the basis of introspective evidence. In this fashion, phenomenology was made the arbiter of psychology. But developments soon after established the psychological as an autonomous domain.

Most notably, Sigmund Freud and his contemporaries solidified the idea that many activities of the mind are unconscious, and that there can be such things as unconscious beliefs and desires. The very fact that this notion seemed coherent is evidence that a nonphenomenal analysis of thought was being used. It appears that Freud construed the notions *causally*. Desire, very roughly, was implicitly construed as the sort of state that brings about a certain kind of behavior associated with the object of the desire. Belief was construed according to its causal role in a similar way. Of course Freud did not make these analyses explicit, but something along these lines clearly underlies his use of the notions. Explicitly, he recognized that accessibility to consciousness is not essential to a state's relevance in the explanation of behavior, and that a conscious quality is not constitutive of something's being a belief or a desire. These conclusions rely on a notion of mentality that is independent of phenomenal notions.

Around the same time, the behaviorist movement in psychology had thoroughly rejected the introspectionist tradition. A new "objective" brand of psychological explanation was developed, with no room for consciousness in its explanations. This mode of explanation had only partial success, but it established the idea that psychological explanation can proceed while the phenomenal is ignored. Behaviorists differed in their theoretical positions: some recognized the existence of consciousness but found it irrelevant to psychological explanation, and some denied its existence altogether. Many went further, denying the existence of *any* kind of mental state. The official reason for this was that internal states were supposed to be irrelevant in the explanation of behavior, which could be carried out entirely in external terms. Perhaps a deeper reason is that all mental notions were tainted with the disreputable odor of the phenomenal.

In any case, these two developments established as orthodoxy the idea that explanation of behavior is in no way dependent on phenomenal notions. The move from behaviorism to computational cognitive science for the most part preserved this orthodoxy. Although the move brought back a role for internal states, which could even be called "mental" states, there was nothing particularly phenomenal about them. These states were admissible precisely on the grounds of their relevance in the explanation of behavior; any associated phenomenal quality was at best beside the point. The concept of the mental as psychological thus had center stage.

In philosophy, the shift in emphasis from the phenomenal to the psychological was codified by Gilbert Ryle (1949), who argued that all our mental concepts can be analyzed in terms of certain kinds of associated behavior, or in terms of dispositions to behave in certain ways.[7] This view, logical behaviorism, is recognizably the precursor of much of what passes for orthodoxy in contemporary philosophy of psychology. In particular, it was the most explicit codification of the link between mental concepts and the causation of behavior.

Ryle did not put this theory forward as an analysis of just *some* mental concepts. He intended all of them to fall within its grasp. It seemed to many people, as it seems to me, that this view is a nonstarter as an analysis of our phenomenal concepts, such as sensation and consciousness itself. To many, it seemed clear that when we talk about phenomenal states, we are certainly not talking about our behavior, or about any behavioral disposition. But in any case, Ryle's analysis provided a suggestive approach to many other mental notions, such as believing, enjoying, wanting, pretending, and remembering.

Apart from its problems with phenomenal states, Ryle's view had some technical problems. First, it is natural to suppose that mental states *cause* behavior, but if mental states are themselves behavioral or behavioral dispositions, as opposed to internal states, then it is hard to see how they could do the job. Second, it was argued (by Chisholm [1957] and Geach [1957]) that no mental state could be defined by a single range of behavioral dispositions, independent of any other mental states. For example, if one believes that it is raining, one's behavioral dispositions will vary depending on whether one has the desire to get wet. It is therefore necessary to invoke other mental states in characterizing the behavioral dispositions associated with a given sort of mental state.

These problems were finessed by what has become known as *functionalism,* which was developed by David Lewis (1966) and most thoroughly by David Armstrong (1968).[8] On this view, a mental state is defined wholly by its *causal role*: that is, in terms of the kinds of stimulation that tend to produce it, the kind of behavior it tends to produce, and the way it interacts with other mental states. This view made mental states fully internal and able to stand in the right kind of causal relation to behavior, answering the first objection, and it allowed mental states to be defined in terms of their interaction with each other, answering the second objection.

On this view, our mental concepts can be analyzed *functionally*: in terms of their actual or typical causes and effects. To give such an analysis for any given mental concept is highly nontrivial; Armstrong (1968) gives a number of analyses, but these are very incomplete. As an in-principle position, however, functionalism may provide a reasonable construal of many of our mental concepts, at least insofar as they play a role in the explanation of behavior. For instance, the notion of learning might be analyzed as the adaptation of one's behavioral capacities in response to environmental stimulation. To take a more complex state, a belief that it is raining might be very roughly analyzed as the sort of state that tends to be produced when it is raining, that leads to behavior that would be appropriate if it were raining, that interacts inferentially with other beliefs and desires in a certain sort of way, and so on. There is a lot of room for working out the details, but many have found the overall idea to be on the right track.

Like Ryle, however, Armstrong and Lewis did not put this forward as an analysis of *some* mental concepts. Rather, it was meant as an analysis of all mental concepts. In particular, they argued that the notions of experience, sensation, consciousness, and so on, could be analyzed in this fashion. This assimilation of the phenomenal to the psychological seems to me to be as great an error as Descartes's assimilation of the psychological to the phenomenal. It is simply a false analysis of what it means to be phenomenal. When we wonder whether somebody is having a color experience, we are not wondering whether they are receiving environmental stimulation and processing it in a certain way. We are wondering whether they are *experiencing* a color sensation, and this is a distinct question. It is a conceptually coherent possibility that something could be playing the causal role without there being an associated experience.

To put the point a different way, note that this analysis of phenomenal concepts leaves it unclear why anybody was ever bothered by the problem in the first place.[9] There is no great mystery about how a state might play some causal role, although there are certainly technical problems there for science. What is mysterious is why that state should *feel* like something; why it should have a phenomenal quality. Why the causal role is played and why the phenomenal quality is present are two entirely different questions. The functionalist analysis denies the distinctness of these questions, and therefore seems to be unsatisfactory.

I will consider this matter in much more detail later, but for now we can note that even if the functionalist account gives an unsatisfactory analysis of phenomenal concepts, it may provide a good analysis of other mental notions, such as learning and memory, and perhaps belief. No parallel worries come up in these cases. It seems no more mysterious that a system should be able to learn than that a system should be able to adapt its behavior in response to environmental stimulation; indeed, these seem to be more or less the same question. Similarly, when we wonder whether somebody has learned something, it seems reasonable to say that in doing this we are wondering whether they have undergone a change that will give rise to an improved capacity to deal with certain situations in the future. Of course, a thorough analysis of the concept of learning will be more subtle than this first approximation, but the further details of the analysis will be spelled out within the same framework.

Indeed, the functionalist account corresponds precisely to the definition I have given of *psychological* properties. Most nonphenomenal mental properties fall into this class, and can therefore be functionally analyzed. There is certainly room to argue over the details of a specific functionalist analysis. There are also significant framework questions about such matters as the role of the environment in characterizing psychological properties, and whether it is causation, explanation, or both that provides the defining link between psychological properties and behavior. These details are relatively unimportant here, though. What matters is that nonphenomenal mental states are largely characterized by their role in our cognitive economy.

The moral of this discussion is that both the psychological and the phenomenal are real and distinct aspects of mind. At a first approximation, phenomenal concepts deal with the first-person aspects of mind, and psychological concepts deal with the third-person aspects. One's approach to the mind will be quite different depending on what aspects of the mind one is interested in. If one is interested in the mind's role in bringing about behavior, one will focus on psychological properties. If one is interested in the conscious experience of mental states, one will focus on phenomenal properties. Neither the phenomenal nor the psychological should be defined away in terms of the other. Conceivably, some deep analysis might reveal a fundamental link between the phenomenal and the psychological, but this would be a nontrivial task, and is not something to be accomplished by prior stipulation. To assimilate the phenomenal to the psychological prior to some deep explanation would be to trivialize the problem of conscious experience; and to assimilate the psychological to the phenomenal would be to vastly limit the role of the mental in explaining behavior.

3. The Double Life of Mental Terms

It seems reasonable to say that together, the psychological and the phenomenal exhaust the mental. That is, every mental property is either a phenomenal property, a psychological property, or some combination of the two. Certainly, if we are concerned with those manifest properties of the mind that cry out for explanation, we find first, the varieties of conscious experience, and second, the causation of behavior. There is no third kind of manifest explanandum, and the first two sources of evidence—experience and behavior—provide no reason to believe in any third kind of nonphenomenal, nonfunctional properties (with perhaps a minor exception for relational properties, discussed shortly). There are certainly other classes of mental states of which we often speak—intentional states, emotional states, and so on—but it is plausible that these can be assimilated to the psychological, the phenomenal, or a combination of the two.

Things are complicated by the fact that many everyday mental concepts straddle the fence, having both a phenomenal and a psychological component. *Pain* provides a clear example. The term is often used to name a particular sort of unpleasant phenomenal quality, in which case a phenomenal notion is central. But there is also a psychological notion associated with the term: roughly, the concept of the sort of state that tends to be produced by damage to the organism, tends to lead to aversion reactions, and so on. Both of these aspects are central to the commonsense notion of pain. We might say that the notion of pain is ambiguous between the phenomenal and the psychological concept, or we might say that both of these are components of a single rich concept.

One can tie oneself into all kinds of knots by worrying about whether the phenomenal quality or the functional role is more essential to pain. For instance, would a hypothetical system in which all the functional criteria were satisfied but in which the conscious experience were not present be truly in pain? One might be tempted to say no, but what of the fact that we speak of pains that last for a day, even though there are times when they are not conscious? There is little point trying to legislate matters one way or the other. Nothing important rests on the semantic decision as to whether some phenomenal quality is *really* essential for something to count as pain. Instead, we can recognize the different components associated with a concept and explicitly distinguish them, speaking for example of "phenomenal pain" and "psychological pain." Our everyday concept of pain presumably combines the two in some subtle weighted combination, but for philosophical discussion things are clearer if we keep them separate.

The reason why phenomenal and psychological properties are often run together is clear: it is because the relevant properties tend to co-occur. Generally, when the processes resulting from tissue damage and leading to aversion reaction take place, some sort of phenomenal quality is instantiated. That is, when psychological pain is present, phenomenal pain is usually also present. It is not a *conceptual* truth that the process should be accompanied by the phenomenal quality, but it is a fact about the world. Once we have this sort of co-occurrence of properties in everyday situations, it is natural that our everyday concepts will bind them together.

Many mental concepts lead this sort of double life. For example, the concept of *perception* can be taken wholly psychologically, denoting the process whereby cognitive systems are sensitive to environmental stimulation in such a way that the resulting states play a certain role in directing cognitive processes. But it can also be taken phenomenally, involving the conscious experience of what is perceived. The possibility of subliminal perception counts against the latter construal, but some would argue that this qualifies as perception only in a weakened sense of the term. Once again, however, the issue is terminological. When we want to be clear, we can simply stipulate whether it is the psychological property, the phenomenal property, or a combination that we are concerned with.

Still, some of these dual concepts lean more strongly toward the phenomenal, and some lean toward the psychological. Take the concept of *sensation,* which is closely related to the concept of perception and which also has both phenomenal and psychological components. The phenomenal component is much more prominent in "sensation" than in "perception," as witnessed by the fact that the idea of unconscious perception seems to make more sense than that of unconscious sensation. Things are still somewhat gray—there remains a sense of "perception" that requires conscious experience, and a sense of "sensation" that does not—but these senses seem less central than the alternatives. Perhaps it is most natural to use "perception" as a psychological term, and "sensation" as a phenomenal term. This way, we can see sensation as something like perception's phenomenal counterpart.

A good test for whether a mental notion M is primarily psychological is to ask oneself: Could something be an instance of M without any particular associated phenomenal quality? If so, then M is likely psychological. If not, then M is phenomenal, or at least a combined notion that centrally involves phenomenology. The latter possibility cannot be ruled out, as some concepts may require both an appropriate sort of phenomenal quality and an appropriate cognitive role; perhaps a central sense of "sensation" has this combined character, for example. But we can at least separate those notions that involve phenomenology from those that do not.

The test suggests that a concept such as *learning,* for example, is largely psychological. To a first approximation, to learn is just for one's cognitive capacities to adapt in a certain way to various new circumstances and stimuli. No particular phenomenal quality is required for a cognitive process to be an instance of learning; such a quality may be present, but it is not what makes the process count as an example of learning. There may be a slight phenomenal tinge inherited from a link with concepts such as belief, discussed below, but this is faint at best. In explaining learning, the central thing we have to explain is how the system manages to adapt in the appropriate way. Something similar goes for concepts such as those of categorization and memory, which seem to be largely psychological notions, in that what is central is the playing of an appropriate cognitive role.

Emotions have a much clearer phenomenal aspect. When we think of happiness and sadness, a distinct variety of conscious experience comes to mind. It is not quite obvious whether the phenomenal aspect is *essential* for a state to be an emotion, however; there is clearly a strong associated psychological property as well. As usual, we need not make any decision on this matter. We can simply talk about the psychological and phenomenal aspects of emotion, and observe that these exhaust the aspects of emotion that require explanation.

The most complex case is that of mental states such as *belief,* often called "propositional attitudes" because they are attitudes to propositions concerning the world. When I believe that Bob Dylan will tour Australia, for example, I endorse a certain proposition concerning Dylan; when I *hope* that Dylan will tour Australia, I have a different attitude toward the same proposition. The central feature of these mental states is their semantic aspect, or *intentionality*: the fact that they are *about* things in the world. That is, a belief has semantic content: the content of my belief cited above is something like the proposition that Dylan will tour Australia (although there is room for debate here).

Belief is most often regarded as a psychological property. On this view, at a rough first approximation, to believe that a proposition is true is to be in a state wherein one acts in a way that would be appropriate if it were true, a state that tends to be brought about by its being the case, and a state in which one's cognitive dynamics of reasoning reflect the appropriate interaction of the belief with other beliefs and desires. The functional criteria for belief are very subtle, however, and no one has yet produced anything like a complete analysis of the relevant criteria. All the same, there is reason to believe that this view captures much of what is significant about belief. It is related to the idea that belief is something of an *explanatory construct*: we attribute beliefs to others largely in order to explain their behavior.

Some would argue that this leaves something out, and that something over and above the relevant sort of psychological process is required for belief. In particular, it leaves out the *experiential* aspects of believing, which some have argued are essential for anything to count as a belief. For example, Searle (1990a) has argued that the intentional content of a belief depends entirely on the associated state of consciousness, or on a state of consciousness that the belief can bring about. Without consciousness, all that is present is "as-if" intentionality.[10]

Certainly, there is often conscious experience in the vicinity of belief: there is something it is like when one has an occurrent (i.e., conscious) belief, and most nonoccurrent beliefs can at least bring about a conscious belief. The crucial questions, though, are whether this conscious quality is what *makes* the state a belief, and whether it is what gives it the content it has. This may be more plausible for some beliefs than for others: for example, one might argue that a conscious quality is required to truly have beliefs about one's *experiences,* and perhaps also certain sorts of experiences are required to have certain sorts of perceptual beliefs about the external world (perhaps one needs red experiences to believe that an object is red?). In other cases, this seems more problematic. For example, when I think that Don Bradman is the greatest cricketer of all time, it seems plausible to say that I would have had the same belief even if I had had a very different conscious experience associated with it. The phenomenology of the belief is relatively faint, and it is hard to see how it could be this phenomenal quality that makes the belief a belief about Bradman. What seems more central to the belief's content is the connection between the belief and Bradman, and the role it plays in my cognitive system.

As a weaker position, it might be suggested that although no *particular* phenomenal quality is required to have a particular belief, a being must at least be *capable* of conscious experience to believe anything at all.[11] There is a certain plausibility in the idea that a being with no conscious inner life would not truly be a believer; at best, it would be only a pseudobeliever. All the same, this would make the role of the phenomenal in intentional concepts quite thin. The most substantial requirements for having a specific belief will lie elsewhere than in the phenomenal. One could even subtract any phenomenal component out, leaving a concept of pseudobelief that resembles belief in most important respects except that it does not involve the concept of consciousness. Indeed, it is plausible that pseudobelief could do most of the explanatory work that is done by the concept of belief.

In any case, I will not try to adjudicate these difficult issues about the relationship between intentionality and consciousness here. We can note that there is at least a *deflationary* concept of belief that is purely psychological, not involving conscious experience; if a being is in the right psychological state, then it is in a state that resembles belief in many important ways, except with respect to any phenomenal aspects. And there is an *inflationary* concept of belief, on which conscious experience is required for truly believing, and perhaps even on which a specific sort of conscious experience is required for truly believing a specific proposition. Which of these is the "true" concept of belief will not matter too much for my purposes.

What is central is that there is not any feature of belief that outstrips the phenomenal and the psychological. Perhaps a small qualification needs to be made to this: one may need to add a *relational* element, to account for the fact that certain beliefs may depend on the state of the environment as well as the internal state of the thinker. It has been argued, for example, that to believe that water is wet, a subject must be related in an appropriate way to water in the environment. This relation is usually taken to be a causal relation, so it is possible that one could build this into the characterization of the relevant psychological property, where the causal roles in question stretch outside the head into the environment. If so, then no extra component would be required. But in any case, it is not much of a burden to note that there might also be a relational component to certain mental states, over and above the psychological and phenomenal components. Either way, no deep further mystery arises.

To see that there is no deep further aspect over and above the phenomenal and the psychological/relational aspects of intentional states, note that the manifest phenomena in the vicinity that need explaining fall into two classes: those we have third-person access to, and those we have first-person access to. Those in the former class ultimately come down to behavior, relations to the environment, and so on, and can be subsumed into the class of the psychological and the relational. Those in the latter class come down to the *experience* associated with believing—for example, the way our concepts seem to reach out into a phenomenal world—and thus constitute part of the problem of consciousness, not a separate mystery. The reasons for believing in any given aspect of belief (including semantic content, "aboutness," and so on) will derive from one of these two classes; there is no independent third class of phenomena forcing itself on us to be explained.

Another way to see this is to note that once we have fixed the psychological, phenomenal, and relational properties of an individual, there seems to be nothing mental that can be independently varied. We cannot even *imagine* someone identical to me in the three respects mentioned above but who believes something different, in the way that we can arguably imagine someone psychologically identical to me who experiences something different. There is simply not enough room in conceptual space for the possibility. Intentional concepts are in some ways less primitive than psychological and phenomenal concepts, in that they cannot be varied independently of the latter.[12]

Everything that I have said here about belief applies equally to other intentional states, such as desire, hope, and so on. All of these states have a psychological and a phenomenal aspect, and we need not legislate which is primary, although a strong case might be made for a psychological analysis. What counts is that there is no aspect of this state that outstrips both the psychological and the phenomenal (with perhaps a relational component thrown in). Psychology and phenomenology together constitute the central aspects of the mind.

The co-occurrence of phenomenal and psychological properties

It is a fact about the human mind that whenever a phenomenal property is instantiated, a corresponding psychological property is instantiated. Conscious experience does not occur in a vacuum. It is always tied to cognitive processing, and it is likely that in some sense it arises from that processing. Whenever one has a sensation, for example, there is some information processing going on: a corresponding perception, if you like. Similarly, whenever one has the conscious experience of happiness, the functional role associated with happiness is generally being played by some internal state. Perhaps it is logically possible that one could have the experience without the causation, but it seems to be an empirical fact that they go together.

In the face of this co-occurrence, the faint-hearted may be tempted to worry whether any real distinction is being made. But it is clear that there is at least a conceptual distinction here, even if the extensions of the concepts involved seem to go together. One can wonder how to explain the phenomenal quality, and one can wonder how to explain the playing of the causal role, and these are two distinct wonderings.

That being said, the co-occurrence of phenomenal and psychological properties reflects something deep about our phenomenal concepts. We have no independent language for describing phenomenal qualities. As we have seen, there is something ineffable about them. Although greenness is a distinct sort of sensation with a rich intrinsic character, there is very little that one can say about it other than that it is green. In talking about phenomenal qualities, we generally have to specify the qualities in question in terms of associated external properties, or in terms of associated causal roles. Our *language* for phenomenal qualities is derivative on our nonphenomenal language. As Ryle said, there are no "neat" sensation words.

If one looks at the catalog of conscious experience that I presented earlier, the experiences in question are never described in terms of their intrinsic qualities. Rather, I used expressions such as "the smell of freshly baked bread," "the patterns one gets when closing one's eyes," and so on. Even with a term like "green sensation," reference is effectively pinned down in extrinsic terms. When we learn the term "green sensation," it is effectively by ostension—we learn to apply it to the sort of experience caused by grass, trees, and so on. Generally, insofar as we have communicable phenomenal categories at all, they are defined with respect either to their typical external associations or to an associated kind of psychological state. For instance, when one speaks of the phenomenal quality of happiness, the reference of the term "happiness" is implicitly fixed via some causal role—the state where one judges all to be good, jumps for joy, and so on. Perhaps this is one interpretation of Wittgenstein's famous remark, "An inner process stands in need of outward criteria."

This dependence of phenomenal concepts on causal criteria has led some (including Wittgenstein and Ryle, in some of their moods) to suggest that there is nothing to the meaning of our mental concepts beyond the associated causal criteria. There is a certain plausibility to this: if a phenomenal property is always picked out by invoking a psychological property, why not suppose that there is only one property involved? But this temptation should be resisted. When we talk of a green sensation, this talk is not equivalent simply to talk of "a state that is caused by grass, trees, and so on." We are talking about the *phenomenal quality* that generally occurs when a state is caused by grass and trees. If there is a causal analysis in the vicinity, it is something like "the kind of *phenomenal* state that is caused by grass, trees, and so on."[13] The phenomenal element in the concept prevents an analysis in purely functional terms.

In general, when a phenomenal property is picked out with the aid of a psychological property *P,* the phenomenal notion is not just *"P."* It is "the sort of conscious experience that tends to accompany *P."* And importantly, the very notion of "phenomenal quality" or "conscious experience" is not defined in psychological terms. Rather, the notion of conscious experience is something of a primitive, as we saw earlier. *If* there were a functional analysis of the notion of experience or phenomenal quality, then the analysis in question would yield functional analyses of specific phenomenal properties, but in the absence of such an analysis we cannot draw such a conclusion.

We cannot identify the notion "phenomenal *P*" with that of "psychological *P*" for all the usual reasons: there are two distinct concepts here, as witnessed by the fact that there are two distinct explananda. Although "phenomenal *P*" is picked out as "the experience that tends to accompany psychological *P,*" we can coherently imagine a situation in which phenomenal *P* occurs without psychological *P,* and vice versa. A Rolls-Royce icon can be roughly analyzed as the kind of icon that is generally found on Rolls-Royce cars, but this does not mean that to be a Rolls-Royce icon is to be a Rolls-Royce car.

This gives us some insight into the sparseness of our specifically phenomenal vocabulary compared to our psychological vocabulary, and it also helps us understand why phenomenal and psychological properties have so often been conflated. For most everyday purposes this conflation does not matter: when one claims that someone is happy, one need not be talking specifically about either the phenomenal quality or the functional role, as they usually go together. However, for philosophical purposes and in particular for the purposes of explanation, to conflate these properties is fatal. The conflation can be tempting, as collapsing the distinction makes the problem of explaining conscious experience suddenly very straightforward; but it is utterly unsatisfactory for the same reason. The problem of consciousness cannot be spirited away on purely verbal grounds.

4. The Two Mind–Body Problems

The division of mental properties into phenomenal and psychological properties has the effect of dividing the mind–body problem into two: an easy part and a hard part. The psychological aspects of mind pose many technical problems for cognitive science, and a number of interesting puzzles for philosophical analysis, but they pose no deep metaphysical enigmas. The question "How could a physical system be the sort of thing that could *learn,* or that could *remember?*" does not have the same bite as the corresponding question about sensations, or about consciousness in general. The reason for this is clear. By our analysis in section 3, learning and memory are functional properties, characterized by causal roles, so the question "How could a physical system have psychological property *P*?" comes to the same thing as "How could a state of a physical system play such-and-such a causal role?" This is a question for the sciences of physical systems. One simply needs to tell a story about the organization of the physical system that allows it to react to environmental stimulation and produce behavior in the appropriate sorts of ways. While the technical problems are enormous, there is a clearly defined research program for their answer. The metaphysical problems are relatively few.

This is not to say that psychological properties pose *no* philosophical difficulties. There are significant problems in coming up with the correct analyses of these notions, for instance. Even if it is widely accepted that these are functional concepts, there can be significant disagreement about just how the requisite functional analyses should run. Intentional properties such as belief and desire, for example, provide fertile grounds for argument. In particular, the question of just what constitutes the content of a given intentional state is still poorly understood. There are also technical problems concerning just how high-level constructs such as these can play a real causal role in the production of behavior, especially if these are partly constituted by properties of the environment, or if there are no strict laws connecting psychological states with behavior. Then there are semi-empirical problems in the foundations of cognitive science concerning just how these properties might be instantiated in existing cognitive systems, or even concerning whether they are instantiated at all.

These problems are all serious, but they have the character of puzzles rather than mysteries. The situation here is analogous to that in the philosophy of biology, where there is no pressing life–body problem; there are merely a host of technical problems about evolution, selection, adaptation, fitness, and species. Just as most of the apparent metaphysical mysteries surrounding biology were disposed of long ago, it is fair to say that the mind–body problem for psychological properties is for all intents and purposes dissolved. What remains is a collection of smaller technical problems with which the normal course of scientific and philosophical analysis can grapple.

The phenomenal aspects of mind are a different matter. Here, the mind–body problem is as baffling as it ever was. The impressive progress of the physical and cognitive sciences has not shed significant light on the question of how and why cognitive functioning is accompanied by conscious experience. The progress in the understanding of the mind has almost entirely centered on the explanation of behavior. This progress leaves the question of conscious experience untouched.

If we like, we can view the psychological–phenomenal distinction not so much as splitting the mind–body problem as factoring it into two separate parts. The hardest part of the mind–body problem is the question: how could a physical system give rise to conscious experience? We might factor the link between the physical and conscious experience into two parts: the link between the physical and the psychological, and the link between the psychological and the phenomenal. As we saw above, we now have a pretty good idea of how a physical system can have psychological properties: the *psychological* mind–body problem has been dissolved. What remains is the question of why and how these psychological properties are accompanied by phenomenal properties: why all the stimulation and reaction associated with pain is accompanied by the *experience* of pain, for instance. Following Jackendoff (1987), we can call this residue the *mind–mind problem*. Current physical explanations take us as far as the psychological mind. What remains ill understood is the link between the psychological mind and the phenomenal mind.[14]

It is conceivable that the link between the phenomenal and the physical might be independent of that between the psychological and the physical, so that factoring would be impossible, but it seems unlikely. The close correlation that we have seen between phenomenal and psychological properties suggests a deep link. In later chapters, I will argue that the link is an extremely strong one and that the factoring strategy is valuable in approaching the mind–body problem. If so, then understanding the link between the psychological and the phenomenal is crucial to understanding conscious experience.

5. Two Concepts of Consciousness

Given that so many mental terms have a dual nature, it will not be surprising to learn that even "consciousness" has both phenomenal and psychological senses. So far, I have been focusing on the phenomenal sense, which itself subsumes all the previously mentioned phenomenal aspects of mind. To be conscious in this sense is just to instantiate some phenomenal quality. This is the key sense of "consciousness," or at least the one that poses the major explanatory problems. But it is not the only sense of the term. "Consciousness" can also be used to refer to a variety of psychological properties, such as reportability or introspective accessibility of information. We can group psychological properties of this sort under the label of *psychological consciousness,* as opposed to the *phenomenal consciousness* on which I have been concentrating.

This ambiguity can lead to much confusion in the discussion of consciousness. Frequently, someone putting forward an explanation of consciousness will start by investing the problem with all the gravity of the problem of phenomenal consciousness, but will end by giving an explanation of some aspect of psychological consciousness, such as the ability to introspect. This explanation might be worthwhile in its own right, but one is left with the sense that more has been promised than has been delivered.

Varieties of psychological consciousness

There are numerous psychological notions for which the term "consciousness" is sometimes used. These include the following:

Awakeness. Sometimes we say that a person is conscious as another way of saying that they are not asleep. It makes sense to suppose that we have experiences while we are asleep, so this notion clearly does not coincide with phenomenal consciousness. Awakeness can plausibly be analyzed in functional terms—perhaps, at a first approximation, in terms of an ability to process information about the world and deal with it in a rational fashion.

Introspection. This is the process by which we can become aware of the contents of our internal states. If you ask me about my mental states, it is by introspection that I determine my answer. This access to one's mental states is an important component of the everyday concept of consciousness, and it is at least partly a functional notion. One might analyze it in terms of one's rational processes being sensitive to information about one's internal states in the right sort of way, and one's being able to use this information appropriately.

Reportability. This is our ability to report the contents of our mental states. It presupposes the ability to introspect, but is more constrained than that ability, as it presupposes a capacity for language. This concept of consciousness has often been the central target of philosophers and psychologists of an operationalist bent.

Self-consciousness. This refers to our ability to think about ourselves, our awareness of our existence as individuals and of our distinctness from others. My self-consciousness might be analyzed in terms of my access to a self-model, or my possession of a certain sort of representation that is associated in some way with myself. It may well be that self-consciousness is limited to humans and a few species of animals.

Attention. We often say that someone is conscious of something precisely when they are paying attention to it; that is, when a significant portion of their cognitive resources is devoted to dealing with the relevant information. We can be phenomenally conscious of something without attending to it, as witnessed by the fringes of a visual field.

Voluntary control. In another sense, we say that a behavioral *act* is conscious when that act is performed deliberately; that is, where the action is caused in the appropriate sort of way by an element of prior thought.

Knowledge. In another everyday sense, we say that someone is conscious of a fact precisely when they know the fact, and that they are conscious of a thing precisely when they know about that thing. This notion is rarely the focus of technical discussion of consciousness, but it is probably as central to the everyday usage of the term as anything else.

That these are all largely functional notions can be seen from how one would explain the phenomena in question. If one were to try to explain attention, one might devise a model of the cognitive processes that lead to resources being concentrated on one aspect of available information rather than another. If one were to try to explain introspection, one would try to explain the processes by which one is sensitive to one's internal states in the appropriate way. Similar stories apply to explanation of the other properties. In each case, a functional explanation seems to capture what is central.

Although these concepts have a psychological core, many or all of them are associated with phenomenal states. There is a certain sort of phenomenal state associated with self-consciousness, for example. The same goes for introspection, attention, and the voluntary control of behavior. As with the other dual-aspect terms that I have discussed, terms such as "introspection" and "self-consciousness" are sometimes used to refer to the phenomenal state, which can lead to confusion. Indeed, some might argue that a phenomenal aspect is required for a process to truly qualify as "introspection," "attention," or whatever. As before, however, this issue is largely verbal. It is clear that there is a phenomenal and a psychological property in the vicinity of each of these concepts. Those who do not like to dignify the psychological property with a mental term such as "attention" can use the term "pseudo-attention" instead. The substantial philosophical issues remain the same, no matter what the properties are called.

The phenomenal and the psychological properties in the vicinity of these notions tend to occur together, but as with other mental concepts, they should not be conflated. We should also be careful not to conflate the phenomenal senses of these terms with phenomenal consciousness in general.

Consciousness and awareness

We have seen that there is a psychological property associated with the experience of emotion, a psychological property associated with the experience of self-consciousness, a psychological property associated with the experience of sensation, and so on. It is natural to suppose that there might be a psychological property associated with experience itself, or with phenomenal consciousness. In fact, I think there is such a property in the vicinity; we can call it "awareness." This is the most general brand of psychological consciousness.

Awareness can be broadly analyzed as a state wherein we have access to some information, and can use that information in the control of behavior. One can be aware of an object in the environment, of a state of one's body, or of one's mental state, among other things. Awareness of information generally brings with it the ability to knowingly direct behavior depending on that information. This is clearly a functional notion. In everyday language, the term "awareness" is often used synonymously with "consciousness," but I will reserve the term for the functional notion I have described here.

In general, wherever there is phenomenal consciousness, there seems to be awareness. My phenomenal experience of the yellow book beside me is accompanied by my functional awareness of the book, and indeed by my awareness of the yellow color. My experience of a pain is accompanied by an awareness of the presence of something nasty, which tends to lead to withdrawal and the like, where possible. The fact that any conscious experience is accompanied by awareness is made clear by the fact that a conscious experience is *reportable*. If I am having an experience, I can talk about the fact that I am having it. I may not be paying attention to it, but I at least have the ability to focus on it and talk about it, if I choose. This reportability immediately implies that I am aware in the relevant sense. Of course, an animal or a prelinguistic human might have conscious experience without the ability to report, but such a being would still plausibly have a degree of awareness. Awareness does not entail the ability to report, although the two tend to go together in creatures with language.

Consciousness is always accompanied by awareness, but awareness as I have described it need not be accompanied by consciousness. One can be aware of a fact without any particular associated phenomenal experience, for instance. However, it may be possible to constrain the notion of awareness so that it turns out to be coextensive with phenomenal consciousness, or nearly so. I will not attempt that project here, but I discuss it further in Chapter 6.

The notion of awareness subsumes most or all of the various psychological notions of consciousness just enumerated. Introspection can be analyzed as awareness of some internal state. Attention can be analyzed as a particularly high degree of awareness of an object or event. Self-consciousness can be understood as awareness of oneself. Voluntary control is trickier, although it might be partly analyzed as requiring attention to the behavior one is performing. Awakeness might be roughly characterized as a state in which one is able to deal rationally with one's environment to some extent, and so implies a particular sort of awareness.

The idea that there is a functional notion of consciousness that can be explicated in terms of access has been fleshed out by Block (1995), who talks about the distinction between "phenomenal consciousness" and "access consciousness." Block's notion of access consciousness corresponds closely to the notion of awareness that I have been describing (I discuss the relationship further in Chapter 6). In a similar fashion, Newell (1992) explicitly distinguishes between "awareness" and "consciousness." He describes awareness as "the ability of a subject to make its behavior depend on some knowledge," and goes on to spell out the distinction between this notion and consciousness, which he says is a nonfunctional phenomenon. Similar distinctions have been made by other philosophers and cognitive scientists.[15]

Explaining consciousness versus explaining awareness

Awareness, like other psychological properties, poses few metaphysical problems. The problems posed by the psychological varieties of consciousness are of the same order of magnitude as those posed by memory, learning, and belief. Certainly, the notion of awareness is not crystal-clear, so there is room for significant philosophical analysis of just what it comes to. Further, there is room for an enormous amount of research in cognitive science, studying how natural and artificial cognitive systems might function in such a way that they are aware. But the outlines of these research programs are reasonably clear. There is little reason to suppose that the normal course of cognitive science, backed by appropriate philosophical analysis, should not eventually succeed.

Insofar as consciousness is the really difficult problem for a science of the mind, it is phenomenal consciousness that is central. The problems here are of a different order of magnitude. Even after we have explained the physical and computational functioning of a conscious system, we still need to explain why the system has conscious experiences. Some dispute this claim, of course, and I will discuss it at greater length soon. For now, though, we can simply note the *prima facie* difference in the problems that the phenomenal and psychological varieties present. It is phenomenal consciousness that poses the *worrying* problem of consciousness.

Given the differences between the psychological and phenomenal notions of consciousness, it is unfortunate that they are often conflated in the literature. This conflation matters little in everyday speech, as awareness and phenomenal consciousness usually go together. But for the purposes of explanation, the conceptual distinction is crucial. Insofar as any remotely satisfactory explanations of "consciousness" have been put forward, it is usually a psychological aspect that is explained. The phenomenal aspects generally go untouched.

Many recent philosophical analyses of consciousness have concerned themselves primarily with the nonphenomenal aspects. Rosenthal (1996) argues that a mental state is conscious precisely when there is a higher-order thought about that mental state. This might be a useful analysis of introspective consciousness, and perhaps of other aspects of awareness, but it does not appear to explain phenomenal experience.[16] Similarly, Dennett (1991) spends much of his book outlining a detailed cognitive model, which he puts forward as an explanation of consciousness. On the face of it, the model is centrally a model of the capacity of a subject to verbally report a mental state. It might thus yield an explanation of reportability, of introspective consciousness, and perhaps of other aspects of awareness, but nothing in the model provides an explanation of phenomenal consciousness (although Dennett would put things differently).

Armstrong (1968), confronted by consciousness as an obstacle for his functionalist theory of mind, analyzes the notion in terms of the presence of some self-scanning mechanism. This might provide a useful account of self-consciousness and introspective consciousness, but it leaves the problem of phenomenal experience to the side. Armstrong (1981) talks about both perceptual consciousness and introspective consciousness, but is concerned with both only as varieties of awareness, and does not address the problems posed by the phenomenal qualities of experience. Thus the sense in which consciousness is really *problematic* for his functionalist theory is sidestepped, by courtesy of the ambiguity in the notion of consciousness.

Others writing on the topic of "consciousness" have been primarily concerned with self-consciousness or introspective consciousness. Van Gulick (1988), in suggesting that consciousness should be analyzed as the possession of "reflexive metapsychological information," is at best providing an analysis of these psychological notions, and indeed concedes that the phenomenal aspects may be left out by such an analysis. Similarly, Jaynes's (1976) elaborate theory of consciousness is concerned only with our awareness of our own thoughts. It says nothing about phenomena associated with perception and therefore could not hope to be a theory of awareness in general, let alone a theory of phenomenal consciousness. Hofstadter (1979) has some interesting things to say about consciousness, but he is more concerned with introspection, free will, and the sense of self than with experience *per se.*

Insofar as consciousness has been a topic for discussion among psychologists, the phenomenal and psychological notions have not often been carefully distinguished. Usually it is some aspect of awareness, such as introspection, attention, or self-consciousness, that psychological studies address. Even the psychological aspects of consciousness have had something of a bad name in psychology, at least until recently. Perhaps this is because of some unclearness in those notions, and the difficulties associated with high-level phenomena such as introspection. One might speculate that to a larger extent this bad reputation is due to their sharing a name with phenomenal consciousness, giving the appearance of partnership in crime.

One sometimes hears that psychological research has been "returning to consciousness" in recent years. The reality seems to be that the psychological aspects of consciousness have been an active subject of research, and that researchers have not been afraid to use the term "consciousness" for the phenomena. For the most part, however, phenomenal consciousness remains off to the side. Perhaps this is understandable. While one can see how the methods of experimental psychology might lead to an understanding of the various kinds of awareness, it is not easy to see how they could explain phenomenal experience.[17]

Cognitive models are well suited to explaining psychological aspects of consciousness. There is no vast metaphysical problem in the idea that a physical system should be able to introspect its internal states, or that it should be able to deal rationally with information from its environment, or that it should be able to focus its attention first in one place and then in the next. It is clear enough that an appropriate functional account should be able to explain these abilities, even if discovering the correct account takes decades or centuries. But the really difficult problem is that of phenomenal consciousness, and this is left untouched by the explanations of psychological consciousness that have been put forward so far.

In what follows, I revert to using "consciousness" to refer to phenomenal consciousness alone. When I wish to use the psychological notions, I will speak of "psychological consciousness" or "awareness." It is phenomenal consciousness with which I will mostly be concerned.

2

Supervenience and Explanation

What is the place of consciousness in the natural order? Is consciousness physical? Can consciousness be explained in physical terms? To come to grips with these issues, we need to build a framework; in this chapter, I build one. The centerpiece of this framework is the concept of *supervenience*: I give an account of this concept and apply it to clarify the idea of reductive explanation. Using this account, I sketch a picture of the relationship between most high-level phenomena and physical facts, one that seems to cover everything except, perhaps, for conscious experience.

1. Supervenience

It is widely believed that the most fundamental facts about our universe are physical facts, and that all other facts are dependent on these. In a weak enough sense of "dependent," this may be almost trivially true; in a strong sense, it is controversial. There is a complex variety of dependence relations between high-level facts and low-level facts in general, and the kind of dependence relation that holds in one domain, such as biology, may not hold in another, such as that of conscious experience. The philosophical notion of supervenience provides a unifying framework within which these dependence relations can be discussed.

The notion of supervenience formalizes the intuitive idea that one set of facts can fully determine another set of facts.[1] The physical facts about the world seem to determine the biological facts, for instance, in that once all the physical facts about the world are fixed, there is no room for the biological facts to vary. (Fixing all the physical facts will simultaneously fix which objects are alive.) This provides a rough characterization of the sense in which biological properties supervene on physical properties. In general, supervenience is a relation between two sets of properties: B-properties—intuitively, the *high-level* properties—and A-properties, which are the more basic *low-level* properties.

For our purposes, the relevant A-properties are usually the physical properties: more precisely, the fundamental properties that are invoked by a completed theory of physics. Perhaps these will include mass, charge, spatiotemporal position; properties characterizing the distribution of various spatiotemporal fields, the exertion of various forces, and the form of various waves; and so on. The precise nature of these properties is not important. If physics changes radically, the relevant class of properties may be quite different from those I mention, but the arguments will go through all the same. Such high-level properties as juiciness, lumpiness, giraffehood, and the like are excluded, even though there is a sense in which these properties are physical. In what follows, talk of physical properties is implicitly restricted to the class of fundamental properties unless otherwise indicated. I will sometimes speak of "microphysical" or "low-level physical" properties to be explicit.

The *A-facts* and *B-facts* about the world are the facts concerning the instantiation and distribution of A-properties and B-properties.[2] So the physical facts about the world encompass all facts about the instantiation of physical properties within the spatiotemporal manifold. It is also useful to stipulate that the world's physical facts include its basic physical laws. On some accounts, these laws are already determined by the totality of particular physical facts, but we cannot take this for granted.

The template for the definition of supervenience is the following:

B-properties *supervene* on A-properties if no two possible situations are identical with respect to their A-properties while differing in their B-properties.

For instance, biological properties supervene on physical properties insofar as any two possible situations that are physically identical are biologically identical. (I use "identical" in the sense of indiscernibility rather than numerical identity here. In this sense, two separate tables might be physically identical.) More precise notions of supervenience can be obtained by filling in this template. Depending on whether we take the "situations" in question to be individuals or entire worlds, we arrive at notions of *local* and *global* supervenience, respectively. And depending on how we construe the notion of possibility, we obtain notions of *logical* supervenience, *natural* supervenience, and perhaps others. I will flesh out these distinctions in what follows.

Local and global supervenience

B-properties supervene *locally* on A-properties if the A-properties of an *individual* determine the B-properties of that individual—if, that is, any two possible individuals that instantiate the same A-properties instantiate the same B-properties. For example, shape supervenes locally on physical properties: any two objects with the same physical properties will necessarily have the same shape. Value does not supervene locally on physical properties, however: an exact physical replica of the Mona Lisa is not worth as much as the Mona Lisa. In general, local supervenience of a property on the physical fails if that property is somehow context-dependent—that is, if an object's possession of that property depends not only on the object's physical constitution but also on its environment and its history. The Mona Lisa is more valuable than its replica because of a difference in their historical context: the Mona Lisa was painted by Leonardo, whereas the replica was not.[3]

B-properties supervene *globally* on A-properties, by contrast, if the A-facts about the entire *world* determine the B-facts: that is, if there are no two possible worlds identical with respect to their A-properties, but differing with respect to their B-properties.[4] A world here is to be thought of as an entire universe; different possible worlds correspond to different ways a universe might be.

Local supervenience implies global supervenience, but not vice versa. For example, it is plausible that biological properties supervene globally on physical properties, in that any world physically identical to ours would also be biologically identical. (There is a small caveat here, which I discuss shortly.) But they probably do not supervene locally. Two physically identical organisms can arguably differ in certain biological characteristics. One might be *fitter* than the other, for example, due to differences in their environmental contexts. It is even conceivable that physically identical organisms could be members of different species, if they had different evolutionary histories.

The distinction between global and local supervenience does not matter too much when it comes to conscious experience, because it is likely that insofar as consciousness supervenes on the physical at all, it supervenes locally. If two creatures are physically identical, then differences in environmental and historical contexts will not prevent them from having identical experiences. Of course, context can affect experience indirectly, but only by virtue of affecting internal structure, as in the case of perception. Phenomena such as hallucination and illusion illustrate the fact that it is internal structure rather than context that is *directly* responsible for experience.

Logical and natural supervenience

more important distinction for our purposes is between *logical* (or conceptual) supervenience, and mere *natural* (or nomic, or empirical) supervenience.

B-properties supervene *logically* on A-properties if no two *logically possible* situations are identical with respect to their A-properties but distinct with respect to their B-properties. I will say more about logical possibility later in this chapter. For now, one can think of it loosely as possibility in the broadest sense, corresponding roughly to conceivability, quite unconstrained by the laws of our world. It is useful to think of a logically possible world as a world that it would have been in God's power (hypothetically!) to create, had he so chosen.[5] God could not have created a world with male vixens, but he could have created a world with flying telephones. In determining whether it is logically possible that some statement is true, the constraints are largely *conceptual*. The notion of a male vixen is contradictory, so a male vixen is logically impossible; the notion of a flying telephone is conceptually coherent, if a little out of the ordinary, so a flying telephone is logically possible.

It should be stressed that the logical supervenience is not defined in terms of deducibility in any system of formal logic. Rather, logical supervenience is defined in terms of logically possible *worlds* (and individuals), where the notion of a logically possible world is independent of these formal considerations. This sort of possibility is often called "broadly logical" possibility in the philosophical literature, as opposed to the "strictly logical" possibility that depends on formal systems.[6]

At the global level, biological properties supervene logically on physical properties. Even God could not have created a world that was physically identical to ours but biologically distinct. There is simply no logical space for the biological facts to independently vary. When we fix all the physical facts about the world—including the facts about the distribution of every last particle across space and time—we will in effect also fix the macroscopic shape of all the objects in the world, the way they move and function, the way they physically interact. If there is a living kangaroo in this world, then *any* world that is physically identical to this world will contain a physically identical kangaroo, and that kangaroo will automatically be alive.

We can imagine that a hypothetical superbeing—Laplace's demon, say, who knows the location of every particle in the universe—would be able to straightforwardly "read off" all the biological facts, once given all the microphysical facts. The microphysical facts are enough for such a being to construct a model of the microscopic structure and dynamics of the world throughout space and time, from which it can straightforwardly deduce the macroscopic structure and dynamics. Given all that information, it has all the information it needs to determine which systems are alive, which systems belong to the same species, and so on. As long as it possesses the biological concepts and has a full specification of the microphysical facts, no other information is relevant.

In general, when B-properties supervene logically on A-properties, we can say that the A-facts *entail* the B-facts, where one fact entails another if it is logically impossible for the first to hold without the second. In such cases, Laplace's demon could read off the B-facts from a specification of the A-facts, as long as it possesses the B-concepts in question. (I will say much more about the connections between these different ways of understanding logical supervenience later in the chapter; the present discussion is largely for illustration.) In a sense, when logical supervenience holds, *all there is* to the B-facts being as they are is that the A-facts are as they are.

There can be supervenience without logical supervenience, however. The weaker variety of supervenience arises when two sets of properties are systematically and perfectly *correlated* in the natural world. For example, the pressure exerted by one mole of a gas systematically depends on its temperature and volume according to the law $pV = KT$, where K is a constant (I pretend for the purposes of illustration that all gases are ideal gases). In the actual world, whenever there is a mole of gas at a given temperature and volume, its pressure will be determined: it is empirically impossible that two distinct moles of gas could have the same temperature and volume, but different pressure. It follows that the pressure of a mole of gas supervenes on its temperature and volume in a certain sense. (In this example, I am taking the class of A-properties to be much narrower than the class of physical properties, for reasons that will become clear.) But this supervenience is weaker than logical supervenience. It is *logically* possible that a mole of gas with a given temperature and volume might have a different pressure; imagine a world in which the gas constant K is larger or smaller, for example. Rather, it is just a fact about *nature* that there is this correlation.

This is an example of *natural* supervenience of one property on others: in this instance, pressure supervenes naturally on temperature, volume, and the property of being a mole of gas. In general, B-properties supervene naturally on A-properties if any two *naturally possible* situations with the same A-properties have the same B-properties.

A naturally possible situation is one that could actually occur in nature, without violating any natural laws. This is a much stronger constraint than mere logical possibility. The scenario with a different gas constant is logically possible, for example, but it could never occur in the real world, so it is not naturally possible. Among naturally possible situations, any two moles of gas with the same temperature and volume will have the same pressure.

Intuitively, natural possibility corresponds to what we think of as real *empirical* possibility—a naturally possible situation is one that could come up in the real world, if the conditions were right. These include not just actual situations but counterfactual situations that might have come up in the world's history, if boundary conditions had been different, or that might come up in the future, depending on how things go. A mile-high skyscraper is almost certainly naturally possible, for example, even though none has actually been constructed. It is even naturally possible (although wildly improbable) that a monkey could type *Hamlet*. We can also think of a naturally possible situation as one that conforms to the laws of nature of our world.[7] For this reason, natural possibility is sometimes called *nomic* or *nomological* possibility,[8] from the Greek term *nomos* for "law."

There are a vast number of logically possible situations that are not naturally possible. Any situation that violates the laws of nature of our world falls into this class: a universe without gravity, for example, or with different values of fundamental constants. Science fiction provides many situations of this sort, such as antigravity devices and perpetual-motion machines. These are easy to imagine, but almost certainly could never come to exist in our world.

In the reverse direction, any situation that is naturally possible will be logically possible. The class of natural possibilities is therefore a subset of the class of logical possiblities. To illustrate this distinction: both a cubic mile of gold and a cubic mile of uranium-235 seem to be logically possible, but as far as we know, only the first is naturally possible—a (stable) cubic mile of uranium-235 could not exist in our world.

Natural supervenience holds when, among all naturally possible situations, those with the same distribution of A-properties have the same distributon of B-properties: that is, when the A-facts about a situation *naturally necessitate* the B-facts. This happens when the same clusters of A-properties in our world are always accompanied by the same B-properties, and when this correlation is not just coincidental but *lawful*: that is, when instantiating the A-properties will always bring about the B-properties, wherever and whenever this happens. (In philosophical terms, the dependence must support counterfactuals.) This co-occurrence need not hold in every logically possible situation, but it must hold in every naturally possible situation.

It is clear that logical supervenience implies natural supervenience. If any two logically possible situations with the same A-properties have the same B-properties, then any two naturally possible situations will also. The reverse does not hold, however, as the gas law illustrates. The temperature and volume of a mole of gas determine pressure across naturally but not logically possible situations, so pressure depends naturally but not logically on temperature and volume. Where we have natural supervenience without logical supervenience, I will say that we have *mere* natural supervenience.

For reasons that will become clear, it is hard to find cases of natural supervenience on the set of *physical* properties without logical supervenience, but consciousness itself can provide a useful illustration. It seems very likely that consciousness is naturally supervenient on physical properties, locally or globally, insofar as in the natural world, any two physically identical creatures will have qualitatively identical experiences. It is not at all clear that consciousness is logically supervenient on physical properties, however.

It seems *logically* possible, at least to many, that a creature physically identical to a conscious creature might have no conscious experiences at all, or that it might have conscious experiences of a different kind. (Some dispute this, but I use it for now only as an illustration.) If this is so, then conscious experience supervenes naturally but not logically on the physical. The necessary connection between physical structure and experience is ensured only by the laws of nature, and not by any logical or conceptual force.

The distinction between logical and natural supervenience is vital for our purposes.[9] We can intuitively understand the distinction as follows. If B-properties supervene logically on A-properties, then once God (hypothetically) creates a world with certain A-facts, the B-facts come along for free as an automatic consequence. If B-properties merely supervene naturally on A-properties, however, then after making sure of the A-facts, God has to do more work in order to make sure of the B-facts: he has to make sure there is a law relating the A-facts and the B-facts. (I borrow this image from Kripke 1972.) Once the law is in place, the relevant A-facts will automatically bring along the B-facts; but one could, in principle, have had a situation where they did not.

One also sometimes hears talk of *metaphysical* supervenience, which is based on neither logical nor natural necessity, but on "necessity *tout court*," or "metaphysical necessity" as it is sometimes known (drawing inspiration from Kripke's [1972] discussion of *a posteriori* necessity). I will argue later that the metaphysically possible worlds are just the logically possible worlds (and that metaphysical possibility of statements is logical possibility with an *a posteriori* semantic twist), but for now it is harmless to assume there is a notion of metaphysical supervenience, to be spelled out by analogy with the notions of logical and natural supervenience above. A notion of "weak" supervenience is also mentioned occasionally, but seems too weak to express an interesting dependence relation between properties.[10]

The logical–natural distinction and the global–local distinction cut across each other. It is reasonable to speak of both global logical supervenience and local logical supervenience, although I will more often be concerned with the former. When I speak of logical supervenience without a further modifier, global logical supervenience is intended. It is also coherent to speak of global and local natural supervenience, but the natural supervenience relations with which we are concerned are generally local or at least localizable, for the simple reason that evidence for a natural supervenience relation generally consists in local regularities between clusters of properties.[11]

A problem with logical supervenience*

A technical problem with the notion of logical supervenience needs to be dealt with. This problem arises from the logical possibility of a world physically identical to ours, but with additional nonphysical stuff that is not present in our own world: angels, ectoplasm, and ghosts, for example. There is a *conceivable* world just like ours except that it has some extra angels hovering in a non-physical realm, made of ectoplasm. These angels might have biological properties of their own, if they reproduced and evolved. Presumably the angels could have all sorts of beliefs, and their communities might have complex social structure.

The problem these examples pose is clear. The angel world is physically identical to ours, but it is biologically distinct. If the angel world is logically possible, then according to our definition biological properties are not supervenient on physical properties. But we certainly *want* to say that biological properties are supervenient on physical properties, at least in *this* world if not in the angel world (assuming there are no angels in the actual world!). Intuitively, it seems undesirable for the mere logical possibility of the angel world to stand in the way of the determination of biological properties by physical properties in our own world.

This sort of problem has caused some (e.g., Haugeland 1982; Petrie 1987) to suggest that logical possibility and necessity are too strong to serve as the relevant sort of possibility and necessity in supervenience relations, and that a weaker variety such as natural possibility and necessity should be used instead. But this would render useless the very useful distinction between logical and natural supervenience outlined above, and would also ignore the fact that there is a very real sense in which the biological facts about our world are logically determined by the physical facts. Others (e.g., Teller 1989) have bitten the bullet by stipulating that worlds with extra nonphysical stuff are not logically or metaphysically possible, despite appearances, but this makes logical and metaphysical possibility seem quite arbitrary. Fortunately, such moves are not required. It turns out that it is possible to retain a useful notion of logical supervenience compatible with the possibility of these worlds, as long as we fix the definition appropriately.[12]

The key to the solution is to turn supervenience into a thesis about *our* world (or more generally, about particular worlds). This accords with the intuition that biological facts are logically determined by the physical facts in our world, despite the existence of bizarre worlds where they are not so determined. According to a revised definition, B-properties are logically supervenient on A-properties if the B-properties in our world are logically determined by the A-properties in the following sense: in any possible world with the same A-facts, the same B-facts will hold.[13] The existence of possible worlds with *extra* B-facts will thus not count against logical supervenience in our world, as long as *at least* the B-facts true in our world are true in all physically identical worlds. And this they generally will be (with an exception discussed below). If there is a koala eating in a gum tree in this world, there will be an identical koala eating in a gum tree in any physically identical world, whether or not that world has any angels hanging around.

There is a minor complication. There is a certain sort of biological fact about our world that does not hold in the angel world: the fact that our world has no living ectoplasm, for example, and the fact that all living things are based on DNA. Perhaps the angel world might even be set up with ectoplasm causally dependent on physical processes, so that wombat copulation on the physical plane sometimes gives rise to baby ectoplasmic wombats on the nonphysical plane. If so, then there might be a wombat that is childless (in a certain sense) in our world, with a counterpart that is not childless in the physically identical angel world. It follows that the property of being childless does not supervene according to our definition, and nor do the world-level properties such as that of having no living ectoplasm. Not all the facts about our world follow from the physical facts alone.

To analyze the problem, note that these facts all involve negative existence claims, and so depend not only on what is going on in our world but on what is not. We cannot expect these facts to be determined by any sort of localized facts, as they depend not just on local goings-on in the world but on the world's limits. Supervenience theses should apply only to *positive* facts and properties, those that cannot be negated simply by enlarging a world. We can define a positive fact in W as one that holds in every world that contains W as a proper part;[14] a positive property is one that if instantiated in a world W, is also instantiated by the corresponding individual in all worlds that contain W as a proper part.[15] Most everyday facts and properties are positive—think of the property of being a kangaroo, or of being six feet tall, or of having a child. Negative facts and properties will always involve negative existence claims in one form or another. These include explicitly negative existential facts such as the nonexistence of ectoplasm, universally quantified facts such as the fact that all living things are made of DNA, negative relational properties such as childlessness, and superlatives such as the property of being the most fecund organism in existence.

In future, the supervenience relations with which we are concerned should be understood to be restricted to positive facts and properties. When claiming that biological properties supervene on physical properties, it is only the positive biological properties that are at issue. All the properties with which we are concerned are positive—local physical and phenomenal properties, for instance—so this is not much of a restriction.

The definition of global logical supervenience of B-properties on A-properties therefore comes to this: for any logically possible world W that is A-indiscernible from our world, then the B-facts true of our world are true of W. We need not build in a clause about positiveness, but it will usually be understood that the only relevant B-facts and properties are positive facts and properties. Similarly, B-properties supervene locally and logically on A-properties when for every actual individual x and every logically possible individual *y*, if *y* is A-indiscernible from *x*, then the B-properties instantiated by *x* are instantiated by *y*. More briefly and more generally: B-properties supervene logically on A-properties if the B-facts about actual situations are entailed by the A-facts, where situations are understood as worlds and individuals in the global and local cases respectively. This definition captures the idea that supervenience claims are usually claims about our world, while retaining the key role of logical necessity.[16]

Supervenience and materialism

Logical and natural supervenience have quite different ramifications for ontology: that is, for the matter of what there is in the world. If B-properties are logically supervenient on A-properties, then there is a sense in which once the A-facts are given, the B-facts are a free lunch. Once God (hypothetically) made sure that all the physical facts in our world held, the biological facts came along for free. The B-facts merely redescribe what is described by the A-facts. They may be *different* facts (a fact about elephants is not a microphysical fact), but they are not *further* facts.

With mere natural supervenience, the ontology is not so straightforward. Contingent lawful connections connect distinct features of the world. In general, if B-properties are merely naturally supervenient on A-properties in our world, then there *could* have been a world in which our A-facts held without the B-facts. As we saw before, once God fixed all the A-facts, in order to fix the B-facts he had more work to do. The B-facts are something over and above the A-facts, and their satisfaction implies that there is something new in the world.

With this in mind we can formulate precisely the widely held doctrine of *materialism* (or *physicalism*), which is generally taken to hold that everything in the world is physical, or that there is nothing over and above the physical, or that the physical facts in a certain sense exhaust all the facts about the world. In our language, materialism is true if all the positive facts about the world are globally logically supervenient on the physical facts. This captures the intuitive notion that if materialism is true, then once God fixed the physical facts about the world, all the facts were fixed.

(Or at least, all the positive facts were fixed. The restriction to positive facts is needed to ensure that worlds with extra ectoplasmic facts do not count against materialism in our world. Negative existential facts such as "There are no angels" are not strictly logically supervenient on the physical, but their nonsupervenience is quite compatible with materialism. In a sense, to fix the negative facts, God had to do more than fix the physical facts; he also had to declare, "That's all." If we wanted, we could add a second-order "That's all" fact to the supervenience base in the definition of materialism, in which case the positive-fact constraint could be removed.)

According to this definition, materialism is true if all the positive facts about our world are entailed by the physical facts.[17] That is, materialism is true if for any logically possible world W that is physically indiscernible from our world, all the positive facts true of our world are true of W. This is equivalent in turn to the thesis that any world that is physically indiscernible from our world contains a copy of our world as a (proper or improper) part, which seems an intuitively correct definition.[18] (This matches the definition of physicalism given by Jackson [1994], whose criterion is that every minimal physical duplicate of our world is a duplicate *simpliciter* of our world.[19])

I will discuss this matter at much greater length in Chapter 4, where this definition of materialism will be further justified. Some may object to the use of logical possibility rather than possibility *tout court* or "metaphysical possibility." Those people may substitute metaphysical possibility for logical possibility in the definition above. Later, I will argue that it comes to the same thing.

2. Reductive Explanation

The remarkable progress of science over the last few centuries has given us good reason to believe that there is very little that is utterly mysterious about the world. For almost every natural phenomenon above the level of microscopic physics, there seems in principle to exist a *reductive explanation*: that is, an explanation wholly in terms of simpler entities. In these cases, when we give an appropriate account of lower-level processes, an explanation of the higher-level phenomenon falls out.

Biological phenomena provide a clear illustration. Reproduction can be explained by giving an account of the genetic and cellular mechanisms that allow organisms to produce other organisms. Adaptation can be explained by giving an account of the mechanisms that lead to appropriate changes in external function in response to environmental stimulation. Life itself is explained by explaining the various mechanisms that bring about reproduction, adaptation, and the like. Once we have told the lower-level story in enough detail, any sense of fundamental mystery goes away: the phenomena that needed to be explained have been explained.

One can tell a similar story for most natural phenomena. In physics, we explain heat by telling an appropriate story about the energy and excitation of molecules. In astronomy, we explain the phases of the moon by going into the details of orbital motion and optical reflection. In geophysics, earthquakes are explained via an account of the interaction of subterranean masses. In cognitive science, to explain a phenomenon such as learning, all we have to do is explain various functional mechanisms—the mechanisms that give rise to appropriate changes in behavior in response to environmental stimulation, at a first approximation (any worries about the *experience* of learning aside). Many of the details of these explanations currently evade our grasp, and are likely to prove very complex, but we know that if we find out enough about the low-level story, the high-level story will eventually come along.

I will not precisely define the notion of reductive explanation until later. For now, it remains characterized by example. However, I can issue some caveats about what reductive explanation is not. A reductive explanation of a phenomenon need not require a *reduction* of that phenomenon, at least in some senses of that ambiguous term. In a certain sense, phenomena that can be realized in many different physical substrates—learning, for example—might not be reducible in that we cannot *identify* learning with any specific lower-level phenomenon. But this multiple realizability does not stand in the way of reductively *explaining* any instance of learning in terms of lower-level phenomena.[20] Reductive explanation of a phenomenon should also not be confused with a reduction of a high-level *theory*. Sometimes a reductive explanation of a phenomenon will provide a reduction of a pre-existing high-level theory, but other times it will show such theories to be on the wrong track. Often there might not even be a high-level theory to reduce.

Reductive explanation is not the be-all and end-all of explanation. There are many other sorts of explanation, some of which may shed more light on a phenomenon than a reductive explanation in a given instance. There are *historical* explanations, for instance, explaining the genesis of a phenomenon such as life, where a reductive explanation only gives a synchronic account of how living systems function. There are also all sorts of *high-level* explanations, such as the explanation of aspects of behavior in terms of beliefs and desires. Even though this behavior might in principle be explainable reductively, a high-level explanation is often more comprehensible and enlightening. Reductive explanations should not be seen as displacing these other sorts of explanation. Each has its place.

Reductive explanation via functional analysis

What is it that allows such diverse phenomena as reproduction, learning, and heat to be reductively explained? In all these cases, the nature of the concepts required to characterize the phenomena is crucial. If someone objected to a cellular explanation of reproduction, "This explains how a cellular process can lead to the production of a complex physical entity that is similar to the original entity, but it doesn't explain *reproduction*," we would have little patience—for that is all that "reproduction" *means*. In general, a reductive explanation of a phenomenon is accompanied by some rough-and-ready *analysis* of the phenomenon in question, whether implicit or explicit. The notion of reproduction can be roughly analyzed in terms of the ability of an organism to produce another organism in a certain sort of way. It follows that once we have explained the processes by which an organism produces another organism, we have explained that instance of reproduction.

The point may seem trivial, but the possibility of this kind of analysis undergirds the possibility of reductive explanation in general. Without such an analysis, there would be no explanatory bridge from the lower-level physical facts to the phenomenon in question. With such an analysis in hand, all we need to do is to show how certain lower-level physical mechanisms allow the analysis to be satisfied, and an explanation will result.

For the most interesting phenomena that require explanation, including phenomena such as reproduction and learning, the relevant notions can usually be analyzed *functionally*. The core of such notions can be characterized in terms of the performance of some function or functions (where "function" is taken causally rather than teleologically), or in terms of the capacity to perform those functions. It follows that once we have explained how those functions are performed, then we have explained the phenomena in question. Once we explain how an organism performs the function of producing another organism, we have explained reproduction, for all it means to reproduce is to perform that function. The same goes for an explanation of learning. All it means for an organism to learn, roughly, is for its behavioral capacities to adapt appropriately in response to environmental stimulation. If we explain how the organism is able to perform the relevant functions, then we have explained learning.

(At most, we may have failed to explain any *phenomenal* aspects of learning, which I leave aside here for obvious reasons. If there is a phenomenal element to the concept of learning, then that part of learning may go unexplained; but I concentrate on the psychological aspects of learning here, which are plausibly the core of the concept.)

Explaining the performance of these functions is quite straightforward, in principle. As long as the results of such functions are themselves characterizable physically, and all physical events have physical causes, then there should be a physical explanation for the performance of any such function. One need only show how certain sorts of states are responsible for the production of appropriate resultant states, by a causal process in accord with the laws of nature. Of course the details of this kind of physical explanation can be nontrivial. Indeed, the details constitute the vast bulk of any reductive explanation, while the analysis component is often trivial. But once the relevant details are in, a story about low-level physical causation will explain how the relevant functions are performed, and will therefore explain the phenomenon in question.

Even a physical notion such as heat can be construed functionally: roughly, heat is the kind of thing that expands metals, is caused by fire, leads to a particular sort of sensation, and the like. Once we have an account of how these various causal relations are fulfilled, then we have an account of heat. Heat is a *causal-role concept*, characterized in terms of what it is typically caused by and of what it typically causes, under appropriate conditions. Once empirical investigation shows how the relevant causal role is played, the phenomenon is explained.

There are some technical complications here, but they are inessential. For example, Kripke (1980) has pointed out a difference between a term such as "heat" and the associated description of a causal role: given that heat is realized by the motion of molecules, then the motion of molecules might qualify as heat in a counterfactual world, whether or not those molecules play the relevant causal role. It remains the case, however, that *explaining* heat involves explaining the fulfillment of the causal role, rather than explaining the motion of molecules. To see this, note that the equivalence of heat with the motion of molecules is known *a posteriori*: we know this *as a result* of explaining heat. The concept of heat that we had *a priori*—before the phenomenon was explained—was roughly that of "the thing that plays this causal role in the actual world." Once we discover how that causal role is played, we have an explanation of the phenomenon. As a bonus, we know what heat *is*. It is the motion of molecules, as the motion of molecules is what plays the relevant causal role in the actual world.

A second minor complication is that many causal-role concepts are somewhat ambiguous between the state that plays a certain causal role and the actual performance of that role. "Heat" can be taken to denote either the molecules that do the causal work or the causal process (heating) itself. Similarly, "perception" can be used to refer to either the act of perceiving or the internal state that arises as a result. Nothing important turns on this ambiguity, however. An explanation of how the causal role is played will explain heat or perception in either of these senses.

A third complication is that many causal-role concepts are partly characterized in terms of their effect on *experience*: for example, heat is naturally construed as the cause of heat sensations. Does this mean that we have to explain heat sensations before we can explain heat? Of course, we have no good account of heat sensations (or of experience generally), so what happens in practice is that that part of the phenomenon is left unexplained. If we can explain how molecular motion comes about in certain conditions, and causes metals to expand, and stimulates our skin in certain ways, then the observation that this motion is *correlated* with heat sensations is good enough. From the correlation, we infer that there is almost certainly a causal connection. To be sure, no explanation of heat will be complete until we have an account of how that causal connection works, but the incomplete account is good enough for most purposes. It is somewhat paradoxical that we end up explaining almost everything about a *phenomenon* except for the details of how it affects our phenomenology, but it is not a problem in practice. It would not be a happy state of affairs if we had to put the rest of science on hold until we had a theory of consciousness.

Reductive explanations in cognitive science

The paradigm of reductive explanation via functional analysis works beautifully in most areas of cognitive science, at least in principle. As we saw in the previous chapter, most nonphenomenal mental concepts can be analyzed functionally. Psychological states are characterizable in terms of the causal role they play. To explain these states, we explain how the relevant causation is performed.

In principle, one can do this by giving an account of the underlying neurophysiology. If we explain how certain neurophysiological states are responsible for the performance of the functions in question, then we have explained the psychological state. We need not always descend to the neurophysiological level, however. We can frequently explain some aspect of mentality by exhibiting an appropriate *cognitive model*—that is, by exhibiting the details of the abstract causal organization of a system whose mechanisms are sufficient to perform the relevant functions, without specifying the physiochemical substrate in which this causal organization is implemented. In this way, we give a *how-possibly* explanation of a given aspect of psychology, in that we have shown how the appropriate causal mechanisms *might* support the relevant mental processes. If we are interested in explaining the mental states of an *actual* organism or type of organism (e.g., learning in humans, as opposed to the possibility of learning in general), this sort of explanation must be supplemented with a demonstration that the causal organization of the model mirrors the causal organization of the organism in question.

To explain the possibility of learning, we can exhibit a model whose mechanisms lead to the appropriate changes in behavioral capacity in response to various kinds of environmental stimulation—a connectionist learning model, for example. To explain human learning, we must also demonstrate that such a model reflects the causal organization responsible for the performance of such functions in humans. The second step is usually difficult: we cannot exhibit such a correspondence directly, due to our ignorance of neurophysiology, so we usually have to look for indirect evidence, such as qualitative similarities in patterns of response, measurements of timing, and the like. This is one reason why cognitive science is currently in an undeveloped state. But as usual, the in-principle possibility of such explanation is a straightforward consequence of the functional nature of psychological concepts.

Unfortunately, the kind of functional explanation that works so well for psychological states does not seem to work in explaining phenomenal states.

The reason for this is straightforward. Whatever functional account of human cognition we give, there is a *further question*: Why is this kind of functioning accompanied by consciousness? No such further question arises for psychological states. If one asked about a given functional model of learning, "Why is this functioning accompanied by learning?" the appropriate answer is a semantic answer: "Because all it *means* to learn is to function like this." There is no corresponding analysis of the concept of consciousness. Phenomenal states, unlike psychological states, are not defined by the causal roles that they play. It follows that explaining how some causal role is played is not sufficient to explain consciousness. After we have explained the performance of a given function, the fact that consciousness accompanies the performance of the function (if indeed it does) remains quite unexplained.

One can put the point the following way. Given an appropriate functional account of learning, it is simply *logically impossible* that something could instantiate that account without learning (except perhaps insofar as learning requires consciousness). However, no matter what functional account of cognition one gives, it seems logically possible that that account could be instantiated without any accompanying consciousness. It may be naturally impossible—consciousness may in fact *arise* from that functional organization in the actual world—but the important thing is that the notion is logically coherent.

If this is indeed logically possible, then any functional and indeed any physical account of mental phenomena will be fundamentally incomplete. To use a phrase coined by Levine (1983), there is an *explanatory gap* between such accounts and consciousness itself. Even if the appropriate functional organization always gives rise to consciousness in practice, the question of *why* it gives rise to consciousness remains unanswered. This point will be developed at length later.

If this is so, it follows that there will be a partial explanatory gap for any mental concept that has a phenomenal element. If conscious experience is required for belief or learning, for example, we may not have a fully reductive explanation for belief or learning. But we at least have reason to believe that the *psychological* aspects of these mental features—which are arguably at the core of the relevant concepts—will be susceptible to reductive explanation in principle. If we leave worries about phenomenology aside, cognitive science seems to have the resources to do a good job of explaining the mind.

3. Logical Supervenience and Reductive Explanation

The epistemology of reductive explanation meets the metaphysics of supervenience in a straightforward way. A natural phenomenon is reductively explainable in terms of some low-level properties precisely when it is logically supervenient on those properties. It is reductively explainable in terms of physical properties—or simply "reductively explainable"—when it is logically supervenient on the physical.

To put things more carefully: A natural phenomenon is reductively explainable in terms of some lower-level properties if the property of instantiating that phenomenon is globally logically supervenient on the low-level properties in question. A phenomenon is reductively explainable *simpliciter* if the property of instantiating that phenomenon is globally logically supervenient on physical properties.

This can be taken as an *explication* of the notion of reductive explanation, with perhaps an element of stipulation. That our prior notion of reductive explanation implies (global) logical supervenience should be clear from the earlier discussion. If the property of exemplifying a phenomenon fails to supervene logically on some lower-level properties, then given any lower-level account of those properties, there will always be a further unanswered question: Why is this lower-level process accompanied by the phenomenon? Reductive explanation requires some kind of analysis of the phenomenon in question, where the low-level facts imply the realization of the analysis. So reductive explanation requires a logical supervenience relation. For example, it is precisely because reproduction is logically supervenient on lower-level facts that it is reductively explainable in terms of those facts.

That logical supervenience *suffices* for reductive explainability is somewhat less clear. If a phenomenon P supervenes logically on some lower-level properties, then given an account of the lower-level facts associated with an instance of P, the exemplification of P is a logical consequence. An account of the lower-level facts will therefore automatically yield an explanation of P. Nevertheless, such an explanation can sometimes seem unsatisfactory, for two reasons. First, the lower-level facts might be a vast hotchpotch of arbitrary-seeming details without any clear explanatory unity. An account of all the molecular motions underlying an instance of learning might be like this, for example. Second, it is possible that different instances of P might be accompanied by very different sets of low-level facts, so that explanations of particular instances do not yield an explanation of the phenomenon as a type.

One option is to hold that logical supervenience is merely *necessary* for reductive explanation, rather than sufficient. This is all that is required for my arguments about consciousness in the next chapter. But it is more useful to note that there is *a* useful notion of reductive explanation such that logical supervenience is both necessary and sufficient. Instead of taking the problems above as indicating that the accounts in question are not *explanations,* we can instead take them to indicate that a reductive explanation is not necessarily an *illuminating* explanation. Rather, a reductive explanation is a *mystery-removing* explanation.

As I noted earlier, reductive explanation is not the be-all and end-all of explanation. Its chief role is to remove any deep sense of mystery surrounding a high-level phenomenon. It does this by reducing the bruteness and arbitrariness of the phenomenon in question to the bruteness and arbitrariness of lower-level processes. Insofar as the low-level processes may themselves be quite brute and arbitrary, a reductive explanation may not give us a *deep* understanding of a phenomenon, but it at least eliminates any sense that there is something "extra" going on.

The gap between a reductive explanation and an illuminating explanation can generally be closed much further than this, however. This is due to two basic facts about the physics of our world: *autonomy* and *simplicity*. Microphysical causation and explanation seem to be autonomous, in that every physical event has a physical explanation; the laws of physics are sufficient to explain the events of physics on their own terms. Further, the laws in question are reasonably simple, so that the explanations in question have a certain compactness. Both of these things might have been otherwise. We might have lived in a world in which there were brutely emergent fundamental laws governing the behavior of high-level configurations such as organisms, with an associated downward causation that overrides any relevant microphysical laws. (The British emergentists, such as Alexander [1920] and Broad [1925], believed our world to be something like this.) Alternatively, our world might have been a world in which the behavior of microphysical entities is governed only by a vast array of baroque laws, or perhaps a world in which microphysical behavior is lawless and chaotic. In worlds like these, there would be little hope of achieving an illuminating reductive explanation, as the bruteness of low-level accounts might never be simplified.

But the actual world, with its low-level autonomy and simplicity, seems to allow that sense can generally be made even of complex processes. The low-level facts underlying a high-level phenomenon often have a basic unity that allows for a comprehensible explanation. Given an instance of high-level causation, such as a released trigger causing a gun to fire, we can not only isolate a bundle of lower-level facts that fix this causation; we can also tell a fairly simple story about how the causation is enabled, by encapsulating those facts under certain simple principles. This may not always work. It may be the case that some domains, such as those of sociology and economics, are so far removed from the simplicity of low-level processes that illuminating reductive explanation is impossible, even if the phenomena are logically supervenient. If so, then so be it: we can content ourselves with high-level explanations of those domains, while noting that logical supervenience implies that there is a reductive explanation in principle, although perhaps one that only a superbeing could understand.

Note also that on this account reductive explanation is fundamentally *particular*, accounting for particular instances of a phenomenon, without necessarily accounting for all instances together. This is what we should expect. If a property can be instantiated in many different ways, we cannot expect a single explanation to cover all the instances. Temperature is instantiated quite differently in different media, for example, and there are different explanations for each. At a much higher level, it is most unlikely that there should be a single explanation covering all instances of murder. Still, there is frequently a certain unity across the explanation of particulars, in that a good explanation of one is often an explanation of many. This is again a consequence of the underlying simplicity of our world, rather than a necessary property of explanation. In our world, the simple unifying stories that one can tell about lower-level processes often apply across the board, or at least across a wide range of particulars. It is also frequently the case, especially in the biological sciences, that the particulars have a common ancestry that leads to a similarity in the low-level processes involved. So the second problem mentioned, that of unifying the explanations of specific instances of a phenomenon, is not as much of a problem as it might be. In any case, it is the explanation of particulars that is central.

There is much more that could be said about closing the gap between reductive explanation and illuminating explanation, but the matter deserves a lengthy treatment in its own right and is not too important for my purposes. What is most important is that if logical supervenience fails (as I will argue it does for consciousness), then *any* kind of reductive explanation fails, even if we are generous about what counts as explanation. Also important is that logical supervenience removes any residual *metaphysical* mystery about a high-level phenomenon, by reducing any brutality in that phenomenon to brutality in lower-level facts. Of secondary importance is that if logical supervenience holds, then some sort of reductive explanation is possible. Although such explanations can fail to be illuminating or useful, this failure is not nearly as fundamental as the failure of explanation in domains where logical supervenience does not hold.

Further notes on reductive explanation

A few further notes: First, a practical reductive explanation of a phenomenon does not usually go all the way to the microphysical level. To do this would be enormously difficult, giving rise to all the brutality problems just discussed. Instead, high-level phenomena are explained in terms of some properties at a slightly more basic level, as when reproduction is explained in terms of cellular mechanisms, or the phases of the moon are explained in terms of orbital motion. In turn, one hopes that the more basic phenomena will themselves be reductively explainable in terms of something more basic still. If all goes well, biological phenomena may be explainable in terms of cellular phenomena, which are explainable in terms of biochemical phenomena, which are explainable in terms of chemical phenomena, which are explainable in terms of physical phenomena. As for the physical phenomena, one tries to unify these as far as possible, but at some level physics has to be taken as brute: there may be no explanation of why the fundamental laws or boundary conditions are the way they are. This ladder of explanation is little more than a pipe dream at the moment, but significant progress has been made. Given logical supervenience, along with the simplicity and autonomy of the lowest level, this sort of explanatory connection between the sciences ought to be possible in principle. Whether the complexities of reality will make it practically infeasible is an open question.

Second, it is at least conceivable that a phenomenon might be reductively explainable in terms of lower-level properties without being reductively explainable *simpliciter*. This might happen in a situation where C-properties are logically supervenient on B-properties, and are therefore explainable in terms of B-properties, but where B-properties themselves are not logically supervenient on the physical. There is clearly one sense in which such an explanation is reductive and another sense in which it is not. For the most part, I will be concerned with reductive explanation in terms of the physical, or in terms of properties that are themselves explainable in terms of the physical, and so on. Even if the C-properties here are reductively explainable in a relative sense, their very existence implies the failure of reductive explanation in general.

Third, *local* logical supervenience is too stringent a requirement for reductive explanation. One can reductively explain even context-dependent properties of an individual by giving an account of how relevant environmental relations come to be satisfied. As long as a phenomenon is globally supervenient, it will be reductively explainable in terms of some lower-level facts, even if these are spread widely in space and time.

Fourth, in principle there are two projects in reductive explanation of a phenomenon such as life, learning, or heat. There is first a project of *explication,* where we clarify just what it is that needs to be explained, by means of analysis. Learning might be analyzed as a certain kind of adaptational process, for example. Second, there is a project of *explanation,* where we see how that analysis comes to be satisfied by the low-level facts. The first project is conceptual, and the second is empirical. For many or most phenomena, the conceptual stage will be quite trivial. For some phenomena, however, such as belief, explication can be a major hurdle in itself. In practice, of course, there is never a clean separation between the projects, as explication and explanation take place in parallel.

4. Conceptual Truth and Necessary Truth*

In my account of supervenience and explanation, I have relied heavily on the notions of logical possibility and necessity. It is now time to say something more about this. The basic way to understand the logical necessity of a statement is in terms of its truth across all logically possible worlds. This requires some care in making sense of both the relevant class of worlds and the way that statements are evaluated in worlds; I will discuss this at some length later in this section. It is also possible to explicate the logical necessity of a statement as truth in virtue of meaning: a statement is logically necessary if its truth is ensured by the meaning of the concepts involved. But again, this requires care in understanding just how the "meanings" should be taken. I will discuss both of these ways of looking at things, and their relation, later in this section.

(As before, the notion of logical necessity is not to be identified with a narrow notion involving derivability in first-order logic, or some other syntactic formalism. Indeed, it is arguable that the justification of the axioms and rules in these formalisms depends precisely on their logical necessity in the broader, more primitive sense.)

All this requires taking seriously, at least to some extent, the notion of *conceptual truth*—that is, the notion that some statements are true or false simply by virtue of the meanings of the terms involved. Key elements of my discussion so far have depended on characterizations of various concepts. I have accounted for the reductive explanation of reproduction, for example, by arguing that low-level details entail that certain functions are performed, and that performance of these functions is all there is to the concept of reproduction.

The notion of conceptual truth has had a bad name in some circles since the critique by Quine (1951), who argued that there is no useful distinction between conceptual truths and empirical truths. The objections to these notions usually cluster around the following points:

1. Most concepts do not have definitions giving necessary and sufficient conditions (this observation has been made many times but is often associated with Wittgenstein 1953).
2. Most apparent conceptual truths are in fact revisable, and could be withdrawn in the face of sufficient empirical evidence (a point raised by Quine).
3. Considerations about *a posteriori* necessity, outlined by Kripke (1972), show that application-conditions of many terms across possible worlds cannot be known *a priori*.

These considerations count against an overly simplistic view of conceptual truth, but not against the way I am using these notions. In particular, it turns out that the class of *supervenience conditionals*—"If the A-facts about a situation are *X,* then the B-facts are *Y,"* where the A-facts fully specify a situation at a fundamental level—are unaffected by these considerations. These are the only conceptual truths that my arguments need, and we will see that none of the considerations above count against them. I will also analyze the relationship between conceptual truth and necessary truth in more detail, and spell out the role these play in understanding logical supervenience.

Definitions

The absence of cut-and-dried definitions is the least serious of the difficulties with conceptual truth. None of my arguments depend on the existence of such definitions. I occasionally rely on analyses of various notions, but these analyses need only be rough and ready, without any pretense at providing precise necessary and sufficient conditions. Most concepts (e.g., "life") are somewhat vague in their application, and there is little point trying to remove that vagueness by arbitrary precision. Instead of saying "A system is alive if and only if it reproduces, adapts with utility 800 or greater, and metabolizes with efficiency 75 percent, or exhibits these in a weighted combination with such-and-such properties," we can simply note that if a system exhibits these phenomena to a sufficient degree then it will be alive, by virtue of the meaning of the term. If an account of relevant low-level facts fixes the facts about a system's reproduction, utility, metabolism, and so on, then it also fixes the facts about whether the system is *alive,* insofar as that matter is factual at all.

We can sum this up with a schematic diagram (Figure 2.1) showing how a high-level property P might depend on two low-level parameters A and B, each of which can take on a range of values. If we had a crisp definition in terms of necessary and sufficient conditions, then we would have something like the picture at left, where the dark rectangle represents the region in which property P is instantiated. Instead, the dependence is invariably something like the picture at right, where the boundaries are vague and there is a large area in which the matter of P-hood is indeterminate, but there is also an area in which the matter is clear. (It may be indeterminate whether bacteria or computer viruses are alive, but there is no doubt that dogs are alive.) Given an example in the determinate area, exemplifying A and B to sufficient degrees that P is exemplified, the conditional "If *x* is A and B to this degree, then *x* is P" is a conceptual truth, despite the lack of a clean definition of P. Any indeterminacy in such conditionals, in the gray areas, will reflect indeterminacy in the facts of the matter, which is as it should be. The picture can straightforwardly be extended to dependence of a property

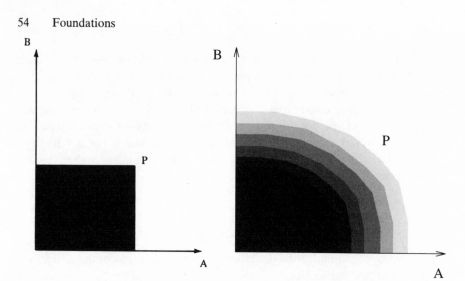

Figure 2.1. Two ways in which a property P might depend on properties A and B.

on an arbitrary number of factors, and to supervenience conditionals in general.

Importantly, then, one set of facts can *entail* another set without there being a clean definition of the latter notions in terms of the former. The above case provides an example: there is no simple definition of P in terms of A and B, but the facts about A and B in an instance entail the facts about P. For another example, think about the *roundness* of closed curves in two-dimensional space (Figure 2.2). There is certainly no perfect definition of roundness in terms of simpler mathematical notions. Nevertheless, take the figure at left, specified by the equation $2x^2 + 3y^2 = 1$. There is a fact of the matter—this figure is round—insofar as there are ever facts about roundness at all (compare to the figure at right, which is certainly not round). Further, this fact is *entailed* by the basic description of the figure in mathematical terms—given that description, and the concept of roundness, the fact that the figure is round is determined. Given that A-facts can entail B-facts without a definition of B-facts in terms of A-facts, the notion of logical supervenience is unaffected by the absence of definitions. (In thinking about more complex issues and objections concerning logical supervenience, it may be worthwhile to keep this example in mind.)

We can put the point by saying that the sort of "meaning" of a concept that is relevant in most cases is not a definition, but an *intension*: a function specifying how the concept applies to different situations. Sometimes an intension might be summarizable in a definition, but it need not be, as these cases suggest. But as long as there is a fact of the matter about how concepts apply in various situations, then we have an intension; and as I will discuss shortly, this will generally be all the "meaning" that my arguments will need.

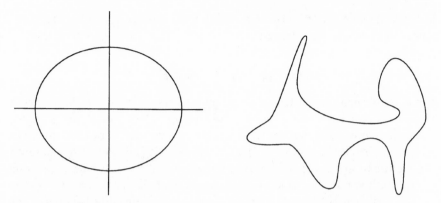

Figure 2.2.   The round curve $2x^2 + 3y^2 = 1$ and nonround friend.

Revisability

The second objection, raised by Quine (1951), is that purported conceptual truths are always subject to revision in the face of sufficient empirical evidence. For instance, if evidence forces us to revise various background statements in a theory, it is possible that a statement that once appeared to be conceptually true might turn out to be false.

This is so for many purported conceptual truths, but it does not apply to the supervenience conditionals that we are considering, which have the form "If the low-level facts turn out like this, then the high-level facts will be like that." The facts specified in the antecedent of this conditional effectively include all relevant empirical factors. Empirical evidence could show us that the antecedent of the conditional is false, but not that the conditional is false. In the extreme case, we can ensure that the antecedent gives a full specification of the low-level facts about the world. The very comprehensiveness of the antecedent ensures that empirical evidence is irrelevant to the conditional's truth-value. (This picture is somewhat complicated by the existence of *a posteriori* necessities, which I discuss shortly. Here, I am only concerned with epistemic conditionals about ways the actual world might turn out.)

While considerations about revisability provide a plausible argument that there are not many *short* conceptual truths, nothing in these considerations counts against the constrained, complex sort of conceptual truth that I have been concerned with. The upshot of these observations is that the truth-conditions of a high-level statement may not be easily *localizable,* as all sorts of factors might have some kind of indirect relevance; but the global truth conditions provided by a supervenience conditional are not threatened. Indeed, if meaning determines a function from possible worlds to reference classes (an intension), and if possible worlds are finitely describable (in terms of arrangement of basic qualities in those worlds, say), then there will automatically be a vast class of conceptually true conditionals that result.

A posteriori *necessity*

It has traditionally been thought that all conceptual truths are knowable *a priori*, as are all necessary truths, and that the classes of *a priori* truths, necessary truths, and conceptual truths are closely related or even coextensive. Saul Kripke's book *Naming and Necessity* (1972) threw a wrench into this picture by arguing that there is a large class of necessarily true statements whose truth is not knowable *a priori*. An example is the statement "Water is H_2O." We cannot know this to be true *a priori*; for all we know (or for all we knew at the beginning of inquiry), water is made out of something else, perhaps XYZ. Kripke argues that nevertheless, given that water is H_2O in the actual world, then water is H_2O in all possible worlds. It follows that "Water is H_2O" is a necessary truth despite its *a posteriori* nature.

This raises a few difficulties for the framework I have presented. For example, on some accounts these necessary truths are conceptual truths, implying that not all conceptual truths are knowable *a priori*. On alternative accounts, such statements are not conceptual truths, but then the link between conceptual truth and necessity is broken. At various points in this book, I use *a priori* methods to gain insight into necessity; this is the sort of thing that Kripke's account is often taken to challenge.

On analysis, I think it can be seen that these complications do not change anything fundamental to my arguments; but it is worth taking the trouble to get clear about what is going on. I will spend some time setting up a systematic framework for dealing with these issues, which will recur. In particular, I will present a natural way of capturing Kripke's insights in a two-dimensional picture of meaning and necessity. This framework is a synthesis of ideas suggested by Kripke, Putnam, Kaplan, Stalnaker, Lewis, Evans, Davies and Humberstone, and others who have addressed these two-dimensional phenomena.

On the traditional view of reference, derived from Frege although cloaked here in modern terminology, a concept determines a function $f : W \rightarrow R$ from possible worlds to referents. Such a function is often called an *intension*; together with a specification of a world w, it determines an *extension* $f(w)$. In Frege's own view, every concept had a *sense,* which was supposed to determine the reference of the concept depending on the state of the world; so these senses correspond closely to intensions. The sense was often thought of as the *meaning* of the concept in question.

More recent work has recognized that no single intension can do all the work that a meaning needs to do. The picture developed by Kripke complicates things by noting that reference in the actual world and in counterfactual possible worlds is determined by quite different mechanisms. In a way, the Kripkean picture can be seen to split the Fregean picture into two separate levels.

Kripke's insight can be expressed by saying that there are in fact *two* intensions associated with a given concept. That is, there are two quite distinct patterns of dependence of the referent of a concept on the state of the world. First, there is the dependence by which reference is fixed in the *actual* world, depending on how the world turns out: if it turns out one way, a concept will pick out one thing, but if it turns out another way, the concept will pick out something else. Second, there is the dependence by which reference in *counterfactual* worlds is determined, given that reference in the actual world is already fixed. Corresponding to each of these dependencies is an intension, which I will call the *primary* and *secondary* intensions, respectively.

The *primary* intension of a concept is a function from worlds to extensions reflecting the way that actual-world reference is fixed. In a given world, it picks out what the referent of the concept would be if that world turned out to be actual. Take the concept "water." If the actual world turned out to have XYZ in the oceans and lakes, then "water" would refer to XYZ,[21] but given that it turns out to have H_2O in the oceans and lakes, "water" refers to H_2O. So the primary intension of "water" maps the XYZ world to XYZ, and the H_2O world to H_2O. At a rough approximation, we might say that the primary intension picks out the dominant clear, drinkable liquid in the oceans and lakes; or more briefly, that it picks out the *watery stuff* in a world.

However, *given* that "water" turns out to refer to H_2O in the actual world, Kripke notes (as does Putnam [1975]) that it is reasonable to say that water is H_2O in every counterfactual world. The *secondary intension* of "water" picks out the water in every counterfactual world; so if Kripke and Putnam are correct, the secondary intension picks out H_2O in all worlds.[22]

It is the primary intension of a concept that is most central for my purposes: for a concept of a natural phenomenon, it is the primary intension that captures what needs explaining. If someone says, "Explain water," long before we know that water is in fact H_2O, what they are asking for is more or less an explanation of the clear, drinkable liquid in their environment. It is only *after* the explanation is complete that we know that water is H_2O. The primary intension of a concept, unlike the secondary intension, is independent of empirical factors: the intension *specifies* how reference depends on the way the external world turns out, so it does not itself depend on the way the external world turns out.

Of course, any brief characterization of the primary intension of a concept along the lines of "the dominant clear, drinkable liquid in the environment" will be a simplification. The true intension can be determined only from detailed consideration of specific scenarios: What would we say if the world turned out this way? What would we say if it turned out that way? For example, if it had turned out that the liquid in lakes was H_2O and the liquid in oceans XYZ, then we probably would have said that both were water; if the stuff in oceans and lakes was a mixture of 95 percent A and 5 percent B, we would probably have said that A but not B was water; if it turned out that a substance neither clear nor drinkable bore an appropriate microphysical relation to the clear, drinkable liquid in our environment, we would probably call that substance "water" too (as we do in the case of ice or of "dirty water"). The full conditions for what it takes to qualify as "water" will be quite vague at the edges and need not be immediately apparent on reflection, but none of this makes much difference to the picture I am describing. I will use "watery stuff" as a term of art to encapsulate the primary intension, whatever it is.[23]

In certain cases, the decision about what a concept refers to in the actual world involves a large amount of reflection about what is the most reasonable thing to say; as, for example, with questions about the reference of "mass" when the actual world turned out to be one in which the theory of general relativity is true,[24] or perhaps with questions about what qualifies as "belief" in the actual world. So consideration of just what the primary intension picks out in various actual-world candidates may involve a corresponding amount of reflection. But this is not to say that the matter is not *a priori*: we have the ability to engage in this reasoning independently of how the world turns out. Perhaps the reports of experiments confirming relativity are disputed, so we are not sure whether the actual world has turned out to be a relativistic world: either way, we have the ability to reason about what "mass" will refer to *if* that state of affairs turns out to be actual.

(Various intricacies arise in analyzing the primary intensions of concepts used by individuals within a linguistic community. These might be handled by noting that an individual's concept may have a primary intension that involves deference to a surrounding community's concept—so my concept "elm" might pick out what those around me call "elms"; but in any case this sort of problem is irrelevant to the issues I will be concerned with, for which we might as well assume that there is just one person in the community, or that all individuals are equally well informed, or even that the community is a giant individual. There are also a few technical problems that might come up in using primary intensions to build a general semantic theory—for example, is the reference of a concept essential to the concept? Might different speakers associate different primary intensions with the same word? But I am not trying to build a full semantic theory here, and we can abstract away from this sort of concern.

Sometimes philosophers are suspicious of entities such as primary intensions because they see them as reminiscent of a "description" theory of reference. But descriptions play no essential part in this framework; I use them merely to flesh out some of the character of the relevant functions from possible worlds to extensions. It is the function itself, rather than any summarizing description, that is truly central. This picture is quite compatible with the "causal" theory of reference: we need simply note that the primary intension of a concept such as "water" may require an appropriate causal connection between the referent and the subject. Indeed, we are led to believe in a causal theory of reference in the first place precisely by considering various ways the actual world might turn out, and noting what the referent of the concept would turn out to be in those cases; that is, by evaluating the primary intension of a concept at those worlds.)

Given that the actual-world reference of "water" is fixed by picking out the watery stuff, one might think that water is watery stuff in all possible worlds. Kripke and Putnam pointed out that this is not so: if water is H_2O in the actual world, then water is H_2O in all possible worlds. In a world (Putnam's "Twin Earth") in which the dominant clear, drinkable liquid is XYZ rather than H_2O, this liquid is not water; it is merely watery stuff. All this is captured by the *secondary* intension of "water," which picks out the water in all worlds: that is, it picks out H_2O in all worlds.

The secondary intension of a concept such as "water" is not determined *a priori*, as it depends on how things turn out in the actual world. But it still has a close relation to the primary intension above. In this case, the secondary intension is determined by first evaluating the primary intension at the actual world, and then *rigidifying* this evaluation so that the same sort of thing is picked out in all possible worlds. Given that the primary intension ("watery stuff") picks out H_2O in the actual world, it follows from rigidification that the secondary intension picks out H_2O in all possible worlds.

We can sum this up by saying "water" is conceptually equivalent to "*dthat* (watery stuff)," where *dthat* is a version of Kaplan's rigidifying operator, converting an intension into a rigid designator by evaluation at the actual world (Kaplan 1979).The single Fregean intension has fragmented into two: a primary intension ("watery stuff") that fixes reference in the actual world, and a secondary intension ("H_2O") that picks out reference in counterfactual possible worlds, and which depends on how the actual world turned out.

(There is sometimes a tendency to suppose that *a posteriori* necessity makes *a priori* conceptual analysis irrelevant, but this supposition is ungrounded. Before we even get to the point where rigid designation and the like become relevant, there is a story to tell about what makes an actual-world X *qualify* as the referent of "X" in the first place. This story can only be told by an analysis of the primary intension. And this project is an *a priori* enterprise, as it involves questions about what our concept *would* refer to if the actual world turned out in various ways. Given that we have the ability to know what our concepts refer to when we know how the actual world turns out, then we have the ability to know what our concepts would refer to *if* the actual world turned out in various ways. Whether or not the actual world *does* turn out a certain way makes little difference in answering this question, except in focusing our attention.)

Both the primary and secondary intensions can be seen as functions f : $W \rightarrow R$ from possible worlds to extensions, where the possible worlds in question are seen in subtly different ways. We might say that the primary intension picks out the referent of a concept in a world when it is *considered as actual*—that is, when it is considered as a candidate for the actual world of the thinker—whereas the secondary intension picks out the referent of a concept in a world when it is *considered as counterfactual,* given that the actual world of the thinker is already fixed. When the XYZ world is considered as actual, my term "water" picks out XYZ in the world, but when it is considered as counterfactual, "water" picks out H_2O.

The distinction between these two ways of looking at worlds corresponds closely to Kaplan's (1989) distinction between the *context of utterance* of an expression and the *circumstances of evaluation.* When we consider a world w as counterfactual, we keep the actual world as the context of utterance, but use w as a circumstance of evaluation. For example, if I utter "There is water in the ocean" in this world and *evaluate* it in the XYZ world, "water" refers to H_2O and the statement is false. But when we consider w as actual, we think of it as a potential context of utterance, and wonder how things would be if the context of the expression turned out to be w. If the context of my sentence "There is water in the ocean" turned out to be the XYZ world, then the statement would be true when evaluated at that world. The primary intension is therefore closely related to what Kaplan calls the *character* of a term, although there are a few differences,[25] and the secondary intension corresponds to what he calls a term's *content.*

There is a slight asymmetry in that a context of utterance but not the circumstance of evaluation is what Quine (1969) calls a *centered* possible world. This is an ordered pair consisting of a world and a *center* representing the viewpoint within that world of an agent using the term in question: the center consists in (at least) a "marked" individual and time. (This suggestion comes from Lewis 1979; Quine suggests that the center might be a point in space-time.) Such a center is necessary to capture the fact that a term like "water" picks out a different extension for me than for my twin on Twin Earth, despite the fact that we live in the same universe.[26] It is only our position in the universe that differs, and it is this position that makes a relevant difference to the reference-fixing process.

This phenomenon arises in an especially obvious way for indexical terms such as "I", whose reference clearly depends on who is using the term and not just on the overall state of the world: the primary intension of "I" picks out the individual at the center of a centered world. (The secondary intension of my concept "I" picks out David Chalmers in all possible worlds.)

There is a less overt indexical element in notions such as "water," however, which can be roughly analyzed as "*dthat*(the dominant clear, drinkable liquid *in our environment*)."[27] It is this indexical element that requires primary intensions to depend on centered worlds. Once actual-world reference is fixed, however, no center is needed to evaluate reference in a counterfactual world. The circumstance of evaluation can therefore be represented by a simple possible world without a center.

All this can be formalized by noting that the full story about reference in counterfactual worlds is not determined *a priori* by a singly indexed function $f : W \to R$. Instead, reference in a counterfactual world depends both on that world and on the way the actual world turns out. That is, a concept determines a doubly indexed function

$$F : W^* \times W \to R$$

where W^* is the space of centered possible worlds, and W is the space of ordinary possible worlds. The first parameter represents contexts of utterance, or ways the actual world might turn out, whereas the second parameter represents circumstances of evaluation, or counterfactual possible worlds. Equivalently, a concept determines a family of functions

$$F_v : W \to R$$

for each $v \in W^*$ representing a way the actual world might turn out, where $F_v(w) = F(v, w)$. For "water," if a is a world in which watery stuff is H_2O, then F_a picks out H_2O in any possible world. Given that in our world water *did* turn out to be H_2O, this F_a specifies the correct application conditions for "water" across counterfactual worlds. If our world had turned out to be a different world b in which watery stuff was XYZ, then the relevant application conditions would have been specified by F_b, a different intension which picks out XYZ in any possible world.

The function F is determined *a priori,* as all *a posteriori* factors are included in its parameters. From F we can recover both of our singly indexed intensions. The primary intension is the function $f : W^* \to R$ determined by the "diagonal" mapping $f : w \mapsto F(w, w')$, where w' is identical to w except that the center is removed. This is the function whereby reference in the actual world is fixed. The secondary intension is the mapping $F_a : w \mapsto F(a, w)$, where a is our actual world. This intension picks out reference in counterfactual worlds. An immediate consequence is that the primary intension and secondary intension coincide in their application to the actual world: $f(a) = F_a(a') = F(a, a')$.

In the reverse direction, the doubly indexed function F and therefore the secondary intension F_a can usually be derived from the primary intension f, with the aid of a "rule" about how the secondary intension depends on the primary intension and the actual world a. This rule depends on the type of concept. For a concept that is a rigid designator, the rule is that in a world w, the secondary intension picks out in w whatever the primary intension picks out in a (or perhaps, for natural-kind terms, whatever has the same underlying structure as what the primary intension picks out in a). More formally, let $D : R \times W \to R$ be a "projection" operator that goes from a class picked out in some world to members of "that" class in another possible world. Then the secondary intension F_a is just the function $D(f(a),-)$, which we can think of as *dthat* applied to the intension given by f.

For other concepts, derivation of the secondary intension from the primary intension will be easier. With "descriptive" expressions such as "doctor," "square," and "watery stuff," rigid designation plays no special role: they apply to counterfactual worlds independently of how the actual world turns out. In these cases, the secondary intension is a simple copy of the primary intension (except for differences due to centering). The framework I have outlined can handle both sorts of concepts.

Property terms, such as "hot," can be represented in one of two ways in an intensional framework. We can see the intension of a property as a function from a world to a class of individuals (the individuals that instantiate the property), or from a world to properties themselves. Either way of doing things is compatible with the current framework: we can easily find a primary and a secondary intension in either case, and it is easy to move back and forth between the two frameworks. I will usually do things the first way, however, so that the primary intension of "hot" picks out the entities that qualify as "hot" things in the actual world, depending on how it turns out, and the secondary intension picks out the hot things in a counterfactual world, given that the actual world has turned out as it has.

Both the primary and the secondary intensions can be thought of as candidates for the "meaning" of a concept. I think there is no point choosing one of these to qualify as *the* meaning; the term "meaning" here is largely an honorific. We might as well think of the primary and secondary intensions as the *a priori* and *a posteriori* aspects of meaning, respectively.

If we make this equation, both of these intensions will back a certain kind of conceptual truth, or truth in virtue of meaning. The primary intension backs *a priori* truths, such as "Water is watery stuff." Such a statement will be true no matter how the actual world turns out, although it need not hold in all nonactual possible worlds. The secondary intension does not back *a priori* truths, but backs truths that hold in all counterfactual possible worlds, such as "Water is H_2O." Both varieties qualify as truths in virtue of meaning; they are simply true in virtue of different aspects of meaning.

It is also possible to see both as varieties of *necessary* truth. The latter corresponds to the more standard construal of a necessary truth. The former, however, can also be construed as truth across possible worlds, as long as these possible worlds are construed as contexts of utterance, or as ways the actual world might turn out. On this subtly different construal, a statement S is necessarily true if no matter how the actual world turns out, it would turn out that S was true. If the actual world turns out to be a world in which watery stuff is XYZ, then my statement "XYZ is water" will turn out to be true. So, according to this construal on which possible worlds are *considered as actual,* "Water is watery stuff" is a necessary truth.

This kind of necessity is what Evans (1979) calls "deep necessity," as opposed to "superficial" necessities like "Water is H_2O." It is analyzed in detail by Davies and Humberstone (1980) by means of a modal operator they call "fixedly actually." Deep necessity, unlike superficial necessity, is unaffected by *a posteriori* considerations. These two varieties of possibility and necessity apply always to *statements.* There is only one relevant kind of possibility of *worlds*; the two approaches differ on how the truth of a statement is evaluated in a world.

We can see this in a different way by noting that there are two sets of *truth conditions* associated with any statement. If we evaluate the terms in a statement according to their primary intensions, we arrive at the *primary* truth conditions of the statement; that is, a set of centered possible worlds in which the statement, evaluated according to the primary intensions of the terms therein, turns out to be true. The primary truth conditions tell us how the actual world has to be for an utterance of the statement to be true in that world; that is, they specify those *contexts* in which the statement would turn out to be true. For instance, the primary truth conditions of "Water is wet" specify roughly that such an utterance will be true in the set of worlds in which watery stuff is wet.

If instead we evaluate the terms involved according to their secondary intensions, we arrive at the more familiar *secondary truth conditions.* These conditions specify the truth-value of a statement in counterfactual worlds, given that the actual world has turned out as it did. For instance, the secondary truth conditions of "Water is wet" (uttered in this world) specifies those worlds in which water is wet: so given that water is H_2O, it specifies those worlds in which H_2O is wet. Note that there is no danger of an ambiguity in actual-world truth: the primary and secondary truth conditions will always specify the same truth-value when evaluated at the actual world.

If we see a proposition as a function from possible worlds to truth-values, then these two sets of truth conditions yield two *propositions* associated with any statement. Composing the primary intensions of the terms involved yields a *primary proposition,* which holds in precisely those contexts of utterance in which the statement would turn out to express a truth. (This is the "diagonal proposition" of Stalnaker 1978. Strictly speaking, it is a centered proposition, or a function from centered worlds to truth-values.) The secondary intensions yield a *secondary* proposition, which holds in those counterfactual circumstances in which the statement, as uttered in the actual world, is true. The secondary proposition is Kaplan's "content" of an utterance and is more commonly seen as the proposition expressed by a statement, but the primary proposition is also central.

The two kinds of necessary truth of a statement correspond precisely to the necessity of the two kinds of associated proposition. A statement is necessarily true in the first (*a priori*) sense if the associated primary proposition holds in all centered possible worlds (that is, if the statement would turn out to express a truth in any context of utterance). A statement is necessarily true in the *a posteriori* sense if the associated secondary proposition holds in all possible worlds (that is, if the statement as uttered in the *actual* world is true in all counterfactual worlds). The first corresponds to Evans's deep necessity, and the second to the more familiar superficial necessity.

To illustrate, take the statement "Water is H_2O." The primary intensions of "water" and "H_2O" differ, so that we cannot know *a priori* that water is H_2O; the associated *primary* proposition is not necessary (it holds in those centered worlds in which the watery stuff has a certain molecular structure). Nevertheless, the secondary intensions coincide, so that "Water is H_2O" is true in all possible worlds when evaluated according to the secondary intensions—that is, the associated *secondary* proposition is necessary. Kripkean *a posteriori* necessity arises just when the secondary intensions in a statement back a necessary proposition, but the primary intensions do not.

Consider by contrast the statement "Water is watery stuff." Here the associated primary intensions of "water" and "watery stuff" are the same, so that we can know this statement to be true *a priori,* as long as we possess the concepts. The associated primary proposition is necessary, so that this statement is necessarily true in Evans's "deep" sense. However, the secondary intensions differ, as "water" is rigidified but "watery stuff" is not: in a world where XYZ is the clear, drinkable liquid, the secondary intension of "watery stuff" picks out XYZ but that of "water" does not. The associated *secondary* proposition is therefore not necessary, and the statement is not a necessary truth in the more familiar sense; it is an example of Kripke's "contingent *a priori.*"

In general, many apparent "problems" that arise from these Kripkean considerations are a consequence of trying to squeeze the doubly indexed picture of reference into a single notion of meaning or of necessity. Such problems can usually be dissolved by explicitly noting the two-dimensional character of reference, and by taking care to explicitly distinguish the notion of meaning or of necessity that is in question.[28]

It is also possible to use this two-dimensional framework to give an account of the semantics of *thought*, as well as of language. I do this at much greater length elsewhere (Chalmers 1994c). This aspect of the framework will not be central here, but it is worth mentioning, as it will come up in one or two minor places. The basic idea is very similar: given an individual's *concept* in thought, we can assign a primary intension corresponding to what it will pick out depending on how the actual world turns out, and a secondary intension corresponding to what it picks out in counterfactual worlds, given that the actual world turns out as it has. Given a *belief*, we can assign a primary proposition and a secondary proposition in a similar way (what I elsewhere call the "notional" and "relational" content of the belief).

For example, concepts such as "Hesperus" and "Phosphorus" will have different primary intensions (one picks out the evening star in a given centered world, the other picks out the morning star), but the same secondary intensions (both pick out Venus in all worlds). The thought "Hesperus is Phosphorus" will have a primary proposition true in all centered worlds in which the evening star is the morning star: the fact that this thought is informative rather than trivial corresponds to the fact that the primary proposition is contingent, as the primary intensions of the two terms differ.

The primary proposition, more than the secondary proposition, captures how things seem from the point of view of the subject: it delivers the set of centered worlds which the subject, in having the belief, is endorsing as potential environments in which he or she might be living (in believing that Hesperus is Phosphorus, I endorse all those centered worlds in which the evening star and the morning star around the center are identical). It is also fairly easy to argue that the primary proposition, rather than the secondary proposition, governs the cognitive and rational relations between thoughts. For this reason it is natural to think of the primary proposition as the *cognitive* content of a thought.[29]

Logical necessity, conceptual truth, and conceivability

With this framework in hand, we can spell out the relationships among logical necessity, conceptual truth, and conceivability. Starting with logical necessity: this is just necessity as explicated above. A statement is logically necessary if and only if it is true in all logically possible worlds. Of course we have two varieties of logical necessity of statements, depending on whether we evaluate truth in a possible world according to primary and secondary intensions. We might call these varieties *1-necessity* and *2-necessity*, respectively.

This analysis explicates the logical necessity and possibility of a *statement* in terms of (a) the logical possibility of *worlds,* and (b) the intensions determined by the terms involved in the statement. I have already discussed the intensions. As for the notion of a logically possible world, this is something of a primitive: as before, we can intuitively think of a logically possible world as a world that God might have created (questions about God himself aside). I will not engage the vexed question of the ontological status of these worlds, but simply take them for granted as a tool, in the same way one takes mathematics for granted.[30] As for the *extent* of the class, the most important feature is that every conceivable world is logically possible, a matter on which I will say more in a moment.

As for conceptual truth, if we equate meaning with intension (primary or secondary), it is easy to make the link between truth in virtue of meaning and logical necessity. If a statement is logically necessary, its truth will be an automatic byproduct of the intensions of the terms (and the compositional structure of the statement). We do not need to bring in the world in any further role, as the intensions in question will be satisfied in every possible world. Similarly, if a statement is true in virtue of its intensions, it will be true in every possible world.

As before, there are two varieties of conceptual truth, depending on whether we equate the "meanings" with primary or secondary intensions, paralleling the two varieties of necessary truth. As long as one makes parallel decisions in the two cases, a statement is conceptually true if and only if it is necessarily true. "Water is watery stuff" is conceptually true and necessarily true in the first sense; and "Water is H_2O" is conceptually true and necessarily true in the second. Only the first variety of conceptual truth will in general be accessible *a priori.* The second variety will include many *a posteriori* truths, as the secondary intension depends on the way the actual world turns out.

(I do not claim that intensions are *the* correct way to think of meanings. Meaning is a many-faceted notion, and some of its facets may not be perfectly reflected by intensions, so one could resist the equation of the two at least in some cases.[31] Rather, the equation of meaning and intension should here be thought of as stipulative: if one makes the equation, then one can make various useful connections. Not much rests on the use of the word "meaning." In any case, truth in virtue of intension is the only sort of truth in virtue of meaning that I will need.)

We can also make a link between the logical possibility of statements and the *conceivability* of statements, if we are careful. Let us say that a statement is conceivable (or conceivably true) if it is true in some conceivable world. This should not be confused with other senses of "conceivable." For example, there is a sense according to which a statement is conceivable if for all we know it is true, or if we do not know that it is impossible. In this sense, both

Goldbach's conjecture and its negation are conceivable. But the false member of the pair will not qualify as conceivable in the sense I am using, as there is no conceivable world in which it is true (it is false in every world).

On this view of conceivability, the conceivability of a statement involves two things: first, the conceivability of a relevant world, and second, the truth of the statement in that world.[32] It follows that in making conceivability judgments, one has to make sure that one describes the world that one is conceiving correctly, by properly evaluating the truth of a statement in the world. One might at first glance think it is conceivable that Goldbach's conjecture is false, by conceiving of a world where mathematicians announce it to be so; but if in fact Goldbach's conjecture is true, then one is *misdescribing* this world; it is really a world in which the conjecture is true and some mathematicians make a mistake.

In practice, to make a conceivability judgment, one need only consider a conceivable *situation*—a small part of a world—and then make sure that one is describing it correctly. If there is a conceivable situation in which a statement is true, there will obviously be a conceivable world in which the statement is true, so this method will give reasonable results while straining our cognitive resources less than conceiving of an entire world!

Sometimes it is said that examples such as "Water is XYZ" show that conceivability does not imply possibility, but I think the situation is subtler than this. In effect, there are two varieties of conceivability, which we might call *1-conceivability* and *2-conceivability,* depending on whether we evaluate a statement in a conceivable world according to the primary or secondary intensions of the terms involved. "Water is XYZ" is 1-conceivable, as there is a conceivable world in which the statement (evaluated according to primary intensions) is true, but it is not 2-conceivable, as there is no conceivable world in which the statement (evaluated according to secondary intension) is true. These two sorts of conceivability precisely mirror the two sorts of logical possibility mentioned previously.

Often, the conceivability of a statement is equated with 1-conceivability (the sense in which "Water is XYZ" is conceivable), as it is this sort of conceivability that is accessible *a priori.* And most often, the *possibility* of a statement is equated with 2-possibility (the sense in which "Water is XYZ" is impossible). Taken *this* way, conceivability does not imply possibility. But it remains the case that 1-conceivability implies 1-possibility, and 2-conceivability implies 2-possibility. One simply has to be careful not to judge 1-conceivability when 2-possibility is relevant. That is, one has to be careful not to describe the world that one is conceiving (the XYZ world, say) according to primary intensions, when secondary intensions would be more appropriate.[33]

It follows from all this that the oft-cited distinction between "logical" and "metaphysical" possibility stemming from the Kripkean cases—on which it is held to be logically possible but not metaphysically possible that water is XYZ—is not a distinction at the level of *worlds,* but at most a distinction at the level of *statements.* A statement is "logically possible" in this sense if it is true in some world when evaluated according to primary intensions; a statement is "metaphysically possible" if it is true in some world when evaluated according to secondary intensions. The relevant space of worlds is the same in both cases.[34]

Most importantly, none of the cases we have seen give reason to believe that any conceivable *worlds* are impossible. Any worries about the gap between conceivability and possibility apply at the level of statements, not worlds: either we use a statement to misdescribe a conceived world (as in the Kripkean case, and the second Goldbach case), or we claim that a statement is conceivable without conceiving of a world at all (as in the first Goldbach case). So there seems to be no reason to deny that conceivability of a world implies possibility. I will henceforth take this for granted as a claim about logical possibility; any variety of possibility for which conceivability does not imply possibility will then be a narrower class. Someone might hold that there is a narrower variety of "metaphysically possible worlds," but any reason for believing in such a class would have to be quite independent of the standard reasons I have considered here. In any case, it is logical possibility that is central to the issues about explanation. (A stronger "metaphysical" modality might at best be relevant to issues about ontology, materialism, and the like; I will discuss it when those issues become relevant in Chapter 4.)

An implication in the other direction, from logical possibility to conceivability, is trickier in that limits on our cognitive capacity imply that there are some possible situations that we cannot conceive, perhaps due to their great complexity. However, if we understand conceivability as conceivability-in-principle—perhaps conceivability by a superbeing—then it is plausible that logical possibility of a world implies conceivability of the world, and therefore that logical possibility of a statement implies conceivability of the statement (in the relevant sense). In any case, I will be more concerned with the other implication.

If a statement is logically possible or necessary according to its primary intension, the possibility or necessity is knowable *a priori,* at least in principle. Modality is not epistemically inaccessible: the possibility of a statement is a function of the intensions involved and the space of possible worlds, both of which are epistemically accessible in principle, and neither of which is dependent on *a posteriori* facts in this case. So matters of 1-possibility and 1-conceivability are in principle accessible from the armchair. By contrast, matters of 2-possibility and 2-conceivability will in many cases be accessible only *a posteriori,* as facts about the external world may play a role in determining the secondary intensions.

The class of 1-necessary truths corresponds directly to the class of *a priori* truths. If a statement is true *a priori,* then it is true no matter how the actual world turns out; that is, it is true in all worlds considered as actual, so it is 1-necessary. And conversely, if a statement is 1-necessary, then it will be true no matter how the actual world turns out, so it will be true *a priori.* In most such cases, the statement's truth will be knowable by us *a priori*; the exceptions may be certain mathematical statements whose truth we cannot determine, and certain statements that are so complex that we cannot comprehend them. Even in these cases, it seems reasonable to say that they are knowable *a priori* at least *in principle,* although they are beyond our limited cognitive capacity. (I will return to this matter when it becomes relevant later.)

Logical necessity and logical supervenience

We obtain two slightly different notions of logical supervenience depending on whether we use the primary or secondary brands of logical necessity. If "gloop" has both a primary and a secondary intension associated with it, then gloopiness may supervene logically on physical properties according to either the primary or the secondary intension of "gloop". Supervenience according to secondary intension—that is, supervenience with *a posteriori* necessity as the relevant modality—corresponds to what some call "metaphysical supervenience," but we have now seen how this can be regarded as a variety of logical supervenience.

(There is really only one kind of logical supervenience of *properties,* just as there is only one kind of logical necessity of *propositions.* But we have seen that terms or concepts effectively determine two properties, one via a primary intension ["watery stuff"] and the other via a secondary intension ["H_2O"]. So for a given concept ["water"], there are two ways in which properties associated with that concept might supervene. I will sometimes talk loosely of the primary and secondary intensions associated with a property, and of the two ways in which a property might supervene.)

I will discuss both the primary and secondary versions of logical supervenience in specific cases, but the former will be more central. Especially when considering questions about explanation, primary intensions are more important than secondary intensions. As noted before, we have only the primary intension to work with at the start of inquiry, and it is this intension that determines whether or not an explanation is satisfactory. To explain water, for example, we have to explain things like its clarity, liquidity, and so on. The secondary intension ("H_2O") does not emerge until after an explanation is complete, and therefore does not itself determine a criterion for explanatory success. It is logical supervenience according to a primary intension that determines whether reductive explanation is possible. Where

I do not specify otherwise, it is logical supervenience according to primary intension that I will generally be discussing.

If we choose one sort of intension—say, the primary intension—and stick with it, then we can see that various ways of formulating logical supervenience are equivalent. According to the definition given at the start of this chapter, B-properties are logically supervenient on A-properties if for any logically possible situation Y that is A-indiscernible from an actual situation X, then all the B-facts true of X are true of Y. Or more simply, B-properties are logically supervenient on A-properties if for any actual situation X, the A-facts about X *entail* the B-facts about X (where "P entails Q" is understood as "It is logically impossible that P and not Q").

Sticking to global supervenience, this means that B-properties supervene logically on A-facts if the B-facts about the actual world are entailed by the A-facts. Similarly, B-properties supervene logically on A-properties if there is no conceivable world with the same A-properties as our world but different B-properties. We can also say that logical supervenience holds if, given the totality of A-facts A^* and any B-fact B about our world W, "$A^*(W) \to B(W)$" is true in virtue of the meanings of the A-terms and the B-terms (where meanings are understood as intensions).

Finally, if B-properties are logically supervenient on A-properties according to primary intensions, then the implication from A-facts to B-facts will be *a priori*. So in principle, someone who knows all the A-facts about an actual situation will be able to ascertain the B-facts about the situation from those facts alone, given that they possess the B-concepts in question. This sort of inference may be difficult or impossible in practice, due to the complexity of the situations involved, but it is at least possible in principle. For logical supervenience according to *secondary* intensions, B-facts about a situation can also be ascertained from the A-facts in principle, but only *a posteriori*. The A-facts will have to be supplemented with contingent facts about the actual world, as those facts will play a role in determining the B-intensions involved.

There are therefore at least three avenues to establishing claims of logical supervenience: these involve conceivability, epistemology, and analysis. To establish that B-properties logically supervene on A-properties, we can (1) argue that instantiation of A-properties without instantiation of the B-properties is inconceivable; (2) argue that someone in possession of the A-facts could come to know the B-facts (at least in cases of supervenience via primary intension); or (3) analyze the intensions of the B-properties in sufficient detail that it becomes clear that B-statements follow from A-statements in virtue of these intensions alone. The same goes for establishing the failure of logical supervenience. I will use all three methods in arguing for central claims involving logical supervenience.

Not everybody may be convinced that the various formulations of logical supervenience are equivalent, so when arguing for important conclusions involving logical supervenience I will run versions of the arguments using each of the different formulations. In this way it will be seen that the arguments are robust, with nothing depending on a subtle equivocation between different notions of supervenience.

5. Almost Everything is Logically Supervenient on the Physical*

In the following chapter I will argue that conscious experience does not supervene logically on the physical, and therefore cannot be reductively explained. A frequent response is that conscious experience is not alone here, and that all sorts of properties fail to supervene logically on the physical. It is suggested that such diverse properties as tablehood, life, and economic prosperity have no *logical* relationship to facts about atoms, electromagnetic fields, and so on. Surely those high-level facts could not be logically entailed by the microphysical facts?

On a careful analysis, I think that it is not hard to see that this is wrong, and that the high-level facts in question are (globally) logically supervenient on the physical insofar as they are facts at all.[35] Conscious experience is almost unique in its failure to supervene logically. The relationship between consciousness and the physical facts is different in kind from the standard relationship between high-level and low-level facts.

There are various ways to make it clear that most properties supervene logically on physical properties. Here I will only be concerned with properties that characterize *natural phenomena*—that is, contingent aspects of the world that need explaining. The property of being an angel might not supervene logically on the physical, but angels are not something that we have reason to believe in, so this failure need not concern us. I will also not concern myself with facts about abstract entities such as mathematical entities and propositions, which need to be treated separately.[36]

It should be noted that in claiming that most high-level properties supervene on the physical, I am not suggesting that high-level facts and laws are entailed by microphysical *laws,* or even by microphysical laws in conjunction with microphysical boundary conditions. That would be a strong claim, and although it might have some plausibility if qualified appropriately, the evidence is not yet in. I am making the much weaker claim that high-level facts are entailed by all the microphysical *facts* (perhaps along with microphysical laws). This enormously comprehensive set includes the facts about the distribution of every last particle and field in every last corner of space-time: from the atoms in Napoleon's hat to the electromagnetic fields in the outer ring of Saturn. Fixing this set of facts leaves very little room for anything else to vary, as we shall see.

Before moving to the arguments I should note some harmless reasons why logical supervenience on the physical sometimes fails. First, some high-level properties fail to supervene logically because of a dependence on conscious experience. Perhaps conscious experience is partly constitutive of a property like love, for example. The primary (although not the secondary) intensions associated with some external properties such as color and heat may also be dependent on phenomenal qualities, as we will see. If so, then love and perhaps heat do not supervene logically on the physical. These should not be seen as providing counterexamples to my thesis, as they introduce no new failure of logical supervenience. Perhaps the best way to phrase the claim is to say that all facts supervene logically on the combination of physical facts and phenomenal facts, or that all facts supervene logically on the physical facts *modulo conscious experience*. Similarly, a dependence on conscious experience may hinder the reductive explainability of some high-level phenomena, but we can still say that they are reductively explainable modulo conscious experience.

Second, an *indexical* element enters into the application of some primary intensions, although not secondary intensions, as we saw earlier. The primary intension of "water," for example, is something like "the clear, drinkable liquid in our environment," so that if there is watery H_2O and watery XYZ in the actual universe, which of them qualifies as "water" depends on which is in the environment of the agent using the term. In principle we therefore need to add a *center* representing the location of an agent to the supervenience base in some cases. This yields logical supervenience and reductive explanation modulo conscious experience and indexicality.

Finally, cases where the high-level facts are indeterminate do not count against logical supervenience. The claim is only that insofar as the high-level facts are determinate, they are determined by the physical facts. If the world itself does not suffice to fix the high-level facts, we cannot expect the physical facts to. Some might suggest that logical supervenience would fail if there were two equally good high-level theories of the world that differed in their description of the high-level facts. One theory might hold that a virus is alive, for instance, whereas another might hold that it is not, so the facts about life are not determined by the physical facts. This is not a counterexample, however, but a case in which the facts about life are indeterminate. Given indeterminacy, we are free to legislate the terms one way or the other where it is convenient. If the facts *are* determinate—for example, if it is true that viruses are alive—then one of the descriptions is simply wrong. Either way, insofar as the facts about the situation are determinate at all, they are entailed by the physical facts.

I will argue for the ubiquity of logical supervenience using arguments that appeal to conceivability, to epistemological considerations, and to analysis of the concepts involved.

Conceivability.   The logical supervenience of most high-level facts is most easily seen by using conceivability as a test for logical possibility. What kind of world could be identical to ours in every last microphysical fact but be biologically distinct? Say a wombat has had two children in our world. The physical facts about our world will include facts about the distribution of every particle in the spatiotemporal hunk corresponding to the wombat, and its children, and their environments, and their evolutionary histories. If a world shared those physical facts with ours, but was not a world in which the wombat had two children, what could that difference consist in? Such a world seems quite inconceivable. Once a possible world is fixed to have all those physical facts the same, then the facts about wombathood and parenthood are automatically fixed. These biological facts are not the sort of thing that can float free of their physical underpinnings even as a conceptual possibility.

The same goes for architectural facts, astronomical facts, behavioral facts, chemical facts, economic facts, meteorological facts, sociological facts, and so on. A world physically identical to ours, but in which these sort of facts differ, is inconceivable. In conceiving of a microphysically identical world, we conceive of a world in which the location of every last particle throughout space and time is the same. It follows that the world will have the same macroscopic structure as ours, and the same macroscopic dynamics. Once all this is fixed there is simply no room for the facts in question to vary (apart, perhaps, from any variation due to variations in conscious experience).

Furthermore, this inconceivability does not seem to be due to any contingent limits in our cognitive capacity. Such a world is inconceivable *in principle*. Even a superbeing, or God, could not imagine such a world. There is simply not anything for them to imagine. Once they imagine a world with all the physical facts, they have automatically imagined a world in which all the high-level facts hold. A physically identical world in which the high-level facts are false is therefore logically impossible, and the high-level properties in question are logically supervenient on the physical.

Epistemology.   Moving beyond conceivability intuitions, we can note that if there *were* a possible world physically identical to ours but biologically distinct, then this would raise radical epistemological problems. How would we know that we were not in that world rather than this one? How would we know that the biological facts in our world are as they are? To see this, note that if I were in the alternative world, it would certainly *look* the same as this one. It instantiates the same distribution of particles found in the plants and animals in this world; indistinguishable patterns of photons are reflected from those entities; no difference would be revealed under even the closest examination. It follows that all the external evidence we possess fails to distinguish the possibilities. Insofar as the biological facts about our world are not logically supervenient, there is no way we can know those facts on the basis of external evidence.

In actuality, however, there is no deep epistemological problem about biology. We come to know biological facts about our world on the basis of external evidence all the time, and there is no special skeptical problem that arises. It follows that the biological facts are logically supervenient on the physical. The same goes for facts about architecture, economics, and meteorology. There is no special skeptical problem about knowing these facts on the basis of external evidence, so they must be logically supervenient on the physical.

We can back up this point by noting that in areas where there *are* epistemological problems, there is an accompanying failure of logical supervenience, and that conversely, in areas where logical supervenience fails, there are accompanying epistemological problems.

Most obviously, there is an epistemological problem about consciousness—the problem of other minds. This problem arises because it seems logically compatible with all the external evidence that beings around us are conscious, and it is logically compatible that they are not. We have no way to peek inside a dog's brain, for instance, and observe the presence or absence of conscious experience. The status of this problem is controversial, but the mere *prima facie* existence of the problem is sufficient to defeat an epistemological argument, parallel to those above, for the logical supervenience of consciousness. By contrast, there is not even a *prima facie* problem of other biologies, or other economies. Those facts are straightforwardly publically accessible, precisely because they are fixed by the physical facts.

(Question: Why doesn't a similar argument force us to the conclusion that if conscious experience fails to supervene logically, then we can't know about even our *own* consciousness? Answer: Because conscious experience is at the very center of our epistemic universe. The skeptical problems about nonsupervenient biological facts arise because we only have access to biological facts by external, physically mediated evidence; external nonsupervenient facts would be out of our direct epistemic reach. There is no such problem with our own consciousness.)

Another famous epistemological problem concerns facts about causation. As Hume argued, external evidence only gives us access to regularities of succession between events; it does not give us access to any further fact of causation. So if causation is construed as something over and above the presence of a regularity (as I will assume it must be), it is not clear that we can know that it exists. Once again, this skeptical problem goes hand in hand with a failure of logical supervenience. In this case, facts about causation fail to supervene logically on matters of particular physical fact. Given all the facts about distribution of physical entities in space-time, it is logically possible that all the regularities therein arose as a giant cosmic coincidence without any real causation. At a smaller scale, given the particular facts about any apparent instance of causation, it is logically possible that it is a mere succession. We infer the existence of causation by a kind of inference to the best explanation—to believe otherwise would be to believe in vast, inexplicable coincidences—but belief in causation is not forced on us in the direct way that belief in biology is forced on us.

I have sidestepped problems about the supervenience of causation by stipulating that the supervenience base for our purposes includes not just particular physical facts but all the physical laws. It is reasonable to suppose that the addition of laws fixes the facts about causation. But of course there is a skeptical problem about laws paralleling the problem about causation: witness Hume's problem of induction, and the logical possibility that any apparent law might be an accidental regularity.

As far as I can tell, these two problems exhaust the epistemological problems that arise from failure of logical supervenience on the physical. There are some other epistemological problems that in a sense precede these, because they concern the existence of the physical facts themselves. First, there is Descartes's problem about the existence of the external world. It is compatible with our experiential evidence that the world we think we are seeing does not exist; perhaps we are hallucinating, or we are brains in vats. This problem can be seen to arise precisely because the facts about the external world do not supervene logically on the facts about our experience. (Idealists, positivists, and others have argued controversially that they do. Note that if these views are accepted the skeptical problem falls away.) There is also an epistemological problem about the theoretical entities postulated by science—electrons, quarks, and such. Their absence would be logically compatible with the directly observable facts about objects in our environment, and some have therefore raised skeptical doubts about them. This problem can be analyzed as arising from the failure of theoretical facts to supervene logically on observational facts. In both these cases, skeptical doubts are perhaps best quelled by a form of inference to the best explanation, just as in the case of causation, but the in-principle possibility that we are wrong remains.

In any case, I am bypassing this sort of skeptical problem by giving myself the physical world for free, and fixing all physical facts about the world in the supervenience base (thereby assuming that the external world exists, and that there are electrons, and so on). Given that those facts are known, there is no room for skeptical doubts about most high-level facts, precisely because they are logically supervenient. To put the matter the other way around: All our sources of external evidence supervene logically on the microphysical facts, so that insofar as some phenomenon does not supervene on those facts, external evidence can give us no reason to believe in it. One might wonder whether some further phenomena might be posited via inference to the best explanation, as above, to explain the microphysical facts. Indeed, this process takes us from particular facts to simple underlying laws (and hence yields causation), but then the process seems to stop. It is in the nature of fundamental laws that they are the end of the explanatory chain (except, perhaps, for theological speculation). This leaves phenomena that we have *internal* evidence for—namely conscious experience—and that is all. Modulo conscious experience, all phenomena are logically supervenient on the physical.

We can also make an epistemological case for logical supervenience more directly, by arguing that someone in possession of all the physical facts could in principle come to know all the high-level facts, given that they possess the high-level concepts involved. True, one could never *in practice* ascertain the high-level facts from the set of microphysical facts. The vastness of the latter set is enough to rule that out. (Even less am I suggesting that one could perform a formal derivation; formal systems are irrelevant for reasons canvased earlier.) But as an in-principle point, there are various ways to see that someone (a superbeing?) armed with only the microphysical facts and the concepts involved could infer the high-level facts.

The simplest way is to note that in principle one could build a big mental simulation of the world and watch it in one's mind's eye, so to speak. Say that a man is carrying an umbrella. From the associated microphysical facts, one could straightforwardly infer facts about the distribution and chemical composition of mass in the man's vicinity, giving a high-level structural characterization of the area. One could determine the existence of a male fleshy biped straightforwardly enough. For instance, from the structural information one could note that there was an organism atop two longish legs that were responsible for its locomotion, that the creature has male anatomy, and so on. It would be clear that he was carrying some device that was preventing drops of water, otherwise prevalent in the neighborhood, from hitting him. Doubts that this device is really an umbrella could be assuaged by noting from its physical structure that it can fold and unfold; from its history that it was hanging on a stand that morning, and was originally made in a factory with others of a similar kind, and so on. Doubts that the fleshy biped is really a human could be assuaged by noting the composition of his DNA, his evolutionary history, his relation to other beings, and so on. We need only assume that the being possesses enough of the concept involved to be able to apply it correctly to instances (that is, the being possesses the intension). If so, then the microphysical facts will give it all the evidence it needs to apply the concepts, and to determine that there really is a person carrying an umbrella here.

The same goes for almost any sort of high-level phenomena: tables, life, economic prosperity. By knowing all the low-level facts, a being in principle can infer all the facts necessary to determine whether or not this is an instance of the property involved. Effectively, what is happening is that a possible world compatible with the microphysical facts is constructed, and the high-level facts are simply read off that world using the appropriate intension (as the relevant facts are invariant across physically identical possible worlds). Hence the high-level facts are logically supervenient on the physical.

Analyzability.   So far, I have argued that microphysical facts fix high-level facts without saying much explicitly about the high-level concepts involved. In any specific case, however, this entailment relationship relies on a concept's intension. If microphysical facts entail a high-level fact, this is because the microphysical facts suffice to fix those features of the world in virtue of which the high-level intension applies. That is, we should be able to *analyze* what it takes for an entity to satisfy the intension of a high-level concept, at least to a sufficient extent that we can see why those conditions for satisfaction could be satisfied by fixing the physical facts. It is therefore useful to look more closely at the intensions of high-level concepts, and to examine the features of the world in virtue of which they apply.

There are some obstacles to elucidating these intensions and to summarizing them in words. As we saw earlier, application conditions of a concept are often indeterminate in places. Is a cup-shaped object made of tissues a cup? Is a computer virus alive? Is a booklike entity that coagulates randomly into existence a book? Our ordinary concepts do not give straightforward answers to these questions. In a sense, it is a matter for stipulation. Hence there will not be determinate application conditions for use in the entailment process. But as we saw earlier, this indeterminacy precisely mirrors an indeterminacy about the facts themselves. Insofar as the intension of "cup" is a matter for stipulation, the facts about cups are also a matter for stipulation. What counts for our purposes is that the intension together with the microphysical facts determines the high-level facts insofar as they are really factual. Vagueness and indeterminacy can make discussion awkward, but they affect nothing important to the issues.

A related problem is that any short analysis of a concept will invariably fail to do justice to it. As we have seen, concepts do not usually have crisp definitions. At a first approximation, we can say something is a table if it has a flat horizontal surface with legs as support; but this lets in too many things (Frankenstein's monster on stilts?) and omits others (a table with no legs, sticking out from a wall?). One can refine the definition, adding further conditions and clauses, but we quickly hit the problems with indeterminacy, and in any case the product will never be perfect. But there is no need to go into all the details required to handle every special case: after a point the details are just more of the same. As long as we know what *sort* of properties the intension applies in virtue of, we will have enough to make the point.

As we saw before, we do not need a definition of B-properties in terms of A-properties in order for A-facts to entail B-facts. Meanings are fundamentally represented by intensions, not definitions. The role of analysis here is simply to characterize the intensions in sufficient detail that the existence of an entailment becomes clear. For this purpose, a rough-and-ready analysis will suffice. Intensions generally apply to individuals in a possible world in virtue of some of their properties and not others; the point of such an analysis is to see what sort of properties the intension applies in virtue of, and to make the case that properties of this sort are compatible with entailment by physical properties.

A third problem stems from the division between the *a priori* and *a posteriori* application conditions of many concepts. As long as we keep primary and secondary intensions separate, however, this is not much of a problem. The secondary intension associated with "water" is something like "H_2O," which is obviously logically supervenient on the physical. But the primary intension, something like "the clear, drinkable liquid in our environment" is equally logically supervenient, as the clarity, drinkability, and liquidity of water is entailed by the physical facts.[37] We can run things either way. As we have seen, it is the primary intension that enters into reductive explanation, so it is this that we are most concerned with. In general, if a primary intension I is logically supervenient on the physical, then so is a rigidified secondary intension $dthat(I)$, as it will generally consist in a projection of some intrinsic physical structure across worlds.

Considerations about *a posteriori* necessity have led some to suppose that there can be no logical entailment from low-level facts to high-level facts. Typically one hears something like "Water is necessarily H_2O, but that is not a truth of meaning, so there is no conceptual relation." But this is a vast oversimplification. For a start, the secondary intension "H_2O" can be seen as part of the meaning of "water" in some sense, and it certainly supervenes logically. But more importantly, the primary intension ("the clear, drinkable liquid . . .") which fixes reference also supervenes, perhaps modulo experience and indexicality. It is precisely in virtue of its satisfying this intension that we deemed that H_2O was water in the first place. Given the primary intension I, the high-level facts are derivable unproblematically from the microphysical facts (modulo the contribution of experience and indexicality). The Kripkean observation that the concept is better represented as *dthat(I)* affects this derivability not at all. The semantic phenomenon of rigidification does not alone make an ontological difference.

With these obstacles out of the way, we can look at the intensions associated with various high-level concepts. In most cases these are characterizable in functional or structural terms, or as a combination of the two. For example, the sorts of things relevant to something's being a table include (1) that it have a flat top and be supported by legs, and (2) that people use it to support various objects. The first of these is a structural condition: that is, a condition on the intrinsic physical structure of the object. The second is a functional condition: that is, it concerns the external causal role of an entity, characterizing the way it interacts with other entities. Structural properties are clearly entailed by microphysical facts. So are functional properties in general, although this is slightly less straightforward. Such properties depend on a much wider supervenience base of microphysical facts, so that facts about an object's environment will often be relevant; and insofar as such properties are characterized dispositionally (something is soluble if it *would* dissolve *if* immersed in water), one needs to appeal to counterfactuals. But the truth-values of those counterfactuals are fixed by the inclusion of physical laws in the antecedent of our supervenience conditionals, so this is not a problem.

To take another example, the conditions on life roughly come down to some combination of the ability to reproduce, to adapt, and to metabolize, among other things (as usual, we need not legislate the weights, or all other relevant factors). These properties are all characterizable functionally, in terms of an entity's relation to other entities, its ability to convert external resources to energy, and its ability to react appropriately to its environment. These functional properties are all derivable, in principle, from the physical facts. As usual, even if there is no perfect definition of life in functional terms, this sort of characterization shows us that life is a functional property, whose instantiation can therefore be entailed by physical facts.

A complication is raised by the fact that functional properties are often characterized in terms of a causal role relative to other high-level entities. It follows that logical supervenience of the properties depends on the logical supervenience of the other high-level notions involved, where these notions may themselves be characterized functionally. This is ultimately not a problem, as long as causal roles are eventually cashed out by nonfunctional properties: typically either by structural or phenomenal properties. There may be some circularity in the interdefinability of various functional properties—perhaps it is partly constitutive of a stapler that it deliver staples, and partly constitutive of staples that they are delivered by staplers. This circularity can be handled by cashing out the causal roles of all the properties simultaneously,[38] as long as the analyses have a noncircular part that is ultimately grounded in structural or phenomenal properties. (The appeal to phenomenal properties may seem to count against logical supervenience on the physical, but see below. In any case, it is compatible with logical supervenience modulo conscious experience.)

Many properties are characterized relationally, in terms of relations to an entity's environment. Usually such relations are causal, so that the properties in question are functional, but this is not always so: witness the property of being on the same continent as a duck. Similarly, some properties are dependent on history (although these can usually be construed causally); to be a kangaroo, a creature must have appropriate ancestors. In any case these properties pose no problems for logical supervenience, as the relevant historical and environmental facts will themselves be fixed by the global physical facts.

Even a complex social fact such as "There was economic prosperity in the 1950s"[39] is characterizable in mostly functional terms, and so can be seen to be entailed by the physical facts. A full analysis would be very complicated and would be made difficult by the vagueness of the notion of prosperity, but to get an idea how it might go, one can ask why we say that there *was* economic prosperity in the 1950s? At a first approximation, because there was high employment, people were able to purchase unusually large amounts of goods, there was low inflation, much development in housing, and so on. We can in turn give rough-and-ready analyses of the notion of housing (the kind of place people sleep and eat in), of employment (organized labor for reward), and of monetary notions (presumably money will be roughly analyzable in terms of the systematic ability to exchange for other items, and its value will be analyzable in terms of how much one gets in exchange). All these analyses are ridiculously oversimplified, but the point is clear enough. These are generally functional properties that can be entailed by physical facts.

Many have been skeptical of the possibility of conceptual analysis. Often this has been for reasons that do not make any difference to the arguments I am making—because of indeterminacy in our concepts, for example, or because they lack crisp definitions. Sometimes this skepticism may have arisen for deeper reasons. Nevertheless, if what I have said earlier in this chapter is correct, and if the physical facts about a possible world fix the high-level facts, we should *expect* to be able to analyze the intension of the high-level concept in question, at least to a good approximation, in order to see how its application can be determined by physical facts. This is what I have tried to do in the examples given here. Other examples can be treated similarly.[40]

I am not advocating a program of performing such analyses in general. Concepts are too complex and unruly for this to do much good, and any explicit analysis is usually a pale shadow of the real thing. What counts is the general point that most high-level concepts are not primitive, unanalyzable notions. They are generally analyzable to the extent that their intensions can be seen to specify functional or structural properties. It is in virtue of this analyzability that high-level facts are in principle derivable from microphysical facts and reductively explainable in terms of physical facts.

Some problem cases

There are some types of properties that might be thought to provide particular difficulties for logical supervenience, and therefore for reductive explanation. I will examine a number of such candidates, paying particular attention to the question of whether the associated phenomena pose problems for reductive explanation analogous to the problems posed by consciousness. It seems to me that with a couple of possible exceptions, no significant new problems arise here.

Consciousness-dependent properties. As discussed already, some concepts' primary intensions involve a relation to conscious experience. An obvious example is redness, taken as a property of external objects. On at least some accounts, the primary intension associated with redness requires that for something to be red, it must be the kind of thing that tends to cause red experiences under appropriate conditions.[41] So in its primary intension, redness is not logically supervenient on the physical, although it supervenes modulo conscious experience. On the other hand, its secondary intension almost certainly supervenes. If it turns out that in the actual world, the sort of thing that tends to cause red experience is a certain surface reflectance, then objects with that reflectance are red even in worlds in which there is no conscious being to see them. Redness is identified *a posteriori* with that reflectance, which is logically supervenient on the physical alone.

We saw earlier that failure of a primary intension to supervene logically is associated with a failure of reductive explanation. So, does reductive explanation fail for redness? The answer is yes, in a weak sense. If redness is construed as the tendency to cause red experiences, then insofar as experience is not reductively explainable, neither is redness. But one can come close. One can note *that* a certain physical quality causes red experiences; and one can even explain the causal relation between the quality and red-*judgments*. It is just the final step to experience that goes unexplained. In practice, our strictures on explanation are weak enough that this sort of thing counts. To explain a phenomenon to which reference is fixed by some experience, we do not require an explanation of experience. Otherwise we would wait a long time.

The same goes for phenomena such as heat, light, and sound. Although their secondary intensions determine structural properties (molecular motion, the presence of photons, waves in air), their primary intensions involve a relation to conscious experience: heat is the thing that causes heat sensations, light causes visual experiences, and so on. But as Nagel (1974) and Searle (1992) have noted, we do not require an explanation of heat sensations when explaining heat. Explanation modulo experience is good enough.

Other properties depend even more directly on conscious experience, in that experience not only plays a role in reference fixation but is partly constitutive of the *a posteriori* notion as well. The property of standing next to a conscious person is an obvious example. On some accounts, mental properties such as love and belief, although not themselves phenomenal properties, have a conceptual dependence on the existence of conscious experience. If so, then in a world without consciousness, such properties would not be exemplified. Such properties therefore are not logically supervenient even *a posteriori,* and reductive explanation fails even more strongly than in the above cases. But they are logically supervenient and reductively explainable modulo conscious experience, so no *further* failure of reductive explanation arises here.

Intentionality.   It is worth separately considering the status of intentionality, as this is sometimes thought to pose problems analogous to those posed by consciousness. It is plausible, however, that any failure of intentional properties to supervene logically is derivative on the nonsupervenience of consciousness. As I noted in Chapter 1, there seems to be no conceivable world that is physically and phenomenally identical to ours, but in which intentional contents differ.[42] If phenomenology is partly constitutive of intentional content, as some philosophers suggest, then intentional properties may fail to supervene logically on the physical, but they will supervene modulo conscious experience. The claim that consciousness is partly constitutive of content is controversial, but in any case there is little reason to believe that intentionality fails to supervene in a separate, nonderivative way.

Leaving any phenomenological aspects aside, intentional properties are best seen as a kind of third-person construct in the explanation of human behavior, and should therefore be analyzable in terms of causal connections to behavior and the environment. If so, then intentional properties are straightforwardly logically supervenient on the physical. Lewis (1974) makes a thorough attempt at explicating the entailment from physical facts to intentional facts by giving an appropriate functional analysis. More recent accounts of intentionality, such as those by Dennett (1987), Dretske (1981), and Fodor (1987) can be seen as contributing to the same project. None of these analyses are entirely compelling, but it may be that a more sophisticated descendant might do the job. There is no argument analogous to the arguments against the supervenience of consciousness showing that intentionality *cannot* supervene logically on physical and phenomenal properties.[43] Indeed, conceivability arguments indicate that intentional properties must be logically supervenient on these if such properties are instantiated at all, and epistemological arguments lead us to a similar conclusion. So there is no separate *ontological* problem of intentionality.

Moral and aesthetic properties.   It is often held that there is no *conceptual* connection from physical properties to moral and aesthetic properties. According to Moore (1922), nothing about the *meaning* of notions such as "goodness" allows that facts about goodness should be entailed by physical facts. In fact, Moore claimed that there is no conceptual connection from *natural* facts to moral facts, where the natural may include the mental as well as the physical (so supervenience modulo conscious experience does not help here). Does this mean that moral properties are as problematic as conscious experience?

There are two disanalogies, however. First, there does not seem to be a conceivable world that is naturally identical to ours but morally distinct, so it is unlikely that moral facts are further facts in any strong sense. Second, moral facts are not phenomena that force themselves on us. When it comes to the crunch, we can deny that moral facts exist at all. Indeed, this reflects the strategy taken by moral antirealists such as Blackburn (1971) and Hare (1984). These antirealists argue that because moral facts are not entailed by natural facts and are not plausibly "queer" further facts, they have no objective existence and morality should be relativized into a construct or projection of our cognitive apparatus. The same strategy cannot be taken for phenomenal properties, whose existence is forced upon us.

For moral properties, there are at least two reasonable alternatives available. The first is antirealism of some sort, perhaps relativizing "objective moral facts" into "subjective moral facts,"[44] or embracing a view on which moral discourse does not state facts at all. The second is to claim that there is an *a priori* connection from natural facts to moral facts, one that (contra Moore) can be seen to hold in virtue of an analysis and explication of moral concepts. If a concept such as "good" determines a stable nonindexical primary intension, then the second position follows: we will have an *a priori* function from naturally specified worlds to moral facts. If it only determines an indexical primary intension, or if different subjects can equally reasonably associate different primary intensions with the concept, or if it determines no primary intension at all, then a version of the first position will follow.

Some other positions are sometimes taken, but none seem tenable. Moore held that there is a nonconceptual *a priori* connection between natural and moral facts that we obtain through a mysterious faculty of "moral intuition," but this view is widely rejected (it is hard to see what could ground such intuitions' truth or falsity). A position on which moral properties supervene by a fundamental nomic link seems out of the question, as there is no conceivable world in which the natural facts are the same as ours but in which the moral facts are different. A popular position among contemporary moral realists (see, e.g., Boyd 1988; Brink 1989) is that moral facts supervene on natural facts with *a posteriori* necessity; that is, they supervene according to the secondary but not the primary intensions of moral concepts. This position is difficult to maintain, however, given that even *a posteriori* equivalences must be grounded in *a priori* reference fixation. Even though it is *a posteriori* that water is H_2O, the facts about water follow from the microphysical facts *a priori*. Similarly, if moral concepts have a primary intension and if naturally identical centered worlds are morally identical, an *a priori* link from natural facts to moral facts would seem to follow. (Horgan and Timmons [1992a; 1992b] provide a critique along these lines.)

Aesthetic properties can be treated in a similar way. If anything, an antirealist treatment is even more plausible here. In the final analysis, although there are interesting conceptual questions about how the moral and aesthetic domains should be treated, they do not pose metaphysical and explanatory problems comparable to those posed by conscious experience.

Names.   On many accounts (e.g., Kaplan 1989), there is no analysis associated with a name such as "Rolf Harris," which simply picks out its referent directly. Does this mean that the property of being Rolf Harris fails to supervene logically on the physical? There is no problem about the supervenience of the secondary intension (e.g., Rolf might be the person conceived from a given sperm and egg in all possible worlds), but the absence of a primary intension might be thought to pose problems for reductive explanation. Still, it is plausible that even though there is no primary intension that is shared across the community, every individual use of the name has a primary intension attached. When I use the name "Rolf Harris," there is *some* systematic way in which its referent depends on the way the world turns out; for me, the primary intension might be something like "the man called 'Rolf Harris' who bangs around on paint cans, and who bears the appropriate causal relation to me."[45] Such an intension will supervene logically. Rather than justifying this in detail, however, it is easier to note that any failure of logical supervenience will not be accompanied by an explanatory mystery. The property of being Rolf Harris does not constitute a phenomenon in need of explanation, as opposed to explication. What needs explaining is the existence of a person named "Rolf Harris" who bangs around on paint cans, and so on. These properties certainly supervene, and are explainable in principle in the usual way.

Indexicals.   Reference fixation of many concepts, from "water" to "my dog," involves an indexical element. The reference of these notions is fixed on the basis of both physical facts and an agent-relative "indexical fact" representing the location of an agent using the term in question. Such a fact is determinate for any given agent, so reference fixation is determinate. Supervenience and explanation succeed modulo that indexical fact.

Does indexicality pose a problem for reductive explanation? For arbitrary speakers, perhaps not, as the "fact" in question can be relativized away. But for myself, it is not so easy. The indexical fact expresses something very salient about the world as I find it: that David Chalmers is *me*. How could one explain this seemingly brute fact? Indeed, is there really a fact here to be explained, as opposed to a tautology? The issue is extraordinarily difficult to get a grip on, but it seems to me that even if the indexical is not an objective fact about the world, it is a fact about the world as I find it, and it is the world as I find it that needs explanation. The nature of the brute indexical is quite obscure, though, and it is most unclear how one might explain it.[46] (Of course, we can give a reductive explanation of why David Chalmers's utterance of "I am David Chalmers" is true. But this nonindexical fact seems quite different from the indexical fact that I am David Chalmers.)

It is tempting to look to consciousness. But while an explanation of consciousness might yield an explanation of "points of view" in general, it is hard to see how it could explain why a seemingly arbitrary one of those points of view is *mine,* unless solipsism is true. The indexical fact may have to be taken as primitive. If so, then we have a failure of reductive explanation distinct from and analogous to the failure with consciousness. Still, the failure is less worrying than that with consciousness, as the unexplained fact is so "thin" by comparison to the facts about consciousness in all its glory. Admitting this primitive indexical fact would require far less revision of our materialist worldview than would admitting irreducible facts about conscious experience.

Negative facts. As we saw earlier, certain facts involving negative existentials and universal quantifiers are not logically determined by the physical facts, or indeed by any set of localized facts. Consider the following facts about our world: there are no angels; Don Bradman is the greatest cricketer; everything alive is based on DNA. All these could be falsified, consistently with all the physical facts about our world, simply by the addition of some new nonphysical stuff: cricket-playing angels made of ectoplasm, for instance. Even addition of facts about conscious experience or indexicality cannot help here.[47]

Does this mean that these facts are not reductively explainable? It seems so, insofar as there is no physical explanation of why there is no extra nonphysical stuff in our world. That is indeed a further fact. The best way to deal with this situation is to introduce a second-order fact that says of the set of basic particular facts, be they microphysical, phenomenal, indexical, or whatever: *That's all.* This fact says that all the particular facts about the world are included in or entailed by the given set of facts. From this second-order fact, in conjunction with all the basic particular facts, all the negative facts will follow.

This does not constitute a very serious failure of reductive explanation. Presumably there will be such a "That's all" fact true of any world, and such a fact will never be entailed by the particular facts. It simply expresses the bounded nature of our world, or of any world. It is a cheap way to bring all the negative existential and universally quantified facts within our grasp.

Physical laws and causation.   On the most plausible accounts of physical laws, these are not logically supervenient on the physical facts, taken as a collection of particular facts about a world's spatiotemporal history. One can see this by noting the logical possibility of a world physically indiscernible from ours over its entire spatiotemporal history, but with different laws. For example, it might be a law of that world that whenever two hundred tons of pure gold are assembled in a vacuum, it will transmute into lead. Otherwise its laws are identical, with minor modifications where necessary. As it happens, in the spatiotemporal history of our world, two hundred tons of gold are never assembled in a vacuum. It follows that our world and the other world have identical histories, but their laws differ nevertheless.

Arguments like this suggest that the laws of nature do not supervene logically on the collection of particular physical facts.[48] By similar arguments one can see that a causal connection between two events is something over and above a regularity between the events. Holders of various Humean views dispute these conclusions, but it seems to me that they have the worse of the arguments here.[49] There is something irreducible in the existence of laws and causation.

I have bypassed these problems elsewhere by including physical laws in the supervenience base, but this steps over the metaphysical puzzle rather than answering it. It is true that laws and causation lead to less significant failure of reductive explanation than consciousness. The laws and causal relations are themselves posited to explain existing physical phenomena, namely the manifold regularities present in nature, whereas consciousness is a brute explanandum. Nevertheless the very existence of such irreducible further facts raises deep questions about their metaphysical nature. Apart from conscious experience and perhaps indexicality, these constitute the only such further facts in which we have any reason to believe. It is not unnatural to speculate that these two nonsupervenient kinds, consciousness and causation, may have a close metaphysical relation.

Recap

The position we are left with is that almost all facts supervene logically on the physical facts (including physical laws), with possible exceptions for conscious experience, indexicality, and negative existential facts. To put the matter differently, we can say that the facts about the world are exhausted by (1) particular physical facts, (2) facts about conscious experience, (3) laws of nature, (4) a second-order "That's all" fact, and perhaps (5) an indexical fact about my location. (The last two are minor compared to the others, and the status of the last is dubious, but I include them for completeness.) Modulo conscious experience and indexicality, it seems that all positive facts are logically supervenient on the physical. To establish this conclusively would require a more detailed examination of all kinds of phenomena, but what we have seen suggests that the conclusion is reasonable. We can sum up the ontological and epistemological situations with a couple of fables. Perhaps there is a grain of truth in the shape of these stories, if not in the details.

Creation myth. Creating the world, all God had to do was fix the facts just mentioned. For maximum economy of effort, he first fixed the laws of nature—the laws of physics, and any laws relating physics to conscious experience. Next, he fixed the boundary conditions: perhaps a time-slice of physical facts, and maybe the values in a random-number generator. These combined with the laws to fix the remaining physical and phenomenal facts. Last, he decreed, "That's all."

Epistemological myth. At first, I have only facts about my conscious experience. From here, I infer facts about middle-sized objects in the world, and eventually microphysical facts. From regularities in these facts, I infer physical laws, and therefore further physical facts. From regularities between my conscious experience and physical facts, I infer psychophysical laws, and therefore facts about conscious experience in others. I seem to have taken the abductive process as far as it can go, so I hypothesize: that's all. The world is much larger than it once seemed, so I single out the original conscious experiences as *mine.*

Note the very different order involved from the two perspectives. One could almost say that epistemology recapitulates ontology backward. Note also that it seems beyond God's powers to fix my indexical fact. Perhaps this is another reason to be skeptical about it.

The logical supervenience of most high-level phenomena is a conclusion that has not been as widely accepted as it might have been, even among those who discuss supervenience. Although the matter is often not discussed, many have been wary about invoking the conceptual modality as relevant to supervenience relations. As far as I can tell there have been a number of separate reasons for this hesitation, none of which are ultimately compelling.

First, the problem with logically possible physically identical worlds with extra nonphysical stuff (angels, ectoplasm) has led some to suppose that supervenience relations cannot be logical (Haugeland 1982; Petrie 1987); but we have seen how to fix this problem. Second, many have supposed that considerations about *a posteriori* necessity demonstrate that supervenience relations cannot be underwritten by meanings (Brink 1989; Teller 1984); but we have seen that supervenience relations based on *a posteriori* necessity can be seen as a variety of logical supervenience. Third, there is a general skepticism about the notion of conceptual truth, deriving from Quine; but we have seen that this is a red herring here. Fourth, worries about "reducibility" have led some to suppose that supervenience is not generally a conceptual relation (Hellman and Thompson 1975); but it is unclear that there are any good arguments against reducibility that are also good arguments against logical supervenience. Fifth, the very phenomenon of conscious experience is sometimes invoked to demonstrate that supervenience relations cannot be logical in general (Seager 1988); but we have seen that conscious experience is almost unique in its failure to supervene logically. Finally, the claim that supervenience relations are not generally logical is often stated without argument, presumably as something that any reasonable person must believe (Bacon 1986; Heil 1992).[50]

It is plausible that every supervenience relation of a high-level property upon the physical is ultimately either (1) a logical supervenience relation of either the primary or secondary variety, or (2) a contingent natural supervenience relation. If neither of these holds for some apparent supervenience relation, then we have good reason to believe that there are no objective high-level facts of the kind in question (as, perhaps, for moral facts). I will argue further in Chapter 4 that there is no deep variety of supervenience intermediate between the logical and the natural.

This provides a unified explanatory picture, in principle. Almost every phenomenon is reductively explainable, in the weak sense outlined earlier, except for conscious experience and perhaps indexicality, along with the rock-bottom microphysical facts and laws, which have to be taken as fundamental.

It is worth taking a moment to answer a query posed by Blackburn (1985) and Horgan (1993): How do we explain the supervenience relations themselves? For a logical supervenience relation based on the primary intension of a concept, this is a simple matter of giving an appropriate analysis of the concept, perhaps in functional or structural terms, and noting that its reference is invariant across physically identical worlds. Here, the supervenience conditional is itself an *a priori* conceptual truth. For a logical supervenience relation based on a secondary intension, the supervenience can be explained by noting that the primary intension of the concept picks out some actual-world referent that is projected (by rigidification) invariantly across physically identical worlds. All we need here for an explanation is an *a priori* conceptual analysis combined with contingent facts about the actual world.[51] On the other hand, a mere natural supervenience relation will itself be a contingent law. At best it will be explainable in terms of more fundamental laws; at worst, the supervenience law will itself be fundamental. In either case, one explains certain regularities in the world by invoking fundamental laws, just as one does in physics, and as always, fundamental laws are where explanation must stop. Mere natural supervenience is ontologically expensive, as we have seen, so it is fortunate that logical supervenience is the rule and natural supervenience the exception.

PART II

The Irreducibility of Consciousness

Can Consciousness
Be Reductively Explained?

1. Is Consciousness Logically Supervenient
on the Physical?

Almost everything in the world can be explained in physical terms; it is
natural to hope that consciousness might be explained this way, too. In this
chapter, however, I will argue that consciousness escapes the net of reductive explanation. No explanation given wholly in physical terms can ever
account for the emergence of conscious experience. This may seem to be a
negative conclusion, but it leads to some strong positive consequences that
I will bring out in later chapters.

To make the case against reductive explanation, we need to show that
consciousness is not logically supervenient on the physical. In principle,
we need to show that it does not supervene *globally*—that is, that all the
microphysical facts in the world do not entail the facts about consciousness. In
practice, it is easier to run the argument *locally,* arguing that in an individual,
microphysical facts do not entail the facts about consciousness. When it
comes to consciousness, local and global supervenience plausibly stand and
fall together, so it does not matter much which way we run the argument:
if consciousness supervenes at all, it almost certainly supervenes locally. If
this is disputed, however, all the arguments can be run at the global level
with straightforward alterations.

How can we argue that consciousness is not logically supervenient on the
physical? There are various ways. We can think about what is conceivable,
in order to argue directly for the logical possibility of a situation in which
the physical facts are the same but the facts about experience are different.
We can appeal to epistemology, arguing that the right sort of link between

knowledge of physical facts and knowledge of consciousness is absent. And we can appeal directly to the concept of consciousness, arguing that there is no analysis of the concept that could ground an entailment from the physical to the phenomenal. In what follows I will give arguments using all three of these strategies. The first two are essentially arguments from conceivability, the second two are arguments from epistemology, and the fifth is an argument from analysis. There is some element of redundancy among the five arguments, but together they make a strong case.

One can also do things more directly, making the case against reductive explanation without explicitly appealing to logical supervenience. I have taken that route elsewhere, but here I will give the more detailed analysis to allow a fuller case. All the same, the case against reductive explanation and the critique of existing reductive accounts (in section 2 onward) should make sense even without this analysis. Some readers might like to proceed there directly, at least on a first reading.

(A technical note: The burden of this chapter is to argue, in effect, that there is no *a priori* entailment from physical facts to phenomenal facts. The sort of necessity that defines the relevant supervenience relation is the *a priori* version of logical necessity, where primary intensions are central. As we saw in Chapter 2, this is the relation that is relevant to issues about explanation; matters of *a posteriori* necessity can be set to one side. In the next chapter, issues of ontology rather than explanation are central, and I argue separately that there is no *a posteriori* necessary connection between physical facts and phenomenal facts.)

Argument 1: The logical possibility of zombies

The most obvious way (although not the only way) to investigate the logical supervenience of consciousness is to consider the logical possibility of a *zombie*: someone or something physically identical to me (or to any other conscious being), but lacking conscious experiences altogether.[1] At the global level, we can consider the logical possibility of a *zombie world*: a world physically identical to ours, but in which there are no conscious experiences at all. In such a world, everybody is a zombie.

So let us consider my zombie twin. This creature is molecule for molecule identical to me, and identical in all the low-level properties postulated by a completed physics, but he lacks conscious experience entirely. (Some might prefer to call a zombie "it," but I use the personal pronoun; I have grown quite fond of my zombie twin.) To fix ideas, we can imagine that right now I am gazing out the window, experiencing some nice green sensations from seeing the trees outside, having pleasant taste experiences through munching on a chocolate bar, and feeling a dull aching sensation in my right shoulder.

Calvin and Hobbes

by Bill Watterson

Figure 3.1. Calvin and Hobbes on zombies. (Calvin and Hobbes © Watterson. Distributed by Universal Press Syndicate. Reprinted with permission. All rights reserved)

What is going on in my zombie twin? He is physically identical to me, and we may as well suppose that he is embedded in an identical environment. He will certainly be identical to me *functionally*: he will be processing the same sort of information, reacting in a similar way to inputs, with his internal configurations being modified appropriately and with indistinguishable behavior resulting. He will be *psychologically* identical to me, in the sense developed in Chapter 1. He will be perceiving the trees outside, in the functional sense, and tasting the chocolate, in the psychological sense. All of this follows logically from the fact that he is physically identical to me, by virtue of the functional analyses of psychological notions. He will even be "conscious" in the functional senses described earlier—he will be awake, able to report the contents of his internal states, able to focus attention in various places, and so on. It is just that none of this functioning will be accompanied by any real conscious experience. There will be no phenomenal feel. There is nothing it is like to be a zombie.

This sort of zombie is quite unlike the zombies found in Hollywood movies, which tend to have significant functional impairments (Figure 3.1). The sort of consciousness that Hollywood zombies most obviously lack is a psychological version: typically, they have little capacity for introspection and lack a refined ability to voluntarily control behavior. They may or may not lack phenomenal consciousness; as Block (1995) points out, it is reasonable to suppose that there is something it tastes like when they eat their victims. We can call these *psychological zombies*; I am concerned with *phenomenal zombies,* which are physically and functionally identical, but which lack experience. (Perhaps it is not surprising that phenomenal zombies have not been popular in Hollywood, as there would be obvious problems with their depiction.)

The idea of zombies as I have described them is a strange one. For a start, it is unlikely that zombies are naturally possible. In the real world, it is likely that any replica of me would be conscious. For this reason, it is most natural to imagine unconscious creatures as physically different from conscious ones—exhibiting impaired behavior, for example. But the question is not whether it is plausible that zombies could exist in our world, or even whether the idea of a zombie replica is a natural one; the question is whether the notion of a zombie is conceptually coherent. The mere intelligibility of the notion is enough to establish the conclusion.

Arguing for a logical possibility is not entirely straightforward. How, for example, would one argue that a mile-high unicycle is logically possible? It just seems obvious. Although no such thing exists in the real world, the description certainly appears to be coherent. If someone objects that it is not logically possible—it merely seems that way—there is little we can say, except to repeat the description and assert its obvious coherence. It seems quite clear that there is no hidden contradiction lurking in the description.

I confess that the logical possibility of zombies seems equally obvious to me. A zombie is just something physically identical to me, but which has no conscious experience—all is dark inside. While this is probably empirically impossible, it certainly seems that a coherent situation is described; I can discern no contradiction in the description. In some ways an assertion of this logical possibility comes down to a brute intuition, but no more so than with the unicycle. Almost everybody, it seems to me, is capable of conceiving of this possibility. Some may be led to deny the possibility in order to make some theory come out right, but the justification of such theories should ride on the question of possibility, rather than the other way around.

In general, a certain burden of proof lies on those who claim that a given description is logically *impossible*. If someone truly believes that a mile-high unicycle is logically impossible, she must give us some idea of where a contradiction lies, whether explicit or implicit. If she cannot point out something about the intensions of the concepts "mile-high" and "unicycle" that might lead to a contradiction, then her case will not be convincing. On the other hand, it is no more convincing to give an obviously false analysis of the notions in question—to assert, for example, that for something to qualify as a unicycle it must be shorter than the Statue of Liberty. If no reasonable analysis of the terms in question points toward a contradiction, or even makes the existence of a contradiction plausible, then there is a natural assumption in favor of logical possibility.

That being said, there are some positive things that proponents of logical possibility can do to bolster their case. They can exhibit various indirect arguments, appealing to what we know about the phenomena in question and the way we think about hypothetical cases involving these phenomena, in order to establish that the obvious logical possibility really is a logical possibility, and really is obvious. One might spin a fantasy about an ordinary person riding a unicycle, when suddenly the whole system expands a thousandfold. Or one might describe a series of unicycles, each bigger than the last. In a sense, these are all appeals to intuition, and an opponent who wishes to deny the possibility can in each case assert that our intuitions have misled us, but the very obviousness of what we are describing works in our favor, and helps shift the burden of proof further onto the other side.

For example, we can indirectly support the claim that zombies are logically possible by considering *nonstandard realizations* of my functional organization.[2] My functional organization—that is, the pattern of causal organization embodied in the mechanisms responsible for the production of my behavior—can in principle be realized in all sorts of strange ways. To use a common example (Block 1978), the people of a large nation such as China might organize themselves so that they realize a causal organization isomorphic to that of my brain, with every person simulating the behavior of a single neuron, and with radio links corresponding to synapses. The population might control an empty shell of a robot body, equipped with sensory transducers and motor effectors.

Many people find it implausible that a set-up like this would give rise to conscious experience—that somehow a "group mind" would emerge from the overall system. I am not concerned here with whether or not conscious experience would *in fact* arise; I suspect that in fact it would, as I argue in Chapter 7. All that matters here is that the idea that such a system lacks conscious experience is *coherent.* A meaningful possibility is being expressed, and it is an open question whether consciousness arises or not. We can make a similar point by considering my silicon isomorph, who is organized like me but who has silicon chips where I have neurons. Whether such an isomorph would *in fact* be conscious is controversial, but it seems to most people that those who deny this are expressing a coherent possibility. From these cases it follows that the existence of my conscious experience is not logically entailed by the facts about my functional organization.

But given that it is conceptually coherent that the group-mind set-up or my silicon isomorph could lack conscious experience, it follows that my zombie twin is an equally coherent possibility. For it is clear that there is no more of a *conceptual* entailment from biochemistry to consciousness than there is from silicon or from a group of homunculi. If the silicon isomorph without conscious experience is conceivable, we need only substitute neurons for silicon in the conception while leaving functional organization constant, and we have my zombie twin. Nothing in this substitution could force experience into the conception; these implementational differences are simply not the sort of thing that could be conceptually relevant to experience. So consciousness fails to logically supervene on the physical.

The argument for zombies can be made without an appeal to these non-standard realizations, but these have a heuristic value in eliminating a source of conceptual confusion. To some people, intuitions about the logical possibility of an unconscious physical replica seem less than clear at first, perhaps because the familiar co-occurrence of biochemistry and consciousness can lead one to suppose a conceptual connection. Considerations of the less familiar cases remove these empirical correlations from the picture, and therefore make judgments of logical possibility more straightforward.[3] But once it is accepted that these nonconscious functional replicas are logically possible, the corresponding conclusion concerning a physical replica cannot be avoided.

Some may think that conceivability arguments are unreliable. For example, sometimes it is objected that we cannot really imagine in detail the many billions of neurons in the human brain. Of course this is true; but we do not need to imagine each of the neurons to make the case. Mere complexity among neurons could not conceptually entail consciousness; if all that neural structure is to be relevant to consciousness, it must be relevant *in virtue* of some higher-level properties that it enables. So it is enough to imagine the system at a coarse level, and to make sure that we conceive it with appropriately sophisticated mechanisms of perception, categorization, high-bandwidth access to information contents, reportability, and the like. No matter how sophisticated we imagine these mechanisms to be, the zombie scenario remains as coherent as ever. Perhaps an opponent might claim that all the unimagined neural detail is conceptually relevant in some way independent of its contribution to sophisticated functioning; but then she owes us an account of what that way might be, and none is available. Those implementational details simply lie at the wrong level to be conceptually relevant to consciousness.

It is also sometimes said that conceivability is an imperfect guide to possibility. The main way that conceivability and possibility can come apart is tied to the phenomenon of *a posteriori* necessity: for example, the hypothesis that water is not H_2O seems conceptually coherent, but water is arguably H_2O in all possible worlds. But *a posteriori* necessity is irrelevant to the concerns of this chapter. As we saw in the last chapter, explanatory connections are grounded in *a priori* entailments from physical facts to high-level facts. The relevant kind of possibility is to be evaluated using the primary intensions of the terms involved, instead of the secondary intensions that are relevant to *a posteriori* necessity. So even if a zombie world is conceivable only in the sense in which it is conceivable that water is not H_2O, that is enough to establish that consciousness cannot be reductively explained.

Those considerations aside, the main way in which conceivability arguments can go wrong is by subtle conceptual confusion: if we are insufficiently reflective we can overlook an incoherence in a purported possibility, by taking a conceived-of situation and *misdescribing* it. For example, one might think that one can conceive of a situation in which Fermat's last theorem is false, by imagining a situation in which leading mathematicians declare that they have found a counterexample. But given that the theorem is actually true, this situation is being misdescribed: it is really a scenario in which Fermat's last theorem is true, and in which some mathematicians make a mistake. Importantly, though, this kind of mistake always lies in the *a priori* domain, as it arises from the incorrect application of the primary intensions of our concepts to a conceived situation. Sufficient reflection will reveal that the concepts are being incorrectly applied, and that the claim of logical possibility is not justified.

So the only route available to an opponent here is to claim that in describing the zombie world as a zombie world, we are misapplying the concepts, and that in fact there is a conceptual contradiction lurking in the description. Perhaps if we thought about it clearly enough we would realize that by imagining a physically identical world we are thereby *automatically* imagining a world in which there is conscious experience. But then the burden is on the opponent to give us some idea of where the contradiction might lie in the apparently quite coherent description. If no internal incoherence can be revealed, then there is a very strong case that the zombie world is logically possible.

As before, I can detect no internal incoherence; I have a clear picture of what I am conceiving when I conceive of a zombie. Still, some people find conceivability arguments difficult to adjudicate, particularly where strange ideas such as this one are concerned. It is therefore fortunate that every point made using zombies can also be made in other ways, for example by considering epistemology and analysis. To many, arguments of the latter sort (such as arguments 3–5 below) are more straightforward and therefore make a stronger foundation in the argument against logical supervenience. But zombies at least provide a vivid illustration of important issues in the vicinity.

Argument 2: The inverted spectrum

Even in making a conceivability argument against logical supervenience, it is not strictly necessary to establish the logical possibility of zombies or a zombie world. It suffices to establish the logical possibility of a world physically identical to ours in which the facts about conscious experience are merely *different* from the facts in our world, without conscious experience being absent entirely. As long as some positive fact about experience in our world does not hold in a physically identical world, then consciousness does not logically supervene.

It is therefore enough to note that one can coherently imagine a physically identical world in which conscious experiences are *inverted,* or (at the local level) imagine a being physically identical to me but with inverted conscious experiences. One might imagine, for example, that where I have a red experience, my inverted twin has a blue experience, and vice versa. Of course he will call his blue experiences "red," but that is irrelevant. What matters is that the experience he has of the things we both call "red"—blood, fire engines, and so on—is of the same kind as the experience I have of the things we both call "blue," such as the sea and the sky.

The rest of his color experiences are systematically inverted with respect to mine, in order that they cohere with the red-blue inversion. Perhaps the best way to imagine this happening with human color experiences is to imagine that two of the axes of our three-dimensional color space are switched—the red–green axis is mapped onto the yellow–blue axis, and vice versa.[4] To achieve such an inversion in the actual world, presumably we would need to rewire neural processes in an appropriate way, but as a *logical* possibility, it seems entirely coherent that experiences could be inverted while physical structure is duplicated exactly. Nothing in the neurophysiology dictates that one sort of processing should be accompanied by red experiences rather than by yellow experiences.

It is sometimes objected (Harrison 1973; Hardin 1987) that human color space is asymmetrical in a way that disallows such an inversion. For instance, certain colors have a warmth or coolness associated with them, and warmth and coolness appear to be directly associated with different functional roles (e.g., warmth is perceived as "positive," whereas coolness is perceived as "negative"). If a warm color and a cool color were switched, then the "warm" phenomenal feel would become dissociated from the "warm" functional role—a "cool" green experience would be reported as positive rather than negative, and so on. In a similar way, there seem to be more discriminable shades of red than of yellow, so swapping red experiences with yellow experiences directly might lead to the odd situation in which a subject could functionally discriminate more shades of yellow than are distinguishable phenomenologically. Perhaps there are enough asymmetries in color space that any such inversion would lead to a strange dissociation of phenomenal feel from the "appropriate" functional role.

There are three things we can say in response to this. First, there does not seem to be anything *incoherent* about the notion of such a dissociation (e.g., cool phenomenology with warm reactions), although it is admittedly an odd idea.[5] Second, instead of mapping red precisely onto blue and vice versa, one can imagine that these are mapped onto slightly different colors. For example, red might be mapped onto a "warm" version of blue (as Levine [1991] suggests), or even onto color not in our color space at all. In the red–yellow case, we might imagine that red is mapped onto an extended range of yellow experiences, in which more discrimination is available. There is no reason why spectrum inversion scenarios *must* involve colors drawn from the usual color space. Third, perhaps the most compelling response is to argue (with Shoemaker [1982]) that even if our own color space is asymmetrical, there certainly *could* be creatures whose color space is symmetrical. For example, there is probably a naturally possible creature who sees (and experiences) precisely two colors, *A* and *B,* which correspond to distinct, well-separated ranges of light wavelengths, and for which the distinction between the two exhausts the structure of the color space. It seems entirely coherent to imagine two such creatures that are physically identical, but whose experiences of *A* and *B* are inverted. That is enough to make the point.

Even many reductive materialists (e.g., Shoemaker [1982]) have conceded that it is coherent that one's color experiences might be inverted while one's functional organization stays constant. It is allowed that a system with different underlying neurophysiological properties, or with something like silicon in place of neurobiology, might have different color experiences. But once this is granted, it follows automatically that inversion of experiences in a physical replica is at least conceptually coherent. The extra neurophysiological properties that are constrained in such a case are again not the kind of thing that could logically determine the nature of the experience. Even if there is some sort of *a posteriori* identification between certain neurophysiological structures and certain experiences (as Shoemaker believes), we must still allow that a different pattern of associations is conceivable, in the sense of conceivability that is relevant to reductive explanation.

While the possibility of inverted spectra and the possibility of zombies both establish that consciousness fails to supervene logically, the first establishes a conclusion strictly weaker than the second. Somebody might conceivably hold that inverted spectra but not zombies are logically possible. If this were the case, then the *existence* of consciousness could be reductively explained, but the specific *character* of particular conscious experiences could not be.

Argument 3: From epistemic asymmetry

As we saw earlier, consciousness is a surprising feature of the universe. Our grounds for belief in consciousness derive solely from our own experience of it. Even if we knew every last detail about the physics of the universe—the configuration, causation, and evolution among all the fields and particles in the spatiotemporal manifold—*that* information would not lead us to postulate the existence of conscious experience. My knowledge of consciousness, in the first instance, comes from my own case, not from any external observation. It is my first-person experience of consciousness that forces the problem on me.

From all the low-level facts about physical configurations and causation, we can in principle derive all sorts of high-level facts about macroscopic systems, their organization, and the causation among them. One could determine all the facts about biological function, and about human behavior and the brain mechanisms by which it is caused. But nothing in this vast causal story would lead one who had not experienced it directly to believe that there should be any *consciousness*. The very idea would be unreasonable; almost mystical, perhaps.

It is true that the physical facts about the world might provide some indirect evidence for the existence of consciousness. For example, from these facts one could ascertain that there were a lot of organisms that *claimed* to be conscious, and said they had mysterious subjective experiences. Still, this evidence would be quite inconclusive, and it might be most natural to draw an eliminativist conclusion—that there was in fact no *experience* present in these creatures, just a lot of talk.

Eliminativism about conscious experience is an unreasonable position *only* because of our own acquaintance with it. If it were not for this direct knowledge, consciousness could go the way of the vital spirit. To put it another way, there is an *epistemic asymmetry* in our knowledge of consciousness that is not present in our knowledge of other phenomena.[6] Our knowledge that conscious experience exists derives primarily from our own case, with external evidence playing at best a secondary role.

The point can also be made by pointing to the existence of a problem of other minds. Even when we know everything physical about other creatures, we do not *know* for certain that they are conscious, or what their experiences are (although we may have good reason to believe that they are). It is striking that there is no problem of "other lives," or of "other economies," or of "other heights." There is no epistemic asymmetry in those cases, precisely because those phenomena are logically supervenient on the physical.

The epistemic asymmetry in knowledge of consciousness makes it clear that consciousness cannot logically supervene. If it were logically supervenient, there would be no such epistemic asymmetry; a logically supervenient property can be detected straightforwardly on the basis of external evidence, and there is no special role for the first-person case. To be sure, there are some supervenient properties—memory, perhaps—that are more easily detected in the first-person case. But this is just a matter of how hard one has to work. The presence of memory is just as accessible from the third person, in principle, as from the first person. The epistemic asymmetry associated with consciousness is much more fundamental, and it tells us that no collection of facts about complex causation in physical systems adds up to a fact about consciousness.

Argument 4: The knowledge argument

The most vivid argument against the logical supervenience of consciousness is suggested by Jackson (1982), following related arguments by Nagel (1974) and others. Imagine that we are living in an age of a completed neuroscience, where we know everything there is to know about the physical processes within our brain responsible for the generation of our behavior. Mary has been brought up in a black-and-white room and has never seen any colors except for black, white, and shades of gray.[7] She is nevertheless one of the world's leading neuroscientists, specializing in the neurophysiology of color vision. She knows everything there is to know about the neural processes involved in visual information processing, about the physics of optical processes, and about the physical makeup of objects in the environment. But she does not know what it is like to see red. No amount of reasoning from the physical facts alone will give her this knowledge.

It follows that the facts about the subjective experience of color vision are not entailed by the physical facts. If they were, Mary could in principle come to know what it is like to see red on the basis of her knowledge of the physical facts. But she cannot. Perhaps Mary could come to know what it is like to see red by some indirect method, such as by manipulating her brain in the appropriate way. The point, however, is that the knowledge does not follow from the physical knowledge alone. Knowledge of all the physical facts will in principle allow Mary to derive all the facts about a system's reactions, abilities, and cognitive capacities; but she will still be entirely in the dark about its experience of red.

A related way to make this point is to consider systems quite different from ourselves, perhaps much simpler—such as bats or mice—and note that the physical facts about these systems do not tell us what their conscious experiences are like, if they have any at all (Nagel focuses on this sort of issue). Once all the physical facts about a mouse are in, the nature of its conscious experience remains an *open question*: it is consistent with the physical facts about a mouse that it has conscious experience, and it is consistent with the physical facts that it does not. From the physical facts about a bat, we can ascertain *all* the facts about a bat, except the facts about its conscious experiences. Knowing all the physical facts, we still do not know what it is like to be a bat.

Along similar lines we can consider a computer, designed as a simple cognitive agent (perhaps it has the intelligence of a dog), but similar to us in certain respects, such as its capacity for perceptual discrimination. In particular it categorizes color stimuli in a manner quite similar to ours, grouping things that we would call "red" under one category and things we would call "green" under another. Even if we know every detail about the computer's circuits, questions remain: (1) Is the computer experiencing anything at all when it looks at roses?; (2) If it is, is it experiencing the same sensory color quality that we have when we look at a rose, or some quite different quality? These are entirely meaningful questions, and knowing all the physical facts does not force one answer rather than another onto us. The physical facts therefore do not logically entail the facts about conscious experience.

Jackson put his argument forward as an argument against materialism rather than against reductive explanation. There have been many replies to the argument; I will discuss them in the next chapter, where materialism rather than reductive explanation will be at issue. But for now it is interesting to note that most of the objections to the argument against materialism have *conceded* the point that is relevant to the argument against reductive explanation: that knowledge of what red is like is factual knowledge that is not entailed *a priori* by knowledge of the physical facts. The only way that the conclusion can be evaded is to deny that knowing what red experience is like gives knowledge of a *fact* at all. This is the strategy taken by Lewis (1990) and Nemirow (1990), who argue that all Mary is lacking is an *ability,* such as the ability to recognize red things. I discuss this suggestion in the next chapter; here, I simply note that insofar as it seems clear that when she sees red for the first time, Mary is *discovering* something about the way the world is, it seems clear that the knowledge she is gaining is knowledge of a fact.

Argument 5: From the absence of analysis

If proponents of reductive explanation are to have any hope of defeating the arguments above, they will have to give us some idea of how the existence of consciousness *might* be entailed by physical facts. While it is not fair to expect all the details, one at least needs an account of how such an entailment might *possibly* go. But any attempt to demonstrate such an entailment is doomed to failure. For consciousness to be entailed by a set of physical facts, one would need some kind of analysis of the notion of consciousness—the kind of analysis whose satisfaction physical facts could imply—and there is no such analysis to be had.

The only analysis of consciousness that seems even remotely tenable for these purposes is a functional analysis. Upon such an analysis, it would be seen that all there is to the notion of something's being conscious is that it should play a certain functional role. For example, one might say that all there is to a state's being conscious is that it be verbally reportable, or that it be the result of certain kinds of perceptual discrimination, or that it make information available to later processes in a certain way, or whatever. But on the face of it, these fail miserably as analyses. They simply miss what it means to be a conscious experience. Although conscious states may play various causal roles, they are not *defined* by their causal roles. Rather, what makes them conscious is that they have a certain phenomenal feel, and this feel is not something that can be functionally defined away.

To see how unsatisfactory these analyses are, note how they trivialize the problem of explaining consciousness. Suddenly, all we have to do to explain consciousness is explain our ability to make certain verbal reports, or to perform certain sorts of discrimination, or to manifest some other capacity. But on the face of it, it is entirely conceivable that one could explain all these things without explaining a thing about consciousness itself; that is, without explaining the *experience* that accompanies the report or the discrimination. To analyze consciousness in terms of some functional notion is either to change the subject or to define away the problem. One might as well define "world peace" as "a ham sandwich." Achieving world peace becomes much easier, but it is a hollow achievement.

Functional analyses of consciousness can also be argued against on more specific grounds. For example, any functionally analyzed concept will have a degree of semantic indeterminancy. Does a mouse have beliefs? Do bacteria learn? Is a computer virus alive? The best answer to these questions is usually in a sense yes, in a sense no. It all depends on how we draw the boundaries in the concepts, and in any high-level functional concepts the boundaries will be vague. But compare: Does a mouse have conscious experience? Does a virus? These are not matters for stipulation. Either there is something that it is like to be a mouse or there is not, and it is not up to us to define the mouse's experience into or out of existence. To be sure, there is probably a continuum of conscious experience from the very faint to the very rich; but if something has conscious experience, however faint, we cannot stipulate it away. This determinacy could not be derived from any functional analysis of the concepts in the vicinity of consciousness, as the functional concepts in the vicinity are all somewhat vague. If so, it follows that the notion of consciousness cannot be functionally analyzed.

Another objection is that the functionalist analysis collapses the important distinction, outlined in Chapter 1, between the notions of awareness and consciousness. Presumably if consciousness is to be functionally analyzed, it will be analyzed roughly as we analyzed awareness then: in terms of a certain accessibility of information in later processing and in the control of behavior. Awareness is a perfectly good concept, but it is quite distinct from the concept of conscious experience. The functionalist treatment collapses the two notions of consciousness and awareness into one, and therefore does not do justice to our conceptual system.

The alternatives to functional analysis look even worse. It is most unclear that there could be any other kind of analysis appropriate for reductive explanation. The only alternative might be a structural analysis—perhaps consciousness could be analyzed as some sort of biochemical structure—but that analysis would be even more clearly inadequate. Whether or not consciousness *is* a biochemical structure, that is not what "consciousness" *means*. To analyze consciousness that way again trivializes the explanatory problem by changing the subject. It seems that the concept of consciousness is irreducible, being characterizable only in terms of concepts that themselves involve consciousness.

Note that this is quite unlike the sort of irreducibility that is sometimes supposed to hold for high-level concepts in general. We have seen that many high-level notions have no crisp definitions, and no manageable analyses in terms of necessary and sufficient conditions. Nevertheless, as we saw in the last chapter, these concepts at least have rough-and-ready analyses that get us into the ballpark, although they will inevitably fail to do justice to the details. Most importantly, it is easy to see that properties such as life, learning, and so on can be analyzed as functional properties, even if spelling out the details of just *which* functional property is a difficult matter. Even though these properties lack crisp functional definitions, they are nevertheless quite compatible with entailment by the physical facts.

The problems with consciousness are in a different league. Here, the purported analyses do not even get into the ballpark. In a much starker way, they completely fail to characterize what needs to be explained. There is no temptation to even *try* to add epicycles to a purported functional analysis of consciousness in order to make it satisfactory, as there is with similar analyses of life and of learning. Consciousness is simply not to be characterized as a functional property in the first place. The same goes for analyses of consciousness as a structural property, or in other reductive terms. There is therefore no way for an entailment from physical facts to consciousness to get off the ground.

2. The Failure of Reductive Explanation

The failure of consciousness to logically supervene on the physical tells us that no reductive explanation of consciousness can succeed. Given any account of the physical processes purported to underlie consciousness, there will always be a further question: Why are these processes accompanied by conscious experience? For most other phenomena, such a question is easily answered: the physical facts about those processes *entail* the existence of the phenomena. For a phenomenon such as life, for example, the physical facts imply that certain functions will be performed, and the performance of those functions is all we need to explain in order to explain life. But no such answer will suffice for consciousness.

Physical explanation is well suited to the explanation of *structure* and of *function.* Structural properties and functional properties can be straightfor- wardly entailed by a low-level physical story, and so are clearly apt for re- ductive explanation. And almost all the high-level phenomena that we need to explain ultimately come down to structure or function: think of the explanation of waterfalls, planets, digestion, reproduction, language. But the explanation of consciousness is not just a matter of explaining structure and function. Once we have explained all the physical structure in the vicinity of the brain, and we have explained how all the various brain functions are performed, there is a further sort of explanandum: consciousness itself. Why should all this structure and function give rise to experience? The story about the physical processes does not say.

We can put this in terms of the thought experiments given earlier. Any story about physical processes applies equally to me and to my zombie twin. It follows that nothing in that story says why, in my case, consciousness arises. Similarly, any story about physical processes applies equally to my inverted twin, who sees blue where I see red: it follows that nothing in that story says why my experience is of one variety rather than another. The very fact that it is logically possible that the physical facts could be the same while the facts about consciousness are different shows us that as Levine (1983) has put it, there is an *explanatory gap* between the physical level and conscious experience.

If this is right, the fact that consciousness accompanies a given physical process is a *further fact,* not explainable simply by telling the story about the physical facts. In a sense, the accompaniment must be taken as brute. We might try to systematize and explain these brute facts in terms of some simple underlying pattern, but there will always remain an element here that is logically independent of the physical story. Perhaps we might get some kind of explanation by combining the underlying physical facts with certain further *bridging* principles that link the physical facts with consciousness, but this explanation will not be a reductive one. The very need for explicit bridging principles shows us that consciousness is not being explained reduc- tively, but is being explained on its own terms.

Of course nothing I have said implies that physical facts are *irrelevant* to the explanation of consciousness. We can still expect physical accounts to play a significant role in a theory of consciousness, giving information about the physical *basis* of consciousness, for example, and perhaps yielding a de- tailed correspondence between various aspects of physical processing and aspects of conscious experience. Such accounts may be especially useful in helping to understand the *structure* of consciousness: the patterns of similar- ity and difference between experiences, the geometric structure of phenomenal fields, and so on. I say much more about these and other things that physical explanation can tell us about experience in a nonreductive framework in Chapter 6. But a physical account, alone, is not *enough*.

At this point, a number of objections naturally arise.

Objection 1: Are we setting the standards too high?

Some might argue that explanation of *any* high-level phenomena will postulate "bridge laws" in addition to a low-level account, and that it is only with the aid of these bridge laws that the details of the high-level phenomena are derived. However, as the discussion in the last chapter suggests (and as is carefully argued by Horgan [1978]), in such cases the bridge laws are not further facts about the world. Rather, the connecting principles themselves are logically supervenient on the low-level facts. The extreme case of such a bridging principle is a supervenience conditional, which we have seen is usually a conceptual truth. Other more "localized" bridging principles, such as the link between molecular motion and heat, can at least be derived from the physical facts. For consciousness, by contrast, such bridging principles must be taken as primitive.

It is interesting to see how a typical high-level property—such as life, say—evades the arguments put forward in the case of consciousness. First, it is straightforwardly inconceivable that there could be a physical replica of a living creature that was not itself alive. Perhaps a problem might arise due to context-dependent properties (would a replica that forms randomly in a swamp be alive, or be human?), but fixing environmental facts eliminates even that possibility. Second, there is no "inverted life" possibility analogous to the inverted spectrum. Third, when one knows all the physical facts about an organism (and possibly about its environment), one has enough material to know all the biological facts. Fourth, there is no epistemic asymmetry with life; facts about life in others are as accessible, in principle, as facts about life in ourselves. Fifth, the concept of life is plausibly analyzable in functional terms: to be alive is roughly to possess certain capacities to adapt, reproduce, and metabolize. As a general point, most high-level phenomena come down to matters of physical structure and function, and we have good reason to believe that structural and functional properties are logically supervenient on the physical.

Objection 2: Couldn't a vitalist have said the same thing about life?

All this notwithstanding, a common reaction to the sort of argument I have given is to reply that a vitalist about life might have said the same things.[8] For example, a vitalist might have claimed that it is logically possible that a physical replica of me might not be *alive*, in order to establish that life cannot be reductively explained. And a vitalist might have argued that life is a further fact, not explained by any account of the physical facts. But the vitalist would have been *wrong*. By analogy, might not the opponent of reductive explanation for consciousness also be wrong?

I think this reaction misplaces the source of vitalist objections. Vitalism was mostly driven by doubt about whether physical mechanisms could perform all the complex *functions* associated with life: adaptive behavior, reproduction, and the like. At the time, very little was known about the enormous sophistication of biochemical mechanisms, so this sort of doubt was quite natural. But implicit in these very doubts is the conceptual point that when it comes to explaining life, it is the performance of various functions that needs to be explained. Indeed, it is notable that as physical explanation of the relevant functions gradually appeared, vitalist doubts mostly melted away. With consciousness, by contrast, the problem persists even when the various functions are explained.

Presented with a full physical account showing how physical processes perform the relevant functions, a reasonable vitalist would concede that life has been explained. There is not even *conceptual* room for the performance of these functions without life. Perhaps some ultrastrong vitalist would deny even this, claiming that something is left out by a functional account of life—the vital spirit, perhaps. But the obvious rejoinder is that unlike experience, the vital spirit is not something we have independent reason to believe in. Insofar as there was ever any reason to believe in it, it was as an explanatory construct—"We *must* have such a thing in order to be able to do such amazing stuff." But as an explanatory construct, the vital spirit can be eliminated when we find a better explanation of how the functions are performed. Conscious experience, by contrast, forces itself on one as an explanandum and cannot be eliminated so easily.

One reason a vitalist might think something is left out of a functional explanation of life is precisely that nothing in a physical account explains why there is something it is like to be alive. Perhaps some element of belief in a "vital spirit" was tied to the phenomena of one's inner life. Many have perceived a link between the concepts of life and experience, and even today it seems reasonable to say that one of the things that needs to be explained about life is the fact that many living creatures are conscious. But the existence of *this* sort of vitalist doubt is of no comfort to the proponent of reductive explanation of consciousness, as it is a doubt that has never been overturned.

Objection 3: Is conceivability a guide to possibility?

Philosophers are often suspicious of arguments that give a key role to conceivability, frequently responding that conceivability does not suffice for possibility. This is a subtle issue that I have discussed earlier and will discuss again: but here, the subtleties are not especially relevant. When it comes to matters of *explanation,* it is clear that conceivability is central. If on reflection we find it conceivable that all these physical processes could take place in the absence of consciousness, then no reductive explanation of consciousness will be satisfactory: the further question of why *we* exist and not zombies will always arise. Even if conceivability is tied to the limits of human capacity, explanation is tied to the limits of human capacity in a similar way.

Another way to put the point is to note that reductive explanation of a phenomenon in terms of the physical requires an *a priori* implication from the physical facts to the relevant high-level facts (logical supervenience according to primary intension, as I put it earlier). If such a connection does not hold, then we will always be able to raise the further question of why the physical processes give rise to consciousness. We have seen that in almost all domains, the right sort of connection holds, making reductive explanation possible; but it does not seem to hold for conscious experience. One can question whether *ontological* views such as materialism turn on these *a priori* links—I discuss that matter in the next chapter—but when it comes to reductive explanation, such links are crucial.

Objection 4: Isn't this a collection of circular intuitions?

It might be further objected that the arguments I have given consist, at bottom, in a collection of intuitions. There is certainly a sense in which all these arguments are based on intuition, but I have tried to make clear just how natural and plain these intuitions are, and how forced it is to deny them. The main intuition at work is that *there is something to be explained*—some phenomenon associated with first-person experience that presents a problem not presented by observation of cognition from the third-person point of view. Given the premise that some explanandum is forced on us by first-person experience that is not forced on us by third-person observation, most of the arguments above fall out. It follows immediately, for example, that what needs to be explained cannot be analyzed as the playing of some functional role, for the latter phenomenon is revealed to us by third-person observation and is much more straightforward.

The "intuition" at work here is the very *raison d'être* of the problem of consciousness. The only consistent way to get around the intuitions is to deny the problem and the phenomenon altogether. One can always, at least when speaking "philosophically," deny the intuitions altogether, and deny that there is anything (apart from the performance of various functions) that needs explaining. But if one takes consciousness seriously, the conclusions for which I am arguing must follow.

Objection 5: Doesn't all explanation have to stop somewhere?

A final objection is that no explanation gives one something for nothing: all explanation has to stop somewhere. In explaining the motion of the planets, for example, one takes the laws of gravity and the existence of mass for granted. Perhaps we should simply take something for granted in this case, too? I am sympathetic with this point; I think we do have to take something for granted in explaining consciousness. But in doing so we inevitably move beyond a *reductive* explanation. Indeed, this sort of analogy lends support to the nonreductive position I am advocating. We take the laws of physics for granted because they are *fundamental* laws. If we take a link between physical processes and conscious experience for granted, this suggests that the link should be taken as fundamental in the same way. I return to this point in the next chapter.

3. Cognitive Modeling

In this and the sections that follow, I illustrate the failure of reductive explanation by giving a critique of a number of accounts of consciousness that have been proposed by researchers in various disciplines. Not all of these proposals have been put forward as reductive explanations of conscious experience, although they have often been interpreted this way; but in any case, it is instructive to see just what these accounts can and cannot achieve. Along the way, it is interesting to note these researchers' varying attitudes to the hard questions about conscious experience.

First, I will consider accounts based on *cognitive modeling*. Cognitive modeling works well for most problems in cognitive science. By exhibiting a model of the causal dynamics involved in cognitive processes, one can explain the causation of behavior in a cognitive agent. This provides a valuable kind of explanation for psychological phenomena, such as learning, memory, perception, control of action, attention, categorization, linguistic behavior, and so on. If we have a model that captures the causal dynamics of someone who is learning, for example, it follows that anything instantiating those dynamics in the right environment will be learning. From the model we can see how certain functions are performed, and this is all we have to explain to explain learning. But this is insufficient to explain consciousness. For any model we exhibit, it remains a further question why realization of the model should be accompanied by consciousness. This is not a question that description and analysis of the model alone can answer.

It is sometimes objected that purported models of consciousness are untestable, as there is no way to verify whether or not instantiations of the model are conscious. This is a problem, but there is a deeper problem. Even if we had (*per impossibile*) an "experience meter" that could peek in and tell us whether an instantiation was conscious, this would only establish a correlation. We would know that whenever the model is instantiated, consciousness goes along with it. But it would not explain consciousness, in the way that such models explain other mental phenomena.

Such models can certainly explain "consciousness" in the psychological senses thereof, where it is construed as some kind of cognitive or functional capacity. Many existing "models of consciousness" can be most charitably interpreted in this light. We can see these as providing explanations of reportability, or of attention, or of introspective abilities, and so on. None of them, however, gives us anything close to an explanation of why these processes should be accompanied by conscious experience. Some examples will illustrate this.

The first example is the cognitive model presented by Bernard Baars (1988), as part of a book-length treatment of consciousness from the standpoint of cognitive psychology. Baars brings all sorts of experimental evidence to bear in establishing his main thesis: consciousness is a kind of *global workspace* in a distributed system of intelligent information processors. When processors gain access to the global workspace, they broadcast a message to the entire system, as if they had written it on a blackboard. The contents of the global workspace are the contents of consciousness.

Baars uses this model to explain a remarkable number of properties of human processing. The model provides a very suggestive framework for explaining a subject's access to information, and its role in attention, reportability, voluntary control, and even the development of a self-concept. The global workspace framework is therefore well suited to explaining consciousness in its whole bundle of psychological senses. There is at least a general theory of *awareness* on offer.

But there is no reductive explanation of *experience* to be found here. The question of why these processes should give rise to experience is simply not addressed. One might suppose that according to the theory, the contents of experience are precisely the contents of the workspace. But even if this is so, nothing internal to the theory *explains* why it is that the information within the global workspace is experienced. The best the theory can do is to say that the information is experienced because it is *globally accessible.* But now the question arises in a different form: Why should global accessibility give rise to conscious experience? This bridging question is not addressed in Baars's work.

Baars mentions this sort of worry briefly: "A skeptical reader may . . . wonder whether we are truly describing conscious experience, or whether, instead, we can only deal with incidental phenomena associated with it" (p. 27). His response is to note that scientific theories tend to at least *approach* the "thing itself"; for instance, biology explains inheritance *itself,* and not just associated phenomena. But this is simply to ignore the ways in which consciousness is different in kind from these phenomena, as we have seen. With inheritance, various functions are all there is to explain. With consciousness, there is a further explanandum: experience itself. Baars's theory can therefore be seen as an interesting approach to the cognitive processes underlying consciousness, and one that gives us much indirect insight into consciousness, but it leaves the key questions—why is there consciousness and how does it arise from cognitive processing?—untouched.

Daniel Dennett has also put forward a cognitive model of consciousness. In fact, he has put forward at least two of them. The first (Dennett 1978c) is a "box-and-lines" model, consisting in an account of the flow of information between various modules (Figure 3.2). Central to the model are (1) a perceptual module, (2) a short-term memory store *M,* which receives

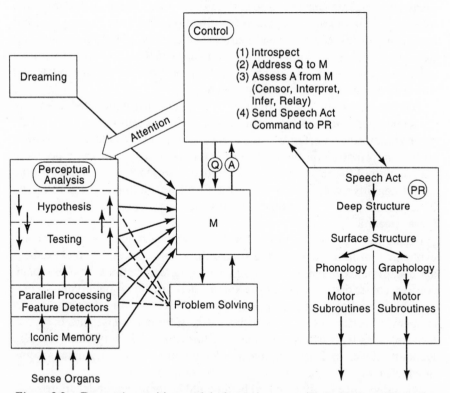

Figure 3.2.   Dennett's cognitive model of consciousness. (Redrawn from Figure 9.1, p. 155, from Daniel C. Dennett, *Brainstorms: Philosophical Essays on Mind and Psychology,* The MIT Press. Copyright © 1987 by Bradford Books, Publishers. By permission of The MIT Press)

information from the perceptual module, (3) a control system, which interacts with the memory store by a question-and-answer-process, and which can direct attention to the contents of the perceptual module, and (4) a "public relations" unit, which receives speech act commands from the control system and converts them into public-language utterances.

What might this model explain? Although it is in a very simplified form (as Dennett would concede), it might be fleshed out to provide an explanation of *reportability*; that is, of our ability to report the contents of our internal states. It also provides the skeleton of an explanation of our ability to bring perceptual information to bear on the control of behavior, to introspect our internal states, and so on. But it tells us nothing about why there should be something it is like to be a system undergoing these processes.

In *Consciousness Explained* (1991), Dennett puts forward a more sophisticated account that draws on much recent work in cognitive science. The model proposed here is essentially a "pandemonium" model, consisting in many small agents competing for attention, with the agent that shouts the loudest playing the primary role in the direction of later processing. On this model there is no central "headquarters" of control, but multiple channels exerting simultaneous influence. Dennett supplements this account with appeals to neuroscience, evolutionary biology, and connectionist models and production systems in artificial intelligence.

The complexity of this account notwithstanding, it is directed at largely the same phenomena as the earlier account. If successful, it would provide an explanation of reportability, and more generally of the influence of various sorts of information on the control of behavior. It also provides a potential explanation of the focus of attention. It gives a provocative account of some of our cognitive capacities, but it goes no further than the previous model in telling us why there should be conscious experience in the vicinity of these capacities.

Unlike most authors who put forward cognitive models, Dennett claims explicitly that his models are the sort of thing that could explain everything about experience that needs explaining. In particular, he thinks that to explain consciousness, one only needs to explain such functional phenomena as reportability and control; any phenomenon that is apparently omitted is a chimera. Sometimes he seems to take it as a basic premise that once one has explained the various functions, one has explained everything (see, e.g., Dennett [1993a], p. 210), but he occasionally puts forward arguments, some of which I will consider later.[9]

The same sort of critique could be directed at cognitive-model approaches to consciousness by Churchland (1995), Johnson-Laird (1988), Shallice (1972, 1988a, 1988b), and many others. All provide intriguing accounts of the performance of cognitive functions, but all leave the really hard questions untouched.

4. Neurobiological Explanation

Neurobiological approaches to consciousness have recently become popular. Like cognitive models, these have much to offer in explaining psychological phenomena, such as the varieties of awareness. They can also tell us something about the brain processes that are *correlated* with consciousness. But none of these accounts explains the correlation: we are not told why brain processes should give rise to experience at all. From the point of view of neuroscience, the correlation is simply a brute fact.

From a methodological standpoint, it is not obvious how one can begin to develop a neuroscientific theory. How does one perform the experiments that detect a correlation between some neural process and consciousness? What usually happens is that theorists implicitly rely on some psychological criterion for consciousness, such as the focus of attention, the control of behavior, and most frequently the ability to make verbal reports about an internal state. One then notes that some neurophysiological property is instantiated when these criteria are present, and one's theory of consciousness is off the ground.

The very fact that such indirect criteria are relied upon, however, makes it clear that no reductive explanation of consciousness is being given. At best, a neurophysiological account might be able to explain why the relevant psychological property is instantiated. The question of why the psychological property in question should be accompanied by conscious experience is left unanswered. Because these theories gain their purchase by *assuming* a link between psychological properties and conscious experience, it is clear that they do nothing to explain that link. We can see this by examining some recent neuroscientific accounts of consciousness.

Much recent attention in neuroscience has focused on certain 40-hertz oscillations in the visual cortex and elsewhere. Francis Crick and Christof Koch (1990) have hypothesized that this sort of oscillation may be the fundamental neural feature responsible for conscious experience, and have advocated the development of a neurobiological theory along these lines.[10]

Why 40-hertz oscillations? Primarily because evidence suggests that these oscillations play an important role in the *binding* of various kinds of information into a unified whole. Two different kinds of information about a scene—the shape and location of an object, for instance—may be represented quite separately, but this theory suggests that the separate neural representations may have a common frequency and phase in their oscillations, allowing the information to be bound together by later processes and stored in working memory. In this way all sorts of disparate information might be integrated into the "contents of consciousness."

Such a theory might indeed provide neurobiological insight into binding and working memory, and perhaps eventually could be elaborated into an account of how information is brought to bear in an integrated way in the control of behavior. But the key question remains unanswered: Why should these oscillations be accompanied by conscious experience? The theory provides a partial answer: because these oscillations are responsible for binding. But the question of why binding itself should be accompanied by experience is not addressed. The theory gains its purchase by assuming a link between binding and consciousness, and therefore does nothing to explain it.

Crick and Koch seem sympathetic with the "big" problem of consciousness, calling it the "major puzzle confronting the neural view of the mind." They argue that pure cognitive-level approaches are doomed to be unsuccessful, and that neural-level theories are required. But they give us no reason to believe that their theory is better suited than cognitive theories when it comes to answering the really difficult questions. Indeed, they do not claim that their project handles the problem of experience. In a published interview, Koch is quite clear about the limitations of the approach:

> Well, let's first forget about the really difficult aspects, like subjective feelings, for they may not have a scientific solution. The subjective state of play, of pain, of pleasure, of seeing blue, of smelling a rose—there seems to be a huge jump between the materialistic level, of explaining molecules and neurons, and the subjective level. Let's focus on things that are easier to study—like visual awareness. You're now talking to me, but you're not looking at me, you're looking at the cappuccino, and so you are aware of it. You can say, "It's a cup and there's some liquid in it." If I give it to you, you'll move your arm and you'll take it—you'll respond in a meaningful manner. That's what I call awareness.[11]

Another neurophysiological theory of consciousness has been outlined by Gerald Edelman in *The Remembered Present* (1989) and other books and articles. The central element of his theory involves re-entrant neural circuits by which perceptual signals can be conceptually categorized before they contribute to memory. Perceptual information and internal state interact in a subtle way (as depicted in Figure 3.3) to give rise to "primary consciousness." His model of "higher-order consciousness" brings in a new memory element through "semantic bootstrapping," which yields concepts of the self, past, and, future. All this is linked to language production through Broca's and Wernicke's areas.

Much of Edelman's work is devoted to the explanation of perception, memory, and language, rather than of consciousness. Insofar as it is devoted to consciousness, the discussion is often vague, but it seems that what ultimately might be explained by this sort of model is perceptual awareness—that is, the effects of perceptual processing on later processes and on the control of behavior—and aspects of self-consciousness, especially the origin of the concept of the self.

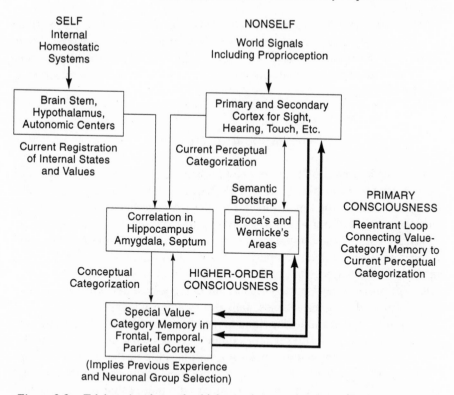

Figure 3.3. Edelman's scheme for higher-order consciousness. (Redrawn from Figure 12-4, p. 132, from *Bright Air, Brilliant Fire* by Gerald M. Edelman. Copyright © 1992 by BasicBooks, Inc. By permission of BasicBooks, a division of HarperCollins, Inc.)

Edelman gives no account of how all this processing should give rise to conscious experience. He simply takes it that there is a correlation. He is up-front about this, noting that phenomenal experience is the hardest problem for a theory of consciousness, and that no physical theory will take us all the way to qualia:

> This suggests an approach to the problem of qualia. As a basis for a theory of consciousness, it is sensible to *assume* that, just as in ourselves, qualia exist in other conscious human beings, whether they are considered as scientific observers or as subjects. . . . We can then take human beings to be the best canonical referent for the study of consciousness. This is justified by the fact that human subjective reports (including those about qualia), actions, and brain structures and function *can all be correlated.* After building a theory based on the assumption that qualia exist in human beings, we can then look anew at some of the properties of qualia based on these correlations. It is our ability to report and correlate while individually experiencing qualia that opens up the possibility of a scientific investigation of consciousness. (Edelman 1992, p. 115)

As before, because this theory is based on the *assumption* of correlation, it is clear that a reductive explanation of experience is not on offer. Most of the time Edelman claims only to be explaining the processes that underlie conscious experience; he does not claim to be explaining experience itself.[12]

5. The Appeal to New Physics

Sometimes it is held that the key to the explanation of consciousness may lie in a new sort of physical theory. Perhaps, in arguing that consciousness is not entailed by the physics of our world, we have been tacitly assuming that the physics of our world is something like physics as we understand it today, consisting in an arrangement of particles and fields in the spatiotemporal manifold, undergoing complex processes of causation and evolution. An opponent might agree that nothing in *this* sort of physics entails the existence of consciousness, but argue that there might be a new kind of physical theory from which consciousness falls out as a consequence.

It is not easy to evaluate this claim in the absence of any detailed proposal. One would at least like to see an example of how such a new physics might *possibly* go. Such an example need not be plausible in the light of current theories, but there would have to be a sense in which it would recognizably be physics. The crucial question is: How could a theory that is recognizably a physical theory entail the existence of consciousness? If such a theory consists in a description of the structure and dynamics of fields, waves, particles, and the like, then all the usual problems will apply. And it is unclear that *any* sort of physical theory could be different enough from this to avoid the problems.

The trouble is that the basic elements of physical theories seem always to come down to two things: the structure and dynamics of physical processes. Different theories invoke different sorts of structure. Newtonian physics invokes a Euclidean space-time; relativity theory invokes a non-Euclidean differential manifold; quantum theory invokes a Hilbert space for wave functions. And different theories invoke different kinds of dynamics within those structures: Newton's laws, the principles of relativity, the wave equations of quantum mechanics. But from structure and dynamics, we can only get more structure and dynamics. This allows the possibility of satisfying explanations of all sorts of high-level structural and functional properties, but conscious experience will remain untouched. No set of facts about physical structure and dynamics can add up to a fact about phenomenology.

Of course, there is a sense in which the physics of the universe *must* entail the existence of consciousness, if one *defines* physics as the fundamental science from whose facts and laws everything else follows. This construal of physics, however, trivializes the question involved. If one allows physics to include theories developed specifically to deal with the phenomenon of consciousness, unmotivated by more basic considerations, then we may get an "explanation" of consciousness, but it will certainly not be a reductive one. For our purposes, it is best to take physics to be the fundamental science developed to explain observations of the external world. If this kind of physics entailed the facts about consciousness, without invoking consciousness itself in a crucial role, then consciousness would truly be reductively explained. For the reasons I have given, however, there is good reason to believe that no such reductive explanation is possible.

Almost all existing proposals concerning the use of physics to explain consciousness focus on the most puzzling part of physics, namely quantum mechanics. This is understandable: for physics to explain consciousness would take something extraordinary, and quantum mechanics is by far the most extraordinary part of contemporary physics. But in the end it does not seem to be extraordinary enough.

For example, Penrose (1994) suggests that the key to understanding consciousness may lie in a theory that reconciles quantum theory with the theory of general relativity. He suggests that gravitational effects not yet understood may be responsible for the collapse of the quantum wave function, leading to a nonalgorithmic element in the laws of nature. Drawing on the ideas of Hameroff (1994), he suggests that human cognition may depend on quantum collapses in microtubules, which are protein structures found in the skeleton of a neuron. Indeed, Penrose and Hameroff suggest that quantum collapse in microtubules may be the physical basis of conscious experience.

These ideas are extremely speculative, but they could at least *conceivably* help to explain certain elements of human cognitive functioning. Penrose suggests that the nonalgorithmic element in collapse could explain certain aspects of our mathematical insight, which he believes goes beyond the capacity of any algorithmic system. Hameroff suggests that the collapse of a superposed wave function might help explain certain aspects of human decision making. But nothing here seems to help with the explanation of conscious experience. Why should quantum processes in microtubules give rise to consciousness? The question here is just as hard as the corresponding question about classical processes in a classical brain. When it comes to the problem of experience, nonalgorithmic and algorithmic processes are in the same boat.

Some have suggested that the *nonlocality* of quantum mechanics, as suggested by recent experiments bearing on the Einstein-Podolsky-Rosen paradox and Bell's theorem, might be the key to a theory of consciousness (see Lahav and Shanks 1992 for suggestions along these lines). But even if physics is nonlocal, it is hard to see how this should help in the explanation of consciousness. Even given a nonlocal physical process, it remains logically possible that the process could take place in the absence of consciousness. The explanatory gap is as wide as ever.

The most frequently noted connection between consciousness and quantum mechanics lies in the fact that on some interpretations of the latter, measurement by a conscious observer is required to bring about the collapse of the wave function. On this sort of interpretation, consciousness plays a central role in the dynamics of the physical theory. These interpretations are highly controversial, but in any case it is notable that they do nothing to provide an *explanation* of consciousness. Rather, they simply *assume* the existence of consciousness, and use it to help explain certain physical phenomena. Theories of consciousness that exploit this relationship are occasionally put forward (e.g., Hodgson 1988; Stapp 1993), but they are certainly not reductive theories.[13]

One cannot rule out the possibility that fundamental physical theories such as quantum mechanics will play a key role in a theory of consciousness. For example, perhaps consciousness will turn out to be associated with certain fundamental physical properties, or with certain configurations of those properties, or perhaps there will be a more subtle link. But all the same, there is little hope that this sort of theory will provide a wholly physical *explanation* of consciousness. When it comes to reductive explanation, physics-based theories are no better off than neurobiological and cognitive theories.

6. Evolutionary Explanation

Even those who take consciousness seriously are often drawn to the idea of an evolutionary explanation of consciousness. After all, consciousness is such a ubiquitous and central feature that it seems that it must have arisen during the evolutionary process for a *reason*. In particular, it is natural to suppose that it arose because there is some function that it serves that could not be achieved without it. If we could get a clear enough idea of the relevant function, then we would have some idea of why consciousness exists.

Unfortunately, this idea overestimates what an evolutionary explanation can provide us. The process of natural selection cannot distinguish between me and my zombie twin. Evolution selects properties according to their functional role, and my zombie twin performs all the functions that I perform just as well as I do; in particular he leaves around just as many copies of his genes. It follows that evolution alone cannot explain why conscious creatures rather than zombies evolved.

Some may be tempted to respond, "But a zombie *couldn't* do all the things that I can." But my zombie twin is by definition physically identical to me over its history, so it certainly produces indistinguishable behavior. Anyone wishing to question zombie capacity must therefore find something wrong with the arguments at the start of this chapter, rather than raising the objection here.

To see the point in a different way, note that the real problem with consciousness is to explain the principles in virtue of which consciousness arises from physical systems. Presumably these principles—whether they are conceptual truths, metaphysical necessities, or natural laws—are constant over space-time: if a physical replica of me had popped into existence a million years ago, it would have been just as conscious as I am. The connecting principles themselves are therefore independent of the evolutionary process. While evolution can be very useful in explaining why particular physical systems have evolved, it is irrelevant to the explanation of the bridging principles in virtue of which some of these systems are conscious.

7. Whither Reductive Explanation?

It is not uncommon for people to agree with critiques of specific reductive accounts, but to qualify this agreement: "Of course *that* doesn't explain consciousness, but if we just wait a while, an explanation will come along." I hope the discussion here has made it clear that the problems with this kind of explanation of consciousness are more fundamental than that. The problems with the models and theories presented here do not lie in the *details*; at least, we have not needed to consider the details in order to see what is wrong with them. The problem lies in the overall explanatory strategy. These models and theories are simply not the *sort* of thing that could explain consciousness.

It is inevitable that increasingly sophisticated reductive "explanations" of consciousness will be put forward, but these will only produce increasingly sophisticated explanations of cognitive functions. Even such "revolutionary" developments as the invocation of connectionist networks, nonlinear dynamics, artificial life, and quantum mechanics will provide only more powerful functional explanations. This may make for some very interesting cognitive science, but the mystery of consciousness will not be removed.

Any account given in purely physical terms will suffer from the same problem. It will ultimately be given in terms of the structural and dynamical properties of physical processes, and no matter how sophisticated such an account is, it will yield only more structure and dynamics. While this is enough to handle most natural phenomena, the problem of consciousness goes beyond any problem about the explanation of structure and function, so a new sort of explanation is needed.

It might be supposed that there could eventually be a reductive explanatory technique that explained something other than structure and function, but it is very hard to see how this could be possible, given that the laws of physics are ultimately cast in terms of structure and dynamics. The existence of consciousness will always be a further fact relative to structural and dynamic facts, and so will always be unexplained by a physical account.

For an explanation of consciousness, then, we must look elsewhere. We certainly need not give up on explanation; we need only give up on *reductive* explanation. The possibility of explaining consciousness nonreductively remains open. This would be a very different sort of explanation, requiring some radical changes in the way we think about the structure of the world. But if we make these changes, the beginnings of a theory of consciousness may become visible in the distance.

4

Naturalistic Dualism

1. An Argument Against Materialism

In the last chapter, I was concerned with the explanatory question, "Can consciousness be explained by physical theories?" rather than the ontological question, "Is consciousness itself physical?" But the two questions are closely related, and in this chapter I will draw out the ontological consequences of the arguments in the last chapter. In particular, the failure of logical supervenience directly implies that materialism is false: there are features of the world over and above the physical features. The basic argument for this goes as follows.

1. In our world, there are conscious experiences.
2. There is a logically possible world physically identical to ours, in which the positive facts about consciousness in our world do not hold.
3. Therefore, facts about consciousness are further facts about our world, over and above the physical facts.
4. So materialism is false.

If a physically identical zombie world is logically possible, it follows that the presence of consciousness is an *extra* fact about our world, not guaranteed by the physical facts alone. The character of our world is not exhausted by the character supplied by the physical facts; there is extra character due to the presence of consciousness. To use a phrase due to Lewis (1990), consciousness carries phenomenal *information*. The physical facts incompletely constrain the way the world is; the facts about consciousness constrain it further.

A similar conclusion can be drawn from the logical possibility of a world with *inverted* conscious experiences. Such a world is physically identical to ours, but some of the facts about conscious experience in our world do not hold in that world. It follows that the facts about conscious experience in our world are further facts over and above the physical facts, and that materialism is false.

Either way, if consciousness is not logically supervenient on the physical, then materialism is false. The failure of logical supervenience implies that some positive fact about our world does not hold in a physically identical world, so that it is a further fact over and above the physical facts. As in Chapter 2, I take materialism to be the doctrine that the physical facts about the world exhaust all the facts, in that every positive fact is entailed by the physical facts. If zombie worlds or inverted worlds are possible, the physical facts do not entail all the positive facts about our world, and materialism is false.

We can use Kripke's image here. When God created the world, after ensuring that the physical facts held, *he had more work to do.* He had to ensure that the facts about consciousness held. The possibility of zombie worlds or inverted worlds shows that he had a choice. The world might have lacked experience, or it might have contained different experiences, even if all the physical facts had been the same. To ensure that the facts about consciousness are as they are, further features had to be included in the world.

What sort of dualism?

This failure of materialism leads to a kind of *dualism*: there are both physical and nonphysical features of the world. The falsity of logical supervenience implies that experience is fundamentally different in kind from any physical feature. But there are many varieties of dualism, and it is important to see just where the argument leads us.

The arguments in the last chapter establish that consciousness does not supervene *logically* on the physical, but this is not to say that it does not supervene at all. There appears to be a systematic dependence of conscious experience on physical structure in the cases with which we are familiar, and nothing in the arguments of the last chapter suggests otherwise. It remains as plausible as ever, for example, that if my physical structure were to be replicated by some creature in the actual world, my conscious experience would be replicated, too. So it remains plausible that consciousness supervenes *naturally* on the physical. It is this view—natural supervenience without logical supervenience—that I will develop.

The arguments do not lead us to a dualism such as that of Descartes, with a separate realm of mental substance that exerts its own influence on physical processes. The best evidence of contemporary science tells us that the physical world is more or less causally closed: for every physical event, there is a physical sufficient cause. If so, there is no room for a mental "ghost in the machine" to do any extra causal work. A small loophole may be opened by the existence of quantum indeterminacy, but I argue later that this probably cannot be exploited to yield a causal role for a nonphysical mind. In any case, for all the arguments in the previous chapter, it remains plausible that *physical* events can be explained in physical terms, so a move to a Cartesian dualism would be a stronger reaction than is warranted.

The dualism implied here is instead a kind of *property* dualism: conscious experience involves properties of an individual that are not entailed by the physical properties of that individual, although they may depend lawfully on those properties. Consciousness is a *feature* of the world over and above the physical features of the world. This is not to say it is a separate "substance"; the issue of what it would take to constitute a dualism of substances seems quite unclear to me. All we know is that there are properties of individuals in this world—the phenomenal properties—that are ontologically independent of physical properties.

There is a weaker sort of property dualism with which this view should not be confused. It is sometimes said that property dualism applies to any domain in which the properties are not themselves properties invoked by physics, or directly reducible to such properties. In this sense, even biological fitness is not a physical property. But this sort of "dualism" is a very weak variety. There is nothing *fundamentally* ontologically new about properties such as fitness, as they are still logically supervenient on microphysical properties. Property dualism of this variety is entirely compatible with materialism. By contrast, the property dualism that I advocate involves fundamentally new features of the world. Because these properties are not even logically supervenient on microphysical properties, they are nonphysical in a much stronger sense. When I speak of property dualism and nonphysical properties, it is this stronger view and the stronger sense of nonphysicality that I have in mind.

It remains plausible, however, that consciousness *arises* from a physical basis, even though it is not *entailed* by that basis. The position we are left with is that consciousness arises from a physical substrate in virtue of certain contingent laws of nature, which are not themselves implied by physical laws. This position is implicitly held by many people who think of themselves as materialists. It is common to hear, "Of course I'm a materialist; the mind certainly arises from the brain." The very presence of the word "arises" should be a tip-off here. One tends not to say "learning arises from the brain," for instance—and if one did, it would be in a temporal sense of "arises." Rather, one would more naturally say that learning *is* a process in the brain. The very fact that the mind needs to *arise* from the brain indicates that there is something further going on, over and above the physical facts.[1]

Some people will think that the view should count as a version of materialism rather than dualism, because it posits such a strong lawful dependence of the phenomenal facts on the physical facts, and because the physical domain remains autonomous. Of course there is little point arguing over a name, but it seems to me that the existence of further contingent facts over and above the physical facts is a significant enough modification to the received materialist world view to deserve a different label. Certainly, if all that is required for materialism is that all facts be lawfully connected to the physical facts, then materialism becomes a weak doctrine indeed.

Although it is a variety of dualism, there is nothing antiscientific or supernatural about this view. The best way to think about it is as follows. Physics postulates a number of *fundamental* features of the world: space-time, mass-energy, charge, spin, and so on. It also posits a number of fundamental laws in virtue of which these fundamental features are related. Fundamental features cannot be explained in terms of more basic features, and fundamental laws cannot be explained in terms of more basic laws; they must simply be taken as primitive. Once the fundamental laws and the distribution of the fundamental features are set in place, however, almost everything about the world follows. That is why a fundamental theory in physics is sometimes known as a "theory of everything." But the fact that consciousness does not supervene on the physical features shows us that this physical theory is not *quite* a theory of everything. To bring consciousness within the scope of a fundamental theory, we need to introduce *new* fundamental properties and laws.

In his book *Dreams of a Final Theory* (1992), physicist Steven Weinberg notes that what makes a fundamental theory in physics special is that it leads to an explanatory chain all the way up, ultimately explaining everything. But he is forced to concede that such a theory may not explain consciousness. At best, he says, we can explain the "objective correlates" of consciousness. "That may not be an explanation of consciousness, but it will be pretty close" (p. 45). But it is not close enough, of course. It does not explain everything that is happening in the world. To be consistent, we must acknowledge that a truly final theory needs an additional component.

There are two ways this might go. Perhaps we might take experience itself as a fundamental feature of the world, alongside space-time, spin, charge, and the like. That is, certain phenomenal properties will have to be taken as *basic* properties. Alternatively, perhaps there is some *other* class of novel fundamental properties from which phenomenal properties are derived. Previous arguments have shown that these cannot be physical properties, but perhaps they are nonphysical properties of a new variety, on which phenomenal properties are logically supervenient. Such properties would be related to experience in the same way that basic physical properties are related to nonbasic properties such as temperature. We could call these properties *protophenomenal* properties, as they are not themselves phenomenal but together they can yield the phenomenal. Of course it is very hard to imagine what a protophenomenal property could be like, but we cannot rule out the possibility that they exist. Most of the time, however, I will speak as if the fundamental properties are themselves phenomenal.

Where we have new fundamental properties, we also have new fundamental laws. Here the fundamental laws will be *psychophysical* laws, specifying how phenomenal (or protophenomenal) properties depend on physical properties. These laws will not interfere with physical laws; physical laws already form a closed system. Instead, they will be *supervenience laws,* telling us how experience arises from physical processes. We have seen that the dependence of experience on the physical cannot be derived from physical laws, so any final theory must include laws of this variety.

Of course, at this stage we have very little idea what the relevant fundamental theory will look like, or what the fundamental psychophysical laws will be. But we have reason to believe that such a theory exists. There is good reason to believe that there is a lawful relationship between physical processes and conscious experience, and any lawful relationship must be supported by fundamental laws. The case of physics tells us that fundamental laws are typically simple and elegant; we should expect the same of the fundamental laws in a theory of consciousness. Once we have a fundamental theory of consciousness to accompany a fundamental theory in physics, we may truly have a theory of everything. Given the basic physical and psychophysical laws, and given the distribution of the fundamental properties, we can expect that all the facts about the world will follow. Developing such a theory will not be straightforward, but it ought to be possible in principle.

In a way, what is going on here with consciousness is analogous to what happened with electromagnetism in the nineteenth century. There had been an attempt to explain electromagnetic phenomena in terms of physical laws that were already understood, involving mechanical principles and the like, but this was unsuccessful. It turned out that to explain electromagnetic phenomena, features such as electromagnetic charge and electromagnetic forces had to be taken as fundamental, and Maxwell introduced new fundamental electromagnetic laws. Only this way could the phenomena be explained. In the same way, to explain consciousness, the features and laws of physical theory are not enough. For a theory of consciousness, new fundamental features and laws are needed.

This view is entirely compatible with a contemporary scientific worldview, and is entirely naturalistic. On this view, the world still consists in a network of fundamental properties related by basic laws, and everything is to be ultimately explained in these terms. All that has happened is that the inventory of properties and laws has been expanded, as happened with Maxwell. Further, nothing about this view contradicts anything in physical theory; rather, it supplements that theory. A physical theory gives a theory of physical processes, and a psychophysical theory tells us how those processes give rise to experience.

To capture the spirit of the view I advocate, I call it *naturalistic dualism*. It is naturalistic because it posits that everything is a consequence of a network of basic properties and laws, and because it is compatible with all the results of contemporary science. And as with naturalistic theories in other domains, this view allows that we can *explain* consciousness in terms of basic natural laws. There need be nothing especially transcendental about consciousness; it is just another natural phenomenon. All that has happened is that our picture of nature has expanded. Sometimes "naturalism" is taken to be synonymous with "materialism," but it seems to me that a commitment to a naturalistic understanding of the world can survive the failure of materialism. (If a reader doubts this, I point to the rest of this work as evidence.) Some might find a certain irony in the name of the view, but what is most important is that it conveys the central message: to embrace dualism is not necessarily to embrace mystery.

In some ways, those who hold this sort of dualism may be temperamentally closer to materialists than to dualists of other varieties. This is partly because of its avoidance of any transcendental element and its commitment to natural explanation, and partly because of its commitment to the physical causation of behavior. Conversely, by avoiding any commitment to a ghost in the machine, this view avoids the worst implausibilities of the traditional dualist views. One often hears that the successes of cognitive science and neuroscience make dualism implausible, but not all varieties of dualism are affected equally. These successes are all grounded in physical explanations of behavior and of other physical phenomena, and so do not distinguish between the materialist and the naturalistic dualist view.

Two final notes. Some will wonder why, if experience is fundamental, it does not qualify as a *physical* property. After all, is not physics just the science of what is truly fundamental? In reply: Certainly if we *define* physics that way, experience will indeed qualify as a physical property, and the supervenience laws will count as laws of physics. But on a more natural reading of "physics" and "physical," experience does not qualify. Experience is not a fundamental property that physicists need to posit in their theory of the external world; physics forms a closed, consistent theory even without experience. Given the possibility of a zombie world, there is a clear sense in which experience is superfluous to physics as it is usually understood. It is therefore more natural to consider experience as a fundamental property that is not a physical property, and to consider the psychophysical laws as fundamental laws of nature that are not laws of physics. But nothing much turns on the terminological issue, as long as the shape of the view is clear.

I should also note that although I call the view a variety of dualism, it is possible that it could turn out to be a kind of monism. Perhaps the physical and the phenomenal will turn out to be two different aspects of a single encompassing kind, in something like the way that matter and energy turn out to be two aspects of a single kind. Nothing that I have said rules this out, and in fact I have some sympathy with the idea. But it remains the case that if a variety of monism is true, it cannot be a *materialist* monism. It must be something broader.

Objections

There are a number of objections that might be raised to the argument against materialism at the beginning of this chapter. Some of these are objections to premise (2), the denial of logical supervenience; I have dealt with objections of that sort in the previous chapter. Here, I will deal with objections to the step from the failure of logical supervenience to the falsity of materialism. The most serious objections of this sort are those that invoke *a posteriori* necessity. I will deal with these in the next section. Here I will deal with some more minor objections.

Sometimes it is argued that consciousness might be an *emergent* property, in a sense that is still compatible with materialism. In recent work on complex systems and artificial life, it is often held that emergent properties are unpredictable from low-level properties, but that they are physical all the same. Examples are the emergence of self-organization in biological systems, or the emergence of flocking patterns from simple rules in simulated birds (Langton 1990; Reynolds 1987). But emergent properties of this sort are not analogous to consciousness. What is interesting about these cases is that the relevant properties are not obvious consequences of low-level laws; but they are still logically supervenient on low-level *facts*. If *all* the physical facts about such a system over time are given, then the fact that self-organization is occurring will be straightforwardly derivable. This is just what we would expect, as properties such as self-organization and flocking are straightforwardly functional and structural.

If consciousness is an emergent property, it is emergent in a much stronger sense. There is a stronger notion of emergence, used by the British emergentists (e.g., Broad [1925]), according to which emergent properties are not even predictable from the entire ensemble of low-level physical facts. It is reasonable to say (as the British emergentists did) that conscious experience is emergent in this sense. But this sort of emergence is best counted as a variety of property dualism. Unlike the more "innocent" examples of emergence given above, the strong variety requires new fundamental laws in order that the emergent properties emerge.

Another objection is that consciousness and the physical might be two aspects of the same thing, in the way that the morning star and the evening star are two aspects of Venus. If so, consciousness might in a sense be physical. But again, we have to ask: Is the phenomenal aspect entailed by the physical aspect? If it is, we have a variety of materialism, but we are back to the arguments in Chapter 3. If it is not, then the phenomenal aspect provides further contingency in the world over and above the physical aspect, and the duality of the aspects gives us a kind of property dualism. Perhaps it may turn out that the duality of the physical and the phenomenal can be subsumed under a grander monism, but this will not be a monism of the physical alone.

A third objection is suggested by the work of Searle (1992). Like me, Searle holds that consciousness is merely naturally supervenient on the physical. He allows that a zombie replica is logically possible, holding that consciousness is merely *caused* by states of the brain. But he denies that this is a variety of dualism, even property dualism. This might seem to be a mere terminological issue, but Searle insists that the ontological status of consciousness is the same as that of physical features such as liquidity, so the issue is not *merely* terminological. Searle's argument that the view is not dualistic is that a similar story holds elsewhere: for example, H_2O causes liquidity, but no one is a dualist about liquidity.

It seems clear that this is a false analogy, however. Given all the microphysical facts about a particular batch of H_2O, it is logically impossible that those facts could hold without liquidity being instantiated. The notion of a nonliquid replica of a batch of liquid H_2O is simply incoherent. It follows that the relation between the microphysical facts and liquidity is much tighter than a simple causal relation. The microphysical features do not *cause* liquidity; they *constitute* it. This is entirely different from what is going on in the case of consciousness, so the analogy fails. Consciousness is ontologically novel in a much more significant way than liquidity.[2]

Finally, some will find the argument for dualism that I have given reminiscent of the argument given by Descartes. Descartes argued that he could imagine his mind existing separately from his body, so his mind could not be identical to his body. This sort of argument is generally regarded to be flawed: just because one can imagine that *A* and *B* are not identical, it does not follow that *A* and *B* are not identical (think of the morning star and the evening star, for example). Might not my argument make a similar mistake? The zombie world only shows that it is *conceivable* that one might have a physical state without consciousness; it does not show that a physical state and consciousness are not identical.

This is to misunderstand the argument, however. It is crucial that the argument as I have put it does not turn on questions of *identity* but of *supervenience.* The form of the argument is not, "One can imagine physical state *P* without consciousness, therefore consciousness is not physical state *P.*" The form of the argument is rather, "One can imagine *all* the physical facts holding without the facts about consciousness holding, so the physical facts do not exhaust all the facts." This is an entirely different sort of argument. In general, modal arguments for dualism that are cast in terms of identity are less conclusive than modal arguments cast in terms of supervenience; this is one reason why I have put things in terms of supervenience throughout, and avoided talk of identity almost entirely. It seems to me that the issues about supervenience are the most fundamental here.

One might nevertheless try to reply to this argument with a strategy analogous to the reply to Descartes. For example, one might note that my strategy still relies on a sort of inference from conceivability to possibility that might be questioned. I consider strategies along these lines in the next section.

2. Objections From *A Posteriori* Necessity*

A popular response to this sort of argument is to object that it only establishes that a zombie world is *logically* possible, which is quite different from being *metaphysically* possible. Whereas conceptual coherence suffices for logical possibility, metaphysical possibility is more constrained. The point is also often made by suggesting that there is a difference between *conceivability* and true *possibility.* Although it may be the case that a zombie world is conceivable, something more is required in order to show that it is possible in the metaphysical sense relevant to the falsity of materialism.

This objection is most often accompanied by an appeal to Kripke's *Naming and Necessity* (1980), which demonstrates the existence of necessary truths such as "Water is H_2O" whose necessity is only knowable *a posteriori.* In the terms of these objectors, it is logically possible that water is not H_2O, but it is not metaphysically possible. It is not unnatural to suppose that zombies might be logically possible but metaphysically impossible in a similar way. If so, this would arguably be enough to save materialism.

This is by far the most common strategy of materialists who are persuaded that there is no entailment between physical and phenomenal concepts. On this view, there can be a conceptual gap without a metaphysical gap. The view offers the enticing prospect of taking consciousness seriously while nevertheless holding on to materialism. Unfortunately, upon close examination the view can be seen quite straightforwardly to fail. The notion of *a posteriori* necessity cannot carry the burden that this argument requires, and in fact is something of a red herring in this context.[3]

We can best see this by using the two-dimensional framework for dealing with *a posteriori* necessity developed in Chapter 2, section 4. Recall that in this framework there are two intensions (functions from possible worlds to referents) associated with any concept: a primary intension (determined *a priori*) that fixes reference in the actual world, and a secondary intension (determined *a posteriori*) that picks out reference in counterfactual worlds. The primary intension associated with "water" is something like "watery stuff." The secondary intension is "H_2O," which is derived from the primary intension by applying Kaplan's *dthat* operator: "*dthat*(watery stuff)" picks out H_2O in all possible worlds, as watery stuff is H_2O in the actual world.

"Logical possibility" comes down to the possible truth of a statement when evaluated according to the primary intensions involved (what I called 1-possibility in Chapter 2). The primary intensions of "water" and "H_2O" differ, so it is logically possible in this sense that water is not H_2O. "Metaphysical possibility" comes down to the possible truth of a statement when evaluated according to the secondary intensions involved (that is, 2-possibility). The secondary intensions of "water" and "H_2O" are the same, so it is metaphysically necessary that water is H_2O.

The objection therefore comes down to the point that in using arguments from conceivability and the like, we have demonstrated the possibility of a zombie world using the *primary* intensions of the notions involved, but not using the more appropriate *secondary* intensions. While the primary intension of phenomenal notions may not correspond to that of any physical notion, the secondary intensions may be the same. If so, then phenomenal and physical/functional concepts may pick out the same properties *a posteriori* despite the *a priori* distinction. Such an objection might be made by an advocate of "psychofunctionalism" (see Block 1980), which equates phenomenal properties with functional properties *a posteriori,* or by an advocate of a view that equates phenomenal properties with certain neurophysiological properties *a posteriori.*

The easiest way to see that none of this affects the argument for dualism is to note that the argument I have given goes through if we concentrate on the primary intension throughout and ignore the secondary intension. We saw in Chapter 2 that it is the primary intension that is most relevant to explanation, but it also serves us well in the argument for dualism. For note that whether or not the primary and secondary intensions coincide, the primary intension determines a perfectly good property of objects in possible worlds. The property of being watery stuff is a perfectly reasonable property, even though it is not the same as the property of being H_2O. If we can show that there are possible worlds that are physically identical to ours but in which the property introduced by the primary intension is lacking, then dualism will follow.

This is just what has been done with consciousness. We have seen that there are worlds physically just like ours that lack consciousness, according to the primary intension thereof. This difference in worlds is sufficient to show that there are properties of our world over and above the physical properties. By analogy, if we could show that there were worlds physically identical to ours in which there was no watery stuff, we would have established dualism about water just as well as if we had established that there were worlds physically identical to ours in which there was no H_2O. And importantly, the difference with respect to the primary intension can be established independently of *a posteriori* factors, so that considerations about *a posteriori* necessity are irrelevant.

(Two technical notes here: Strictly speaking, a primary intension determines a *center-relative* property of an object in a possible world (or a relation between objects and centers), as the primary intension applies to *centered* possible worlds. But this relativity cannot be exploited to help our objector. Once the location of a center is specified, a primary intension determines a perfectly good nonindexical property; and all the arguments of Chapter 3 go through even when the location of the center is included in the supervenience base. For example, even if Mary's facts about the world include facts about where she is located, this will not enable her to know what it is like to see red.

One might also be worried by the fact that the concept of consciousness is arguably not present at the center of the zombie world, whereas the application of a primary intension might require the presence of the relevant concept at the center of the world. (One might even start worrying about the application of the *zombie's* concept!) I think the situation is more subtle than this—primary intensions need not require the presence of the original concept—but in any case, we can bypass this worry altogether simply by considering a *partial* zombie world: one in which I am at the center, conscious, with all the relevant concepts, but in which some other people are zombies.)

The irrelevance of *a posteriori* necessity can be further supported by the observation that with consciousness, the primary and secondary intensions coincide. What it takes for a state to be a conscious experience in the actual world is for it to have a phenomenal feel, and what it takes for something to be a conscious experience in a counterfactual world is for it to have a phenomenal feel. The difference between the primary and secondary intensions for the concept of water reflects the fact that there could be something that looks and feels like water in some counterfactual world that in fact is not water, but merely watery stuff. But if something feels like a conscious experience, even in some counterfactual world, it *is* a conscious experience. All it means to be a conscious experience, in any possible world, is to have a certain feel. (Kripke makes a similar point, although he puts the point in terms of essential properties rather than in terms of meaning.)

Even if someone insists that the primary and the secondary intensions differ, however, the argument still goes through. We simply focus on the primary intension used to fix reference, as above. For instance, if "consciousness" comes to "*dthat* (has a phenomenal feel)", then we simply focus on the intension "has a phenomenal feel." The arguments in Chapter 3 establish that there is a possible world in which my replica lacks a phenomenal feel, so the property of having a phenomenal feel is a fact over and above the physical facts, and the argument for dualism is successful.[4]

The most general way to make the point is to note that nothing about Kripke's *a posteriori* necessity renders any logically possible worlds impossible. It simply tells us that some of them are misdescribed, because we are applying terms according to their primary intensions rather than the more appropriate secondary intensions. One might have thought it possible *a priori* that water is XYZ, rather than H_2O. In conceiving this, one imagines something like a world in which XYZ is the liquid found in oceans and lakes. However, Kripke's analysis shows us that due to the way the actual world turns out, we are misdescribing this world as one in which XYZ is water, as we are describing it with the primary intension instead of the more appropriate secondary intension. Strictly speaking, it is a world in which XYZ is watery stuff. These considerations cannot show the impossibility of this apparently possible world; they simply show us the correct way to describe it.

As we saw in Chapter 2, Kripkean considerations show us that the secondary intension $F_a: W \rightarrow R$ sometimes differs from the primary intension $f: W^* \rightarrow R$. This puts some *a posteriori* constraints on the application conditions of concepts, but the relevant space of worlds stays constant throughout; the only difference between the arguments of the two functions involves the location of a center. So although there may be two kinds of possibility of *statements*, there is only one relevant kind of possibility of *worlds*.

It follows that if there is a conceivable world that is physically identical to ours but which lacks certain positive features of our world, then no considerations about the designation of terms such as "consciousness" can do anything to rule out the metaphysical possibility of the world. We can simply forget the semantics of these terms, and note that the relevant possible world clearly lacks *something,* whether or not we call it "consciousness." The Kripkean considerations might tell us at best how this world and the relevant features should be appropriately described, but they have no effect on its possibility; and the mere possibility of such a world, no matter how it is described, is all the argument for dualism needs to succeed.

An alternative strategy

There is a quite different way in which one might appeal to *a posteriori* necessity in order to avoid dualism. It might be argued that to claim that the zombie world is *physically identical* to ours is to misdescribe it. Just as the XYZ world seems to contain water but does not, the zombie world *seems* physically identical while being physically different. This may sound strange, but there is a way to cash it out. An opponent might argue that there are properties essential to the physical constitution of the world that are not accessible to physical investigation. In conceiving of a "physically identical" world, we are really only conceiving of a world that is identical from the standpoint of physical investigation, while differing in the inaccessible essential properties, which are also the properties that guarantee consciousness.

For example, it might be that for something to qualify as an electron in a counterfactual world, it is not sufficient that it be causally related to other physical entities in the way that an electron is. Some hidden essence of electronhood might also be required. On this view, the concept of an electron is something like "*dthat*(the entity that plays the electron role)." Reference to electrons is fixed by an extrinsic characterization, but is then rigidified so that entities with the same intrinsic nature are picked out in counterfactual worlds, regardless of whether they play the appropriate role, and so that entities that play the role in those worlds do not qualify as electrons unless they have the appropriate intrinsic nature. The same might go for properties such as mass, which might be understood as "*dthat*(the property that plays the mass role)." The essential nature of electrons or of mass would then be hidden to physical theory, which characterizes electrons and mass only extrinsically. If so, it might be that the relevant essential properties are themselves phenomenal or protophenomenal properties, so that their instantiation could guarantee the existence of consciousness in our world.

If this were the case, the zombie world that we are conceiving would lack these hidden essential properties and would therefore fail to be physically identical to our world. The zombie world would give the same results as our world when evaluated according to the primary intensions of physical predicates, which apply on the basis of extrinsic relations, but not when evaluated according to the secondary intensions, which require the hidden essence. Given this, conscious experience might supervene "metaphysically" on physical properties after all. (An argument very much like this is given by Maxwell [1978], and is also suggested by the approach in Lockwood [1989]. As Maxwell puts it, the basic idea is that even though phenomenal concepts cannot be given topic-neutral analyses that pick out underlying physical properties, physical concepts can be given topic-neutral analyses that might pick out underlying phenomenal properties.[5])

This is in many ways a more interesting objection than the previous one. It certainly relies on a speculative metaphysics, but this does not prevent it from being a coherent position. A more direct reply is that it relies on an incorrect view of the semantics of physical terms. Arguably, physical predicates apply even *a posteriori* on the basis of extrinsic relations between physical entities, irrespective of any hidden properties. This is a purely conceptual question: if electrons in our world have hidden protophenomenal properties, would we call an otherwise identical counterfactual entity that lacks those properties an electron? I think we would. Not only is reference to electrons fixed by the role that electrons play in a theory; the very concept of an electron is defined by that role, which determines the application of the concept across all worlds. The notion of an electron that has all the extrinsic properties of actual protons does not appear to be coherent, and neither does the notion that there is a world in which mass plays the role that charge actually plays. The semantic account given above predicts that these notions should be coherent, and so gives a false account of the concepts.

Semantic intuitions may differ, but as usual there is a reply that runs deeper than the semantic intuitions. Even if we allow that certain hidden properties could be constitutive of physical properties, the difference between this view and the property dualism that I have advocated is small. It remains the case that the world has phenomenal properties that are not fixed by the properties that physics reveals. After ensuring that a world is identical to ours from the standpoint of our physical theories, God has to expend further effort to make that world identical to ours across the board. The dualism of "physical" and "nonphysical" properties is replaced on this view by a dualism of "accessible" and "hidden" physical properties, but the essential point remains.

The view that physical entities have an intrinsic protophenomenal nature is one to which I will return, but the metaphysics of the view remains much the same regardless of the approach we take to the semantics of physical predicates. As before, secondary intensions and *a posteriori* necessity make only a semantic and not a metaphysical difference. However the view is spelled out, it admits phenomenal or protophenomenal properties as fundamental, and so remains closer to a version of dualism (or perhaps an idealism or a neutral monism, as I discuss later) than to a version of materialism.

Strong metaphysical necessity

The two-dimensional analysis just discussed establishes that an invocation of Kripkean *a posteriori* necessity has no force against the argument from supervenience. This sort of necessity does not put *a posteriori* constraints on the space of possible worlds, but merely constrains the way in which certain terms are used to describe them; so if there is a logically possible world that is identical to ours in all physical respects but not in all positive respects, then these considerations cannot count against the world's metaphysical possibility.

Some may claim, however, that the relevant worlds might be metaphysically impossible *nevertheless*. It could be held that there is a modality of metaphysical possibility that is distinct from and more constrained than logical possibility, and that arises for reasons independent of the Kripkean considerations. On this view, there are fewer metaphysically possible worlds than there are logically possible worlds, and the *a posteriori* necessity of certain statements can stem from factors quite independent of the semantics of the terms involved. We can call this hypothesized modality *strong metaphysical necessity,* as opposed to the *weak metaphysical necessity* introduced by the Kripkean framework.

On this view, there are worlds that are entirely conceivable, even according to the strongest strictures on conceivability, but which are not possible at all. This is a gap between conceivability and possibility much stronger than any gap found elsewhere. There is a sense in which the truth of *statements* such as "Water is XYZ" is conceivable but not possible, but these examples never rule out the possibility of any conceivable *world.* They are merely instances in which such a world is misdescribed. Strong metaphysical necessity goes beyond this. On this position, "zombie world" may correctly describe the world that we are conceiving, even according to a secondary intension. It is just that the world is not metaphysically possible.[6]

The short answer to this objection is that there is no reason to believe that such a modality exists. Such "metaphysical necessities" will put constraints on the space of possible worlds that are brute and inexplicable. It may be reasonable to countenance brute, inexplicable facts about *our* world, but the existence of such facts about the space of possible worlds would be quite bizarre. The realm of the possible (as opposed to the realm of the natural) has no room for this sort of arbitrary constraint.

The position cannot be supported by analogy, as no analogies are available.[7] We have already seen that analogies with the necessity of "Water is H_2O," "Hesperus is Phosphorus," and so on fail, as these examples require only a single space of worlds. Indeed, if some worlds are logically possible but metaphysically impossible, it seems that we could never know it. By assumption the information is not available *a priori,* and *a posteriori* information only tells us about *our* world. This can serve to locate our world in the space of possible worlds, but it is hard to see how it could give information about the extent of that space. Any claims about the added constraints of metaphysical possibility would seem to be a matter of arbitrary stipulation; one might as well stipulate that it is metaphysically impossible that a stone could move upward when one lets go of it.

Further, the position leads to an *ad hoc* proliferation of modalities. If it were accepted, we would have to countenance *four* kind of possibility and necessity of statements, even leaving the natural modality aside: possibility and necessity according to primary or secondary intensions, over the space of logically possible or metaphysically possible worlds. And considering the possibility of worlds rather than statements, we would now have *three* objective classes of possible worlds: logically possible worlds, metaphysically possible worlds, and naturally possible worlds. We have good reason to believe in the first and the last of these classes, but we have very little reason to believe in a third, distinct class as a metaphysical given.

Someone who holds that a zombie world is logically possible but metaphysically impossible has to answer the key question: *Why couldn't God have created a zombie world?* Presumably it is in God's powers, when creating the world, to do anything that is logically possible. Yet the advocate of metaphysical necessity must say either the possibility is coherent, but God could not have created it, or God could have created it, but it is nevertheless metaphysically impossible. The first is quite unjustified, and the second is entirely arbitrary. If the second holds, in any case, an argument against materialism still goes through; after fixing the physical facts about the world, God still had more work to do.

Even if this view were accepted, it would look very much like the property dualism I advocate, in many crucial respects. On this view, it would still be the case that the existence of consciousness cannot be derived from physical knowledge, so that consciousness cannot be reductively explained. And it would remain the case that we would need certain primitive connecting principles to explain the supervenience of the phenomenal on the physical. The only difference between the views is that the relevant psychophysical principles are deemed to be brute "laws of necessity" rather than laws of nature. For all *explanatory* purposes in constructing a theory, we are left in the same position in which property dualism leaves us; the main difference is in an ontological stipulation.

The only real motivation for this view would seem to be to save materialism at all costs, perhaps because of perceived problems with dualism. But this sort of materialism seems far more mysterious than the dualist alternative. The invocation of brute "metaphysically necessary" principles constraining the space of possible worlds introduces an element much more problematic, and indeed far less naturalistic, than the mere invocation of further natural laws postulated by property dualism. In the end, the invocation of a new degree of necessity is a sort of solution by *ad hoc* stipulation that raises as many problems as it answers. The view saves materialism only at the cost of making it entirely mysterious how consciousness *could* be physical.[8]

Cognitive limitations

There is a final position that might be taken by a materialist who finds the zombie world conceivable but still wants to save materialism. In the position discussed above, the materialist accepts that the zombie notion is entirely coherent, even to a maximally rational being, but nevertheless denies its metaphysical possibility, thus leading to a "two-layered" picture of logically and metaphysically possible worlds. But a materialist might also argue that the apparent conceivability arises from some sort of impaired rationality, so that if we were only more intelligent we would see that the description of the world is not coherent after all. On this view, the world is not really even *logically* possible; it is just that the limitations of human cognitive faculties mislead us into believeing that it is. (This may be one interpretation of the position of McGinn [1989].)

One might try to support this position by analogy with the necessity of certain complex mathematical truths that lie beyond our powers of mathematical insight. If our mathematical powers are computable, such truths must exist (by Gödel's theorem), and even if not, they may well exist all the same. (Perhaps Goldbach's conjecture is an example, or perhaps the continuum hypothesis or its negation.) These truths are necessary even though they are not knowable *a priori* by us, nor are they grounded in a combination of *a priori* knowable and empirical factors in the manner of Kripkean necessities. Perhaps the implication from physical facts to phenomenal facts is a necessity of this form, somehow beyond our powers of modal comprehension?[9]

The analogy is imperfect, however. In the mathematical case, our modal reasoning leaves the matter *open*; our conceivability intuitions do not tell us anything one way or the other. There may be some weak sense in which it is "conceivable" that the statements are false—for example, they are false for all we know—but this is not a sense that delivers a conceivable world where they fail. In the zombie case, by contrast, the matter is not left open: there seems to be a clearly conceivable world in which the implication is false. To save materialism, the possibility of this world has to be ruled out despite the best evidence of our modal powers; but nothing in the mathematical case comes close to providing an example whereby an apparently possible world is ruled out in this way. Once again, any gap between conceivability and possibility that the materialist might invoke here must be *sui generis,* unsupported by relevant analogies elsewhere.[10]

Of course, a materialist might bite the bullet and make a case for a *sui generis* cognitive impairment. To do this, she would have to hold that the arguments in Chapter 3 all go wrong in ways that we cannot appreciate. Apart from requiring that imperfect rationality leads our conceivability intuitions to go massively astray, the view also requires that a smarter version of Mary really could know what it is like to see red on the basis of physical information, and that there is an analysis of phenomenal concepts to support the implication from physical to phenomenal facts (perhaps a structural or functional analysis), although one whose correctness lies beyond our powers of appreciation.

While it must be conceded that any philosophical argument *could* go wrong because of cognitive impairment, in the absence of any substantial reason to believe this, this sort of objection seems quite *ad hoc.* As before, the main motivation would seem to be a desire to hang onto materialism at all costs. Such an option should always be the *last* option considered, only after we have given up on both substantial *arguments* pointing out where we have gone wrong and substantial attempts to develop an alternative to materialism. If we find a substantial alternative that is satisfactory, then any motivation for this view will disappear.[11]

3. Other Arguments for Dualism*

I am not the first to use the argument from logical possibility against material-ism.[12] Indeed, I think that in one form or another it is the fundamental antimaterialist argument in the philosophy of mind. Nevertheless, it has not received the careful attention it deserves. More attention has focused on two antimaterialist arguments by Jackson (1982) and Kripke (1972). These arguments strike me as related, but as perhaps less fundamental. Jackson's argument is important for the entry it provides to the argument from logical supervenience, and the most compelling portion of Kripke's argument de-pends on the argument from logical supervenience, as we will see.

Jackson's argument

I have already discussed Jackson's argument, the knowledge argument, in the context of establishing the failure of logical supervenience, where it plays a supporting role. Recall that the argument is concerned with Mary, a neuroscientist brought up in a black-and-white room, who knows all the physical facts about color processing in the brain. Later, when she first sees a red object, she learns some new facts. In particular, she learns what it is like to see red. The argument concludes that the physical facts do not exhaust all the facts, and that materialism is false.

This argument is closely related to the arguments from zombies or inverted spectra, in that both revolve around the failure of phenomenal facts to be entailed by physical facts. In a way, they are flip sides of the same argument. As a direct argument against materialism, however, Jackson's argument is often seen as vulnerable due to its use of the intensional notion of knowl-edge. Many attacks on the argument have centered on this intensionality—arguing, for example, that the same fact can be known in two different ways. These attacks fail, I think, but the most straightforward way to see this is to proceed directly to the failure of supervenience, which is cast in terms of metaphysics rather than epistemology. The framework I have developed helps bring out just why the various objections do not succeed. I will discuss some of these objections in what follows.

First, various respondents have argued that although Mary gains new knowledge upon seeing red, this knowledge does not correspond to any new *fact*. She simply comes to know an old fact in a new way, under a new "mode of presentation," due to the intensionality of knowledge (Churchland 1985; Horgan 1984b; Lycan 1995; McMullen 1985; Papineau 1993; Teller 1992; Tye 1986). For example, Tye and Lycan appeal to the intensional difference between "This liquid is water" and "This liquid is H_2O": in a sense these express the same fact, but one can be known without the other. Similarly, Churchland appeals to the gap between knowledge of temperature and knowledge of mean kinetic energy, Horgan discusses the difference between knowledge of Clark Kent and knowledge of Superman, while McMullen points to Mark Twain and Samuel Clemens.

These gaps arise precisely because of the difference between primary and secondary intensions. One can know things about water without knowing things about H_2O because the primary intensions differ—there is no *a priori* connection between water thoughts and H_2O thoughts. Nevertheless, in a sense there is only one set of facts about the two: because of the *a posteriori* identity between water and H_2O, the relevant secondary intensions coincide. (It is not obvious that one *has* to individuate facts this way, so that water facts and H_2O facts are the same facts, but I will go along with this for the sake of argument.[13]) In the terminology used earlier, "If this is water, it is H_2O" is logically contingent but metaphysically necessary. This objection therefore comes to precisely the same thing as the objection from the distinction between logical necessity and (Kripkean) metaphysical necessity discussed earlier, and the discussion there of primary and secondary intensions is sufficient to refute it.

We can also put the point a more direct way. Whenever one knows a fact under one mode of presentation but not under another, there will always be a *different* fact that one lacks knowledge of—a fact that connects the two modes of presentation.[14] If one knows that Hesperus is visible but not that Phosphorus is visible (because one does not know that Hesperus is Phosphorus), then one does not know that one object is both the brightest star in the morning sky and the brightest star in the evening sky. This is a separate fact that one lacks knowledge of entirely. Similarly, if one knows that Superman can fly but not that Clark Kent can fly, then one does not know that there is an individual who is both the lead reporter at the *Daily Planet* and who wears a cape. If one knows that water is wet but not that H_2O is wet, one does not know that the stuff in the lakes is made out of H_2O molecules. And so on.

More formally: Say that "a is G" and "b is G" are the same fact in this sense, but one cannot connect the two facts *a priori*. This must be because $a = b$ and the secondary intensions are the same, but the primary intensions are different: perhaps a is equivalent to $dthat(P)$ and b to $dthat(Q)$. If one knows that a is G but not that b is G, then one lacks the factual knowledge that something is both P and Q. More generally, one lacks the factual knowledge that something is both P' and Q', where these are any identifying descriptions such that one knows that a is P' and that b is Q'. This fact is quite separate from the facts that one initially possessed. Even when interpreted according to secondary intensions, there will be a possible world in which a is F but in which nothing is both P and Q (or both P' and Q').

(As in section 2, there is the complication that P and Q may be index-relative properties, but this changes nothing fundamental. To make the unknown novel fact strictly nonindexical, one need only move to the fact "There exists a point [with property X] from which P and Q pick out the same thing." X is a backup just in case one knows of some *other* location from which P and Q pick out the same thing; in such a case, we simply make X specific enough to distinguish oneself from those other locations. The extreme case where one lacks any distinguishing self-knowledge reduces to the pure indexical case, discussed below.)

It follows that if Mary gains any factual knowledge that she previously lacked—even if it is only knowledge of an old fact under a different mode of presentation—then there must be some truly novel fact that she gains knowledge of. In particular, she must come to know a new fact *involving* that mode of presentation. Given that she already knew all the physical facts, it follows that materialism is false. The physical facts are in no sense exhaustive.

This rejoinder may seem less straightforward than the corresponding rejoinder to the argument from logical possibility. The supervenience framework eliminates the less clear-cut question of how to individuate pieces of knowledge, and so makes discussion less confusing. All the same, close analysis shows that water–H_2O analogies and related objections fail equally either way. Despite the fact that this is easily the most popular response to the knowledge argument, it is also easily the weakest of the major replies. It simply does not hold up to scrutiny.

A second, more sophisticated objection, due to Loar (1990), also holds that Mary gains new knowledge of old facts because of intensionality, but explicitly goes beyond the usual water–H_2O analogies. Loar recognizes that analogies with the usual examples cannot do the job for the materialist, as (in our terminology) such analogies allow that physical and phenomenal notions have distinct primary intensions, and the antimaterialist can simply apply the argument to the property corresponding to the primary intension. As Loar puts it, even though "heat" and some statistical-mechanical predicate *designate* the same property (secondary intension), they nevertheless *introduce* distinct properties (primary intension). So he takes the argument further, and argues that two predicates can introduce the same property—that is, share the same primary intension—even when this sameness is not knowable *a priori*. If so, then Mary's knowledge of phenomenal properties may just be knowledge of physical/functional properties, even though she could not have connected the two beforehand.

But how can two primary intensions coincide without our being able to know it *a priori*? Only if the space of possible worlds is smaller than we would have thought *a priori*. We think the intensions differ because we conceive of a world where they have different reference, such as a zombie world. Loar's position therefore requires that this world is not really possible, despite the fact that we cannot rule it out on conceptual grounds, and despite the fact that Kripkean *a posteriori* necessity cannot do any work for us. This position therefore comes to precisely the same thing as the "strong metaphysical necessity" objection considered above. Like that objection, Loar's position requires that a conditional from physical facts to phenomenal facts be metaphysically necessary despite being logically contingent, where this gap cannot be explained by a difference in primary intensions. Like that objection, Loar's position requires a brute and arbitrary restriction on possible worlds. Loar offers no argument for this restriction, and his position is subject to precisely the same criticisms.[15]

One might expect there to be a third objection analogous to the intermediate "alternative strategy" from section 2. This would be cashed out in the claim that Mary does not really know all the physical facts. She knows all the facts couched in the terms of physics, but she lacks knowledge about the hidden (phenomenal or protophenomenal) essences of physical entities. If she had this knowledge, she would thereby know the phenomenal facts. As before, however, this view has only a very tenuous claim to the name "materialism." Like my own view, this view must take phenomenal or protophenomenal properties to be fundamental properties.

A fourth objection draws a connection between Mary's plight and a lack of indexical knowledge (Bigelow and Pargetter 1990; McMullen 1985; Papineau 1993). Although Mary gains new knowledge, it is argued that this is no more puzzling than other cases where someone who knows all the relevant objective facts discovers something new: for example, an omniscient amnesiac who discovers "*I* am Rudolf Lingens," or a well-informed insomniac who does not know that it is 3:49 A.M. *now* (see Perry 1979 and Lewis 1979). In these cases, there is gap between physical knowledge and indexical knowledge, just as there is a gap between physical knowledge and phenomenal knowledge in Mary's case.

The connection might be drawn in two ways. First, an objector might try to *reduce* phenomenal knowledge to indexical knowledge, arguing that all that Mary lacks is indexical knowledge. Second, one might try to draw an *analogy* between the two cases, arguing that in the indexical case the epistemic gap does not lead to an ontological gap (indexicality does not falsify materialism), so that the phenomenal case need not lead to an ontological gap either.

The reduction strategy clearly fails. As we saw in Chapter 2, indexicals accompany facts about conscious experience in their failure to supervene logically on physical facts, but they are all settled by the addition of a thin "indexical fact" about the location of the agent in question. But even when we give Mary perfect knowledge about her indexical relation to everything in the physical world, her knowledge of red experiences will not be improved in the slightest. In lacking phenomenal knowledge, she lacks far more than someone lacking indexical knowledge.

The analogy strategy is more interesting. One might respond by arguing for an ontological gap even in the indexical case (see, e.g., Nagel 1983), but a more straightforward response is available. To see this, note that in the indexical case, an argument analogous to that in section 1 does not get off the ground: there is no conceivable uncentered world in which the physical facts are the same as ours, but in which the indexical facts differ. In uncentered worlds, indexical facts do not even apply. There is a relevant conceivable *centered* world, to be sure, but it is uncentered worlds that are relevant to the ontological question. (If not, there is an ontological gap in the indexical case as well, so the objector's argument does not get started.[16]) So in this case alone we can explain away the epistemic gap by noting that epistemic connections are determined by *centered* primary intensions, whereas ontological connections are determined by properties corresponding to uncentered intensions. Indeed, this is reflected in the single loophole that was found in the argument of section 2, and in the analogous argument in this section: the fact that primary intensions determine only center-relative properties. This loophole allows through a single piece of irreducible indexical knowledge (the location of a centered world's center) without ontological cost, but nothing further. Once the location of a center is specified, the loophole is closed. The phenomenal facts remain unsettled even when the location of a center is specified, so conscious experience remains out in the cold.[17]

If a materialist is to hold on to materialism, she really needs to deny that Mary makes any *discovery* about the world at all. Materialism requires logical supervenience, which requires that Mary can gain no new factual knowledge of any sort when she first experiences red. Thus, in a fifth strategy, Lewis (1990) and Nemirow (1990) argue that at most Mary gains a new *ability*. For example, she gains the ability to imagine the sight of red things, and to recognize them when she sees them. But this is only knowledge *how*, not knowledge *that*. When she first experiences red, she learns no facts about the world.[18]

Unlike the previous options, this strategy does not suffer from internal problems. Its main problem is that it is deeply implausible. No doubt Mary does gain some abilities when she first experiences red, as she gains some abilities when she learns to ride a bicycle. But it certainly seems that she learns something else: some *facts* about the nature of experience. For all she knew before, the experience of red things might have been like this, or it might have been like that, or it might even have been like nothing at all. But now she knows that it is like *this*. She has narrowed down the space of epistemic possibilities. No such new knowledge comes along when an omniscient mechanic learns to ride a bicycle (except perhaps for knowledge about the phenomenology of bicycle riding). So this reply fails to come to grips with what goes on when Mary learns what it is like to see red.

We can also use more indirect methods to see that Mary's discovery involves factual knowledge. For example, Loar (1990) points out that this sort of knowledge can be embedded in conditionals: "If seeing red things is like this and seeing blue things is like this, then seeing purple things is probably like that"; "If it is like this for dogs to see red, then such-and-such follows"; and so on. Another example: as Lycan (1995) points out,[19] what we imagine can turn out to be right or wrong; thus, after seeing a few colors, Mary might imagine what it is like to see another one, and her imagination might be correct or incorrect. If so, then to know what something is like is to know a truth about the world, and the ability analysis fails.

Dennett (1991) takes a related but more extreme position, arguing that Mary learns nothing at all. He notes that Mary could use her neurophysiological knowledge to recognize that a red object is red when she sees it, by noticing its effects on her reactions, which may differ from the effects of something blue. (If a team of experimenters tries to fool her by holding up a blue apple, she might not be fooled.) Perhaps this is so, but all that follows is that *contra* Lewis and Nemirow, Mary had certain abilities to recognize even before she had her first experience of red. It does nothing to show that she had the crucial knowledge: knowledge of what seeing red would be like. That would only follow if we had already accepted the ability analysis of "knowing what it is like"; but if we had accepted that analysis, the argument against materialism would already have been defeated. So Dennett's argument is a red herring here.

Ultimately, the strategy that a materialist *must* take is to deny that Mary gains knowledge about the world. And the only tenable way to do this seems to be via an ability analysis of "knowing what it is like." This is the only position with the internal coherence to ensure that it is not defeated by technical objections, just as analytic functionalism is ultimately the most coherent way for a materialist to resist the argument from logical supervenience. But contraposing, the very implausibility of the denial that Mary gains knowledge about the world is evidence that materialism is doomed.[20]

We have seen that the modal argument (the argument from logical possibility) and the knowledge argument are two sides of the same coin. I think that in principle each succeeds on its own, but in practice they work best in tandem.[21] Taking the knowledge argument alone: most materialists find it hard to deny that Mary gains knowledge about the world, but often deny the step from there to the failure of materialism. Taking the modal argument alone: most materialists find it hard to deny the argument from the conceivability of zombies or inverted spectra to the failure of materialism, but often deny the premise. But taking the two together, the modal argument buttresses the knowledge argument where help is needed, and vice versa. In perhaps the most powerful combination of the two arguments, we can use the knowledge argument to compellingly establish the failure of logical supervenience, and the modal argument to compellingly make the step from that failure to the falsity of materialism.

Kripke's argument

Kripke's argument was directed at the identity thesis put forward by Place (1957) and Smart (1959), but it can be seen to have a broad force against all forms of materialism. I will discuss the strengths and weaknesses of this argument in some detail, to support the conclusion that the parts that succeed are precisely those parts that correspond to the argument from logical supervenience.

The argument goes roughly as follows: According to the identity thesis, certain mental states (such as pains) and brain states (such as C-fibers firing) are identical, even though "pain" and "C-fibers firing" do not *mean* the same thing. The identity here was originally supposed to be contingent rather than necessary, just as the identity between water and H_2O is contingent. Against this, Kripke argues that all identities are necessary: If X is Y, then X is *necessarily Y,* as long as the terms X and Y designate rigidly, picking out the same individual or kind across worlds. Water is *necessarily* H_2O, he argues; that is, water is H_2O in every possible world. The identity may *seem* contingent—that is, it might seem that there is a possible world in which water is not H_2O but XYZ—but this is illusory. In fact, the possible world that one is imagining contains no water at all. It is just a world in which there is some watery stuff—stuff that looks and behaves like water—made out of XYZ. In asserting that this watery stuff is water, one is misdescribing it.

Similarly, Kripke argues, if pains are identical to the firing of C-fibers, then this identity must be necessary. But the identity does not *seem* to be necessary. On the face of it, one can imagine a possible world where a pain occurs without any brain state whatsoever (disembodied pain), and one can imagine a world in which C-fibers fire without any accompanying pain (in a zombie, say). Further, he argues, these possibilities cannot be explained away as merely apparent possibilities, in the way that the possibility of water without H_2O was explained away. For that to be the case, we would have to be *misdescribing* the "disembodied pain" world as one in which pain occurred, when really there was just "painy stuff" (something that feels like pain) going on. Similarly, we would have to be misdescribing the zombie as lacking pain, when all it really lacks is painy stuff. On such an account, the zombie would presumably have real pain, which is the firing of C-fibers; it is just that it doesn't feel like real pain.

But this cannot be the case, according to Kripke: *all it is* for something to be pain is for it to feel like pain. There is no distinction between pain and painy stuff, in the way that there is a distinction between water and watery stuff. One could have something that felt like water without it being water, but one could not have something that felt like pain without it being pain. Pain's feel is *essential* to it. So the possibility of the pains without the brain states (and vice versa) cannot be dismissed as before. Those possible worlds really are possible, and mental states are not necessarily identical to brain states. It follows that they cannot be identical to brain states at all.

Kripke runs the argument in two different ways, once against token-identity theories and once against type-identity theories. Token-identity theories hold that *particular* pains (such as my pain now) are identical to particular brain states (such as the C-fibers firing in my head now). Kripke argues in the above fashion that a particular pain could occur without the particular associated brain state, and vice versa, so they cannot be identical. Type-identity theories hold that mental states and brain states are identical as *types*: pain, for example, might be identical as a type to the firing of C-fibers. Kripke holds that this is straightforwardly refuted by the fact that one could instantiate the mental-state type without the brain-state type, and vice versa. Overall, we can count four separate arguments here, divided according to the target (token- or type-identity theories) and according to the method of argument (from the possibility of disembodiment or from the possibility of zombies).

There are some obvious differences between Kripke's argument and the argument I have given. For a start, Kripke's argument is couched entirely in terms of identity, whereas I have relied on the notion of supervenience. Second, Kripke's argument is closely tied to his theoretical apparatus involving rigid designators and *a posteriori* necessity, whereas that apparatus plays only a secondary role in my argument, in answering certain objections. Third, Kripke's argument is usually seen to rely on a certain essentialism about various states, whereas no such doctrine is invoked in my argument. Fourth, my argument nowhere appeals to the possibility of disembodiment, as Kripke's does. Nevertheless there are obvious similarities. Both are modal arguments, involving necessity and possibility in key roles. And both appeal to the logical possibility of dissociating physical states from the associated phenomenal states.

I will now discuss what succeeds and what fails in Kripke's arguments, starting with those against token identity. These are generally held to be inconclusive. This is largely because they rely on intuitions about what counts as *that very thing* across possible worlds, and such intuitions are notoriously unreliable. Kripke's claim that one could have *that very* pain state without *that very* brain state relies on the claim that what is essential to that pain state is its feel, and only its feel. But such claims about the essential properties of individuals are hard to justify. The token-identity theorist can respond by arguing that it is just as plausible that the firing of C-fibers is an essential property of the state. Of course, C-fiber firing does not seem to be essential to pain as a *type,* but who is to say that it is not essential to this particular pain token, especially if that token is identical to a brain state? If it is, then one simply could not have the particular pain in question without the particular brain state. (A line like this is taken by Feldman [1974], who argues that painfulness need not be essential to a particular pain, and by McGinn [1977], who in effect argues that both painfulness *and* C-fiber firing might be essential to a particular pain.) If so, then in imagining a disembodied version of my pain, one is not imagining *that very* pain but a separate, numerically distinct pain. The same goes for imagining my C-fiber firing without pain. So the arguments against token identity are inconclusive, although the arguments against type identity may survive.

Next, the argument from disembodiment does not establish a conclusive case against materialism. It might refute a type-identity thesis of the kind put forward by Place and Smart, but materialism does not require such a thesis.[22] As Boyd (1980) notes, the materialist need not hold that mental states are physical states in all possible worlds—it is compatible with materialism that in some worlds mental states are constituted out of nonphysical stuff, as long as in *this* world they are physically constituted. The possibility of disembodiment only establishes the possibility of dualism, rather than its truth.[23] To illustrate this, we can note that that few would argue that the possibility of nonphysical life implies dualism about biology. An argument against the identity thesis may be all that Kripke intended, but in any case the more general version of materialism survives.

This leaves the argument from the possibility of instantiating physical states without the corresponding phenomenal states—essentially an argument from the possibility of zombies. Curiously, this is the part of Kripke's argument that has received the least critical attention, with most commentators focusing on the possibility of disembodiment. As before, the argument that zombies yield against strong type-identity theses may be irrelevant, due to the fact that materialism does not require such a thesis, but there is a more general argument lurking here. The possibility of instantiating the relevant physical states without pain, Kripke argues (pp. 153–54), shows that even after God created all the physical stuff going on when one has a pain—perhaps a brain with C-fibers firing—*he had to do more work* in order that those firings be felt as pain. This is enough to establish that materialism is false.[24]

This argument from physical states without phenomenal states corresponds directly to the argument I have given against materialism. Even the further maneuvers correspond. To the objection that this situation is merely conceivable and not truly possible, Kripke will respond: One cannot explain away the conceived situation as one that lacks the feeling of pain but not pain itself, as to be a pain is to feel like pain in any possible world. (That is, the secondary intension and the primary intension of "pain" coincide.) To this we might add (with Jackson [1980]) that even if the equivalence is disputed, the argument against materialism will succeed when applied to *feelings* of pain rather than pain. (That is, even if the intensions differ, the argument still goes through using the primary intension.) These are isomorphic to the responses that I gave to the same sort of objection earlier in this chapter.

(Note that with his thesis that an apparently-conceivable-but-impossible situation should be explained away as an epistemically possible situation that is misdescribed, Kripke is in effect endorsing the "weak" treatment of *a posteriori* necessity: the spaces of conceivable and possible worlds are the same, but *a posteriori* factors put constraints on their correct description.[25] To see this, note that an advocate of "strong" metaphysical necessity, on which the space of possible worlds is a proper subset of the space of conceivable worlds, would not advocate such a thesis. On such a view, we might *correctly* describe an epistemically possible situation, but it might still be (brutely) metaphysically impossible. Kripke's reliance on the misdescription strategy, by contrast, suggests an implicit endorsement of the two-dimensional framework: indeed, all his examples of misdescription can be seen as cases in which a world is described under primary rather than secondary intensions.)

This argument from physical states without phenomenal states strikes me as the most conclusive part of Kripke's discussion. It is frequently overlooked amidst the discussion of identity theses, disembodiment, and the like; even Kripke assigns this aspect of his discussion a noncentral role. All the same, I think it is this part of the discussion that ultimately carries the burden of Kripke's argument.

To summarize, it seems to me that insofar as Kripke's argument against materialism succeeds, (1) the possibility of disembodiment is inconclusive as an argument against materialism but inessential to the case; (2) arguments phrased in terms of identity are similarly inconclusive but inessential; (3) an essentialist metaphysics is inessential, except insofar as the feel of pain is essential to pain as a type—but that is just a fact about what "pain" *means*; and (4) Kripke's apparatus of rigid designation and the like is not central, although it is required to answer a certain sort of objection.[26] But his argument contains a sound core, in what is essentially an argument from the failure of logical supervenience.

4. Is This Epiphenomenalism?*

A problem with the view I have advocated is that if consciousness is merely
naturally supervenient on the physical, then it seems to lack causal efficacy.
The physical world is more or less causally closed, in that for any given
physical event, it seems that there is a physical explanation (modulo a small
amount of quantum indeterminacy). This implies that there is no room for
a nonphysical consciousness to do any independent causal work. It seems
to be a mere epiphenomenon, hanging off the engine of physical causation,
but making no difference in the physical world. It exists, but as far as the
physical world is concerned it might as well not. Huxley (1874) advocated
such a view, but many people find it counterintuitive and repugnant. Indeed,
this consequence has been enough to cause some (e.g., Kirk [1979]; Seager
[1991]) to question the conclusions of their arguments against materialism,
and to consider the possibility that consciousness might be logically supervenient on the physical after all.

   This argument has been formalized in different but related ways by Kirk
(1979), Horgan (1987), and Seager (1991). If we assume that the physical
world is causally closed and that consciousness causes some physical events,
then it follows under certain natural assumptions about causation that consciousness must supervene logically (or metaphysically) on the physical.[27] If
so, then given that the physical world is causally closed, the mere natural
supervenience of consciousness implies that consciousness is epiphenomenal.
The basic shape of the argument is clear: if it is possible to subtract the
phenomenal from our world and still retain a causally closed world Z, then
everything that happens in Z has a causal explanation that is independent
of the phenomenal, as there is nothing phenomenal in Z. But everything
that happens in Z also happens in our world, so the causal explanation that
applies in Z applies equally here. So the phenomenal is causally irrelevant.
Even if conscious experience were absent, the behavior might have been
caused in exactly the same way.

   In responding to this, I will pursue a two-pronged strategy. First, it is not
obvious that mere natural supervenience must imply epiphenomenalism in
the strongest sense. It is clear that the picture it produces looks *something
like* epiphenomenalism. Nevertheless, the very nature of causation itself is
quite mysterious, and it is possible that when causation is better understood
we will be in a position to understand a subtle way in which conscious
experience may be causally relevant. (In effect, it may turn out that background assumptions in arguments above are false.) I will outline some ways
in which such an analysis might be made below. On the second prong, I will
consider the *reasons* why epiphenomenalism might be found unpalatable,
and analyze their force as arguments. If these intuitions do not translate into
compelling arguments, it may turn out the sort of epiphenomenalism that

this position implies is *only* counterintuitive, and that ultimately a degree of epiphenomenalism can be accepted.

Strategies for avoiding epiphenomenalism

There are a number of ways in which one might try to preserve the failure of logical supervenience while nevertheless avoiding epiphenomenalism. The most obvious of these is to deny the causal closure of the physical, and to embrace a strong form of interactionist dualism in which the mental fills causal gaps in physical processing. I think this strategy should be avoided, for reasons I discuss shortly. However, there are a number of more subtle options that depend on an appropriate view of metaphysics and especially of causation. I discuss four such options.

1. Regularity-based causation.   The first option is to accept a strong Humean account of causation, upon which all it is for A to cause B is for there to be a uniform regularity between events of type A and events of type B. Such a view would allow a "causal" role for the phenomenal: the mere fact that pain sensations are generally followed by withdrawal reactions would imply that pain causes withdrawal reactions.

A related non-Humean option identifies a causal connection with any *nomic* (or lawful) connection, even if a nomic regularity is something more than a uniform regularity. The natural supervenience view is entirely compatible with the existence of a nomic connection between experience and behavior (for example, there might be a lawful connection between experience and an underlying brain state, and a lawful connection between that brain state and behavior). One might claim that this is enough for causation. This might be supported by noting that the counterfactual "Behavior would have been the same even in the absence of experience" is *false* on the most natural interpretation: if the experience were absent, the brain state would have been different, and behavior would have been different. Here, the counterfactual is assessed by considering *naturally* possible worlds, rather than logically possible worlds.

I find both of these positions implausible. I have argued against Humean views of causation in Chapter 2, and even on the non-Humean view it is implausible that just any nomic connection suffices for causation—think of the correlation between the hair color of identical twins, for instance. Nevertheless, considerations like these at least give us an idea of why consciousness *appears* to play a causal role. There are all sorts of systematic regularities between conscious experiences and later physical events, each of which leads us to *infer* a causal connection. Faced with such regularities, we would expect people to infer a causal relation for broadly Humean reasons. This can therefore explain away some of our intuitions that consciousness is causally efficacious, thus supporting the second prong of the strategy.

2. *Causal overdetermination.*   Perhaps we might claim that a physical state and a phenomenal state, though wholly distinct, might both qualify as causing a later physical state. If physical state P_1 is associated with phenomenal state Q_1, then perhaps it is true both that P_1 causes a later physical state P_2 and that Q_1 causes P_2. This is counterintuitive: P_1 is already a sufficient cause of P_2, so Q_1 would seem to be causally redundant. But it is not obvious that Q_1 could not stand in a causal relation to P_1 nevertheless. This may be especially reasonable if we adopt a nonreductive view of causation (of the sort advocated by Tooley 1987). Perhaps there is an irreducible causal connection between the two physical states, and a separate irreducible causal connection between the phenomenal state and the physical state.

This sort of causal overdetermination of events is often regarded with suspicion, but it is hard to demonstrate conclusively that there is something wrong with it. The nature of causation is sufficiently ill understood that overdetermination cannot yet be ruled out. I will not pursue this line myself, but it nevertheless deserves to be taken seriously.

3. *The nonsupervenience of causation.*   A third strategy rests with the very nature of causation itself. We saw in Chapter 2 that there are two classes of facts that do not supervene logically on particular physical facts: facts about consciousness and facts about causation. It is natural to speculate that these two failures might be intimately related, and that consciousness and causation have some deep metaphysical tie. Both are quite mysterious, after all, and two mysteries might be more neatly wrapped into one. Perhaps, for instance, experience itself is a kind of causal nexus; perhaps it somehow realizes Hume's "unknowable causal relation"; or perhaps the relationship is more complex. A relationship like this might suggest a role for experience in causation that is more subtle than the usual sort of causation, but nevertheless avoids the strongest form of epiphenomenalism.

A proposal like this has been developed by Rosenberg (1996), who argues that many of the problems of consciousness are precisely paralleled by problems about causation. He argues that because of these parallels, it may be that experience *realizes* causation, or some aspects of causation, in the actual world. On this view, causation needs to be realized by something in order to support its many properties, and experience is a natural candidate. If this is so, it may be that it is the very existence of experience that allows for causal relations to exist, so that there is a subtle sort of relevance for experience in causation.

Of course, this proposal is extremely speculative, and faces some problems. For a start, it seems to lead to a version of panpsychism, the view that everything is conscious, which many find counterintuitive. Further, the zombie world is still a problem—it seems that we can imagine all that causation going on without experience, so that experience might still seem epiphenomenal. A response might be that causation has to be realized by something; in the zombie world it is realized by something else, but experience is still relevant in this world in virtue of realizing causation here. It is not obvious to me that causation *has* to be realized by something with any further properties; if it need not be, then the phenomenal nature of causation might still be redundant. But again, the metaphysics of causation is as yet far from clear, and this proposal is certainly worth investigating.

4. The intrinsic nature of the physical.   The strategy to which I am most drawn stems from the observation that physical theory only characterizes its basic entities *relationally,* in terms of their causal and other relations to other entities. Basic particles, for instance, are largely characterized in terms of their propensity to interact with other particles. Their mass and charge is specified, to be sure, but all that a specification of mass ultimately comes to is a propensity to be accelerated in certain ways by forces, and so on. Each entity is characterized by its relation to other entities, and these entities are characterized by their relations to other entities, and so on forever (except, perhaps, for some entities that are characterized by their relation to an observer). The picture of the physical world that this yields is that of a giant causal flux, but the picture tells us nothing about what all this causation *relates.* Reference to the proton is fixed as the thing that causes interactions of a certain kind, that combines in certain ways with other entities, and so on; but what is the thing that is doing the causing and combining? As Russell (1927) notes, this is a matter about which physical theory is silent.[28]

One might be attracted to the view of the world as pure causal flux, with no further properties for the causation to relate, but this would lead to a strangely insubstantial view of the physical world.[29] It would contain only causal and nomic relations between empty placeholders with no properties of their own. Intuitively, it is more reasonable to suppose that the basic entities that all this causation relates have some internal nature of their own, some *intrinsic* properties, so that the world has some substance to it. But physics can at best fix reference to those properties by virtue of their extrinsic relations; it tells us nothing directly about what those properties might be. We have some vague intuitions about these properties based on our experience of their macroscopic analogs—intuitions about the very "massiveness" of mass, for example—but it is hard to flesh these intuitions out, and it is not clear on reflection that there is anything to them.

There is only one class of intrinsic, nonrelational property with which we have any direct familiarity, and that is the class of phenomenal properties.

It is natural to speculate that there may be some relation or even overlap between the uncharacterized intrinsic properties of physical entities, and the familiar intrinsic properties of experience. Perhaps, as Russell suggested, at least some of the intrinsic properties of the physical are themselves a variety of phenomenal property?[30] The idea sounds wild at first, but on reflection it becomes less so. After all, we really have *no idea* about the intrinsic properties of the physical. Their nature is up for grabs, and phenomenal properties seem as likely a candidate as any other.

There is of course the threat of panpsychism. I am not sure that this is such a bad prospect—if phenomenal properties are fundamental, it is natural to suppose that they might be widespread—but it is not a necessary consequence. An alternative is that the relevant properties are protophenomenal properties. In this case the mere instantiation of such a property does not entail experience, but instantiation of numerous such properties could do so jointly. It is hard to imagine how this would work (we know that it cannot work for standard physical properties), but these intrinsic properties are quite foreign to our conception. The possibility cannot be ruled out *a priori*.

Either way, this sort of intimate link suggests a kind of causal role for the phenomenal. If there are intrinsic properties of the physical, it is instantiations of these properties that physical causation ultimately relates. If these are phenomenal properties, then there is phenomenal causation; and if these are protophenomenal properties, then phenomenal properties inherit causal relevance by their supervenient status, just as billiard balls inherit causal relevance from molecules. In either case, the phenomenology of experience in human agents may inherit causal relevance from the causal role of the intrinsic properties of the physical.

Of course, this would be a subtler kind of causal relevance than the usual kind. It remains the case, for example, that one can imagine removing the phenomenal properties, with the pattern of causal flux remaining the same. But now the response is that in imagining such a scenario, one is effectively altering the intrinsic properties of physical entities and replacing them by something else (of course, the trouble is that we are not used to imagining intrinsic properties of the physical at all). Thus one is simply moving to a world where something else is doing the causation. If there could be a world of *pure* causal flux, this argument would fail, but such a world is arguably logically impossible, as there is nothing in such a world for causation to relate.

This position is rather akin to the second position described in section 2, where electrons have a hidden essence to which physical descriptions merely fix reference. I think that for the reasons given there, the intrinsic properties should not be *identified* with physical properties such as mass. It seems reasonable to say that there is still mass in the zombie world, despite differences in its intrinsic nature. If so, then mass is an extrinsic property that can be "realized" by different intrinsic properties in different worlds. But whichever way we make this semantic decision, the position retains an essential duality between the properties that physics deals with directly and the hidden intrinsic properties that constitute phenomenology.

There is a sense in which this view can be seen as a monism rather than a dualism, but it is not a materialist monism. Unlike physicalism, this view takes certain phenomenal or protophenomenal properties as fundamental. What it finally delivers is a network of intrinsic properties, at least some of which are phenomenal or protophenomenal, and which are related according to certain causal/dynamic laws. These properties "realize" the extrinsic physical properties, and the laws connecting them realize the physical laws. In the extreme case in which all the intrinsic properties are phenomenal, the view might be best seen as a version of idealism. It is an idealism very unlike Berkeley's, however. The world is not supervenient on the mind of an observer, but rather consists in a vast causal network of phenomenal properties underlying the physical laws that science postulates. A less extreme case in which intrinsic properties are protophenomenal, or in which some are neither phenomenal nor protophenomenal, is perhaps best regarded as a version of Russell's neutral monism. The basic properties of the world are neither physical nor phenomenal, but the physical and the phenomenal are constructed out of them. From their intrinsic natures in combination, the phenomenal is constructed; and from their extrinsic relations, the physical is constructed.

On this view, the most basic laws will be those that connect the basic intrinsic properties. The familiar physical laws capture the relational shape of these laws, while abstracting away from the intrinsic properties. Psychophysical laws can be reinterpreted as laws that connect intrinsic properties (or properties constructed out of these) to their relational profiles (or to complex relational structures). Thus these laws do not "dangle" ontologically from physical laws. Rather, both are consequences of the truly basic laws. But the epistemological order differs from the ontological order: we are led first to the relational structure of the causal network, and only slowly to the underlying intrinsic properties. For everyday explanatory purposes, it is therefore most useful to continue to think of this view in terms of a network of physical laws, with further principles connecting the physical to the phenomenal.

All this metaphysical speculation may need to be taken with a pinch of salt, but it shows that the issue of epiphenomenalism is not cut and dried. There are a number of subtle issues about causation and about the nature of experience that will need to be understood better before we can say for certain whether experience is epiphenomenal. In any case, I will now set aside the metaphysical speculation and return to a less lofty plane (although I will return to some of these issues in Chapter 8).

It remains the case that natural supervenience *feels* epiphenomenalistic. We might say that the view is epiphenomenalistic *to a first approximation*: if it allows some causal relevance for experience, it does so in a subtle way. I think we can capture this first-approximation sense by noting that the view makes experience *explanatorily irrelevant*. We can give explanations of behavior in purely physical or computational terms, terms that neither involve nor imply phenomenology. If experience is tied in some intimate way to causation, it is in a way that these explanations can abstract away from. One might find even explanatory irrelevance troubling; I will say much more about it in the next chapter.

Some have been tempted to avoid epiphenomenalism by leaping into the "strong metaphysical necessity" position of section 2 of this chapter. If experience does not supervene logically on the physical, it has seemed to some that the only way to preserve its causal role is to declare it brutely identical to or metaphysically supervenient on some physical property or properties. Apart from the problems that I have already mentioned, however, the view still has serious problems with explanatory irrelevance. The very conceivability of a zombie shows that on this view, behavior can be explained in terms that neither involve nor imply the existence of experience. Explanatory relations are conceptual relations, so that strong metaphysical necessity is irrelevant here. The view still leaves behavior independent of experience in a strong sense and has to face up to most of the same difficulties as a property dualism. There is therefore not much to be gained by taking such a position.

Interactionist dualism?

Some people, persuaded by the arguments for dualism but convinced that phenomenal consciousness must play a significant causal role, may be tempted by an interactionist variety of dualism, in which experience fills causal gaps in physical processes. Giving in to this temptation raises more problems than it solves, however. For a start, it requires a hefty bet on the future of physics, one that does not currently seem at all promising; physical events seem inexorably to be explained in terms of other physical events. It also requires a large wager on the future of cognitive science, as it suggests that the usual kinds of physical/functional models will be insufficient to explain behavior. But the deepest problem is that this view may be no better at getting around the problems with epiphenomenalism than the view with causal closure, for reasons I will discuss shortly.

The only form of interactionist dualism that has seemed even remotely tenable in the contemporary picture is one that exploits certain properties of quantum mechanics. There are two ways this might go. First, some have appealed to the existence of quantum indeterminacy, and have suggested that a nonphysical consciousness might be responsible for filling the resultant causal gaps, determining which values some physical magnitudes might take within an apparently "probabilistic" distribution (e.g., Eccles 1986). Although these decisions would have only a tiny proximate effect, perhaps nonlinear dynamics could amplify these tiny fluctuations into significant macroscopic effects on behavior.

This is an audacious and interesting suggestion, but it has a number of problems. First, the theory contradicts the quantum-mechanical postulate that these microscopic "decisions" are entirely random, and in principle it implies that there should be some detectable pattern to them—a testable hypothesis. Second, in order that this theory allows that consciousness does any *interesting* causal work, it needs to be the case that the behavior produced by *these* microscopic decisions is somehow different in kind than that produced by most other sets of decisions that might have been made by a purely random process. Presumably the behavior is more rational than it would have been otherwise, and it leads to remarks such as "I am seeing red now" that the random processes would not have produced. This again is testable in principle, by running a simulation of a brain with real random processes determining those decisions. Of course we do not know for certain which way this test would come out, but to hold that the random version would lead to unusually degraded behavior would be to make a bet at long odds.

A second way in which quantum mechanics bears on the issue of causal closure lies with the fact that in some interpretations of the quantum formalism, consciousness itself plays a vital causal role, being required to bring about the so-called "collapse of the wave-function." This collapse is supposed to occur upon any act of measurement; and in one interpretation, the only way to distinguish a measurement from a nonmeasurement is via the presence of consciousness. This theory is certainly not universally accepted (for a start, it *presupposes* that consciousness is not itself physical, surely contrary to the views of most physicists), and I do not accept it myself, but in any case it seems that the kind of causal work consciousness performs here is quite different from the kind required for consciousness to play a role in directing behavior.[31] It is unclear how a collapse in external perceived objects allows consciousness to affect physical processing within the brain; such theories are usually silent on what happens to the brain during collapse. And even if consciousness somehow manages to collapse the brain state, then all the above remarks about apparently random processes and their connection with behavior still apply.

In any case, all versions of interactionist dualism have a conceptual problem that suggests that they are less successful in avoiding epiphenomenalism than they might seem; or at least that they are no better off than the view I have advocated. Even on these views, there is a sense in which the phenomenal is irrelevant. We can always subtract the phenomenal component from any explanatory account, yielding a purely causal component. Imagine (with Eccles) that "psychons" in the nonphysical mind push around physical processes in the brain, and that psychons are the seat of experience. We can tell a story about the causal relations between psychons and physical processes, and a story about the causal dynamics among psychons, without ever invoking the fact that psychons have phenomenal properties. Just as with physical processes, we can imagine subtracting the *phenomenal* properties of psychons, yielding a situation in which the causal dynamics are isomorphic. It follows that the fact that psychons are the seat of experience plays no essential role in a causal explanation, and that even in this picture experience is explanatorily irrelevant.

Some might object that psychons (or ectoplasm, or whatever) are entirely *constituted* by their phenomenal properties. Even so, there is a sense in which their phenomenal properties are irrelevant to the explanation of behavior; it is only their relational properties that matter in the story about causal dynamics. If one objects that still, they have further intrinsic properties that are *causally* relevant, we have a situation like the one that arose above with phenomenal properties intrinsic to *physical* entities. Either way, we have a sort of causal relevance but explanatory irrelevance. Indeed, nothing especially is gained by moving away from the causal closure of the physical. We still have a broader causal network that is closed, and it remains the case that the phenomenal nature of entities in the network is explanatorily superfluous.

We can even imagine that if interactionism is true, then for reasons quite independent of conscious experience we would be led eventually to postulate psychons in order to explain behavior, to fill the observed causal gaps and account for the data. If so, psychons would have the status of a kind of theoretical entity like the theoretical entities of physics. Nothing in this story would involve or imply experience, which would be as explanatorily superfluous as in the usual case; we could still tell a zombie story involving psychons, and so on. The additional observation that these psychons might have phenomenal properties works no better or worse as a response to epiphenomenalism than the analogous observation that physical entities (perhaps basic entities, perhaps quite complex ones) might have phenomenal properties over and above their extrinsic features. The denial of the causal closure of the physical therefore makes no significant difference in the avoidance of epiphenomenalism.[32]

The problems of epiphenomenalism

Any view that takes consciousness seriously will at least have to face up to a limited form of epiphenomenalism. The very fact that experience can be coherently subtracted from any causal account implies that experience is superfluous in the *explanation* of behavior, whether or not it has some subtle causal relevance. It is possible that it will turn out to be causally irrelevant in a stronger sense; that question is open. We therefore need to pursue the second prong of the strategy, and see just what are the problems with the causal or explanatory irrelevance of experience, and whether they are ultimately fatal. I will do this at much greater length in Chapter 5, but here we can briefly survey the field.

The most common objection to epiphenomenalism is simply that it is counterintuitive or even "repugnant." Finding a conclusion counterintuitive or repugnant is not *sufficient* reason to reject the conclusion, however, especially if it is the conclusion of a strong argument. Epiphenomenalism may be counterintuitive, but it is not *obviously* false, so if a sound argument forces it on us, we should accept it. Of course, a counterintuitive conclusion may give us reason to go back and reexamine the argument, but we still need to find something wrong with the argument on independent grounds. If it turns out that the falsity of logical supervenience implies epiphenomenalism, then logical supervenience may be *desirable,* but we cannot simply assert it as a brute fact. To hold logical supervenience, one needs some account of how the physical facts might entail the facts about consciousness, and this is precisely what I have argued cannot be given.

More detailed objections to epiphenomenalism fall into three classes: those concerning the relationship of experience to ordinary behavior, those concerning the relationship of experience to *judgments* about experience, and those concerning the overall picture of the world that it gives rise to.

Take the first class first. Many find it simply obvious that their feelings of pain cause them to withdraw their hand from a flame, or that my experience of a headache cannot be irrelevant to the explanation of why I take pills. There is certainly a strong intuition to this effect. On the other hand, we can easily explain away the source of this intuition, in terms of the systematic regularities between these events. We are much more directly aware of experience and of behavior than we are of an underlying brain state; upon exposure to systematic regularities between experience and behavior, it is natural that a strong causal connection should be inferred. Even if the connection were only an indirect nomic connection due to relations to the underlying brain state, we would still expect the inference to be made. So this intuition can be explained away. In any case, this sort of objection cannot be fatal to the view, as it is an intuition that does not extend directly into an argument. It is an instance of the *merely* counterintuitive.

The second class of objections is more worrying. It seems very strange that our experiences should be irrelevant to the explanation of why we *talk* about experiences, for instance, or perhaps even to our internal *judgments* about experiences; this seems much stranger than the mere irrelevance of my pain to the explanation of my hand's withdrawal. Some claim that this sort of problem is not merely counterintuitive but fatal. For example, it might be claimed that this is incompatible with our *knowledge* of experience, or with our ability to *refer* to experiences. I believe that when these arguments are spelled out they do not ultimately gain their conclusion, but these questions are certainly challenging. I devote Chapter 5 to these issues.

Objections in the third class concern the overall structure of the view. One objection is that the picture is ugly and implausible, with experience hanging off the physical by "nomological danglers" that are not integrated with the other laws of nature. I think this can be combated by developing a theory that leads to a more integrated picture. The label "epiphenomenalism" tends to suggest a view on which experience is dangling "up there," floating free of processing in some way; a better picture that is still compatible with natural supervenience is a picture of experience sitting down among the causal cracks. At the very least, we can try to make the psychophysical laws as simple and elegant as possible. Also falling into this class is a worry about how consciousness might *evolve* in an epiphenomenalist account, but it is not hard to see that this poses no problem for the view I advocate; I discuss this further at the end of this chapter.

On examination, there are not many *arguments* that do serious damage to epiphenomenalism. The main class of worrying arguments are those concerning judgments about experience, which I will discuss in the next chapter. Arguments aside, some have the *intuition* that epiphenomenalism must be wrong, but the intuition does not suffice to reject the position in the face of strong arguments in its favor.

I do not describe my view as epiphenomenalism. The question of the causal relevance of experience remains open, and a more detailed theory of both causation and of experience will be required before the issue can be settled. But the view implies at least a weak form of epiphenomenalism, and it may end up leading to a stronger sort. Even if it does, however, I think the arguments for natural supervenience are sufficiently compelling that one should accept them. Epiphenomenalism is counterintuitive, but the alternatives are more than counterintuitive. They are simply *wrong,* as we have already seen and will see again. The overall moral is that if the arguments suggest that natural supervenience is true, then we should learn to live with natural supervenience.

Some will find that nevertheless the epiphenomenalist nature of this position is a fatal flaw. I have some sympathy with this position, which can be seen as an expression of the paradox of consciousness: when it comes to consciousness, it can seem that *all* the alternatives are bad. However, I think the problems with all other views are fatal in a much stronger way than the counterintuitiveness of this one. Given that some option in logical space has to be correct, this view seems to be the only reasonable candidate.

5. The Logical Geography of the Issues

The argument for my view is an inference from roughly four premises:

1. Conscious experience exists.
2. Conscious experience is not logically supervenient on the physical.
3. If there are phenomena that are not logically supervenient on the physical facts, then materialism is false.
4. The physical domain is causally closed.

Premises (1), (2), and (3) clearly imply the falsity of materialism. This, taken in conjunction with premise (4) and the plausible assumption that physically identical beings will have identical conscious experiences, implies the view that I have called natural supervenience: conscious experience arises from the physical according to some laws of nature, but is not itself physical. The various alternative positions can be catalogued according to whether they deny premises (1), (2), (3), or (4). Of course, some of these premises can be denied in more than one way.

Denying premise (1):

    i. *Eliminativism.* On this view, there are no positive facts about conscious experience. Nobody is conscious in the phenomenal sense.

Denying premise (2):

Premise (2) can be denied in various ways, depending on how the entailment in question proceeds—that is, depending on what sort of physical properties are centrally responsible for entailing consciousness. I call all of these views "reductive materialist" views, as they all suppose an analysis of the notion of consciousness that is compatible with reductive explanation.

    ii. *Reductive functionalism.* This view takes consciousness to be conceptually entailed by the physical in virtue of functional or dispositional properties. On this view, what it means for a state to be conscious is for it to play a certain causal role. In a world physically identical to ours, all the relevant causal roles would be played, and therefore the conscious states would all be the same. The zombie world is therefore logically impossible.

    iii. *Nonfunctionalist reductive materialism.* On this view, the facts about consciousness are conceptually entailed by the physical facts in virtue of some nonfunctional property. Possible candidates might include biochemical and quantum properties, or properties yet to be determined.

    iv. *New-physics materialism.* According to this view, we have no current idea of how physical facts could explain consciousness, but that is because our current conception of physical facts is too narrow. When one argues that a zombie world is logically possible, one is really arguing that all the fields and particles interacting in the space-time manifold, postulated by current physics, could exist in the absence of consciousness. But with a new physics, things might be different. The entities in a radically different theoretical framework might be sufficient to entail and explain consciousness.

Denying premise (3):

    v. *Nonreductive materialism.* This is the view that although there may be no logical entailment from the physical facts to the facts about consciousness, and therefore no reductive explanation of consciousness, consciousness *just is* physical. The physical facts "metaphysically necessitate" the facts about consciousness. Even though the idea of a zombie world is quite coherent, such a world is metaphysically impossible.

Denying premise (4):

    vi. *Interactionist dualism.* This view accepts that consciousness is nonphysical, but denies that the physical world is causally closed, so that consciousness can play an autonomous causal role.

Then there is my view, which accepts premises (1), (2), (3), and (4):

    vii. *Naturalistic dualism.* Consciousness supervenes naturally on the physical, without supervening logically or "metaphysically."

There is also an eighth common view, which is generally underspecified:

    viii. *Don't-have-a-clue materialism.* "I don't have a clue about consciousness. It seems utterly mysterious to me. But it must be physical, as materialism must be true." Such a view is held widely, but rarely in print (although see Fodor 1992).

To quickly summarize the situation as I see it, option (i) seems to be manifestly false; (ii) and (iii) rely on false analyses of the notion of consciousness and therefore change the subject; (iv) and (vi) place large and implausible bets on the way that physics will turn out, and also have fatal conceptual problems; and (v) either makes an invalid appeal to Kripkean *a posteriori* necessity or relies on a bizarre metaphysics. I have a certain amount of sympathy with (viii), but it presumably must eventually reduce to some more specific view, and none of these seem to work. This leaves (vii) as the only tenable option.

More slowly, starting with options (iv) and (vi): Option (vi), interactionist dualism, requires that physics will turn out to have gaps that can be filled by the action of a nonphysical mind. Current evidence suggests that this is unlikely. Option (iv) requires that the shape of physics will be transformed so radically that it could entail facts about conscious experience; but nobody has an idea of how *any* physics could do this. Indeed, given that physics ultimately deals in structural and dynamical properties, it seems that all physics will ever entail is more structure and dynamics, which (unless one of the other reductive options is embraced) will never entail the existence of experience.

The deepest reason to reject options (iv) and (vi) is that they ultimately suffer from the same problem as a more standard physics: the phenomenal component can be coherently subtracted from the causal component. On the interactionist view, we have seen that even if the nonphysical entities have a phenomenal aspect, we can coherently imagine subtracting the phenomenal component, leaving a purely causal/dynamic story characterizing the interaction and behavior of the relevant entities. On the new physics view, even if it explicitly incorporates phenomenal properties, the fact that these properties are *phenomenal* can play no essential role in the causal/dynamic story; we would be left with a coherent physics even if that aspect were subtracted. Either way, the dynamics is all we need to explain causal interactions, and no set of facts about dynamics adds up to a fact about phenomenology. A zombie story can therefore still be told.

Various moves can be made in reply, but each of these moves can also be made on the standard physical story. For example, perhaps the abstract dynamics misses the fact that the nonphysical stuff in the interactionist story is intrinsically phenomenal, so that phenomenal properties are deeply involved in the causal network. But equally, perhaps the abstract dynamics of physics misses the fact that its basic entities are intrinsically phenomenal (physics characterizes them only extrinsically, after all), and the upshot would be the same. Either way, we have the same kind of explanatory irrelevance of the intrinsic phenomenal properties to the causal/dynamic story. The move to interactionism or new physics therefore does not solve any problems inherent in the property dualism I advocate. At the end of the day, they can be seen as more complicated versions of the same sort of view.

As for option (iii), the most tempting version is the one that gestures toward unknown properties that we have so far overlooked as the key to the entailment. But ultimately the problem is the same: physics only gives us structure and dynamics, and structure and dynamics does not add up to phenomenology. The only available properties would seem to be those characterizing physical structure or function, or properties constructed out of the two. But structural properties are obviously inappropriate analyses of the concept of experience, and functional properties are not much better (although I consider them below). Any view of this sort will ultimately change the subject.

This leaves options (i), (ii), (v), and (vii), which correspond to the options taken most seriously in the contemporary literature: eliminativism, reductive functionalism, nonreductive materialism, and property dualism. Of these I reject option (i) as being in conflict with the manifest facts. Perhaps an *extraordinary* argument could establish that conscious experience does not exist, but I have never seen an argument that comes remotely close to making this case. In the absence of such an argument, to take option (i) is simply to evade the problem by denying the phenomenon.

Option (v) is often attractive to those who want to take consciousness seriously and also retain materialism. But I have argued that it simply does not work. The nonreductive materialism advocated by Searle turns out to have internal problems and collapses into one of the other views (most likely property dualism). Other proponents of this view rely on an appeal to Kripke's *a posteriori* necessity, but the sort of *a posteriori* necessity demonstrated by Kripke cannot save materialism. The only consistent way to take option (v) is to appeal to a strong *a posteriori* necessity that goes well beyond Kripke's, and to invoke brute constraints on the space of "metaphysically possible" worlds. We have seen that there is no reason to believe in such constraints, or to believe in such a third, intermediate grade of the possibility of worlds. This metaphysics gains no support from any other phenomena, and it is hard to see how it *could* be supported.

Even if this metaphysics of necessity is accepted, for most explanatory purposes the view ends up looking like the view I advocate. It implies that consciousness cannot be reductively explained. It implies that conscious experience is explanatorily irrelevant to the physical domain. And it implies that a theory of consciousness must invoke bridging principles to connect the physical and phenomenal domains, principles that are not themselves entailed by physical laws. This view calls these principles "metaphysically necessary," but for all practical purposes the upshot is the same. This sort of theory will have the same *shape* as the dualist theories I advocate, and almost everything I say in developing a nonreductive theory in the next few chapters will apply equally here.

Option (ii), reductive functionalism, is the most serious materialist option. Leaving aside various wild options, if materialism is true, then consciousness is logically supervenient, and the only remotely reasonable way for it to be logically supervenient is via a functional analysis. On this view, then, all it *means* for something to be a conscious experience is for it to play a certain causal role in a system. Phenomenal properties are treated exactly the same way as psychological properties, such as learning or categorization.

The problem with this view, of course, is that it misrepresents what it means to be a conscious experience, or to be conscious. When I wonder whether other beings are conscious, I am not wondering about their abilities or their internal mechanisms, which I may know all about already; I am wondering whether there is something it is like to be them. This point can be supported in various familiar ways. One way is to note that even once we have explained various functional capacities, the problem of explaining experience may still remain. Another rests on the observation that we can imagine any functional role being played in the absence of conscious experience. A third derives from the fact that knowledge of functional roles does not automatically yield knowledge of consciousness. There are also the objections, made earlier, that a functionalist analysis cannot account for the semantic determinacy of attributions of consciousness and that it collapses the conceptual distinction between consciousness and awareness.

At the end of the day, reductive functionalism does not differ much from eliminativism. Both of these views hold that there is discrimination, categorization, accessibility, reportability, and the like; and both deny that there is anything else that even needs to be explained. The main difference is that the reductive line holds that some of these explananda deserve the name "experience," whereas the eliminative line holds that none of them do. Apart from this terminological issue, the substance of the views is largely the same. It is often noted that the line between reductionism and eliminativism is blurry, with reduction gradually sliding into elimination the more we are forced to modify the relevant concepts in order to perform a reduction. In allowing that consciousness exists only insofar as it is defined as some functional capacity, the reductive functionalist view does sufficient violence to the concept of consciousness that it is probably best viewed as a version of eliminativism. Neither is a view that takes consciousness seriously.

This leaves view (vii), the property dualism that I have advocated, as the only tenable option. Certainly it seems to be a consequence of well-justified premises. In some ways it is counterintuitive, but it is the only view without a fatal flaw. Some will find its dualistic nature unpalatable; but I will argue shortly that dualism of this variety is not as unreasonable as many have thought, and that it is open to few serious objections. The biggest worry about this view is that it implies a certain irrelevance of phenomenal properties in the explanation of behavior, and may lead to epiphenomenalism, although this is not automatic. I will argue in the next chapter, however, that this explanatory irrelevance has no fatal consequences. Ultimately, this view gives us a coherent, naturalistic, unmysterious view of consciousness and its place in the natural order.

Type A, type B, and type C

Taking a broader view of the logical geography, we can say that there are three main classes of views about conscious experience. *Type-A* views hold that consciousness, insofar as it exists, supervenes logically on the physical, for broadly functionalist or eliminativist reasons. *Type-B* views accept that consciousness is not logically supervenient, holding that there is no *a priori* implication from the physical to the phenomenal, but maintain materialism all the same. *Type-C* views deny both logical supervenience and materialism.

Type-A views come in numerous varieties—eliminativism, behaviorism, various versions of reductive functionalism—but they have certain things in common. A type-A theorist will hold that (1) physical and functional duplicates that lack the sort of experience that we have are inconceivable; (2) Mary learns nothing about the world when she first sees red (at best she gains an ability); and (3) everything there is to be explained about consciousness can be explained by explaining the performance of various functions. Archetypal type-A theorists include Armstrong (1968), Dennett (1991), Lewis (1966), and Ryle (1949). Others may include Dretske (1995), Rey (1982), Rosenthal (1996), Smart (1959), White (1986), and Wilkes (1984).

Type-B views, or nonreductive versions of materialism, usually fall prey to internal difficulties. The only type-B view that seems to be even internally coherent is the view that invokes strong metaphysical necessity in a crucial role. Taking this view, a type-B theorist must hold that (1) zombies and inverted spectra are conceivable but metaphysically impossible; (2) Mary learns something when she sees red, but that this learning can be explained away with a Loar-style analysis; and (3) consciousness cannot be reductively explained, but is physical nevertheless. The central type-B view has never received a definitive statement, but the closest thing to such a statement is given by Levine (1983, 1993) and Loar (1990). Others who appear to endorse physicalism without logical supervenience include Byrne (1993), Flanagan (1992), Hill (1991), Horgan (1984b), Lycan (1995), Papineau (1993), Tye (1995), and van Gulick (1992).

Type-C positions include various kinds of property dualism, in which materialism is taken to be false and some sort of phenomenal or protophenomenal properties are taken as irreducible. On such a view, (1) zombies and inverted spectra are logically and metaphysically possible; (2) Mary learns something new, and her knowledge is of nonphysical facts; and (3) consciousness cannot be reductively explained, but might be nonreductively explained in terms of further laws of nature. Type-C positions are taken by Campbell (1970), Honderich (1981), Jackson (1982), H. Robinson (1982), W. Robinson (1988), Sprigge (1994), and in the present work.

It is perhaps worth mentioning separately the position discussed earlier in which phenomenal properties are identified with the intrinsic properties of physical entities. This sort of view is endorsed by Feigl (1958), Lockwood (1989), Maxwell (1978), and Russell (1926), and I have some sympathy with it myself. I include this as a version of type C, as it takes phenomenal or protophenomenal properties as fundamental, but it has its own metaphysical shape. In particular, it is more of a monism than the natural interpretation of type C. Perhaps we can call this position type C', but I will usually include it under type C.

There are two main choice points between types A, B, and C. First, is consciousness logically supervenient (type A versus the rest)? Second, is physicalism true (type B versus type C)? Taking the second choice point first, I have little difficulty in rejecting type B. While it has the virtue of taking consciousness seriously, it relies on a metaphysics that is either incoherent or obscure, and one that is largely unmotivated; the main motivation is simply to avoid dualism at all costs. In the end, this view shares the same explanatory shape as type C, but with an added dose of metaphysical mystery. Type C is straightforward by comparison.

The central choice is the choice between type A and the rest. For myself, reductive functionalism and eliminativism seem so clearly false that I find it hard to fathom how anyone could accept a type-A view. To me, it seems that one could only accept such a view if one believed that there was no significant problem about consciousness in the first place. Nevertheless, experience indicates that almost one-third of the population are willing to accept a type-A position and do not budge. This indicates the Great Divide mentioned in the preface: the divide between views that take consciousness seriously and those that do not.

In many ways, the divide between type A and the others is deeper than that between type B and type C. The latter division involves relatively subtle issues of metaphysics, but the former involves some very basic intuitions. Even though type B and type A are both "materialist" views, type-B views are much closer to type-C views in their spirit. Both these views acknowledge the depth of the problem of consciousness where type-A views do not.

Ultimately, argument can take us only so far in settling this issue. If someone insists that explaining access and reportability explains everything, that Mary discovers nothing about the world when she first has a red experience, and that a functional isomorph differing in conscious experience is inconceivable, then I can only conclude that when it comes to experience we are on different planes. Perhaps our inner lives differ dramatically. Perhaps one of us is "cognitively closed" to the insights of the other. More likely, one of us is confused or is in the grip of a dogma. In any case, once the dialectic reaches this point, it is a bridge that argument cannot cross. Rather, we have reached a brute clash of intuitions of a sort that is common in the discussion of deep philosophical questions. Explicit argument can help us to isolate and characterize the clash, but not to resolve it.

At the beginning of this work, I said that my approach was premised on taking consciousness seriously. We can now see just what this comes to. To take consciousness seriously is to accept just this: that there is something interesting that needs explaining, over and above the performance of various functions.[33] This has the status of a *prima facie* premise that only an extremely strong argument could overturn. No argument that I have ever seen comes close to overturning the premise. Indeed, type-A theorists do not usually *argue* against the premise, but simply deny it. Conversely, beyond a certain point it is almost impossible to argue *for* the premise, any more than one can argue that conscious experience exists. At best, one can try to clarify the issues in the hope that enlightenment sets in.

With the issues clarified, readers can decide for themselves whether to take consciousness seriously. All I claim is that *if* one takes consciousness seriously, then property dualism is the only reasonable option. Once we reject reductive functionalism and eliminativism, it follows inexorably that consciousness is not logically supervenient on the physical. And once we reject logical supervenience, the path to property dualism is unswerving. Type-B views are popular, but do not appear to stand up to close philosophical scrutiny. The main metaphysical choice that remains open is whether to accept a standard type-C view or a type-C' view. This is not a question that we have to settle immediately—I do not have a settled opinion on it myself—but in any case, it follows either way that if we want to take consciousness seriously, we must admit phenomenal or protophenomenal properties as fundamental.

Some other views found in the philosophical literature do not fall explicitly into the framework I have outlined. With this framework in place, however, it is not hard to locate them and to analyze their problems. I briefly discuss nine such positions in the endnotes: biological materialism,[34] physicalist-functionalism,[35] psychofunctionalism,[36] anomalous monism,[37] representationalism,[38] consciousness as higher-order thought,[39] reductive teleofunctionalism,[40] emergent causation,[40] and mysterianism.[42]

6. Reflections on Naturalistic Dualism

Many people, including a past self of mine, have thought that they could simultaneously take consciousness seriously and remain a materialist. In this chapter I have argued that this is not possible, and for straightforward reasons. The moral is that those who want to come to grips with the phenomenon must embrace a form of dualism. One might say: You can't have your materialist cake and eat your consciousness too.

All the same, many will be searching for an alternative to the position I have put forward, because they find its dualistic nature unacceptable. This reaction is natural, given the various negative associations of dualism, but I suspect that it is not grounded in anything more solid than contemporary dogma. To see this, it is worthwhile to consider the various reasons that one might have for rejecting dualism in favor of materialism, and to measure the force of these reasons as things stand.

The first reason to prefer materialism is *simplicity*. This is a good reason. Other things being equal, one should prefer a simpler theory over one that is ontologically profligate. Ockham's razor tells us that we should not multiply entities without necessity. But other things are not equal, and in this case there *is* necessity. We have seen that materialism cannot account for the phenomena that need to be explained. Just as Maxwell sacrificed a simple mechanistic worldview by postulating electromagnetic fields in order to explain certain natural phenomena, we need to sacrifice a simple physicalistic worldview in order to explain consciousness. We have paid due respect to Ockham by recognizing that for materialism to be overthrown, one will need good arguments. But when the arguments against materialism are there, Ockham's razor cannot save it.

The second and perhaps the most pervasive reason to believe in materialism is inductive: materialism has always worked elsewhere. With phenomena such as life, cognition, and the weather, we either have materialist accounts already or we have good reason to suppose that they are not far off. Why should consciousness be any different?

But this reason is easy to defeat. As we have seen, there is a simple explanation for the success of materialist accounts in various external domains. With phenomena such as learning, life, and the weather, all that needs to be explained are structures and functions. Given the causal closure of the physical, one should expect a physical account of this structure and function. But with consciousness, uniquely, we need to explain more than structures and functions, so there is little reason to expect an explanation to be similar in kind.

Indeed, we saw in Chapter 2 that given the nature of our access to external phenomena, we should *expect* a materialist account of any such phenomena to succeed. Our knowledge of these phenomena is physically mediated, by light, sound, and other perceptual media. Given the causal closure of the physical, we should expect phenomena that we observe by these means to be logically supervenient on the physical—otherwise we would never know about them. But our epistemic access to conscious experience is of an entirely different kind. Consciousness is at the very center of our epistemic universe, and our access to it is not perceptually mediated. The reasons for expecting a materialist account of external phenomena therefore break down in the case of consciousness, and any induction from those phenomena will be shaky at best.

Third, many have preferred materialism in order to *take science seriously*. It has been thought that a dualist view would challenge science on its own grounds. According to Churchland (1988), "[D]ualism is inconsistent with evolutionary biology and modern physics and chemistry." But this is quite false. Nothing about the dualist view I advocate requires us to take the physical sciences at anything other than their word. The causal closure of the physical is preserved; physics, chemistry, neuroscience, and cognitive science can proceed as usual. In their own domains, the physical sciences are entirely successful. They explain physical phenomena admirably; they simply fail to explain conscious experience.

Churchland suggests a number of other reasons to reject dualism: (1) the systematic dependence of mental phenomena on neurobiological phenomena; (2) modern computational results that suggest that complex results can be achieved without a nonphysical homunculus; and (3) a lack of evidence, explanation, or methodology for dualism. The first two reasons offer no evidence against my view. As for the third, arguments for dualism have already been presented, while dualist explanation and methodology will be illustrated in the remainder of this work.

A fourth motivation to avoid dualism, for many, has arisen from various spiritualistic, religious, supernatural, and other antiscientific overtones of the view. But those are quite inessential. On the view I advocate, consciousness is governed by natural law, and there may eventually be a reasonable scientific theory of it. There is no *a priori* principle that says that all natural laws will be physical laws; to deny materialism is not to deny naturalism. A naturalistic dualism expands our view of the world, but it does not invoke the forces of darkness.

In a related concern, many have thought that to accept dualism would be to give up on explanation. In the words of Dennett (1991), "[G]iven the way that dualism wallows in mystery, accepting dualism is giving up" (p. 37). Perhaps some dualist views have this feature, but it is far from an automatic corollary, as I hope the remainder of this work will make clear.

One occasionally hears a fifth objection to dualism, which is that it cannot explain how the physical and the nonphysical interact. But the answer to this is simple on the natural supervenience framework: they interact by virtue of psychophysical laws. There is a system of laws that ensures that a given physical configuration will be accompanied by a given experience, just as there are laws that dictate that a given physical object will gravitationally affect others in a certain way.

It might be objected that this does not tell us what the *connection* is, or *how* a physical configuration gives rise to experience. But the search for such a connection is misguided. Even with fundamental physical laws, we cannot find a "connection" that does the work. Things simply happen in accordance with the law; beyond a certain point, there is no asking "how." As Hume showed, the quest for such ultimate connections is fruitless. If there are indeed such connections, they are entirely mysterious in both the physical and psychophysical cases, so the latter poses no *special* problem here.

It is notable that Newton's opponents made a similar objection to his theory of gravitation: *How* does one body exert a force on another far away? But the force of the question dissolved over time. We have learned to live with taking certain things as fundamental.

There is also a worry, raised occasionally, about how consciousness might have *evolved* on a dualist framework: did a new element suddenly pop into nature, as if by magic? But this is not a problem. Like the fundamental laws of physics, psychophysical laws are eternal, having existed since the beginning of time. It may be that in the early stages of the universe there was nothing that satisfied the physical antecedents of the laws, and so no consciousness, although this depends on the nature of the laws. In any case, as the universe developed, it came about that certain physical systems evolved that satisfied the relevant conditions. When these systems came into existence, conscious experience automatically accompanied them by virtue of the laws in question. Given that psychophysical laws exist and are timeless, as naturalistic dualism holds, the evolution of consciousness poses no special problem.

In short, very few of the usual reasons for rejecting dualism have any force against the view I am advocating. The main residual motivation to reject dualism may simply lie in the term's negative connotations, and the fact that it goes against what many of us have been brought up to believe. But once we see past these associations, we see that there is no reason why dualism cannot be a reasonable and palatable view. Indeed, I think that the position I have outlined is one that those who think of themselves as materialists, but who want to take conscious experience seriously, can learn to live with and even to appreciate.

Indeed, mine is a view that many who think of themselves as "materialists" may already implicitly share. All I have done is bring the ontological implications of a natural view—that consciousness "arises" from the physical, for example—out into the open. Some dualists may even find my view all too materialistic for their tastes, in which case so be it. Ideally, it is a view that takes the best of both worlds and the worst of neither.

This dualism, then, requires us to give up little that is *important* about our current scientific worldview. It merely requires us to give up a dogma. Otherwise, the view is merely a supplement to the worldview; it is a necessary broadening in order to bring consciousness within its scope. Our credo: If this is dualism, then we should learn to love dualism.

The Paradox of Phenomenal Judgment

1. Consciousness and Cognition

So far, the distinctions and divisions between consciousness and cognition have been stressed above all else. Consciousness is mysterious; cognition is not. Consciousness is ontologically novel; cognition is an ontological free lunch. Cognition can be explained functionally; consciousness resists such explanation. Cognition is governed entirely by the laws of physics; consciousness is governed in part by independent psychophysical laws.

While the focus on these distinctions has been necessary in order to come to grips with the many subtle metaphysical and explanatory issues surrounding conscious experience, it may encourage a misleading picture of the mind. In this picture, consciousness and cognition are utterly detached from each other, living independent lives. One might get the impression that a theory of consciousness and a theory of cognition will have little to do with one another.

This picture is misleading. Our mental life is not alienated from itself in the way that the picture suggests. There are deep and fundamental ties between consciousness and cognition. On one side, the contents of our conscious experiences are closely related to the contents of our cognitive states. Whenever one has a green sensation, individuated phenomenally, one has a corresponding green *perception*, individuated psychologically. On the other side, much cognitive activity can be centered on conscious experience. We know about our experiences, and make judgments about them; as I write this, a great deal of my thought is being devoted to consciousness. These relations between consciousness and cognition are not arbitrary and capricious, but systematic.

An analysis of this systematic relationship may provide much of the basic material for a theory of consciousness. In this way, we can see that the nature of cognition is not irrelevant to consciousness, but central to its explanation. Of course a theory of cognition cannot do all the explanatory work on its own, but it can nevertheless play a major role. After all, it is through cognition that we get a handle on consciousness in the first place. A thorough investigation of the links between consciousness and cognition can provide the purchase we need to constrain a theory of consciousness in a significant way, perhaps ultimately leading to an account of consciousness that neither mystifies nor trivializes the phenomenon.

In this chapter, I lay the groundwork for a study of the relationship between consciousness and cognition. The next section introduces some notions that are at the center of this relationship. The remainder of the chapter is largely defensive, addressing various problems that the relationship between consciousness and cognition might seem to pose for a nonreductive view. In the next chapter, I begin the task of building a positive theory that systematizes the relationship between consciousness and cognition, with the goal of drawing them together into a unified picture of the mind.

Phenomenal judgments

The primary nexus of the relationship between consciousness and cognition lies in *phenomenal judgments*. Our conscious experience does not reside in an isolated phenomenal void. We are aware of our experience and its contents, we form judgments about it, and we are led to make claims about it. When I have a red sensation, I sometimes form a belief that I am having a red sensation, which can issue in a verbal report. At a more abstract level, when one stops to reflect on the mysteries that consciousness poses, as I have been doing throughout this book, one is making judgments about consciousness. At a more concrete level, we frequently form judgments about the *objects* of our conscious experience (in the environment, for example), as when we think, "There is something red." The various judgments in the vicinity of consciousness I call *phenomenal judgments,* not because they are phenomenal states themselves, but because they are concerned with phenomenology or with its objects.

Phenomenal judgments are often reflected in *claims* about consciousness: verbal expressions of those judgments. At various times, people make claims about consciousness ranging from "I have a throbbing pain now" through "LSD gives me bizarre color sensations" to "The problem of consciousness is utterly baffling." These claims and judgments are intimately related to our phenomenology, but they are ultimately part of our psychology. Verbal reports are behavioral acts, and are therefore susceptible to functional explanation. In a similar way phenomenal judgments are themselves cognitive acts, and fall within the domain of psychology.

It is often taken that beliefs should be understood as functional states, characterized by their causal ties to behavior, the environment, and other beliefs, but this view is not universally accepted. Some hold that phenomenal experience can be partly constitutive of belief or of belief contents. For beliefs about consciousness, the functional view is likely to be particularly controversial: if any beliefs are dependent on conscious experience, beliefs about consciousness are the most likely candidates. I will therefore adopt the less loaded label "judgment" for the functional states in question, and will leave open the question of whether a judgment about consciousness is all there is to a belief about consciousness. We can think of a judgment as what is left of a belief after any associated phenomenal quality is subtracted.

That there are purely psychological states that qualify as these judgments should not be a controversial matter. For a start, the disposition to make verbal reports of a certain form is a psychological state; at the very least, we can use the label "judgment" for this disposition. Moreover, whenever I form a belief about my conscious experience, there are all sorts of accompanying functional processes, just as there are with any belief. These processes underlie the disposition to make verbal reports, and all sorts of other dispositions. If one believes that LSD produces bizarre color sensations, the accompanying processes may underlie a tendency to indulge in or to avoid LSD in future, and so on. We can use the term "judgment" as a coverall for the states or processes that play the causal role in question. At a first approximation, a system judges that a proposition is true if it tends to respond affirmatively when queried about the proposition, to behave in an appropriate manner given its other beliefs and desires, and so on.

Judgments can perhaps be understood as what I and my zombie twin have in common. My zombie twin does not have any conscious experience, but he *claims* that he does; at least, his detailed verbal reports sound the same as my own. As I am using the term, I think it is natural to say that my zombie twin *judges* that he has conscious experience, and that his judgments in this vicinity correspond one-to-one with mine.

At the end of this chapter, I argue that the semantic *content* of my phenomenal beliefs is partly constituted in subtle ways by conscious experience itself (for example, red sensations may play a role in constituting the content of certain beliefs about red sensations). If this is so, then some of the zombie's judgments will have contents that are not as rich as my corresponding belief contents. Nevertheless, they will at least correspond one-to-one to mine, will have the same *form,* and will *function* in the same way in directing behavior as mine. So when I talk of a zombie's judgment that he is having a red sensation, I am talking about *something* interesting in his psychology: at the very least, my words can be taken to refer in a deflationary way to the judgment that he expresses using the words "I am having a red sensation" (or words with that sound!). I will talk about "claims" in a similar way, abstracting away from these subtle issues of content.

Strictly speaking, all descriptions of phenomenal claims and judgments in terms of their content (e.g., references to the judgment that one is having a red sensation) should be read in this deflationary way. The full content attributed will certainly be possessed by a subject's phenomenal *beliefs*, but the question of the content of a judgment is not so clear, precisely because it is not clear what role consciousness plays in constituting the content of a phenomenal belief. I will not make too much of this distinction for much of this chapter, as I will be trying to raise some problems that phenomenal judgments pose for my view in the most acute way possible. At the end of the chapter, I will consider these questions about content in more detail.

Three kinds of phenomenal judgment

Judgments related to conscious experience fall into at least three groups. There are what I will call *first-order, second-order,* and *third-order* phenomenal judgments. I will usually drop the qualifier and speak of "first-order judgments," and so on, where it is understood that these are always phenomenal judgments.

First-order judgments are the judgments that go along with conscious experiences, concerning not the experience itself but the *object* of the experience. When I have a red sensation—upon looking at a red book, for instance—there is generally an explicit or implicit judgment, "There is something red." When I have the experience of hearing a musical note, there is an accompanying psychological state concerning that musical note. It seems fair to say that any object that is *consciously experienced* is also *cognitively represented,* although there is more to say about this. Alongside every conscious experience there is a content-bearing cognitive state. This cognitive state is what I am calling a first-order judgment. (One might argue that this state is unlike a belief or judgment in certain ways, as for example it need not be endorsed on reflection. I discuss this at more length in the next chapter, but for now I will speak of "judgments" at least as a first approximation.)

We may think of the contents of these first-order judgments as making up the contents of *awareness,* where awareness is the psychological counterpart of consciousness mentioned in Chapter 1: information of which we are aware is roughly information that is accessible to the cognitive system, available for verbal report, and so on. These judgments are not strictly *about* consciousness. Rather, they are *parallel* to consciousness, and generally *about* objects and properties in the environment, or even in the head. In fact, it is reasonable to say that a first-order judgment is about what the corresponding experience is about. Where I have an experience of a red book, there is a corresponding first-order judgment about the red book. In a certain sense, we can therefore say that experience and first-order judgments—and therefore consciousness and awareness—share their contents. I will give a more refined account of this relationship in the next chapter.

In this chapter, I will be most concerned with *second-order* judgments. These are more straightforwardly judgments about conscious experiences. When I have a red sensation, I sometimes notice that I am having a red sensation. I judge that I have a pain, that I experience certain emotional qualities, and so on. In general, it seems that for any conscious experience, if one possesses the relevant conceptual resources, then one at least has the capacity to judge that one is having that experience.

One can also make more detailed judgments about conscious experiences. One can note that one is experiencing a particularly vivid shade of purple, or that a pain has an all-consuming quality, or even that a green after-image is the third such after-image one has had today. Apart from judgments about specific conscious experiences, second-order judgments also include judgments about particular *kinds* of conscious experiences, as when one notes that some drug produces particularly intense sensations, or that the tingle one gets before a sneeze is particularly pleasurable.

What I will call *third-order* judgments are judgments about conscious experience as a type. These go beyond judgments about particular experiences. We make third-order judgments when we reflect on the fact that we have conscious experiences in the first place, and when we reflect on their nature. I have been making third-order judgments throughout this work. A typical third-order judgment might be, "Consciousness is baffling; I don't see how it could be reductively explained." Others include "Conscious experience is ineffable," and even "Conscious experience does not exist."

Third-order judgments are particularly common among philosophers, and among those with a tendency to speculate on the mysteries of existence. It is possible that many people go through life without making any third-order judgments. Still, such judgments occur in a significant class of people. The very fact that people make such judgments is something that needs explanation.

To help keep the distinctions in mind, the various kinds of judgments related to consciousness can be represented by the following:

- First-order judgment: *That's red!*
- Second-order judgment: *I'm having a red sensation now.*
- Third-order judgment: *Sensations are mysterious.*

2. The Paradox of Phenomenal Judgment

The existence of phenomenal judgments reveals a central tension within a nonreductive theory of consciousness. The problem is this. We have seen that consciousness itself cannot be reductively explained. But phenomenal judgments lie in the domain of psychology and in principle should be reductively explainable by the usual methods of cognitive science. There should be a physical or functional explanation of why we are disposed to make the *claims* about consciousness that we do, for instance, and of how we make the *judgments* we do about conscious experience. It then follows that our claims and judgments about consciousness can be explained in terms quite independent of consciousness. More strongly, it seems that consciousness is *explanatorily irrelevant* to our claims and judgments about consciousness. This result I call the *paradox of phenomenal judgment.*

The paradox of phenomenal judgment does not seem to have received a great deal of attention, but it is put forward vividly by physicist Avshalom Elitzur (1989) as an argument against views that take consciousness to be "passive"; he argues instead for an interactionist dualism.[1] The paradox is also expressed by psychologist Roger Shepard (1993), who suggests that it is something we should become reconciled to:

> In short, we still seem to be left with a dilemma: No analysis of the purely physical processes in a brain (or in a computer) seems capable of capturing the particular quality of the subjective experience corresponding to those processes. Yet, some such analysis should surely be able to give a causal account of how an individual comes to type a sentence such as the preceding. Perhaps we shall have to reconcile ourselves to accepting that although both the existence of conscious experiences and the similarity relations among their qualia have physical embodiments with physical causes and effects, the conscious experiences or qualia themselves are neither characterizable as physical events nor communicable between physical systems. (p. 242)

As we saw in the last chapter, the question of whether consciousness is *causally* irrelevant in the production of behavior is a complex metaphysical issue that is best left open. But the *explanatory* irrelevance of consciousness is clearer, and raises many of the same difficulties that would be raised by causal irrelevance. However the metaphysics of causation turns out, it seems relatively straightforward that a physical explanation of behavior can be given that neither appeals to nor implies the existence of consciousness.

When I say in conversation, "Consciousness is the most mysterious thing there is," that is a behavioral act. When I wrote in an earlier chapter "Consciousness cannot be reductively explained," that was a behavioral act. When I comment on some particularly intense purple qualia that I am experiencing, that is a behavioral act. Like all behavioral acts, these are in principle explainable in terms of the internal causal organization of my cognitive system. There is some story about firing patterns in neurons that will explain why these acts occurred; at a higher level, there is probably a story about cognitive representations and their high-level relations that will do the relevant explanatory work. We certainly do not know the details of the explanation now, but if the physical domain is causally closed, then there will be some reductive explanation in physical or functional terms.

In giving this explanation of my claims in physical or functional terms, we will never have to invoke the existence of conscious experience itself. The physical or functional explanation will be given independently, applying equally well to a zombie as to an honest-to-goodness conscious experiencer. It therefore seems that conscious experience is irrelevant to the explanations of phenomenal claims and irrelevant in a similar way to the explanation of phenomenal judgments, even though these claims and judgments are centrally concerned with conscious experience!

One way to resist this claim would be to argue that the full *content* of my phenomenal claims and beliefs cannot be reductively explained, because consciousness plays a role in constituting that content. One might argue that a zombie's claims and beliefs are *different* claims and beliefs, for example (although they look and sound just the same!), because a zombie would not have the full concept of consciousness. But at the very least it is still puzzling that consciousness should be irrelevant to the *sounds* we make when talking about consciousness, to the finger movements I am making now, and so on; so this response does not remove the full sense of bafflement. So I will set aside this way of thinking about things for now, and will continue to think about claims and judgments in the "deflationary" way that allows that they can be reductively explained.

Another way to resist the point would be to argue that for *any* high-level property that might be thought relevant in explanation, there will be a low-level explanation that does not invoke the existence of that property. One could argue that a psychological property such as memory is explanatorily irrelevant, as one can give neurophysiological explanations of actions that never once mention memory; one could even argue that temperature is explanatorily irrelevant in physics, as explanatory appeals to temperature can in principle be replaced by a molecular account. (Kim [1989] calls this the problem of *explanatory exclusion*.) This might suggest that consciousness is no worse off than any other high-level property when it comes to explanatory irrelevance. If consciousness is on a par with memory or temperature, this is not bad company to be in.

We have seen, however, that high-level properties such as temperature and memory are all logically supervenient on the physical. It follows that when one gives an explanation of some action in neurophysiological terms, this does not make memory explanatorily irrelevant. Memory can *inherit* explanatory relevance by virtue of its logically supervenient status. When we explain a man's desire for female companionship in terms of the fact that he is male and unmarried, this does not make the fact that he is a bachelor explanatorily irrelevant! The general principle here is that when two sets of properties are *conceptually* related, the existence of an explanation in terms of one set does not render the other set explanatorily irrelevant. In a sense, one of the explanations can be a retelling of the other, due to the conceptual relation between the terms involved.

When we tell a story about the interaction of memories, there is a sense in which we are retelling the physical story at a higher level of abstraction. This higher level will omit many details from the physical story, and will therefore often make for a much more satisfying explanation (all those details may have been irrelevant clutter), but it is nevertheless logically related to the lower-level story. The same goes for temperature. These high-level properties are no more rendered explanatorily irrelevant by the existence of a low-level explanation than the velocity of a billiard ball is rendered explanatorily irrelevant by the existence of molecular processes within the ball. In general, the high-level properties in question will constitute a more parsimonious *redescription* of what a low-level explanation describes. One might say that even a low-level description will often *implicitly* involve high-level properties, by virtue of their logically supervenient status, even if it does not invoke them explicitly. Where there is logical supervenience, there is no problem of explanatory irrelevance.

The problems with consciousness are much more serious. Consciousness is not logically supervenient on the physical, so we cannot claim that a physical or functional explanation implicitly involves consciousness, or that consciousness inherits explanatory relevance by logically supervening on the properties involved in such an explanation. A physical or functional explanation of behavior is independent of consciousness in a much stronger sense. It can be given in terms that do not even *imply* the existence of conscious experience. Consciousness is conceptually independent of what goes into the explanation of our claims and judgments about consciousness.

This is not to say that one can *never* appeal to conscious experience in the explanation of behavior. It is perfectly reasonable to explain the fact of someone's withdrawal from a flame by noting that they experienced pain. After all, even on the nonreductive view there are lawful regularities between experience and subsequent behavior. Such regularities ultimately depend on regularities at the physical level, however. For any explanation of behavior that appeals to a pain sensation, there is a more fundamental explanation in purely physical/functional terms—perhaps in terms of psychological pain or pain perception—that do not invoke or imply any properties of experience. Experience gains a sort of indirect explanatory relevance in virtue of its nomic connection to these physical and functional processes, but it nevertheless remains superfluous to the basic explanation.

To see the problem in a particularly vivid way, think of my zombie twin in the universe next door. He talks about conscious experience all the time—in fact, he seems obsessed by it. He spends ridiculous amounts of time hunched over a computer, writing chapter after chapter on the mysteries of consciousness. He often comments on the pleasure he gets from certain sensory qualia, professing a particular love for deep greens and purples. He frequently gets into arguments with zombie materialists, arguing that their position cannot do justice to the realities of conscious experience.

And yet he has no conscious experience at all! In his universe, the materialists are right and he is wrong. Most of his claims about conscious experience are utterly false. But there is certainly a physical or functional explanation of why he makes the claims he makes. After all, his universe is fully law-governed, and no events therein are miraculous, so there must be *some* explanation of his claims. But such an explanation must ultimately be in terms of physical processes and laws, for these are the *only* processes and laws in his universe.

(As before, one might plausibly argue that a zombie does not refer to consciousness in the full sense with his word "consciousness." For now, talk of a zombie's claims and judgments about consciousness should be read in the deflationary way discussed earlier. But even if he does not have the full concept, there is no doubt that he judges that he has *some* property over and above his structural and functional properties—a property that he calls "consciousness"—and the problem arises as strongly in this form.)

Now my zombie twin is only a logical possibility, not an empirical one, and we should not get *too* worried about odd things that happen in logically possible worlds. Still, there is room to be perturbed by what is going on. After all, any explanation of my twin's behavior will equally count as an explanation of *my* behavior, as the processes inside his body are precisely mirrored by those inside mine. The explanation of *his* claims obviously does not depend on the existence of consciousness, as there is no consciousness in his world. It follows that the explanation of my claims is also independent of the existence of consciousness.

To strengthen the sense of paradox, note that my zombie twin is himself engaging in reasoning just like this. He has been known to lament the fate of *his* zombie twin, who spends all his time worrying about consciousness despite the fact that he has none. He worries about what that must say about the explanatory irrelevance of consciousness in his own universe. Still, he remains utterly confident that consciousness exists and cannot be reductively explained. But all this, for him, is a monumental delusion. There *is* no consciousness in his universe—in his world, the eliminativists have been right all along. Despite the fact that his cognitive mechanisms function in the same way as mine, *his* judgments about consciousness are quite deluded.

This paradoxical situation is at once delightful and disturbing. It is not *obviously* fatal to the nonreductive position, but it is at least something that we need to come to grips with. It is certainly the greatest tension that a nonreductive theory is faced with, and any such theory that does not at least face up to the problem cannot be fully satisfactory. We have to carefully examine the consequences of the situation and separate what is merely counterintuitive from what threatens the viability of a nonreductive view of consciousness.

Nietzsche said, "What does not kill us, makes us stronger." If we can cope with this paradox, we may be led to valuable insights about the relationship between consciousness and cognition. I devote the remainder of this chapter to facing up to the paradox, and related issues about the connection between consciousness and cognition will recur throughout the next few chapters. In this way a theory of consciousness can be set onto much firmer ground.

(One might think one could evade the paradox by embracing what I have called a type-B position, in which consciousness supervenes with metaphysical necessity but not with conceptual necessity, or a type-C′ positions, in which phenomenal properties constitute the intrinsic nature of the physical. But the paradox arises almost as strongly for these views. Even if these views salvage a sort of causal relevance for consciousness, they still lead to explanatory irrelevance, as explanatory relevance must be supported by *conceptual* connections. Even on these views, one can give a reductive explanation of phenomenal judgments but not of consciousness itself, making consciousness explanatorily irrelevant to the judgments. There will be a processing explanation of the judgments that does not invoke or imply the existence of experience at any stage; the presence of any further "metaphysically necessary" connection or intrinsic phenomenal properties will be conceptually quite independent of anything that goes into the explanation of behavior.

Another way to see this: on these views, zombies are still conceivable, and there will be a perfectly good explanation of the zombie's behavior. Because this explanation applies to a zombie, the existence of consciousness will play no essential role in the explanation. But what is going on within the zombies is also going on within us, so the same explanation will apply equally to us. So even on these views there will be an explanation of our phenomenal judgments to which consciousness is quite superfluous.)

Facing up to the paradox

When it comes to the explanation of *most* of our behavior, the fact that consciousness is explanatorily irrelevant may be counterintuitive, but it is not too paradoxical. To explain my reaching for the book in front of me, we need not invoke my phenomenal *sensation* of the book; it is enough to invoke my *perception* instead. When a concert-goer sighs at a particularly exquisite movement, one might have thought that the experienced quality of auditory sensations might be central to an explanation of this behavior, but it turns out that an explanation can be given entirely in terms of auditory perception and functional responses. Even in explaining why I withdraw my hand from a flame, a functional explanation in terms of the psychological notion of pain will suffice.

In general, it turns out that where one might think that one would need to invoke phenomenal properties in the explanation of behavior, one can usually invoke psychological properties instead. We saw in Chapter 1 that there is a psychological state underlying every phenomenal state. Where one might have invoked a sensation, one invokes a perceptual registration; where one might have invoked the phenomenal quality of an emotion, one invokes a corresponding functional state; where one might have invoked an occurrent thought, one need only invoke the content of that thought. It is this correspondence between phenomenal and psychological properties that makes the explanatory irrelevance of phenomenal properties not *too* serious a problem in general. It is counterintuitive at first, but it is only counterintuitive. At least for behavior that is not directly concerned with conscious experience, there does not seem to be a pressing need to invoke phenomenal properties in explanation.

It is with our claims and judgments about consciousness that the explanatory irrelevance of conscious experience becomes troubling. True, it may not be especially worrying that consciousness is explanatorily irrelevant to our *first-order* phenomenal judgments, such as "That is a red thing." It is reasonable that these should be explained purely in terms of perception and other psychological processes; after all, the judgments in question are not directly concerned with conscious experience, but with the state of the world. For second- and third-order phenomenal judgments, however, explanatory irrelevance seems to raise real problems. It is these judgments that are *about* conscious experience, and that are responsible for our talking about our sensations and for philosophers' worries about the mysteries of consciousness. It is one thing to accept that consciousness is irrelevant to explaining how I walk around the room; it is another to accept that it is irrelevant to explaining why I talk about consciousness. One would surely be inclined to think that the fact that I am conscious will be part of the explanation of why I *say* that I am conscious, or why I *judge* that I am conscious; and yet it seems that this is not so.

After all, part of the explanation of why we claim and judge that there is water will involve the fact that there is indeed water. In a similar way, it seems that the existence of stars and planets is almost certainly explanatorily relevant to our judging that there are stars and planets. As a rule, when we judge truly and reliably that *P,* the fact that *P* is true generally plays a central role in the explanation of the judgment. There are *some* judgments for which the objects of those judgments are explanatorily irrelevant to the judgments themselves. Think of religious beliefs, for instance, or beliefs about UFOs, which can arguably be explained without invoking any gods or UFOs. But these are all quite possibly *false* beliefs, and not obviously instances of *knowledge.* By contrast, we *know* that we are conscious.

Here we are faced with a difficult situation: how can knowledge of consciousness be reconciled with the fact that consciousness is explanatorily irrelevant to phenomenal judgments? If phenomenal judgments arise for reasons independent of consciousness itself, does this not mean that they are unjustified? This, above all, is the central difficulty posed by the paradox of phenomenal judgment, and I will address it at length later in this chapter.

The paradox is a consequence of the facts that (1) the physical domain is causally closed; (2) judgments about consciousness are logically supervenient on the physical; (3) consciousness is not logically supervenient on the physical; and (4) we know we are conscious. From premises (1) and (2) it follows that judgments about consciousness can be reductively explained. In combination with premise (3), this implies that consciousness is explanatorily irrelevant to our judgments, which lies in tension with premise (4). Thus we have the paradox. One might try to escape the paradox by denying any one of these premises. I will consider each of these escape routes briefly.

Some dualists will deny premise (1). Traditionally, a Cartesian interactionist dualism has been motivated by the thought that only this can give consciousness the relevance to action that it deserves. Indeed, Elitzur (1989) argues directly from the existence of claims about consciousness to the conclusion that the laws of physics cannot be complete, and that consciousness plays an active role in directing physical processes (he suggests that the second law of thermodynamics might be false). But I have already argued that interactionist dualism is of little help in avoiding the problem of explanatory irrelevance.

Some might be tempted to deny premise (2), but recall that we have *defined* judgments so that they are functional states, logically supervenient on the physical. Now, some might argue that there is no such functional state that remotely resembles what we think of as a judgment; but even so, we can simply retreat to *claims* about consciousness, which are behavioral acts and so more straightforwardly logically supervenient, and which raise the difficulties almost as strongly. Even if someone argued that behavioral acts are not purely physical (they might argue that conscious experience is required for something to qualify as a *claim* rather than a noise, or as a claim about consciousness), it is still surprising that consciousness is explanatorily irrelevant to the sounds we produce, and to the marks we write, all of which can be systematically interpreted as concerning consciousness. So some analogous problems will arise no matter how we define the relevant states. Still, this sort of consideration can play at least a subsidiary role in dealing with the paradox, as it is plausibly *beliefs* rather than *claims* that are most closely connected to knowledge, and some sort of phenomenal belief content may be constituted by experience itself. I return to this matter later in the chapter.

Reductionists and eliminativists will of course deny premise (3) or (4). I have argued exhaustively for (3) already, so I will not repeat the arguments here. Similarly, the denial of premise (4) leads to eliminativism, an option I have already rejected. Still, I will examine a way that a reductionist might exploit the paradox of phenomenal judgment shortly.

It seems to me that the most reasonable attitude to take is to recognize that all the premises are probably true; and to see how they can be reconciled with one other. We know there is conscious experience; the physical domain is almost certainly causally closed; and we have established earlier that consciousness is not logically supervenient on the physical. The trick is to learn to live with the combination.

3. On Explaining Phenomenal Judgments

Given what has gone before, explaining why we say the things we do about consciousness emerges as a reasonable and interesting project for cognitive science. These claims are behavioral acts, and should be as susceptible to explanation as any other behavioral act. Indeed, there should be rich pickings for any cognitive scientist who takes this path. Explaining our claims and judgments about consciousness may be difficult, but it will not be as difficult as explaining consciousness itself. This explanation will not automatically yield an explanation of consciousness, of course, but it may well point us in the right direction.

We can do more than accept the possibility of such an explanation as an intellectual conclusion, derived from the causal closure of physics and the logical supervenience of behavior. There are independent reasons for think- ing that phenomenal judgments will be natural concomitants of certain kinds of cognitive processes, and that on reflection one should *expect* such judg- ments from an intelligent system with a certain design. If so, then the explana- tion of the claims and judgments may not be as difficult as one might think; they might fall out of some basic principles about cognitive design.

Here, I will provide just a very brief sketch of why one might think this; I go into this matter in more detail in Chapter 8. To get some feel for the sit- uation, imagine that we have created computational intelligence in the form of an autonomous agent that perceives its environment and has the capacity to reflect rationally on what it perceives. What would such a system be like? Would it have any concept of consciousness, or any related notions?

To see that it might, note that on the most natural design such a system would surely have some concept of self—for instance, it would have the ability to distinguish itself from the rest of the world, and from other entities resembling it. It also seems reasonable that such a system would be able to access its own cognitive contents much more directly than it could those of others. If it had the capacity to reflect, it would presumably have a certain direct awareness of its own thought contents, and could reason about that fact. Furthermore, such a system would most naturally have direct access to perceptual information, much as our own cognitive system does.

When we asked the system what perception was like, what would it say? Would it say, "It's not like anything"? Might it say, "Well, I know there is a red tricycle over there, but I have no idea *how* I know. The information just appeared in my database"? Perhaps, but it seems unlikely. A system designed this way would be quite inefficient and unnatural; its access to its own perceptual contents would be curiously indirect. It seems much more likely that it would say, "I know there is a red tricycle because I *see* it there." When we ask it in turn how it knows that it is *seeing* the tricycle, the answer would very likely be something along the lines of "I just see it."

It would be an odd system that replied, "I know I see it because sensors 78–84 are activated in such-and-such a way." As Hofstadter (1979) points out, there is no need to give a system such detailed access to its low-level parts. Even Winograd's program SHRDLU (1972) did not have knowledge about the code it was written in, despite the fact that it could perceive a virtual world, make inferences about that world, and even justify its knowledge to a limited degree. Such extra knowledge would seem to be quite unnecessary, and would only complicate the processes of awareness and inference.

Instead, it seems likely that such a system would have the same kind of attitude toward its perceptual contents as we do toward ours, with its knowledge of them being direct and unmediated, at least as far as the system is concerned. When we ask how it knows that it sees the red tricycle, an efficiently designed system would say, "I just *see* it!" When we ask how it knows that the tricycle is red, it would say the same sort of thing that we do: "It just looks red." If such a system were reflective, it might start wondering about how it is that things look red, and about why it is that red *just is* a particular way, and blue another. From the system's point of view it is just a brute fact that red looks one way, and blue another. Of course from our vantage point we know that this is just because red throws the system into one state, and blue throws it into another; but from the machine's point of view this does not help.

As it reflected, it might start to wonder about the very fact that it seems to have some access to what it is thinking, and that it has a sense of self. A reflective machine that was designed to have direct access to the contents of its perception and thought might very soon start wondering about the mysteries of consciousness (Hofstadter 1985a gives a rich discussion of this idea): "Why is it that heat *feels* this way?"; "Why am I *me,* and not someone else?"; "I know my processes are just electronic circuits, but how does this explain my *experience* of thought and perception?"

Of course, the speculation I have engaged in here is not to be taken too seriously, but it helps to bring out the *naturalness* of the fact that we judge and claim that we are conscious, given a reasonable design. It would be a strange kind of cognitive system that had no idea what we were talking about when we asked what it was like to be it. The fact that we think and talk about consciousness may be a consequence of very natural features of our design, just as it is with these systems. And certainly, in the explanation of why these systems think and talk as they do, we will never need to invoke full-fledged *consciousness.* Perhaps these systems are really conscious and perhaps they are not, but the explanation works independently of this fact. Any explanation of how these systems function can be given solely in computational terms. In such a case it is obvious that there is no room for a ghost in the machine to play an explanatory role.

All this is to say (expanding on a claim in Chapter 1) that consciousness is surprising, but claims about consciousness are not. Although consciousness is a feature of the world that we would not predict from the physical facts, the things we *say* about consciousness are a garden-variety cognitive phenomenon. Somebody who knew enough about cognitive structure would immediately be able to predict the likelihood of utterances such as "I *feel* conscious, in a way that no physical object could be," or even Descartes's "Cogito ergo sum." In principle, some reductive explanation in terms of internal processes should render claims about consciousness no more deeply surprising than any other aspect of behavior. I have gestured toward such an explanation above, and will consider the matter in more detail in a later chapter.

We will see later that the details of an appropriate explanation can be very useful in getting a theory of consciousness off the ground. The relationship between an explanation of phenomenal judgments and an explanation of consciousness is a subtle one, however. Before proceeding, I will consider a less subtle response to the situation we are placed in.

Is explaining the judgments enough?

At this point a natural thought has probably occurred to many readers, especially those of a reductionist bent: If one has explained why we *say* we are consciousness, and why we *judge* that we are conscious, haven't we explained all that there is to be explained? Why not simply give up on the quest for a theory of consciousness, declaring consciousness itself a chimera?

Even better, why not declare one's theory of why we judge that we are conscious to be a theory of consciousness in its own right? It might well be suggested that a theory of our judgments is all the theory of consciousness that we need.

This position gets some support from considerations about judgments in other domains. It might be thought that the widespread belief in gods, found in all sorts of diverse cultures, provides an excellent reason to believe that gods exist. But there is an alternative explanation of this belief, in terms of social and psychological forces. Atheists might appeal to people's psychological insecurity in the face of the cosmos, to the need for a common outlet for spiritual or emotional expression, and to the intrinsically self-propagating nature of certain idea systems, to explain why it is all but inevitable that religious beliefs should be widespread, given our nature and circumstances. One can even point to the existence of certain highly plausible but faulty arguments for the existence of a god, such as the argument from design and the cosmological arguments. Although these arguments are faulty, they are not *obviously* faulty (in particular, the argument from design could reasonably have been seen as compelling before the time of Darwin), and it is not hard to see why they should generally contribute toward the naturalness of religious belief.

The observation that widespread religious belief might be explained in this way, without appeal to the existence of any gods, is generally taken to provide further evidence that no gods in fact exist. On this interpretation, the atheistic hypothesis can not only explain the complex structure of nature as well as the theistic hypothesis; it can even explain why the theistic hypothesis is so popular. This is a powerful way to cut the support from underneath an opposing view. In the case of religious belief, the argument seems very strong. It makes a tempting argument in the case of consciousness, too.

This is surely the single most powerful argument for a reductive or eliminativist view of consciousness. But it is not enough. The analogy fails. Explaining our judgments about consciousness does not come close to removing the mysteries of consciousness. Why? Because consciousness is itself an *explanandum*. The existence of God was arguably hypothesized largely in order to explain all sorts of evident facts about the world, such as its orderliness and its apparent design. When it turns out that an alternate hypothesis can explain the evidence just as well, then there is no need for the hypothesis of God. There is no separate phenomenon *God* that we can point to and say: *that* needs explaining. At best, there is indirect evidence.[2] Similarly, the existence of UFOs is often postulated to explain strange events in the sky, markings in the ground, disappearances in the Bermuda Triangle, the claims of UFO "survivors," and so on. If it turns out that this evidence can be explained without postulating the existence of UFOs, then our reason for believing in UFOs disappears.

But consciousness is not an explanatory construct, postulated to help explain behavior or events in the world. Rather, it is a brute explanandum, a phenomenon in its own right that is in need of explanation. It therefore does not matter if it turns out that consciousness is not required to do any work in explaining other phenomena. Our evidence for consciousness never lay with these other phenomena in the first place. Even if our judgments about consciousness are explained reductively, *all* this shows is that our judgments can be explained reductively. The mind–body problem is not that of explaining our judgments about consciousness. If it were, it would be a relatively trivial problem. Rather, the mind–body problem is that of explaining consciousness itself. If the judgments can be explained without explaining consciousness, then that is interesting and perhaps surprising, but it does not remove the mind–body problem.

To take the line that explaining our judgments about consciousness is enough (just as explaining our judgments about God is enough) is most naturally understood as an eliminativist position about consciousness (as one analogously takes an eliminativist position about God). As such it suffers from all the problems that eliminativism naturally faces. In particular, it denies the evidence of our own experience. This is the sort of thing that can only be done by a philosopher—or by someone else tying themselves in intellectual knots. Our experiences of red do not go away upon making such a denial. It is still like something to be us, and that is still something that needs explanation. To throw out consciousness itself as a result of the paradox of phenomenal judgment would be to throw out the baby with the bathwater.

There is a certain intellectual appeal to the position that explaining phenomenal judgments is enough. It has the feel of a bold stroke that cleanly dissolves all the problems, leaving our confusion lying on the ground in front of us exposed for all to see. Yet it is the kind of "solution" that is satisfying only for about half a minute. When we stop to reflect, we realize that all we have done is to explain certain aspects of our behavior. We have explained why we talk in certain ways, and why we are disposed to do so, but we have not remotely come to grips with the central problem, namely conscious experience itself. When thirty seconds are up, we find ourselves looking at a red rose, inhaling its fragrance, and wondering: "Why do I experience it like *this*?" And we realize that this explanation has nothing to say about the matter.

If this position is not taken as a kind of eliminativism, it can perhaps be taken as a kind of functionalist position, in which the notion of consciousness is construed as "the thing responsible for judgments about consciousness." But this is as inadequate as any other functional definition of consciousness. Whether or not consciousness is *in fact* responsible for judgments about consciousness, this does not seem to be a conceptual truth. After all, it is at least *logically* possible that one could explain the judgments without explaining consciousness, whether or not it is plausible; and that is enough to show that this construal of consciousness is a false one.

There are other variations on this line of argument. For instance, one could argue that there is a purely reductive explanation of why I think that consciousness cannot be reductively explained, or of why I think consciousness is not logically supervenient, or of why I think it cannot be functionally defined. We might even reductively explain why I think conscious experience is an explanandum. This might be thought to undercut my arguments in earlier sections entirely, opening the way for a reductive view of consciousness. But again this view can be satisfying only as a kind of intellectual cut and thrust. At the end of the day, we still need to explain why it is *like this* to be a conscious agent. An explanation of behavior or of some causal role is simply explaining the wrong thing. This might seem to be mule-headed stubbornness, but it is grounded in a simple principle: our theories must explain what cries out for explanation.

This line of argument is perhaps the most interesting that a reductionist or eliminativist can take—if I were a reductionist, I would be this sort of reductionist—but at the end of the day it suffers from the problem that all such positions face: it does not explain what needs to be explained. Tempting as this position is, it ends up failing to take the problem seriously. The puzzle of consciousness cannot be removed by such simple means.[3]

Dennett on phenomenal judgments

One advocate of the position that our judgments about consciousness are all we need to explain is Daniel Dennett. In a 1979 paper he writes:

> I am left defending the view that such judgments *exhaust* our immediate consciousness, that our individual stream of consciousness consists of nothing but such propositional episodes, or better: that such streams of consciousness, composed exclusively of such propositional episodes, are the reality that inspires the variety of misdescriptions that pass for theories of consciousness, both homegrown and academic. . . . My view, put bluntly, is that there is no phenomenological manifold in any such relation to our reports. There are the public reports we issue, and then there are the episodes of our propositional awareness, our judgments, and then there is—so far as introspection is concerned—darkness. (1979, p. 95)

To this, all I can say is that Dennett's introspection is very different from mine. When I introspect, I find sensations, experiences of pain and emotion, and all sorts of other accoutrements that, although *accompanied* by judgments, are not *only* judgments—unless one *redefines* the notion of judgment, or of "episodes of our propositional awareness," to include such experiences. If we redefine the terms in this way, then Dennett's position is reasonable, but there is no longer any reason to suppose that our judgments can be reductively explained. If judgments are instead construed as functionally individuated states such as dispositions to report, as I think Dennett intends, then his thesis becomes implausible. It simply consists in a denial of the data that a theory of consciousness must explain.

What might be going on when someone claims that introspection reveals only judgments? Perhaps Dennett is a zombie.[4] Perhaps he means something unusual by "judgment." Most likely, however, he has taken something else for introspection: what we might call *extrospection,* the process of observing one's own cognitive mechanisms "from the outside," as it were, and reflecting on what is going on. Observing one's *mechanisms,* it is easy to come to the conclusion that it is judgments that are doing all the work. All that is going on in the relevant cognitive processes is a lot of categorization, distinction, and reaction. The processes involved with my perception of a yellow object can plausibly be fully explained in terms of certain retinal sensitivities, transformations into internal representations, and categorization and labeling of these representations. But this does not explain the contents of introspection; it explains only the *processes* involved. Extrospection is not introspection, although it is easy to see how a philosopher inclined to speculate on his own internal mechanisms could take one for the other. Conscious experience remains untouched by this explanatory method. (Perhaps the descriptions just given might provide an excellent account of the phenomenology of *blindsight* (described in Chapter 6), if not of ordinary consciousness!)

A similar move is made by Dennett in what is perhaps the central argument of *Consciousness Explained* (1991). Having presented his theory of reportability, Dennett needs to argue that it explains everything that needs to be explained, and in particular that it explains experience insofar as experience needs to be explained. After much preliminary skirmishing, he makes the crucial argument (pp. 363–64) that a theory of experience needs to explain why things *seem* the way they do to us. And he argues that his theory can explain why things seem the way they do to us. Hence, he concludes, his theory explains everything that needs to be explained.

This is an elegant argument, with a ring of plausibility that many reductionist arguments about consciousness lack. But its elegance derives from the way it exploits a subtle ambiguity in the notion of "seeming," which balances on the knife-edge between the phenomenal and psychological realms. There is a phenomenal sense of "seem," in which for things to seem a certain way is just for them to be *experienced* a certain way. And there is a psychological sense of "seem," in which for things to seem a certain way is for us to be disposed to judge that they are that way. It is in the first sense that a theory of experience must explain the way things seem. But it is in the second sense that Dennett's theory explains it.[5]

Once this subtle equivocation is noted, the argument loses most of its force. When Dennett says that his theory explains the way things seem to us, what this ultimately comes to is that it explains why we *say* that things are that way, and why we behave correspondingly in other fashions. (As Dennett himself notes, his theory of consciousness is grounded in his quasi-behaviorist theory of content.) But that sort of explanation falls far short of what a theory of consciousness needs to explain. At the end of the day, calling a theory of this sort a theory of consciousness begs all the important questions.

In general, when one starts from phenomenal judgments as the explananda of one's theory of consciousness, one will inevitably be led to a reductive view. But the ultimate explananda are not the judgments but experiences themselves. No mere explanation of dispositions to behave will explain why there is something it is like to be a conscious agent.

4. Arguments Against Explanatory Irrelevance

We have seen that the paradox of phenomenal judgment leads to counterintuitive consequences. But so far this is all that we have seen. Some people will think that the consequences are not just counterintuitive but fatal. To establish this, these objectors need an *argument*. Such an argument would show us why the explanatory irrelevance of consciousness simply cannot be true.

Such arguments are surprisingly hard to come by, but they can be made. The general idea is to argue that explanatory irrelevance is inconsistent with some well-established fact about ourselves. I can see three ways this might go. It might be argued that explanatory irrelevance is inconsistent with the fact that we *know* about our conscious experiences; or that it is inconsistent with the fact that we *remember* our conscious experiences; or that it is inconsistent with the fact that we *refer* to our conscious experiences. I do not think that any of these arguments are compelling, but they all raise interesting issues and all need to be expressed.

Some of these arguments are most naturally framed in terms of *causal* irrelevance rather than explanatory irrelevance. In order to give these arguments their full power, I will temporarily concede the causal irrelevance of experience, in order to see whether the arguments succeed. It is possible that similar arguments could be made wholly in terms of explanatory irrelevance, but they would be more complicated. In any case, I have at least allowed that it *might* turn out that experience is causally irrelevant, and it is interesting to see whether this would have fatal consequences.

In order to allow an opponent's objections their full force, I will also occasionally speak of "beliefs" rather than "judgments" in what follows. As

I noted earlier, my main line of defense will not turn on the distinction between beliefs and judgments, so I will not make too much of it here. That issue might still have a supporting role to play, though. In what follows, it should at least be kept in the back of one's mind that (1) when talking about a zombie's beliefs and judgments, a deflationary notion is being stipulated, and (2) my own phenomenal beliefs, in the full sense, may be partly constituted by conscious experience.

5. The Argument from Self-Knowledge*

The most difficult problem posed by explanatory irrelevance is the one I have already discussed: our knowledge of our own conscious experiences. On the face of it, we do not just *judge* that we have conscious experiences; we *know* that we have conscious experiences. But if a nonreductive view is right, then experience is explanatorily irrelevant to the formation of the judgment; the same judgment would have been formed even if experience were absent. It may therefore seem hard to see how that judgment can qualify as *knowledge*.

This might simply be phrased as a *challenge*: If experience is explanatorily irrelevant, how can we know about experience? As such, it is an important challenge, and one of the central questions about conscious experience. There are already many such difficult questions, however, and we may not be able to answer them before we develop a detailed theory of consciousness. It can also be phrased more strongly as an *argument*: If experience is explanatorily irrelevant, then we *could not* know that we have experiences. It is arguments of this sort that I am concerned to answer here. I will also make some suggestions in answer to the challenge, but that is a project that will recur.

I can see two related ways that such an argument might go. First, it might proceed directly from the possibility of my zombie twin. My zombie twin makes the same phenomenal judgments that I do. Where I judge that I am conscious, he judges that he is conscious. Further, his judgments are produced by the same *mechanisms* as my judgments. If *justification* accrues to judgments solely in virtue of the mechanisms by which they are formed, as is often supposed, then the zombie's judgments will be as justified as mine. But surely his judgments are not justified at all. After all, they are utterly and systematically false. It seems to follow that *my* judgments cannot be justified, either. They are produced by the same mechanisms that are responsible for deluded judgments in a zombie, and so they surely cannot qualify as knowledge.

If my phenomenal judgments are no more justified than a zombie's, then the ground is cut out from under the nonreductive position. The very starting point of the nonreductive position, our knowledge of the fact of experience, would be destroyed. It follows that this point functions as both a challenge and an argument. As a challenge: How can my judgments be any more justified than a zombie's, given that they are formed by the same mechanisms? As an argument: If my judgments are formed by the same mechanisms as a zombie's, they cannot be any more justified.

The second argument appeals to a *causal theory of knowledge.* It is often held that the crucial factor in justifying a belief about an entity is an appropriate causal connection between the belief and the entity it is about. My beliefs about the table I am looking at, for example, are justified at least in part by the fact that the table is causally responsible for the beliefs. Proponents of a causal theory hold that a judgment about some object or state of affairs must bear a causal relation to that object or state of affairs if it is to count as knowledge (perhaps with exceptions in *a priori* domains such as conceptual or mathematical knowledge). Certainly, it seems that if my belief that John is in the pool bears no causal relation to John or the pool, then I do not know that John is in the pool.

But experience is causally irrelevant, or so I am conceding for now. A conscious experience plays no causal role in the formation of a judgment about that experience. If a causal theory of knowledge is correct, it follows that we cannot know anything about our experiences. Again, there is a challenge and an argument. The challenge: How can I know about experience, given that experience does not cause my judgments? The argument: If experience plays no causal role in the formation of my judgments, then they cannot count as knowledge.

Shoemaker (1975a) uses arguments like these to argue for materialism about consciousness, and in fact to argue for reductive functionalism. Shoemaker explicitly assumes a causal theory of knowledge, arguing that if we are to know about experience, then it must cause our introspective beliefs about experience. He also uses a version of the zombie argument to support reductive functionalism. If zombies or their functional equivalents are logically possible, then experience is inaccessible to introspection: zombies have the same introspective mechanisms that we do, so those mechanisms do not allow us to determine whether or not we are zombies. Shoemaker concludes that zombies and their functional equivalents must be logically impossible.

The response to all of these arguments is fairly clear, I think. A property dualist should argue that a causal theory of knowledge is not appropriate for our knowledge of consciousness, and that the justification of our judgments about consciousness does not lie with the mechanisms by which those judgments are formed. Knowledge of conscious experience is in many important respects quite different from knowledge in other domains. Our knowledge of conscious experience does not consist in a causal relationship to experience, but in another sort of relationship entirely.

This conclusion can be supported on independent grounds. One way to come to this independent support is to first consider another way that a property dualist might try to respond: through a *reliabilist* theory of knowledge. This might seem a promising response at first, but I think that one can see that a reliabilist theory is inappropriate for dealing with our knowledge of consciousness. It turns out that a causal theory is inappropriate for the same reason.

On a reliabilist theory, beliefs about a subject matter are justified if they are formed by a *reliable* process; that is, if they are formed by a process that tends to produce true beliefs. Perceptual beliefs, for example, are justified if they come about via optical stimulation from objects in the environment, a process that generally produces true beliefs; they are not justified if they are produced by hallucination, which is a very unreliable mechanism. It is entirely compatible with a nonreductive theory of experience that in the actual world, our phenomenal judgments are reliable: at least as a matter of nomic correlation, it seems likely that when one judges that one is having a visual experience, one is having a visual experience. The phenomenal judgments of my zombie twin, by contrast, are entirely unreliable; his judgments are generally false.

It might therefore seem that a reliabilist theory is the answer to our difficulties: it implies that our judgments about experience might be justified even in the absence of a direct causal connection, and it has the resources to explain the fact that my judgments are justified while my zombie twin's are not. But many will find that the appeal to a reliabilist theory is unsatisfying all the same; it has the feeling of a slippery maneuver that cannot meet the burden it is being asked to carry. The knowledge that a reliabilist theory grants us seems too weak to count as the kind of knowledge that we have of our conscious experience. On reflection, it is not hard to see why.

The trouble is that if our beliefs about consciousness were justified *only* by a reliable connection, then we could not be *certain* that we are conscious. The mere existence of a reliable connection cannot deliver certainty, for we have no way to rule out the possibility that the reliable connection is absent and that there is no consciousness at the other end. The only way to be sure here would be to have some *further* access to the other end of the connection; but that would be to say that we have some further basis to our knowledge of consciousness. This situation is often deemed acceptable for our knowledge of the external world: we do not need to be certain that chairs exist in order to *know* (in an everyday sense) that chairs exist, so it is not a problem that we are not certain that there is a reliable connection between chairs and our judgments about chairs. But we are certain that we are conscious; at least, this certainty is at the foundation of the position I have advocated. Perhaps the knowledge that we are conscious can be doubted in various "philosophical" ways, but not in the very direct way—analogous to doubting our knowledge of the external world—that would be granted if our beliefs were justified only by a reliable connection.

Beliefs justified only by a reliable connection are always compatible with the existence of *skeptical hypotheses*. These concern scenarios where things seem exactly the same to a subject but in which the beliefs are false, because the reliable connection does not hold. In the case of perceptual knowledge, for example, one can construct a case in which the reliable connection is absent—a case where the subject is a brain in the vat, say—and everything will still seem the same to the subject. Nothing about a subject's core epistemic situation rules this scenario out. But in the case of consciousness, one cannot construct these skeptical hypotheses. Our core epistemic situation already *includes* our conscious experience. There is no situation in which everything seems just the same to us but in which we are not conscious, as our conscious experience is (at least partly) constitutive of the way things seem.

It is notable that in constructing skeptical scenarios relevant to other sorts of knowledge, such as our knowledge of the external world, philosophers are always careful to stipulate that a skeptical scenario is *experientially* identical to the original scenario. As Descartes noted, skepticism goes only so far. If a skeptical scenario involves a vastly different set of experiences at its center—a host of bright flashing yellow and green experiences with a deafening noise, say—then it is ruled out automatically. We *know* (in a much stronger sense than before) that such a situation is not our situation.

It follows that a reliabilist account of knowledge cannot deliver knowledge that is strong enough to have the character of our knowledge of conscious experience, and is therefore inappropriate in this case. But everything I have said about a reliabilist account of knowledge also applies to a causal account of knowledge. Where there is causation, there is contingency: a causal connection that holds might not have held. If the sole source of justification for a belief about X is a causal connection to X, then a subject cannot know for certain that the causal connection exists. The only way they might know this for certain would be if they had some *independent* access to X or to the causal chain, but this would imply knowledge grounded in something more than the causal chain itself. There will always be a skeptical scenario in which everything seems just the same to the subject, but in which the causal connection is absent and in which X does not exist; so the subject cannot know for certain about X. But we do know for certain that we are conscious; so a causal account of this knowledge is inappropriate.

Of course, an opponent might simply deny that our knowledge of consciousness is certain, and assert that there *are* skeptical scenarios that we cannot rule out—a zombie scenario, for example. But anyone who takes this view will likely be an eliminativist (or a reductive functionalist) about consciousness from the start. If one accepts that our immediate evidence does not rule out the possibility that we are zombies, then one should embrace the conclusion that we *are* zombies: it leads to a much simpler view of the world, for a start. But the reason there is a problem about consciousness is that our immediate evidence *does* rule out that possibility. To take consciousness seriously is to accept that we have immediate evidence that rules out its nonexistence. Of course, all this is open to argument in the usual way; but the point is that there is no special reason to start disputing this at *this* point in the argument. Eliminativists and reductive functionalists have departed long ago. *If* one takes consciousness seriously, then one has good reason to believe that a causal or reliabilist account of our phenomenal knowledge is inappropriate.

What justifies phenomenal judgments?

The basic problem with the accounts above is that they make our access to consciousness *mediated,* in the way that our access to objects in the environment is mediated, by some sort of causal chain or reliable mechanism. This sort of mediation is appropriate when there is a gap between our core epistemic situation and the phenomena in question, as in the case of the external world: we are connected to objects in the environment from a distance. But intuitively, our access to consciousness is not mediated at all. Conscious experience lies at the center of our epistemic universe; we have access to it *directly*.

This raises a question. What is it that justifies our beliefs about our experiences, if it is not a causal link to those experiences, and if it is not the mechanisms by which the beliefs are formed? I think the answer to this is clear: it is *having* the experiences that justifies the beliefs. For example, the very fact that I have a red experience now provides justification for my belief that I am having a red experience. Change the red experience to a different sort of experience, or remove it altogether, and the chief source of justification for my belief is removed. When I believe that I am experiencing a loud noise, my warrant for that belief stems chiefly from my experience of a loud noise. Indeed, one might ask, from where else could it stem?

We can put the point by noting, as before, that experience is part of our core epistemic situation. Replace my bright red experiences by dull green experiences, and you change my evidence for some of my beliefs, including my belief that I am having a bright red experience. This is mirrored in the fact that there is no way to construct a skeptical scenario in which I am in a qualitatively equivalent epistemic position, but in which my experiences are radically different. My experiences are *part* of my epistemic situation, and simply having them gives me evidence for some of my beliefs.

All this is to say that there is something intrinsically epistemic about experience. To have an experience is automatically to stand in some sort of intimate epistemic relation to the experience—a relation that we might call "acquaintance." There is not even a conceptual possibility that a subject could have a red experience like this one without having *any* epistemic contact with it: to have the experience is to be related to it in this way.

Note that I do not say that to have an experience is automatically to *know* about it, in the sense in which knowledge requires belief. I think that thesis would be false: we have many experiences that we do not have beliefs about, and so do not know about. Further, one might have an experience without conceptualizing the experience in any way. To have an experience, and consequently to be acquainted with the experience, is to stand in a relationship to it more primitive than belief: it provides *evidence* for our beliefs, but it does not in itself constitute belief.

Indeed, nothing I have said implies that all beliefs about experiences are incorrigible, in that every such belief is automatically fully justified. Because beliefs about experiences lie at a distance from experiences, they can be formed for all sorts of reasons, and sometimes unjustified beliefs will be formed. If one is distracted, for example, one may make judgments about one's experiences that are quite false. The claim is not that having an experience is the *only* factor that may be relevant to the justification or lack of justification of a belief about experience. The claim is simply that it is *a* factor—perhaps the primary factor—and provides a potential source of justification that is not present when the experience is absent.

Some might find all this an *ad hoc* construction to save a troubled theory, but I do not think it is *ad hoc*. We have very good reason, quite independent of any considerations about explanatory irrelevance, to believe that the epistemology of experience is special, and very different in kind from epistemology in other domains. Many have spoken of our "direct knowledge" of or "acquaintance" with experience, without being forced into the position as a defensive maneuver. Many have even claimed that knowledge of experience is the foundation of all knowledge, precisely because we stand in such a direct epistemic relationship to it. The claim that all knowledge derives from knowledge of experience may have been overblown, but the general point that there is something special about our knowledge of experience has never been overturned.[6]

Similarly, the claim that experiences themselves justify our beliefs about experience is easy to motivate on independent grounds. For example, in his careful discussion of our knowledge of our own minds, Siewert (1994)—who takes consciousness seriously, but who shows no signs of sympathy with the view that consciousness is explanatorily irrelevant—gives an in-depth defense of the view that we have a "first-person warrant" for our beliefs about our experiences, a warrant that is grounded at least partly in our having the experiences. So it is not going out on a limb to see experience as providing a direct source of justification.

Answering the arguments

Given all this, the answer to the arguments against explanatory irrelevance is straightforward. In response to the argument from the causal theory of knowledge, we note that there is independent reason to believe that the causal theory is inappropriate to explicate our knowledge of experience: our knowledge of experience is grounded in a more immediate relation. And in response to the argument from my zombie twin, we note that the justification of my beliefs about experience involves more than the mechanisms by which the beliefs are formed: it crucially involves experiences themselves. Because my zombie twin lacks experiences, he is in a very different epistemic situation from me, and his judgments lack the corresponding justification.

It may be tempting to object that if my belief lies in the physical realm, its justification must lie in the physical realm; but this is a nonsequitur. From the fact that there is no justification in the physical realm, one might conclude that the *physical* portion of me (my brain, say) is not justified in its belief. But the question is whether *I* am justified in the belief, not whether my *brain* is justified in the belief, and if property dualism is correct then there is more to me than my brain. I am constituted by both physical and nonphysical properties, and the full story about me cannot be told by focusing on only one half. In particular, the justification of my belief accrues not just in virtue of my physical features but in virtue of some of my nonphysical features—namely the experiences themselves.

It might still be objected, "But the belief would still have been formed even if the experience had been absent!" To this, the answer is, "So what?" In *this* case, I have *evidence* for my belief, namely my immediate acquaintance with experience. In a different case, that evidence is absent. To note that in a different case the belief might have been formed in the absence of the evidence is not to say that the evidence does not justify the belief in this case.[7] I *know* I am conscious, and the knowledge is based solely on my immediate experience. To say that the experience makes no difference to my psychological functioning is not to say that the experience makes no difference to *me*.

Finally, there is a persistent refrain that comes up in these situations: "But your zombie twin would say the same thing!" If I say I know I am conscious, it is noted that my zombie twin says the same. If I say my belief is justified by my immediate acquaintance with experience, it is noted that my zombie twin says the same. To this, the answer is again, "So what?" At most this shows that from the *third-person* point of view, my zombie twin and I are identical, so that *you* cannot be certain that I am conscious; but we knew this all along. But it does nothing to imply that from the *first-person* view, I cannot know I am conscious. From the first-person point of view, my zombie twin and I are very different: I have experiences, and he does not. Because of this, I have evidence for my belief where he does not. Despite the fact that he says the same things I do, I know that I am not him (though *you* might not be sure) because of my direct first-person acquaintance with my experiences. This may sound somewhat paradoxical at first, but really it is simply saying the obvious: our experience of consciousness enables us to know that we are conscious.

Even when it is objected that my zombie twin would *believe* the same things that I would, this does nothing to make plausible the first-person skeptical hypothesis that I might be a zombie. Underlying this sort of objection may be the implicit assumption that the beliefs themselves are the primary determinants of my epistemic situation; so if there is a situation in which I believe exactly the same things that I do now, it is a situation that is evidentially equivalent to my current one. But of course this is false. The evidence for my beliefs about experiences is much more primitive than the beliefs themselves. It is experience itself that is primary; the beliefs are largely a secondary phenomenon.

It should also be remembered that we are stipulating a *deflationary* (i.e., functional) notion of belief, so to say that my zombie twin believes the same things as me is still only to make a claim about our commonalities from the third-person point of view: he is disposed to make the same sorts of claims, the same sort of inferences, and so on. This says nothing about how things are from the inside. The feeling that "a zombie would have the same beliefs" provides an objection here may stem from assuming an *inflationary* notion of belief, in which belief is at least in part an experiential phenomenon. Only in that sense might it be the case that identity in beliefs would make the situations indistinguishable from the first-person point of view; but of course in that sense there is no reason to accept that a zombie has the same beliefs in the first place.

The upshot of all this is that arguments about self-knowledge provide no reason to reject the view I advocate. If one takes consciousness seriously, one will already have good reason to embrace an epistemology of consciousness that renders these arguments toothless. Although there are many tempting arguments that can be made, none of them appear to stand up to scrutiny.

Very much remains to be done in clarifying the first-person epistemology of consciousness, of course. At best I have sketched the bare outline of a framework for thinking about these things; many issues remain to be dealt with. In particular, one would like an analysis of just *how* an experience justifies a belief; of what other factors are relevant in justifying beliefs about experiences; of under just what circumstances a belief about experience is fully justified; and so on. All of these are important questions that deserve to be taken up at length in a study of the epistemology of consciousness. But all of these are part of the *challenge,* and on the face of it there is no reason to believe that the challenge cannot be met. What is important is that the *arguments* that self-knowledge might appear to provide against a nonreductive view of experience do not succeed.

6. The Argument from Memory*

The second objection to the causal or explanatory irrelevance of experience is that it is incompatible with the fact that we *remember* our experiences. It certainly seems that I often remember my old experiences, as when I recall the tangy odor of mothballs in a closet when I was a child, or when I recollect a particularly vivid experience of orange while I was watching the sun set last night. But to remember something, it is often held, is to stand in an appropriate causal relation to it; this is sometimes known as the *causal theory of memory.* If experiences are causally irrelevant to my psychological functioning, however, it seems that my old experiences are not causally related to any of my current states. If so, then we could not remember our experiences at all.

The causal theory of memory is not written in stone, however. It comes from an analysis of what seems the appropriate thing to say about various cases. As with the case of knowledge, it may be that a causal theory is appropriate in many domains without being appropriate across the board. In particular, it is not obvious that it is appropriate in the domain of experience. Causal theories might not be *as* inappropriate in the case of memory as they are in the case of knowledge, as there is no doubt that our relation to a remembered experience is mediated, and it is plausible that much of that mediation involves a causal chain. But this is not to say that the causal chain tells the whole story.

In the case of remembered experiences, there will certainly be a causal connection at the level of *psychology*: the underlying cognitive state at the time of the original experience will be causally connected to the cognitive state at the time of the memory. And it seems plausible that an appropriate causal connection of this sort is all that is required for memory of experience. For example, there may be a causal connection between a phenomenal *belief* at the earlier time and beliefs at the later time; and if what I have said in the previous section is correct, this original belief may count as *knowledge,* being justified by an acquaintance with the experience itself. This sort of causal connection between a belief justified by acquaintance and a later belief seems quite sufficient for the later belief to count as an instance of memory. So there seems to be good reason to believe that a causal connection to an experience is not required to remember that experience.

Of course the question of just what counts as a "memory" and what counts as merely a justified true belief about the past is largely a semantic decision in these cases. What is important is that a nonreductive theory can save the appearances by giving a mechanism by which true beliefs about one's past experiences are formed. As long as a nonreductive theory can do this, then any *argument* that memory provides against such a theory is defanged. If someone *insists* that a causal connection to an object is required for memory, then we can simply say that we "pseudo-remember" experiences instead, or some such, and nothing important will be lost. But in any case it seems to me that a causal connection to a relevant original psychological state is quite enough for these beliefs to qualify as memories.

7. The Argument from Reference*

The third argument against the causal or explanatory irrelevance of consciousness is that it is incompatible with our ability to *refer* to our conscious experiences. Certainly, it seems that we can think about our conscious experiences, and talk about them—I have been doing that throughout this book. But it is sometimes held that reference to an entity requires a causal connection to that entity; this is known as the causal theory of reference. If so, then it would be impossible to refer to causally irrelevant experiences.

There seems to be no principled reason why reference to an entity *requires* a causal connection to that entity, however. Reference frequently involves a causal connection, but it is not clear that things have to be that way. In referring to an entity, all that is required is that our concepts have *intensions* (in particular, primary intensions) that the entity might satisfy. For example, my concept "the largest star in the universe" has a primary intension, picking out a referent in any given centered world. In the actual world, this intension picks out a certain star S—whether or not I am causally connected to S—so S qualifies as the referent of the concept. Given that there is a primary intension that an entity in the actual world might satisfy, we have the basic ingredients needed for reference.

It happens that for many of our concepts, primary intensions are characterized causally: at a given centered world, they pick out an appropriate entity that is causally connected to the center. This is the insight of the so-called causal theory of reference. But there is no reason why a primary intension *has* to work this way. There are many other functions that pick out, in a hypothetical centered world, an entity that has no causal connection to the center. Such functions might make perfectly good primary intensions, with a perfectly good referent.

Further, the *existence* of a primary intension—even in cases where a primary intension is characterized causally—does not depend in any way on a causal connection to the referent. The primary intension is independent of those actual-world goings on. A causal connection may often play a role in *evaluating* the primary intension at a world, but this is very different from playing a role in determining the primary intension itself. Indeed, some of our concepts (e.g., "Santa Claus") have no referent at all, but they still have a primary intension—an intension that *could* have picked out a referent if the world had turned out the right way.

It will often be the case that causal connection to a referent plays a role in *acquiring* a concept, and thus in forming a primary intension. One might argue that even in the case of "the largest star in the universe," causal connections to the world play a role in acquiring the basic concepts from which this compositional concept is formed. But again, there seems to be no principled reason why the existence of a primary intension *requires* a causal connection to relevant subject matter. Even a brain in a vat might have concepts with primary intensions, despite its causal isolation (though most of them would be intensions that nothing in its world satisfies). Again, the *constitution* of a primary intension is independent of such causal connections.

There is a natural reason why causation is central to so many of our concepts: it is because we generally refer to what we *know* about, and the things we know about are generally things we are causally connected to. But we have already seen that there is good reason to reject the causal model of knowledge at least in the case of consciousness: in that case we have knowledge of a more immediate variety. So to refer to consciousness, we do not need to refer via an intension that picks out something that the center is causally connected to; instead, we can refer via an intension that picks out something that the center is immediately acquainted with.

In any case, what is important is that (1) my concept of "consciousness" can have a primary intension, whether or not there is a causal connection to the referent (for the existence of a primary intension never depends on such a causal connection); and (2) the primary intension can pick out a referent whether or not there is a causal connection to the referent (for there is no reason why a primary intension must pick out its referent in virtue of a causal connection). The intension specifies a perfectly good function from centered worlds to features of those worlds; in this world, there is something that satisfies the intension, so my concept has a referent. As we have seen, consciousness is something of a primitive concept (like space and time, perhaps), so there is no hope of characterizing the intension in detail in the way one might for some concepts; but there is no reason to believe that it should not be perfectly capable of picking out a referent in a world.

8. The Content of Phenomenal Beliefs*

Even if it is accepted that property dualism is compatible with referring to consciousness, there remain many interesting puzzles about the content of our phenomenal concepts and beliefs. First, there are questions about the nature of our concepts' intensions, both for general concepts such as "consciousness" and for more specific concepts such as "red experience": Just what do they pick out in a given world? And second, there are questions about what *constitutes* the content of our concepts: Is the content constituted by our psychological nature alone, or by our psychological and phenomenal nature, and what role do each of these play? I do not have settled opinions on these matters, but I will at least scratch the surface here.

An interesting way to get at some of these questions is to ask whether there is a difference between the content of my phenomenal beliefs and those of a zombie; and if so, what is it? I return to speaking of "beliefs" here rather than "judgments," as the question is precisely whether there is an element to the content of a phenomenal belief over and above the content of a phenomenal judgment, which was stipulated to be a purely psychological entity. I will allow, at least for the purposes of discussion, that a zombie has beliefs (although his beliefs are certainly nothing over and above his judgments). The question is whether there is any difference between the content of his beliefs and mine. In particular, what is the difference, if any, between the truth conditions of our respective beliefs, and between the intensions of our respective concepts?

One line that could be taken is that the content of our beliefs and concepts is exactly the same. On this view, the zombie has concepts of "consciousness" and of "red experience" with the same primary intensions as my corresponding concepts, and beliefs with the same (primary) truth conditions. His concept "conscious being," for example, still picks out the conscious beings in a given centered world. It is just that in his world, there are no such beings; or at least, he is not such a being. So his belief "I am conscious" has the same (primary) truth conditions as my belief; the only difference is that his belief is false where mine is true.

To evaluate this line, one needs to consider some specific questions. First, when a zombie says, "I am conscious," does he speak falsely? Some might say no: we should interpret the zombie's remark charitably, so that his concept refers to some functional property that he instantiates, and the remark comes out true.[8] But the zombie (at least if he is my zombie twin) will certainly insist that his is not a functional concept: he means to refer to a property of his over and above his ability to discriminate, categorize, report, and so on. It seems reasonable to take his word on this. Of course we can also allow a "deflationary" interpretation of his words, so that claims such as "I have regained consciousness" might come out true in everyday contexts; but at least in philosophical contexts, it seems reasonable to hold his concepts to the higher standard that he intends, so that his beliefs come out false. It is not as if he is suffering under a conceptual confusion that could be cleared up by more careful conceptual analysis. (If he could do that, I could do it too; but this discussion is premised on the idea that I am not suffering from such a conceptual confusion.) So there seems to be a reasonable sense in which his claims of consciousness are false.[9]

This is not enough to show that the zombie's concept has the *same* intension as mine, however. Perhaps this only shows that he has a concept something like "property over and above any physical and functional property," without possessing the full-blown concept of consciousness. The real test is whether there are any centered worlds in which everything relevant is identical, but in which a zombie's belief has a different truth-value from mine. For example, what if we are both talking to a conscious being? I say, "You are conscious," and speak truly. If he says, "You are conscious," does he speak truly? Some might say no, because he lacks the immediate acquaintance with consciousness to give him the full concept. But there is also an intuition that "yes" may be reasonable.

Perhaps the most relevant examples involve a hypothetical being with some nonstructural, nonfunctional intrinsic property that is *not* a phenomenal property—if there could be such a property—where the property stands in the usual sort of relations that phenomenal properties stand in. When I say, "You are conscious," to such a being, I speak falsely; but perhaps when my zombie twin says this, then if he spoke truly in the previous case, he also speaks truly here? In the absence of any acquaintance with consciousness, it is hard to see how the zombie's concept could be specific enough to distinguish the two cases. If so, then the zombie's concept of consciousness falls short of the full-blown concept.

If our acquaintance with consciousness plays a role in constituting the primary intension of our concept, this would mean that the concept of "consciousness" is interestingly different from other concepts, such as "water." In these cases the primary intension is independent of the actual referent; a cognitive system with a different referent, or with no referent at all, might have the same primary intension. But consciousness is not an ordinary referent: our relation to it is unmediated, and it is at the center of our mental lives, so it might play an unusually strong role in constituting a primary intension. In any case, I leave the question open.

What about *specific* phenomenal concepts, such as the concept of "red experience"? These are somewhat more complicated, as there may be more than one concept in the vicinity of such a term. One way to get at these concepts is to consider how to describe individuals with inverted spectra: for example, someone who, when looking at red things, has the sort of experience I have when looking at green things. When I say that such a person (on looking at a red rose) is having a red experience, there may be a loose sense in which the remark can be taken to be true: in this sense, "red experience" comes to something like "experience of the sort typically caused (in the individual having the experience) by red things." Perhaps there is a public-language concept of "red experience" that works something like this, but in any case I set this one aside.

More natural, perhaps, is a sense in which such a remark is false: the person is not having a red experience but a green experience. In one way of explicating such a sense, the primary intension of my concept "red experience" might come to something like "experience of the sort typically caused (in me) by red things." This sense has some interesting properties: for example, if you and I have spectra inverted relative to each other, then your concept "green experience" will pick out (what I call) *red* experiences. It follows that your remark "Grass gives me green experiences" might be true, even though my remark "Grass gives you green experiences" is false. This is occasionally found distasteful,[10] but it is a natural consequence of the indexicality of the concept (a similar phenomenon arises with "I"-remarks, and with the "water"-remarks of me and my Twin Earth twin). If one wants to avoid this sort of thing, the more "public" concept characterized above is always available.[11]

The primary intension of this concept "red experience" should be quite straightforward, if the general concept of experience is already granted. Your concept "red experience" may have the same primary intension as mine, even if our spectra are inverted: both pick out the same entities at a given centered world (experiences of the sort typically caused at the center by red things), although of course our concepts will have different *referents,* as we inhabit different centered worlds (mine is centered on me, and yours on you). Because of this, our concepts may also have different secondary intensions: mine picks out red experiences in a counterfactual world, whereas yours picks out green experiences. Even a zombie might have the same primary intension as the two of us, at least insofar as it has the concept of experience at all, although of course its intension will not pick out anything at its centered world, and its concept "red experience" will fail to refer.

There is more to the story than this, however. This relational construal of the concept "red experience" is still relatively peripheral. One has a concept in the vicinity—perhaps the most important concept in these discussions—that is not exhausted by the relational characterization. In particular, one has a concept of the *quality* of red experiences. Nothing in the relational characterization above captures the concept of this quality, as witnessed by the fact that the primary intension characterized above is compatible with many different qualities. Someone with an inverted spectrum would share that intension, but I have a concept of this quality—call it "*R*"—that is *distinct* from the corresponding concept—call it "*G*"—in my inverted counterpart.

At first glance, one might think it enough that this quality is captured by the *secondary* intension of my concept "red experience" as characterized above. As we have seen, my inverted counterpart and I have different secondary intensions corresponding to the different qualities picked out by our "red experience" concepts. But capturing it in a secondary intension is not enough. To see this, note that it is *informative* to learn that red experiences (that is, experiences caused by red objects) have their specific quality. That is, it is far from *a priori* that red experiences should be *R*. In learning this, one narrows down one's model of the way the actual world is: the sort of experience that is caused by red things might have been *this* way or *this* way, but instead it is *this* way. And this sort of informativeness requires a difference in primary intension: when two concepts have the same primary intension, it is *a priori* that they are coextensive.[12]

Another way to see this is to note that when Mary has a red experience for the first time, she learns something *different* from what is learned by her inverted twin, who has green experiences where Mary has red. Mary learns that red things cause experiences like *this,* whereas her counterpart learns that they cause experiences like *that.* Their models of the world are narrowed down in different ways: Mary now endorses one set of centered worlds, where her twin endorses another. It follows that their concepts of the qualities in question must have different primary intensions. Mary's primary intension picks out experiences of one sort (*this* sort) in any given centered world, whereas her counterpart's picks out experiences of a different sort.

My qualitative concept "*R*" plays little direct role in communicative practices. In that way, it resembles Wittgenstein's "beetle in a box."[13] My inverted counterpart has a different concept "*G*" in the vicinity, but others understand him to be saying the same things that they understand me to be saying, assuming that their own situations remain constant across the two scenarios. This reflects the "ineffability" that I noted in Chapter 1: despite the rich intrinsic nature of red sensations, there is little I can say to communicate this difference apart from pinning it down via various relational properties, and assuming that others have the same associated experiences. That is, it appears to be the relational concept of "red experience" that carries the communicative burden. This ineffability can be seen as providing indirect support for the explanatory irrelevance of experience: the fact that there is little one can *say* that captures the intrinsic quality of the experience meshes well with the fact that the quality plays no direct role in governing cognitive processes.[14]

(Of course, one can still *talk* about these qualities, as I have done on occasion throughout this book. I can express my phenomenal beliefs in language; it is just that my language will communicate the full content of my beliefs to others only if they have the relevant qualities for themselves, standing in the same sort of relevant relations.)

This clearly provides a case where the content of our concepts and beliefs is constituted by something over and above our physical and functional structure, so that no reductive account of the belief contents will succeed.[15] My inverted twin and I might be physically identical, but our corresponding qualitative concepts are distinct, not just in reference but in primary intension. Here, even more clearly than in the case of "consciousness," is a case where the content of a phenomenal belief is constituted by phenomenology itself. Something undeniably interesting is going on here: somehow a sort of experience, which one might think of as the *referent* of a qualitative concept, is getting inside the concept and constituting its *sense* (where sense is equated with primary intension). This is quite unlike standard cases where the object of a concept might play a role in constituting a secondary intension but not a primary intension.[16] It is made possible only by the fact that experience is at the *heart* of the mind.

We see then that there is in fact something more to a phenomenal belief than to a phenomenal judgment, at least in these cases. It is possible that this might help in understanding the epistemology of consciousness. For example, the most specific case of this sort of constitution relation will arise when only a single S experience is involved in constituting a phenomenal concept S ("*this* sort of experience"[17]). The direct constitution relation—the way the experience gets inside the concept, so to speak—might help us in understanding how the experience itself could justify a belief to the effect that the experience is S. Certainly, this gives a tight relation between the experience and the belief of a sort that might be thought appropriate. And given this sort of specific justified phenomenal belief, one can see how more general justified phenomenal beliefs (such as the belief that one is conscious) might follow. I leave this issue here, as we are entering deep water, but this relation between experiences and phenomenal concepts provides much food for thought.

(Perhaps one might put forward a thesis to the effect that a belief that an experience is S, where the concept S is constituted by the experience itself in the above fashion, is always justified. There would still be unjustified phenomenal beliefs, but these would arise in cases where there is a different relation between the concept and the experience, such as when a concept constituted by one experience—or one set of experiences, or an extrinsic description—is applied to another experience. Perhaps this relatively weak thesis might capture an element of what is plausible in standard "incorrigibility" theses, while at the same time leaving room for all the usual counterexamples; it might even serve as the central plank in a detailed account of the epistemology of experience. But I am unsure about this.)

The fact that there is an element in my belief that is not present in my zombie twin's corresponding belief may also help deflate any intuitions supporting the epistemological arguments mentioned previously. It is *only* our judgments (functionally construed) that are the same: it is not true that the same *beliefs* would have been present even if the experience had been absent.[18] And it is beliefs, after all, that are most central here. We have seen that this sort of distinctness in beliefs is not required to defeat the epistemological arguments (I did not assume it in the earlier discussion), but it may nevertheless help remove any lingering doubts in the vicinity.

It is natural to wonder how far this sort of constitution of content by experience might extend. The fact that this holds for specific phenomenal concepts lends further support to the idea that it does so for the more general concept of "consciousness," although the question of the relationship between my concept and that of a zombie remains unclear. One might then wonder whether experience could play a role in constituting the content of *non*phenomenal concepts, such as concepts of external kinds, as some philosophers have suggested. It is not obvious how the extension would be made, but perhaps the fact that experience plays this role in one case lends some support to the idea that it might in others.

In any case, nothing here requires a causal theory of reference. Indeed, a causal connection to experience would probably be inappropriate in allowing the sort of direct relationship that we find between experiences and the primary intensions of phenomenal concepts: in all the usual cases in which there is a causal connection ("water," for example), there is no such relationship. Instead, it appears to be our immediate acquaintance with experience that makes this sort of constitution possible. So a causal connection to experience is not required to constitute possession of the relevant primary intensions; and certainly no causal connections are required for the primary intensions to pick out a referent in these cases; so there is no principled difficulty with referring to experience, even on a property dualist view.

It appears, then, that while the explanatory irrelevance of experience to physical behavior may be counterintuitive at first, there are no strong arguments against it. What might appear to be strong arguments, from epistemology and reference, turn out merely to be challenges. Consideration of these points raises a large number of interesting issues, but at the end of the day we have seen that there is good reason to believe that the epistemology and semantics of experience cannot be essentially causal, and should instead be understood in other terms. I have said a little here about how one might go about understanding those things on a property dualist view. A full understanding of these issues would require a lengthy separate investigation; but I hope I have said enough to make clear that the nonreductive view provides a natural framework for making sense of these issues.

PART III

Toward a Theory of Consciousness

6

The Coherence Between Consciousness and Cognition

1. Toward a Nonreductive Theory

Even if consciousness cannot be reductively explained, there can still be a theory of consciousness. We simply need to move to a *nonreductive* theory instead. We can give up on the project of trying to explain the existence of consciousness wholly in terms of something more basic, and instead admit it as fundamental, giving an account of how it relates to everything else in the world.

Such a theory will be similar in kind to the theories that physics gives us of matter, of motion, or of space and time. Physical theories do not derive the existence of these features from anything more basic, but they still give substantial, detailed accounts of these features and of how they interrelate, with the result that we have satisfying explanations of many specific phenomena involving mass, space, and time. They do this by giving a simple, powerful set of *laws* involving the various features, from which all sorts of specific phenomena follow as a consequence.

By analogy, the cornerstone of a theory of consciousness will be a set of *psychophysical laws* governing the relationship between consciousness and physical systems. We have already granted that consciousness supervenes naturally (although not logically) on the physical. This supervenience must be underwritten by psychophysical laws; an account of these laws will tell us just *how* consciousness depends on physical processes. Given the physical facts about a system, such laws will enable us to infer what sort of conscious experience will be associated with the system, if any. These laws will be on a par with the laws of physics as part of the basic furniture of the universe.

It follows that while this theory will not explain the existence of consciousness in the sense of telling us "why consciousness exists," it will be able to explain specific instances of consciousness, in terms of the underlying physical structure and the psychophysical laws. Again, this is analogous to explanation in physics, which accounts for why specific instances of matter or motion have the character they do by invoking general underlying principles in combination with certain local properties. All sorts of macroscopic physical phenomena can be explained in terms of underlying physical laws; similarly, we might expect that all sorts of "macroscopic" experiential phenomena might be explained by the psychophysical laws in a theory of consciousness.

There need be nothing especially supernatural about these laws. They are part of the basic furniture of nature, just as the laws of physics are. There will be something "brute" about them, it is true. At some level, the laws will have to be taken as true and not further explained. But the same holds in physics: the ultimate laws of nature will always at some point seem arbitrary. It is this that makes them laws of nature rather than laws of logic.

In science, we never get something for nothing: something, somewhere must always be taken for granted. It is a remarkable fact that in most areas of science, all we ultimately need to take for granted are the laws of physics and perhaps some boundary conditions. But there is no reason why the laws of physics should be absolutely privileged in this way. If it turns out that in the study of consciousness one needs to take some aspect of the relationship between physical processes and consciousness for granted, then so be it. That is the price of constructing a theory.

Still, we certainly want to take as little for granted as we possibly can. An ultimate theory will not leave the connection at the level of "Brain state X produces conscious state Y" for a vast collection of complex physical states and associated experiences. Instead, it will systematize this connection via an underlying explanatory framework, specifying simple underlying laws in virtue of which the connection holds. Physics does not content itself with being a mere mass of observations about the positions, velocities, and charges of various objects at various times; it systematizes these observations and shows how they are consequences of underlying laws, where the underlying laws are as simple and as powerful as possible. The same should hold of a theory of consciousness. We should seek to explain the supervenience of consciousness upon the physical in terms of the simplest possible set of laws.

Ultimately, we will wish for a set of *fundamental laws*. Physicists seek a set of basic laws simple enough that one might write them on the front of a T-shirt; in a theory of consciousness, we should expect the same thing. In both cases, we are questing for the basic structure of the universe, and we have good reason to believe that the basic structure has a remarkable simplicity. The discovery of fundamental laws may be a distant goal, however. In physics, we first had laws characterizing macroscopic regularities, and only later proceeded to the underlying fundamental laws. In a theory of consciousness, we might similarly expect to start with *nonbasic* laws, characterizing the relationship between physical processes and conscious experience at a fairly high level. Even this sort of high-level principle might give us significant explanatory purchase in the meantime, just as the principles of thermodynamics were useful well before we had the underlying principles of statistical mechanics. And these high-level laws, once discovered, will put strong constraints on any underlying fundamental laws, thus guiding us in the search for an ultimate theory.

When we finally have fundamental theories of physics and of consciousness in hand, we may have what truly counts as a theory of everything. The fundamental physical laws will explain the character of physical processes; the psychophysical laws will explain the conscious experiences that are associated; and everything else will be a consequence.

Of course, it may be that in the quest for such theories, there will be developments that change our conception of an ultimate theory. It may be, for example, that we will find overarching laws that subsume the phenomena of both physics and consciousness into a grander theory, just as we found a theory that subsumed electricity and magnetism, and as physicists are now searching for a theory that unifies all the basic physical forces. Perhaps there will be developments that are more surprising still. But the current framework at least provides a start in the search for a theory that might serve as a first approximation, providing a springboard for any more radical successor theories that might be in the distance.

How might we build a theory of consciousness?

All this metaphysical grandeur is well and good, one might reply, but how does it cash out in practice? In particular, how can we *discover* the psychophysical laws that will constitute a theory of consciousness? After all, there is an enormous problem for a theory of consciousness that does not confront a theory of physics: the lack of data. Because consciousness is not directly observable in experimental contexts, we cannot simply run experiments measuring the experiences that are associated with various physical processes, thereby confirming and disconfirming various psychophysical hypotheses. Perhaps these laws, even if they exist, might remain in an unknowable limbo? Indeed, it might seem that the untestability of any theory of consciousness that we might put forward would relegate such theories to the status of pseudoscience.

There is certainly something to this worry: it is this that makes a theory of consciousness more difficult to get a grip on than a theory in physics. But it does not disbar us from the search for a theory of consciousness altogether. For a start, we each have access to a rich source of data in our own case.

We know about our own detailed and specific conscious experiences, and we also know about the underlying physical processes, so there is a significant set of regularities right there. Given these regularities, we can invoke some sort of inference to the best explanation to find the simplest possible underlying laws that might generate the regularities. Right now, we do not have even a single set of laws that might do this, so this is far from a trivial constraint on a theory. It might well turn out that there is only one reasonably simple set of laws that gives the right results, in which case we would have good reason to believe that those laws are part of a correct theory.

It might still be objected that all sorts of theories remain compatible with the first-person data: from solipsistic theories (in which only I am conscious) to panpsychist theories (in which everything is conscious); from biochemicalist theories (in which consciousness arises only from certain biochemical organizations) to computationalist theories (in which consciousness arises from anything with the right sort of computational organization); including along the way such bizarre theories as the theory that people are only conscious in odd-numbered years (right now, it is 1995). How can we rule out any of these theories, given that we cannot poke inside others' minds to measure their conscious experience?

All such theories are *logically compatible* with the data, but this is not enough to make them *plausible*. Solipsistic theories, for example, are extremely implausible due to their great arbitrariness (why should only *this* person be conscious?) and their great heterogeneity in space and time (my conscious experience is systematically tied to my physical structure, but a physical duplicate of me located elsewhere will not be conscious at all). All sorts of plausibility considerations play a role in shaping our theories, over and above the role played by empirical evidence, in all sorts of domains. Consider, for example, our acceptance of the theory of evolution, as opposed to the theory that the world was created fifty years ago with memories and fossil record intact. Or consider the acceptance of certain simple theories of quantum mechanics instead of other empirically equivalent but highly jury-rigged theories. Empirical evidence is not all that we have to go on in theory formation; there are also principles of plausibility, simplicity, and aesthetics, among other considerations.

The role played by simplicity, in particular, cannot be overstated. Without this constraint, scientific theorizing in general would be woefully underconstrained. For any scientific theory one can easily construct an *ad hoc* hypothesis that is empirically equivalent. No one will accept such a hypothesis, however, precisely because of its unnecessary complexity. So if we can find a simple set of underlying laws that are compatible with the data we have, we have good reason to reject more complex alternatives.

Other plausibility constraints can take us a long way in generating a theory of consciousness. The most obvious is the principle we rely on whenever we take someone's verbal report as an indicator of their conscious experience: that people's reports concerning their experiences by and large accurately reflect the contents of their experiences. This is not a principle that we can prove to be true, but it is antecedently much more plausible than the alternative. This plausibility is based to some extent on an inference from our own case, but it also has the character of a methodological constraint in developing a theory of consciousness. If the principle turned out to be entirely false, all bets would be off: in that case, the world would simply be an unreasonable place, and a theory of consciousness would be beyond us. In developing any sort of theory, we assume that the world is a reasonable place, where planets do not suddenly pop into existence with fossil records fully formed, and where complex laws are not jury-rigged to reproduce the predictions of simpler ones. Otherwise, anything goes.

With a plausibility assumption such as this one in hand, we have a very useful constraint on a theory of consciousness, and indeed a rich source of data even from the third-person case: to find out whether someone is consciously experiencing a stimulus, just ask them! This principle allows us to draw much stronger conclusions about the association between conscious experiences and their physical bases. Of course, the assumption is so plausible that researchers rely on it all the time, and few would think of questioning it. Related assumptions can also play a useful role, as with the principle that people's memories of their experiences are not radically incorrect, by and large. Of course, there may be occasional exceptions to these principles; but there is at least a presumption that reports and memories are likely to be accurate reflections of experience in the absence of good reasons to believe otherwise.

Some other plausibility assumptions might include the following: that fundamental laws are homogeneous in space and time; that conscious experience depends only on the internal physical state of an organism; that arbitrary factors such as the distribution of molecules within a neuron are unlikely to be reflected in conscious experience, unless perhaps they affect the neuron's functioning; and so on. Of course it is logically possible that any of these assumptions be false, but in the absence of reasons to believe otherwise, there is a reasonable presumption that each is true. Together, these plausibility assumptions place strong constraints on a theory of consciousness, and can help us considerably in generating such a theory.

What of the worry that a theory of consciousness is untestable, then? This worry will only come into play in a strong way if it turns out that there are two equally simple theories, both of which fit the data perfectly, and both of which meet the relevant plausibility constraints. This may well not happen: a single theory may emerge that is clearly superior to all competitors. If two equally good theories do come along, we may be hard pressed to choose between them, but even so we will have gained significant insight into consciousness by narrowing things down so far. In any case, it is clearly premature to worry about untestability before we have even a single theory that can handle the phenomena in a remotely satisfactory way.

Of course this reliance on first-person data and on plausibility constraints means that a theory of consciousness will have a speculative character not shared by theories in most scientific domains. Because rigorous intersubjective testing is impossible, we will never be quite as certain that our theories are on the right track. For this reason, the science of consciousness will probably always lack the strong empirical credentials of other sciences, and the most hard-headed researchers will always keep their distance. But consciousness is such a central phenomenon that it is better to have some understanding of it than no understanding at all: if a reasonable theory of consciousness can be devised and found superior to all competitors, this will be an achievement of some importance even if the theory can never be given absolutely conclusive support. This is simply the boat in which we find ourselves, in trying to understand the universe: we take the materials that we have, and we work with them.

In this chapter and the next two, I take some initial steps toward a theory of consciousness. The first two of these chapters discuss possible *nonbasic* psychophysical laws, arguing for certain principles that express high-level regularities in the dependence of consciousness on physical processes. The third chapter speculates on the character of the underlying fundamental laws. All this has the character of a preliminary investigation, but we have to start somewhere.

2. Principles of Coherence

The most promising way to get started in developing a theory of consciousness is to focus on the remarkable *coherence* between conscious experience and cognitive structure. The phenomenology and the psychology of the mind do not float free of each other; they are systematically related. The many lawful relations between consciousness and cognition can provide much of what we need to get a theory of consciousness off the ground. The best way to get a handle on this relationship is to focus on phenomenal judgments. These judgments are part of psychology, but they are closely bound up with phenomenology, and as such they provide a bridge between the domains. By thinking about these judgments and the way they function in our own case, we can come up with a number of principles connecting the phenomenal to the psychological.

The most obvious principle of this sort is the one I mentioned in section 1: our second-order judgments about consciousness are by and large correct. We can call this the *reliability* principle. When I judge that I am having an auditory sensation, I am usually having an auditory sensation. When I think I have just experienced a pain, I have usually just experienced a pain. There is also a converse principle, which we might call the *detectability* principle: where there is an experience, we generally have the capacity to form a second-order judgment about it. Of course many experiences slip by without our paying any attention to them, but we usually have the *ability* to notice them: it would be an odd sort of experience that was unnoticeable by us in principle.[1]

The principles I have outlined are not absolute. Our second-order judgments can sometimes go wrong, providing exceptions to the reliability principle. This might happen due to inattention (when distracted, I might believe I have just experienced pain when I only experienced loud noise), failure to grasp relevant categories (as when I mislabel a crimson experience maroon), mental illness or neurophysiological pathology (as with cases such as blindness denial, when subjects make false claims about their experiences), and for various other reasons. In the reverse direction, it is arguable that experiences can be unnoticeable if they occur while one is asleep, for example, or if they flicker by too fast for one to attend to them. But all the same, these principles at least encapsulate significant regularities. In a typical case, a second-order judgment will usually be correct, and an experience will usually be noticeable. These regularities are not exceptionless laws, but they hold far too often to be a mere coincidence. Something systematic is going on.

I will not try to justify these claims in detail, as they will not be the central coherence principles on which I will be focusing. But consideration of the first-person case makes it clear that the principles are plausible at least there, and they can naturally be extended to other cases by principles of homogeneity and simplicity. The principles are also endorsed by common sense, which carries some weight; of course common sense can be overridden if we have have compelling grounds to do so, but other things being equal, one should come down on the side of common sense rather than against it. Finally, as I noted above, these principles have the status of a sort of methodological constraint in developing a theory of consciousness. If second-order judgments were unreliable across the board, or if most of our experiences were entirely unnoticeable, then our judgments about experience would bear so little relation to the reality that a theory of consciousness could not even get off the ground.

The coherence between consciousness and awareness

The most fundamental coherence principle between consciousness and cognition does not involve second-order phenomenal judgments. Rather, it concerns the relationship between consciousness and first-order judgments. The principles with which we will deal here concern the coherence between consciousness and *awareness*. Recall that awareness is the psychological correlate of consciousness, roughly explicable as a state wherein some information is directly accessible and available for the deliberate control of behavior and for verbal report. The contents of awareness correspond to the contents of first-order phenomenal judgments (with a caveat to be mentioned), the contentful states—such as "That object is red"—that are not about consciousness, but parallel to it.

Where there is consciousness, there is awareness. My visual experience of a red book upon my table is accompanied by a functional *perception* of the book. Optical stimulation is processed and transformed, and my perceptual systems register that there is an object of such-and-such shape and color on the table, with this information available in the control of behavior. The same goes for the specific details in what is experienced. Each detail is cognitively represented in awareness. To see that each detail must be so represented, simply observe that I am able to comment on those details and to direct my behavior in ways that depend on them; for instance, I can point to appropriate parts of the book. Such systematic availability of information implies the existence of an internal state carrying that content.

This internal state is a first-order phenomenal judgment—at least to a first approximation. I include the qualification because one might question whether this state should strictly be called a "judgment" at all. The content of this state need not be something that the subject would endorse on reflection, and indeed it might not be conceptualized by the subject at all. Such a state might qualify as a judgment only in a weak sense; it may be better to speak of it as a sort of informational registration, or as an implicit or subpersonal judgment at best. I will discuss this issue in more depth later in this chapter, but for now, when I speak of these states as judgments, this talk should be understood broadly as picking out a class of representational states that need not be reflectively endorsed by the subject, and which need not have conceptualized content.

What goes for visual experience here goes equally for any sensory experience. What is experienced in audition is represented in our auditory system, in such a way that later processes have access to it in the control of behavior; in particular, the contents are available for verbal report. In principle, somebody who knew nothing about consciousness might examine our cognitive processes and ascertain these contents of awareness by observing the role that information plays in directing later processes. In the same sort of way we can handle hallucinations and other cases of sensations without a real object being sensed. Although there is no real object for the contents of perception to concern, there is still representation in our perceptual system. Macbeth had a first-order cognitive state with the content "dagger there" to accompany his experience of a dagger, despite the fact that there was no dagger to be perceived or experienced.

Even nonperceptual experience falls under this umbrella. Although there may be no *object* of a pain experience, contents along the line of "something hurts"—or perhaps better, "something bad"—are still cognitively represented. The very fact that we can comment on the pain and direct our behavior appropriately brings out this fact. There is awareness here just as there is awareness in visual perception, even though the object of the awareness is not so clear-cut. A similar story goes for our experience of emotion, and other "internal" experiences. In all these cases, there are cognitive states corresponding to the experiences; if there were not, then the content of the experience could not be reflected in behavior at all.

Note that the principle is not that whenever we have a conscious experience we are aware *of the experience.* It is first-order judgments that are central here, not second-order judgments. The principle is that when we have an experience, we are aware of the *contents* of the experience. When we experience a book, we are aware of the book; when we experience a pain, we are aware of something hurtful; when we experience a thought, we are aware of whatever it is that the thought is about. It is not a matter of an experience followed by a separate judgment, as might be the case for second-order judgments; these first-order judgments are concomitants of experiences, existing alongside them.

The tie between experiences and second-order judgments is much more indirect: although we have the *ability* to notice our experiences, most of the time we notice only the contents of the experience, not the experience itself. Only occasionally do we sit back and take notice of our *experience* of the red book; usually we just think about the book. Where second-order judgments are infrequent, first-order judgments are ubiquitous. The most direct link is therefore the link between consciousness and first-order judgments.

So far I have argued that where there is consciousness there is awareness. But the arrow goes both ways. Where there is awareness, there is generally consciousness. When we are aware of something in our environment, with some reportable content directing our behavior, there is generally a corresponding conscious experience. When my cognitive system represents a dog barking, I have an experience of a dog barking. When I am aware of heat around me, I feel hot. And so on.

Things get a little tricky here. It may seem that there are various kinds of awareness that do not have corresponding experiences. Awareness involving information in memory provides an example. I am aware that Clinton is president, in the sense that I have access to this information, can verbally report it, and can use it in the deliberate direction of my behavior. If I am not having an occurrent thought to this effect, however, there does not seem to be a corresponding conscious experience; or if there is, it is an extremely weak one. Similarly, I may be (nonoccurrently) aware that there is a bicycle downstairs, without there being an associated bicycle experience. This sort of awareness without experience is most pronounced with propositional awareness—I am aware *that* my bicycle is downstairs—although it also applies to a kind of objectual awareness, in that it seems reasonable to say that I am aware *of my bicycle.*

We could leave this matter as it stands, but it is more satisfying to put restrictions on the notion of awareness so that it is more truly parallel to consciousness. It seems plausible that there is *some* kind of functional difference between the processes involved in one sort of case and in the other—the very fact that I can report on the difference between them bears witness to that. It is this functional difference that needs to be isolated.

Perhaps the most salient difference is that in cases of awareness with consciousness, there is a kind of *direct* access that cases of awareness without consciousness lack. The information that Clinton is president, for example, needs to be "called up" in order for it to make a difference in the deliberate control of behavior, at least if it is not the content of an occurrent thought. It is not as immediately poised to make a difference in control as are the cognitive states associated with experiences and occurrent thoughts. That is, the cognitive access to the information in this case is somewhat more indirect. It is this that provides the functional distinction between occurrent and nonoccurrent thoughts.

We can therefore build this directness of access into a revised notion of awareness. According to the revised notion, nonoccurrent thoughts do not qualify as part of the contents of awareness, but occurrent thoughts do. Correspondingly, we should expect that occurrent thoughts will be associated with experiences, even if nonoccurrent thoughts are not. This is just what we find. My nonoccurrent thought that Clinton is president has no impact on my phenomenology, but an occurrent thought to that effect will be associated with an experience. To see this, note that there is *something* it is like to think to oneself that Clinton is president; if I had not been thinking that thought just now, it would have been like something subtly different to be me.[2]

Thus it is plausible that with awareness appropriately defined, consciousness is always accompanied by awareness, and vice versa. There is more to be said in characterizing the relevant sort of awareness; I will refine the characterization further in what follows, partly by considering various interesting cases. Even at the coarse level, however, we can see that this relationship provides a useful focal point in understanding the coherence between consciousness and cognition.

The principle of structural coherence

So far we have a hypothesis: where there is consciousness, there is awareness, and where there is (the right kind of) awareness, there is consciousness. The correlation between these can be made more detailed than this. In particular, various *structural* features of consciousness correspond directly to structural features that are represented in awareness.

An individual's conscious experience is not in general a homogeneous blob; it has a detailed internal structure. My visual field, for example, has a definite geometry to it. There is a large red patch here, with a small yellow patch in close proximity, with some white in between; there are patterns of stripes, squares, and triangles; and so on. In three dimensions, I have experiences of shapes such as cubes, experiences of one thing as being behind another thing, and other manifestations of the geometry of depth. My visual field consists in a vast mass of details, which fit together into an encompassing structure.

Crucially, all of these details are cognitively represented, within what we can think of as the structure of awareness. The size and shape of various patches is represented in my visual system, for example: perhaps in a fairly direct topographic map, but even if not, we know that it is represented somehow. It must be, as witnessed by the fact that the relevant information is available to guide the control of behavior. The same goes for perceptual representation of the stripes, and of cubical shapes, and so on. Each of these structural details is accessible to the cognitive system, and available for use in the control of behavior, so each is represented in the contents of awareness.

In principle, someone with complete knowledge of my cognitive processes would be able to recover all of these structural details. The geometry of the visual field can be recovered by an analysis of the information that the visual system makes available for later control processes; the very fact that each of these details can be reflected in the behavioral capacities of the subject—a subject might trace the various structural details with arm movements, for example, or comment on them in verbal reports—implies that the information must be present somewhere. Of course the details of the analysis would be very tricky, and far beyond present-day methods, but we know that the information is there. In this way we can see that the structure of consciousness is mirrored in the structure of awareness.

The same goes for *implicit* structure in the phenomenal field, such as relations between colors. Even if I am only seeing one color at a given time, there are a host of colors I *could* have been seeing, colors to which this color bears a structural relation. One color is very similar to another color, and quite different from another. Two colors can seem complementary, or one color group can seem "warm" and another "cold." On a close analysis, our phenomenal colors turn out to fall into a three-dimensional structure, ordered along a red–green dimension, a yellow–blue dimension, and a white–black dimension (the choice of axes is somewhat arbitrary, but there will always be three of them). It turns out that this three-dimensional phenomenal structure is mirrored by a three-dimensional structure in the color information processed within our perceptual systems. Of course it is predictable that it would be, as we know the relevant information is available in the control of behavior, but it is interesting to see that the structure is currently being worked out in detail in studies of the visual system (see Hardin 1988 for discussion). We might say that in this case there is a *difference structure* in our conscious experience (a space of differences between possible experiences) that is mirrored by a difference structure in awareness: to the manifold of color experiences and relations among them, there corresponds a manifold of color representations and corresponding relations among them.

We can find similar sorts of implicit structure in other phenomenal domains, and a similar correspondence to implicit structures at the processing level. The phenomenological structure in a musical chord must be mirrored by structure in what is represented, for example, in order that it can be reported and reflected in other processes of control. The same holds for the implicit structure of tastes. Such correspondences are found in empirical studies of the relevant processes with considerable frequency; but even without such studies, one can see that there must be some sort of correspondence, by reflecting on the fact that these structural details are available to play a control role. In general, this sort of reasoning leads us to the conclusion that any detailed structure that one might find in a phenomenal field will be mirrored in the structures represented in awareness.

There are various more specific features of experience that are also mirrored within awareness. The most obvious of these is *intensity* of experience. It is clear that intensity makes a difference to later processes, so it must somehow be represented in the structure of awareness. Indeed, it is plausible that the intensity of an experience corresponds directly to the extent to which an underlying representation tends to play a control role, occupying the resources of later processes (think of the difference between an intense pain and a faint one, or between an all-consuming emotion and a background emotion). Another such feature is the *resolution* of experiences, as found for example in the difference between the high resolution at the center of a visual field and the low resolution at the fringes. This resolution is something that we would expect to be mirrored in the resolution of underlying representations, and indeed that is what we find.

In general, even if experiences are in some sense "ineffable," relations between experiences are not; we have no trouble discussing these relations, whether they be relations of similarity and difference, geometric relations, relations of intensity, and so on. As Schlick (1938) pointed out, the *form* of experience seems to be straightforwardly communicable, even if the *content* (intrinsic quality) is not: I can characterize the relationship between a red and a green experience, if not the redness and greenness themselves.[3] So we should expect that these relations will be cognitively represented, and this is indeed what we find. Similarities and differences between experiences correspond to similarities and differences represented in awareness; the geometry of experience corresponds to the geometry of awareness; and so on. If we refine the notion of awareness as suggested above, so that states of awareness are always accompanied by states of experience, then a structural correspondence in the other direction will also be plausible: the structure represented in awareness is mirrored in the structure of experience.

So alongside the general principle that where there is consciousness, there is awareness, and vice versa, we have a more specific principle: the structure of consciousness is mirrored by the structure of awareness, and the structure of awareness is mirrored by the structure of consciousness. I will call this the *principle of structural coherence*.[4] This is a central and systematic relation between phenomenology and psychology, and ultimately can be cashed out into a relation between phenomenology and underlying physical processes. As we will see, it is useful in a number of ways.

3. More on the Notion of Awareness

One of the most interesting philosophical projects in the study of consciousness is that of refining the notion of awareness so that it becomes a more perfect psychological correlate of consciousness. On an initial definition, awareness corresponds only imperfectly to consciousness, but the notion can be refined to handle problem cases. Ultimately we would like to characterize a psychological state that plausibly correlates with conscious experience across the board, at least in a range of cases with which we are familiar.

I defined awareness initially as the state wherein some information is accessible for verbal report and the deliberate control of behavior. Considerations about propositional awareness in the absence of experience suggested modifying this to require *direct* access. Other modifications are possible. The most obvious is that availability for verbal report is not strictly required for conscious experience, as considerations about experience in mammals suggest, although it is a good heuristic in cases where language is present. A natural suggestion is to modify the definition of awareness to something like *direct availability for global control.* That is, a subject is aware of some information when that information is directly available to bring to bear in the direction of a wide range of behavioral processes. This allows for the possibility of experience in nonhuman animals, and also squares nicely with the reportability criterion. In cases where information is reportable, it is generally available for global control (for example, in the deliberate direction of a wide range of behaviors). The reverse implication does not always hold (as witnessed by the animal case), but at least in subjects that have the *capacity* to report, availability of information for global control generally implies its availability for report.

Of course this project of refinement can only go so far, as we lack an experience meter with which to confirm and refine these hypotheses empirically. Still, we have a good idea from the first-person case about states in which we have experiences and states in which we do not, and an analysis of what is going on in these cases usually allows us to characterize those states in functional terms. So reflection on the relationship between experience and function in familiar cases gives us considerable leverage. We might also try to empirically refine these hypotheses via first-person experimentation. For example, we can place ourselves into a given functional state, and see what sort of experience we have. With a little help from principles of homogeneity and reliability, we can draw conclusions from the investigation of corresponding situations in others.

There is also a role for the empirical consideration of cases farther from home, for example by considering what sorts of experiences are plausibly had by subjects suffering from certain pathologies, or by nonhuman animals. Of course, we can never be completely certain about what experiences are present in these cases, but some conclusions are much more plausible than others. In effect, these cases act as a focus for our reasoning and an aid to the imagination in distilling plausible principles on the connection between experience and function. The principles may be ultimately grounded in nonempirical analysis, but focus on empirical cases at least ties this sort of reasoning to the real world.

For example, reflection on the attribution of experience to mammals squares with the refined criterion I have suggested above. We are generally prepared to attribute perceptual experience of a stimulus to mammals in cases where the direction of behavior can be made to depend on that stimulus, especially if this is exhibited in a number of different kinds of behavior. If we found that information about a stimulus could only be exhibited in a single, relatively minor behavioral reaction, we might suppose that the information is entirely unconscious. As its availability for use becomes more widespread, it becomes more plausible to suppose that it is experienced. So the coherence between consciousness and this notion of awareness is compatible both with the first-person data and with the natural reasoning concerning nonhuman cases.

There are a number of other interesting problem cases for analysis. One example is *blindsight* (described in Weiskrantz 1986). This is a deficit arising from damage to the visual cortex, in which the usual route for visual information processing is damaged, but in which visual information nevertheless seems to be processed in a limited way. Subjects with blindsight can see nothing in certain areas of their visual field, or so they say. If one puts a red or green light in their "blind area" they claim to see nothing. But when one *forces* them to make a choice about what is in that area—on whether a red or green light is present, for example—it turns out that they are right far more often than they are wrong. Somehow they are "seeing" what is in the area without really *seeing* it.

Blindsight is sometimes put forward as a case in which consciousness and the associated functional role come apart. After all, in blindsight there is discrimination, categorization, and even verbal report of a sort, but it seems that there is no conscious experience. If this were truly a case in which functional role and experience where dissociated, it would clearly raise problems for the coherence principle. Fortunately, the conclusion that this is an example of awareness without consciousness is ungrounded. For a start, it is not *obvious* that there is no experience in these cases; perhaps there is a faint experience that bears an unusual relation to verbal report. More to the point, however, this is far from a standard case of *awareness*. There is a large difference between the functional roles played here and those played in the usual case—it is precisely because of this difference in functional roles that we notice something amiss in the first place.[5]

In particular, subjects with blindsight seem to lack the usual sort of access to the information at hand. Their access is curiously indirect, as witnessed by the fact that it is not straightforwardly available for verbal report, and in the deliberate control of behavior. The information is available to many fewer control processes than is standard perceptual information; it can be made available to other processes, but only by unusual methods such as prompting and forced choice. So this information does not qualify as directly available for global control, and the subjects are not truly aware of the information in the relevant sense. The lack of experience corresponds directly to a lack of awareness. It is also possible, perhaps, that blindsight subjects have a weak sort of experience, in which case one might also want to say that they have a weak sort of awareness, by drawing the standards of directness and globality appropriately. The description of the situation is somewhat underdetermined, given our lack of access to the facts of the matter, but either way it is compatible with the coherence between consciousness and awareness.

In general, this sort of case cannot provide evidence *against* a link between functional organization and conscious experience, as our conclusions about the presence or absence of consciousness in these cases are drawn precisely on functional grounds. In particular, the evidence for unusual states of consciousness in these pathological cases usually relies entirely on evidence for unusual states of awareness. Such cases therefore cannot damage the principle of coherence; they can only bolster and refine it.

A tricky problem case is provided by experiences during sleep. It is plausible that we have experiences when we dream (although see Dennett 1978b), but reportability and any role in the control of action are missing, as action is missing entirely. Still, these cases might plausibly be analyzed in terms of *availability* for global control; it is just that the relevant control processes themselves are mostly shut down. Perhaps the information makes it into the sort of position from which it can usually be used for control purposes; this suggestion is supported by the accessibility of current dream content in a half-waking state. We could then still run the counterfactual: if reportability and control had been enabled (e.g., if the motor cortex had been functioning normally), then the information could have played a role. But this deserves a more careful analysis, along with empirical investigation of what is really going on during sleep.

Some interesting cases are presented by Block (1995) in his extended discussion of the distinction between phenomenal consciousness and "access consciousness." In Block's account, a state is "access-conscious" if its content is poised to be used as a premise in reasoning, poised for rational control of action, and poised for rational control of speech. So access consciousness corresponds roughly to my initial definition of awareness, although my definition gives less of a role to rationality. Block presents some cases where the two varieties of consciousness might come apart. It is instructive to see how a coherence principle might handle them.

On the possibility of access consciousness without phenomenal consciousness, Block appeals only to cases that are conceptually possible, such as zombies; these nonactual cases clearly cannot threaten the coherence principle. He mentions blindsight, but notes that blindsight only yields access consciousness in a weak sense. He also discusses cases such as "superblindsight," which is like blindsight except that a subject is trained to have much better access to the information in the blind field. There are clearly *conceivable* cases of awareness without consciousness in the vicinity, but Block himself notes that there is no reason to believe such cases are actual. Interestingly, he notes that in the closest thing to empirical examples of such a case (a monkey described in Humphrey 1992 and a human patient described in Weiskrantz 1992; see also Cowey and Stoerig 1992), there is reason to believe that phenomenal consciousness is actually present.

On phenomenal consciousness without access consciousness, Block mentions some actual cases. One is a situation in which a subject suddenly becomes aware of the fact that there has been a loud drill in the background for some time. Block suggests that before realizing this, the subject was phenomenally conscious but not access-conscious of the drilling noise. Using the account of awareness I have given, however, it seems reasonable to say that the subject was aware of the drill all along. It is plausible that relevant information about the drill was *available* the whole time; it simply was not *accessed.* So if access consciousness or awareness is defined dispositionally, this case is no problem for a coherence principle. Block also mentions a case in which a three-by-three array of letters is flashed briefly at a subject (Sperling 1960). If asked to name the letters in the top row, subjects can name those but then cannot name the others; the same for the other rows. Block argues that a subject is phenomenally conscious of all nine of the letters, but is access-conscious of only three at a time. But once again it is plausible that information about all nine letters was initially available; it is just that information about only three letters was accessed, and the very process of access destroyed the accessibility of the other information. So this case is also compatible with the coherence principle, on a dispositional account of awareness.

There are many other cases that might be considered. All I have done here is to present some cases and some brief analysis as illustration, to give some idea of the shape of an interesting philosophical project. In a more careful analysis, one might seek to put stronger constraints on just what *kind* of accessibility goes along with conscious experience, and just what kind of global control role is relevant. The account of awareness in terms of direct availability for global control is just a start. This is a fertile area for further analysis.

*Relationship to functionalist theories of consciousness**

The project I have outlined can be seen as a search for a sort of functionalist account of consciousness. It is not a *reductive* functionalist account—it does not say that the playing of some functional role is all there is to consciousness, or all there is to be explained. Rather, it is a *nonreductive* account, one that gives functional criteria for when consciousness arises. All the same, there is a sense in which it is playing in the same ballpark as reductive functionalist accounts; these also give functional criteria for when consciousness arises, alongside their more ambitious metaphysical claims. It is interesting to leave the metaphysical differences aside and compare various accounts in terms of their functional criteria alone.

For example, the proposal that consciousness goes along with direct availability for global control is reminiscent of Dennett's (1993b) proposal that consciousness is *cerebral celebrity*: "Consciousness is cerebral celebrity—nothing more and nothing less. Those contents are conscious that persevere, that monopolize resources long enough to achieve certain typical and 'symptomatic' effects—on memory, on the control of behavior and so forth" (p. 929).

Leaving aside the fact that Dennett takes this to be a conceptual truth, it is quite close to the present account. The main difference is that my account takes consciousness to go along with *potential* cerebral celebrity. It is not required that a content actually play a global control role to be conscious, but it must be available to do so. This seems to square better with the properties of experience. For example, we experience the fringes of our visual field, but most of the time these do not play much of a role in global control; they are merely available to do so if required. Many of the noises

Figure 6.1. Zippy the Pinhead on higher-order theories of consciousness. (Reprinted with special permission of King Features Syndicate)

we experience may pass without leaving significant effects on memory, behavior, and the like, but the information *could* have done so. Of course, Dennett may simply be using the term"consciousness" in a stronger sense, a sense in which we are not conscious of those fringes and noises (Dennett is dubious about the very idea of experience, after all), but the comparison is interesting all the same.

Another functionalist account is Rosenthal's (1996) proposal that for a state to be conscious is for it to be the object of a higher-order thought. In the language I have been using, this means that a first-order state is a content of consciousness precisely when there is a second-order judgment about it. This is considerably stronger than my proposal, in the same sort of way that Dennett's proposal is stronger. On the face of it, there is little reason to believe that we form second-order judgments about all of our experiences, including experiences of every detail of the visual field, of background noises, and so on. Rosenthal holds that the second-order judgments are usually themselves unconscious, which is why we do not notice they are present, but even third-person considerations seem to militate against them. All these second-order judgments seem quite unnecessary in the design of a cognitive system. One might expect a system to have the ability to form such judgments when necessary, as we do about our more salient experiences, but a system with a second-order judgment for every detail of the visual field would seem quite redundant (Figure 6.1).

In Rosenthal's account, conscious states are states that we are conscious *of.* This may have a ring of plausibility, but I think it is only in the weak sense (of the last chapter) in which we are *acquainted* with all of our experiences.[6] It is not at all clear that most of our experiences are objects of our thoughts. To suppose that there are two separate cognitive states for every detail of experience, a first-order and a second-order judgment, leads to a cluttered picture of the mind. It is hard to see why evolution would bother to build in these second-order judgments across the board, when a simple availability for global control would serve its purposes just as well. Rosenthal's account is better taken as an account of introspective consciousness, although he puts it forward as an account of consciousness in the "what it is like" sense.

It is useful to divide functional accounts of consciousness into *first-order* and *second-order* varieties. On the second-order varieties (which include Rosenthal's higher-order thought account, as well as the higher-order perception account of Lycan [1995] and others), what is central to consciousness is the presence of some second-order cognitive state. In first-order theories, only a first-order cognitive state is required, with some restrictions on the role that it plays. Second-order theories may give a good account of introspection or of reflective consciousness, but first-order theories seem more closely linked to conscious experience.[7]

Of course not *all* first-order cognitive states correspond to conscious experiences; there can be first-order judgments about the world that correspond to no experience at all. One therefore needs an additional component in such a theory to distinguish those relevant class of first-order states. The obvious way to do this is to constrain the *role* of those states. This is what I have done, suggesting that the relevant first-order judgments are precisely those that are directly available for global control. Other first-order accounts suggest related constraints, as we will see. One might argue that the causation of a higher-order thought is just another constraint of this kind; the trouble is that the constraint seems to be much too strong.

An interesting intermediate proposal is that a conscious state corresponds to a first-order judgment that has the *capacity* to cause a second-order judgment about it.[8] This avoids the clutter of the previous proposal, and has an element of plausibility. Indeed, it is not all that different from the notion that a conscious state corresponds to a first-order judgment that is available for global control: presumably the availability for global control and the availability for second-order judgment will go together much of the time. Such a proposal may falter when it comes to systems such as babies and animals that arguably have experiences but lack the capacity for second-order judgments, however; it seems to require more conceptual sophistication than may be required for the possession of experiences. If so, the characterization in terms of availability for global control is superior.

It is likely that any first-order functionalist account will invoke a constraint involving some sort of availability. An examination of existing reductive accounts bears this out. For example, Kirk (1992) suggests that perceptual consciousness requires that incoming information is "present" to a system's main decision-making processes, and Kirk (1994) suggests that "directly active" information is required. The suggestion by Dretske (1995) that experience is information that is represented *to* a system also has this flavor, as does the suggestion by Tye (1995) that information must be "poised" for cognitive processing in an appropriate way. One could probably reconcile these suggestions with each other without too many difficulties. All of them seem intended to express a similar idea.

In any case, it is interesting that a nonreductionist about consciousness need not regard the issues between the various first-order and second-order functionalist accounts as internecine warfare among doomed theories. Although these accounts cannot explain consciousness, they are still quite relevant as candidate theories of consciousness's cognitive basis, and some of them succeed here better than others. Even a property dualist can acknowledge an element of truth in them, and can attach some significance to the differences between them.

First-order judgments and first-order registrations*

I have argued that states of experience correspond directly to underlying cognitive states, which I have called first-order judgments. But as I noted before, and as Dretske (1995) has stressed, it may be misleading to call these states *judgments*. Judgments, recall, were originally defined to come to much the same thing as beliefs (with the stipulation that any phenomenal element is excluded). But while it is reasonable to suppose that there is a representational state corresponding to every detail in an experienced visual field, it is not clear that the subject has beliefs about all those details. The contents of the fringes of my visual field, for example, might seem to be something about which I do not have beliefs one way or another, at least until I pay attention to them. Nevertheless, even in the absence of beliefs, there is some sort of cognitive state carrying the relevant information, as the information is at least *available*.

We might simply stipulate that we are using the term "judgment" in a broader way to cover this sort of cognitive state in addition to explicit beliefs. After all, it is plausible that representations of the fringes of the visual field can be seen as "microjudgments," or as implicit judgments made by processes within the cognitive systems, even if they are not judgments of the whole person. But it is probably best to avoid confusion on this matter and introduce a broader term for representational states that are not necessarily judgments. I will use the term "registrations" for this purpose. The cognitive contents of perceptual states, for example, will be carried by first-order registrations rather than by first-order judgments. A first-order registration need not be a state that is endorsed by the subject, but it is nevertheless a contentful state that is available to the subject and that plays a role in the cognitive system.

First-order registrations may even on occasion be contradicted by first-order judgments. Optical illusions provide a clear example: a subject might know that two objects have the same size, but perception can represent them as having different sizes anyway. Dretske gives another example: You hold up seven fingers, and I see all seven. But I do not have time to count them, and I mistakenly take there to be eight fingers before me. So I *judge* that there are eight fingers before me, but my phenomenal experience is of seven fingers. The judgment therefore does not directly parallel the phenomenology. But somewhere within the perceptual system, the visual information of seven fingers is represented and made available to later systems. It is this earlier representation that I am calling a first-order registration. We can think of first-order registrations as the immediate product of perceptual and introspective processes, before they are rationally integrated into a coherent whole.[9]

The contents of awareness, then, will strictly speaking be constituted by first-order registrations rather than by first-order judgments. In particular, the contents of awareness will consist approximately of those first-order registrations that are directly available for use in global control. So defined, the contents of awareness correspond directly to the contents of consciousness. Of course, there will be some first-order registrations that fall outside the contents of awareness, as with states of subliminal perception, for example. As with judgments, we can speak of first-order *phenomenal* registrations to distinguish those registrations that correspond to experiences from those that do not. It is always those in the first class that I will be concerned with, however, so I will usually speak simply of "first-order registrations" and leave the qualifier implicit.

(The representational content of a first-order registration is probably best taken to be *nonconceptual* content, as is the parallel content of experience. I discuss this and some other issues about the contents of awareness and experience in an endnote.)[10]

4. The Explanatory Role of Coherence Principles

The principles of coherence that I have outlined are not just metaphysical set pieces. They can play a central role in empirical work on conscious experience. Any empirical study of consciousness requires some preexperimental reasoning to even get off the ground, in order to draw conclusions about conscious experience on the basis of physical data. The coherence principles provide the necessary purchase. With them in place, there is a methodological foundation for empirical research on conscious experience in a number of areas. A lot of work along these lines is already taking place; the coherence principles simply bring the assumptions that lie behind the work into the open.

There are at least three main projects in which these principles might play an explanatory role. First, the principle of structural coherence can help us in the project of using facts about physical processing to help explain the structure of specific sorts of experience. Second, the coherence between consciousness and awareness acts as a kind of epistemic lever in allowing researchers to infer conclusions about experience from third-person data. And third, the coherence between consciousness and awareness can serve as a background principle in the search for the physical correlates of consciousness. I will discuss each of these in turn.

The first of these provides the clearest example in contemporary practice. It is common to see empirical work on neurobiological and cognitive processes used to shed light on structural features of experience. As I have already discussed, for example, a study of the processes underlying color vision is very useful in helping to explain the structure of phenomenal color space. Similarly, the study of topographic maps in the visual cortex helps shed light on the structure of the phenomenal visual field, and the study of processing in the auditory cortex helps us understand many structural aspects of auditory experiences (pitch relationships and directional aspects, for example). Something similar applies in many other phenomenal domains.

One might wonder how any story about physical processes could be used to shed light on features of experience, given what I have said about the impossibility of reductive explanation. The principle of structural coherence allows us to understand what is going on. In essence, this principle is being used as a *background assumption,* to provide a bridge from features of physical processes to features of experience. If we take for granted the coherence between the structure of consciousness and the structure of awareness, then in order to explain some specific aspect of the former, we need only explain the corresponding aspect of the latter. The bridging principle does the rest of the work.

In the case of color, for example, what happens is that a story about physical processes gives us a reductive account of the structure of awareness, by explaining the relevant similarities and differences between the visual stimuli that the color system processes and makes available to later systems. Once we have this account of the relevant structure of color awareness in hand, then the coherence principle tells us that this structure will be mirrored in the structure of color experience. So if the coherence principle is taken for granted, a functional account of visual processing serves as an indirect account of the structure of phenomenal color space. The same method can be exploited to explain many other features of experience.

Some have been sufficiently impressed by the coherence between the structure in consciousness and in cognition to suggest that this is all we need for a physical explanation of consciousness. Van Gulick (1993), for instance, notes the fact that the structure of our color space corresponds directly to a structure that is represented in visual processing, and suggests that this closes the "explanatory gap" by providing a functional explanation of color sensation. Clark (1993) devotes an entire book to this strategy, arguing that sensory qualities can be completely explained by accounting for the relations of similarity and difference within quality spaces.

If what I have said before is correct, these claims are a little too strong. First, this method does not explain the *intrinsic* nature of a color experience, as the possibility of a structure-preserving spectrum inversion shows. At best, it explains the relational structure *between* such experiences or between parts of a complex experience; so more is required for a full account of consciousness. Second and more important, no account of the structure of awareness explains why there is any accompanying experience at all, precisely because it cannot explain why the principle of structural coherence holds in the first place. By taking the principle as a background assumption we have already moved beyond *reductive* explanation: the principle simply assumes the existence of consciousness, and does nothing to explain it. This counts as a kind of *nonreductive* explanation, taking the existence of consciousness for granted and trying to explain some of its properties.

Within these limits, the principle of structural coherence provides an enormously useful explanatory relation between the physical and the phenomenal. If we want to explain some apparent structure in a phenomenal domain— say, the relations we find between our experiences of musical chords—then we can investigate the functional organization of the corresponding psychological domain, taking advantage of insights from cognitive science and neuroscience to reductively explain the structure of awareness in that domain. In doing so we have explained the structure of the phenomenal domain, modulo the contribution of the principle of structural coherence. Because of our appeal to this principle we will not have explained consciousness itself by doing so, but we will still have explained much of what is special about a *particular* phenomenal domain.

This way, the principle of structural coherence can serve as the backbone of a project that Crick and Koch[11] call "the natural history of qualia." Even if neuroscience cannot explain the existence of experience, it can explain a vast number of facts about experience. Neuroscience can indirectly explain the similarity and difference relations between experiences; the geometry of experiential spaces such as taste space and color space; the detailed structure of experiential fields, such as the visual field; the perceived location associated with experiences within such a field; the intensity of experiences; the duration of experiences; associations between experiences; and much more. As Crick and Koch put it, neuroscience can give an account of all those features of experiences that are objectively communicable. The very communicability of those features implies that they are mirrored in physical features of the system, and indeed in features of awareness. The structural coherence between consciousness and awareness is the implicit or explicit foundation on which this sort of explanation rests. (Such a foundation is particularly crucial in the field of psychophysics, as I discuss in an endnote.)[12]

Using these methods, we might even get some insight into what it is like to be a bat! Functional organization can tell us much about the kind of information that a bat has access to—the kinds of discriminations it can make, the ways it categorizes things, the most salient properties in its perceptual field, and so on—and about the way in which it uses it. Eventually we should be able to build up a detailed picture about the structure of awareness in a bat's cognitive system. By the principle of structural coherence, we will then have a good idea about the structure of the bat's experiences. We will not know *everything* about what it is like to be a bat—we will not have a clear conception of the intrinsic nature of the experiences, for instance—but we will know quite a bit. An interesting paper by Akins (1993) about the mental lives of bats can be read as contributing to this project.

In a similar way, Cheney and Seyfarth's (1990) book *How Monkeys See the World* is put forward as an answer to a question like the one about bats, taking us inside the mind of another species. In effect the work uses the principle of structural coherence as a background assumption throughout, giving an account of certain functional processes and the structure of awareness that they entail, and inviting us to infer a corresponding structure of experience. Of course this does not answer Nagel's real worry, for the usual reasons, but it is nevertheless a striking achievement. We do not need to engage the ultimate mystery of consciousness every time we want to account for a specific phenomenal domain.

Coherence principles as epistemic levers

Empirical researchers in neuroscience, psychology, ethology, and related fields sometimes want to make claims about the presence of conscious experience in a system. Although consciousness is most often set to one side in these fields, there is a nonnegligible body of work in which conclusions about conscious experience are drawn from empirical results. How is this possible, given the difficulties in observing experience directly? If all that can be observed are physical processes, what justifies any conclusion at all?

The answer must be that whenever conclusions about experience are drawn from empirical results, a bridging principle linking physical processes to experience is doing the work. A bridging principle will give a *criterion* for the presence of consciousness in a system, a criterion that applies at the physical level. Such a principle will act as an *epistemic lever* leading from knowledge about physical processes to knowledge about experience. The epistemic lever is not itself experimentally testable, at least from the third-person viewpoint; instead, it acts as a kind of prior background assumption. These assumptions are not always made explicit, but they are the only way that this sort of work gets any purchase on conscious experience.

Bridging principles are so crucial here that it makes sense to be explicit about them. There is a sense in which anyone who appeals to a bridging principle—which means anyone who draws conclusions about experience from external observations—is doing "philosophy," as bridging principles are not themselves experimental conclusions. Such principles must be based on considerations from the first-person case, and on general principles of plausibility. These principles effectively precede any experimental results, as it is the principles themselves that tell us how to interpret those results. Of course there are *a priori* assumptions involved in any experimental enterprise, but here they play an unusually significant role. It is therefore important to justify those assumptions as well as we can, by a careful analysis. That is one way to interpret the project in which I have been engaged in this chapter.

The bridging principle that I have recommended is that of the coherence between consciousness and awareness: when a system is aware of some information, in the sense that the information is directly available for global control, then the information is conscious. I suspect that if one undertook a careful study of the bridging principles used by empirical researchers and by those who interpret empirical research, almost all such principles would be compatible with this one and indeed derivable from it. The most common bridging principle, of course, is the use of reportability as a criterion for experience: at least in a language-using system, it is generally held that information is conscious if it is reportable. Reportability is a version of awareness—when information is reportable, it is always available for control—so this criterion clearly squares with the coherence principle, although it is more limited in its scope.

Other criteria are also occasionally used; sometimes researchers want to make claims about experience in animals without language, or in humans whose report mechanisms are not functioning normally. In these cases, the best sign of experience is usually taken to be a strong effect of some information in the control of behavior. For example, Logothetis and Schall (1989) present their work as isolating the "neuronal correlates of subjective visual perception" in monkeys. Here, a monkey is taken to be having perceptual experience of a moving object in its environment when it can reliably make an eye movement or press a bar in response to that movement. This again squares perfectly with the criterion provided by awareness, or direct availability for global control.

Some may find an appeal to preexperimental bridging principles disturbing in an experimental science; indeed, the need for such epistemic levers may be the reason that such sciences have so often stayed away from consciousness. Nevertheless, this is the boat we find ourselves in, and conclusions drawn on the basis of these principles are better than no conclusions at all. It makes sense for the relevant principles to be made explicit, though, and justified by careful analysis, rather than being swept under the rug. In this way the underlying reasoning that leads to empirical conclusions about conscious experience will be clarified.

The physical correlates of consciousness

What are the neural and information-processing *correlates* of consciousness? This is one of the central questions about consciousness that empirical research is often taken to address. Various empirical hypotheses have been put forward. For example, Crick and Koch (1990) put forward the hypothesis that certain 40-hertz oscillations in the cortex are the neural correlates of experience. Baars (1988) can be interpreted as suggesting that a global workspace is the information-processing basis for experience, with the contents of experience corresponding directly to the contents of the workspace. Farah (1994) argues that consciousness is associated with "high-quality" representations in the brain. Libet (1993) puts forward a neural "time-on" theory, in which consciousness is associated with neuronal activities that persist for a long enough time, with a minimal duration of around 500 milliseconds. There have been numerous other proposals in a similar vein.

The coherence between consciousness and awareness provides a natural way to make sense of much of this work. It is striking that each of these candidates is itself a plausible candidate to play a role in facilitating *awareness*—direct availability for global control. Crick and Koch's oscillations are put forward because of the role they may play in binding information and placing that information in working memory; and of course working memory is just a system whereby contents are made available for control. Libet's temporally extended neural activity may be relevant precisely because that sort of activity has the widespread robust effects on the cognitive system required for awareness. The same goes for Farah's "high-quality" representations; it is arguable that "low-quality" representations might not be able to permeate cognitive functioning in the appropriate way. For Baars's global workspace, the link is clearest of all: the workspace is put forward precisely in virtue of its role in mediating global access and control.

A deflationary interpretation of what is going on here would be that these researchers simply *mean* awareness when they say "consciousness," so that this commonality is unremarkable. But I think it is clear from context that most of them—at least Crick and Koch and Farah, and probably Libet—are talking about consciousness in the full phenomenal sense, and are trying to isolate physical correlates for it. All of them make remarks that suggest they would accept a *conceptual* distinction between consciousness and awareness as I am defining it.

A more interesting interpretation is to take these researchers to be talking about consciousness in the phenomenal sense, and to note that all their proposals are compatible with the overarching bridging principle of coherence between consciousness and awareness. Indeed, these hypotheses may be *derivable* from the coherence principle, together with relevant empirical results. Say we accept the coherence principle as a background assumption, so we take it that experience is directly associated with direct availability for global control. If empirical results suggest that in a particular species (such as *Homo sapiens*), 40-hertz oscillations subserve global availability, then we have reason to believe that the oscillations are a correlate of experience in that species. If results suggest that temporally extended activity subserves global availability, then we have reason to believe that that sort of activity is a correlate of experience. And so on.

Of course, more than one of these hypotheses might be correct. Perhaps both oscillations and temporally extended activity subserve global availability in different instances, or perhaps they simultaneously play a role at different stages of the access/control process. Perhaps the oscillations subserve high-quality representations in the global workspace. Those are empirical issues. But the hypotheses could also turn out to be false. Perhaps it will turn out that the oscillations play no special role in global control, and instead are involved only with peripheral operations. Perhaps they have only very limited effects on later processes and on behavior.

What is notable is that *if* we had reason to believe that oscillations were dissociated from awareness in this way, we would also have reason to believe that they were dissociated from experience. If it turned out that oscillations had no special relationship with reportability and awareness, for example, the ground would be cut from under the correlation hypothesis. After all, we do not have independent evidence for the hypothesis: all our evidence comes from the link with reportability and awareness. Because we lack an "experience meter," we must always rely on such indirect criteria, and the criteria of reportability and awareness seem to be the best we can do. It follows that we can only have empirical evidence for a link between a process N and consciousness if we already have evidence for a link between N and awareness.

This suggests a clear methodology for finding physical correlates of experience. Preexperimental considerations suggest that the basic processing correlate of consciousness is awareness, or global availability. Empirical results suggest that the physical states that play a role in awareness in a given species are of a certain type N. The prior bridging principle and the empirical results combine to suggest that in this species, N is a physical correlate of consciousness.

(Interestingly, Dennett [1993b] suggests almost the same methodology. He suggests that specific proposals about the basis of consciousness, such as the oscillation proposal, are plausible precisely insofar as the relevant processes play a role in securing "cerebral celebrity". I can agree with almost all of this, except that I require only *potential* cerebral celebrity, and I think the link between consciousness and celebrity is a nomic principle rather than a conceptual truth. Indeed, *anyone* empirically investigating consciousness will need a nonempirical bridging principle to interpret physical results in terms of conscious experience. For the reductionist this will be a conceptual truth, and for the property dualist it will be a nomic principle based on first-person considerations and plausible analysis. But many of the points I make here apply either way.)

It seems natural to say that the *central* correlation between physical processing and experience is the coherence between consciousness and awareness. What gives rise *directly* to experience is not oscillations or temporally extended activity or high-quality representations, but the process of direct availability for global control. Any more specific physical state will qualify as a correlate only insofar as it plays a role in global availability; so the more specific correlations are derivative on the overarching correlation.

There may be many such correlates. Different types of physical process may subserve availability in different modalities, for example. There may also be different correlates at different stages of the processing path; even taking visual experience alone, there may be one sort of correlate in the visual cortex and another in areas further downstream. Of course, there is no guarantee that even within a particular modality, there will be a neural correlate of any simple type. Perhaps there will be no straightforward characterization of the processes in the visual cortex that subserve experience; it might happen that they could be grouped together *only* by their functional role (that is, by the fact that they subserve awareness). But we can at least hope that there might be a more straightforward characterization to be found: if not in the perceptual cortices, then perhaps at some later point on the processing path.

We might also find correlates at levels higher than the neural. On constructing an appropriate cognitive or computational model, we might be able to find some way of characterizing in information-processing terms those entities that are responsible for awareness and that therefore underlie experience. Of course the simplest such characterization is tautologous—the processes subserving awareness are those responsible for global access, control, and verbal report. But a substantial cognitive model might give us less tautologous characterizations. Perhaps we might be able to characterize in relatively local terms the type of information that turns out to play a significant global role, for example, given the overall design of the system. An example is the suggestion of Shallice (1972) that the contents of consciousness correspond to the contents of "selector inputs" to certain action systems. According to the design of the model, the selector inputs determine which action systems become "dominant," or play a role in global control. If so, selector inputs facilitate awareness and are a plausible correlate of conscious experience.

Other information-processing correlates fall somewhere between the tautologous and the nontautologous. An example is Baars's global workspace. We might *define* the global workspace as a kind of "virtual" area, corresponding precisely to those contents that are widely disseminated; if so the contents of the workspace are the contents of awareness almost by definition. Baars's model has more empirical bite than this: he proposes that the workspace is a single unified system (one that we can localize at least in information-processing terms) in which information is integrated and disseminated. This could turn out to be false, so the proposal has empirical substance that experimental work might support or deny. But the characterization of the workspace is still sufficiently close to the characterization of awareness to explain the slight flavor of the *a priori* that the proposal retains; it sometimes seems that almost any empirical results could be made compatible with such a framework. (Of course Baars makes many more specific claims about the operations of the workspace, and these claims carry significant empirical substance.) Farah's "high-quality representation" proposal also has a slight whiff of tautology, though it depends on how a high-quality representation is defined: if to be a "high-quality" representation is just to be able to play a significant global role, then the *a priori* flavor is strong, but if it is defined in terms of the way that such a representation is formed, the flavor is much weaker.

Even at the cognitive level, there is no special reason to believe that there will be a single isolable mechanism that underlies experience. Schacter (1989) suggests that there may be a single mechanism, such as a module, but this is only one way things might go. It *might* turn out that a role in global control is always facilitated by some central mechanism (such as Baars's global workspace), but on the face of it, it is equally likely that processes of many different kinds are responsible at different times for securing the appropriate availability, even within a single species or a single subject.

Sometimes people want to draw stronger conclusions about physical correlates than I have suggested. For example, if we find that 40-hertz oscillations are the basis for experience in familiar cases, might we not hypothesize that 40-hertz oscillations are the *ultimate* basis of experience? Perhaps those oscillations give rise to experience even when they are not associated with awareness, and perhaps well-functioning systems without the oscillations might lack experience? Such a conclusion would be unjustified, however. The 40-hertz oscillations were taken to be relevant *because* of their association with awareness; we have no reason to believe that when they do not play that role, there is anything special about them. Certainly there is no reason to believe that 40-hertz oscillations in a test-tube should give rise to experiences like mine! And even in intermediate cases, such as those of animals or anesthetized systems, it would be dangerous to infer anything about experience from the presence of the oscillations, except insofar as the presence of the oscillations gives us reason to believe that some sort of awareness is present.

In general, we cannot expect these empirical methods to yield universal psychophysical principles incompatible with those we started with. They can yield more *specific* principles, applying within a given species, but these will be derived by a direct application of preexisting bridging principles. Given that the preexisting principles bear the entire burden in drawing conclusions about experience from physical data, it is impossible for the data to support a conclusion that contradicts the principles.

We should therefore not expect the search for a neural correlate of consciousness to lead to the holy grail of a universal theory. We might expect it to be valuable in helping us to understand consciousness in specific cases, such as the human case: learning more about the processes underlying awareness will certainly help us understand the structure and dynamics of consciousness, for example. But in holding up the bridge from physical processes to conscious experience, preexperimental coherence principles will always play a central role.

5. Coherence as a Psychophysical Law

So far I have mostly considered coherence within a range of relatively familiar cases, involving humans and other biological systems. But it is natural to suppose that these principles of coherence may have the status of universal laws. If consciousness is always accompanied by awareness, and vice versa, in my own case and in the case of all humans, one is led to suspect that something systematic is going on. There is certainly a lawlike correlation in the familiar cases. We can therefore put forward the hypothesis that this coherence is a law of nature: in any system, consciousness will be accompanied by awareness, and vice versa. The same goes for the full-blown principle of structural coherence. The remarkable correlation between the structure of consciousness and the structure of awareness seems too specific to be an accident. It is natural to infer an underlying law: for any system, anywhere in space-time, the structure of consciousness will mirror and be mirrored by the structure of awareness.

Laws such as these would make a significant contribution to a theory of consciousness. So far, all we know is that consciousness arises from the physical somehow, but we do not know in virtue of what physical properties it so arises; that is, we do not know what properties enter into the physical side of the connection. Given the laws of coherence, we have a partial answer: consciousness arises in virtue of the functional organization associated with awareness. We can even arrive at a fairly specific understanding of parts of the supervenience relation by virtue of the principle of structural coherence: not only does consciousness arise from awareness, but the structure of consciousness is determined by the structure of awareness.

Of course this law will probably not be a *fundamental* psychophysical law. Fundamental laws connect properties more basic or at least more cleanly defined than a high-level construct such as "awareness." But not all laws are fundamental laws. It may even be that the coherence principles are not *strict* laws; there may be some exceptions around the edges, especially given the underdetermined nature of the concept of awareness. But even if these laws are neither fundamental nor strict, they nevertheless provide a strong constraint that any fundamental psychophysical laws must satisfy. A proposed theory of consciousness that does not have the coherence principles as a consequence will be in trouble. Conversely, if a proposed fundamental psychophysical law is simple, well motivated, and has the coherence principles as a consequence, then that may provide good reason to accept it.

What, then, are the grounds for accepting the coherence principles as laws? The basic evidence comes from the correlations in familiar cases: ultimately, for me, from my own case. The apparent correlations between awareness and consciousness in my own case are so detailed and remarkable that there must be something more than a mere chance regularity. There must be some underlying law. The only question is *what* law? This law must entail that in my own case, awareness will always be accompanied by consciousness, and vice versa, and further that the structures of the two will correspond. The principles of coherence I have put forward will do the job. Might some different principle also suffice?

It is very plausible that some kind of awareness is *necessary* for consciousness. Certainly all the instances of consciousness that I know about are accompanied by awareness. There seems to be little reason to believe in any instances of consciousness *without* the accompanying functional processes. If there are any, we have no evidence for them, not even indirect evidence, and we could not in principle. It therefore is reasonable to suppose on the grounds of parsimony that wherever there is consciousness, there is awareness. If we are wrong about this—if for example a static electron has the rich conscious life of a Proust—then we will certainly never know about it.

The question of the *sufficiency* of awareness is more difficult. Given the necessity of awareness, any candidates for an underlying law will have the form "Awareness plus something gives rise to consciousness." At least, any underlying laws must *entail* a principle of this form, in order to explain the regularities in my own case. The remaining question then, is: What is the extra something, or is nothing extra required?

Call the hypothetical extra ingredient the *X-factor*. Either I am conscious in virtue of awareness alone, or I am conscious in virtue of awareness and the X-factor. The X-factor might consistently be any property, as long as it is possessed by me now, and preferably throughout my life. Perhaps the X-factor is a matter of nationality, and awareness gives rise to consciousness only in Australians. Perhaps it is a matter of location, and awareness gives rise to consciousness only within a hundred million miles of a star. Perhaps it is a matter of *identity,* and awareness gives rise to consciousness only in David Chalmers.

All of these laws would be compatible with my evidence, and would explain the correlation, so why do they all seem so unreasonable? It is because in each of these cases, the X-factor seems quite *arbitrary.* There is no reason to believe that consciousness should depend on these things; they seem to be irrelevant frills. It is not as if the X-factor plays a role in explaining any of the phenomena associated with consciousness. At least awareness might help explain our phenomenal judgments, which have a close tie to consciousness, so there is some reason to believe in a connection there. By contrast, each of these X-factors seems to appear out of nowhere. Why would the universe be such that awareness gives rise to consciousness in one person, and one person only? It would be a strange, arbitrary way for a world to be.

The same goes for more "plausible" X-factors that someone might put forward seriously. A natural candidate for such an X-factor is cell-based biology, or even human neurophysiology. Certainly some people have supposed that consciousness is limited to beings with the right kind of biological make-up. In a similar way, some have suggested that consciousness arises from functional organization only when that organization is not implemented in a "homunculi-headed" manner, as in the example of the Chinese nation. But X-factors like these are equally arbitrary. They only complicate the laws without any added compensation. Why should the world be set up so that awareness gives rise to consciousness only in beings with a particular biology, or such that internal homunculi are ruled out? The hypotheses seem baroque, with extraneous distractions built in.

Why might someone believe in an X-factor? I think such beliefs arise for a natural but misleading reason. There is a basic intuition that consciousness is something over and above functional organization. This is an intuition that of course I share—consciousness is a further fact, for which no functional organization is logically sufficient. There is also a natural tendency to believe that everything is physical, and that consciousness must be physically explainable one way or another. Faced with these two pressures, there is a natural reaction: we have to add something extra, and the extra something must be physical. Human biology is a natural candidate for that extra ingredient. In this way, it might be thought that we have bridged the gap from functional organization to human biology.

But this is quite misguided. The addition of biology into the picture has not helped the original problem at all. The gap is as large as ever: consciousness seems to be something over and above biology, too. As argued earlier, *no* physical facts suffice to explain consciousness. The X-factor can do no work for us; we are looking in the wrong place for a solution to our problem. The problem was the assumption of materialism in the first place. Once we accept that materialism is false, it becomes clear that the search for a physical X-factor is irrelevant; instead, we have to look for a "Y-factor," something *additional* to the physical facts that will help explain consciousness. We find such a Y-factor in the postulation of irreducible psychophysical laws. Once we have imported these into our framework, the intuition that consciousness is a further fact is preserved, and the problem is removed.

The desire for a physical X-factor is a holdover from the attempt to have one's materialist cake and eat one's consciousness too. Once we recognize that consciousness is a further nonphysical fact and that there are independent psychophysical laws, the X-factor becomes quite redundant. To ask for an independent psychophysical connection *and* an X-factor is to ask for two gifts when we only need one.

The X-factor therefore has no explanatory role to play in a theory of consciousness, and only complicates the story. Any such factor only makes the fundamental laws more complex than they need to be. Given the simplicity of the picture in which awareness gives rise to consciousness, a universe in which consciousness depends on a separate X-factor begins to look like an unreasonable place. One might as well have a clause in Newton's laws saying every action has an equal and opposite reaction unless the objects involved are made of gold. Principles of simplicity dictate that the best hypothesis is that no X-factor is required, and that awareness gives rise to consciousness without qualifications.

Some people will still be unsure about the functionalist conclusion that I have reached, even if it is a dualist version of functionalism. It is true that the argument from X-factors is somewhat tentative and relies strongly on simplicity assumptions. I will give more concrete arguments for the same conclusion in the next chapter, using thought experiments to make the case that a functional replica of a conscious being will have precisely the same kind of conscious experience. But for now I note that these considerations at least provide a strong *prima facie* case for this sort of functionalism.

It is worthwhile taking a moment to grasp the overall epistemological framework. What we have here is essentially an inference to the best explanation. We note remarkable regularities between consciousness and awareness in our own case, and postulate the simplest possible underlying law. This is the same sort of reasoning that goes on in formulating physical theories, and even in combating skeptical hypotheses about causation and about the external world. In all these cases, the underlying assumption is that the world is a simple and reasonable place. Failing such an assumption, anything goes. With such an assumption, things fall into place.

It also seems that this is as good a solution to the problem of other minds as we are going to get. We note regularities between experience and physical or functional states in our own case, postulate simple and homogeneous underlying laws to explain them, and use those laws to infer the existence of consciousness in others. This may or may not be the reasoning that we implicitly use in believing that others are conscious, but in any case it seems to provide a reasonable justification for our beliefs.

It is interesting to speculate on just what our principles of coherence imply for the existence of consciousness outside the human race, and in particular in much simpler organisms. The matter is unclear, as our notion of awareness is only clearly defined for cases approximating human complexity. It seems reasonable to say that a dog is aware, and even that a mouse is aware (perhaps they are not self-aware, but that is a different matter). For example, it seems reasonable to say that a dog is aware of a fire hydrant in the basic sense of the term "aware." The dog's control systems certainly have access to information about the hydrant, and can use it to control behavior appropriately. By the coherence principle, it seems likely that the dog *experiences* the hydrant, in a way not unlike our visual experience of the world. This squares with common sense; all I am doing here is making the common-sense reasoning a little more explicit.

The same is arguably true for mice and even for flies. Flies have some limited perceptual access to environmental information, and their perceptual contents presumably permeate their cognitive systems and are available to direct behavior. It seems reasonable to suppose that this qualifies as awareness, and that by the coherence principle there is some kind of accompanying experience. Around here the matter gets tricky. It is tempting to extend the coherence further down the information-processing scale; but sooner or later, the notion of "awareness" gives out on us and can do no explanatory work, due to its indeterminacy. I will not speculate further on this matter for now, but I return to it later.

7

Absent Qualia, Fading Qualia, Dancing Qualia

1. The Principle of Organizational Invariance

If consciousness arises from the physical, in virtue of what sort of physical properties does it arise? Presumably these will be properties that brains can instantiate, but it is not obvious just which properties are the right ones. Some have suggested biochemical properties; some have suggested quantum properties; many have professed uncertainty. A natural suggestion is that consciousness arises in virtue of the *functional organization* of the brain. On this view, the chemical and indeed the quantum substrate of the brain is irrelevant to the production of consciousness. What counts is the brain's abstract causal organization, an organization that might be realized in many different physical substrates.

Functional organization is best understood as the *abstract pattern of causal interaction* between various parts of a system, and perhaps between these parts and external inputs and outputs. A functional organization is determined by specifying (1) a number of abstract components, (2) for each component, a number of different possible states, and (3) a system of dependency relations, specifying how the state of each component depends on previous states of all components and on inputs to the system, and how outputs from the system depend on previous component states. Beyond specifying their number and their dependency relations, the nature of the components and the states is left unspecified.

A physical system *realizes* a given functional organization when the system can be divided into an appropriate number of physical components each with the appropriate number of states, such that the causal dependency relations among the components of the system, inputs, and outputs precisely reflect the dependency relations given in the specification of the functional organization. (A more formal account along these lines is given in Chalmers [1994a, 1994b] and is summarized in Chapter 9, but the informal understanding will suffice for now.)

A given functional organization can be realized by diverse physical systems. For example, the organization realized by the brain at the neural level might in principle be realized by a silicon system. A description of the brain's functional organization abstracts away from the physical nature of the parts involved, and from the way that the causal connections are implemented. All that counts is the existence of the parts, and the dependency relations between their states.

A physical system has functional organization at many different levels, depending on how finely we individuate its parts and on how finely we divide the states of those parts. At a coarse level, for instance, it is likely that the two hemispheres of the brain can be seen as realizing a simple two-component organization, if we choose appropriate interdependent states of the hemispheres. It is generally more useful to view cognitive systems at a finer level, however. If we are interested in cognition, we will usually focus on a level fine enough to determine the behavioral capacities associated with the brain, where behavior is individuated to some appropriate level of precision. Organization at too coarse a level (e.g., the two-component organization above) will fall far short of determining behavioral capacities, as the mechanisms that drive behavior will fall between the cracks of this description; a simple system might share the organization without sharing the behavior. At a fine enough level, though—perhaps the neural level—functional organization will determine behavioral capacities. Even if our neurons were replaced with silicon chips, then as long as these chips had states with the same pattern of causal interactions as we find in the neurons, the system would produce the same behavior.

In what follows, the relevant sort of functional organization of a system will always be at a level fine enough to determine behavioral capacities. Call such an organization a *fine-grained* functional organization. For the purposes of illustration, I will usually focus on the neural level of organization in the brain, although a higher level might suffice, and it is not impossible that a lower level could be required. In any case, the arguments generalize. For the purposes of what follows, we need also stipulate that for two systems to share their functional organization, they must be in corresponding states at the relevant times; although my sleeping twin might count as sharing my organization in a broad sense, he will not count in the strict sense required below. When two systems share their functional organization in this strict sense, I will say that they are *functional isomorphs*.

I claim that conscious experience arises from fine-grained functional organization. More specifically, I will argue for a *principle of organizational invariance,* holding that given any system that has conscious experiences, then any system that has the same fine-grained functional organization will have qualitatively identical experiences. According to this principle, consciousness is an organizational invariant: a property that remains constant over all functional isomorphs of a given system. Whether the organization is realized in silicon chips, in the population of China, or in beer cans and ping-pong balls does not matter. As long as the functional organization is right, conscious experience will be determined.

This thesis has often been associated with a reductive functionalist view about consciousness, such as the view that all it *is* to be conscious is to be in the appropriate functional state. From such a view the invariance principle would naturally follow, but the invariance principle can be held independently. Just as one can believe that consciousness arises from a physical system but is not a physical state, one can believe that consciousness arises from functional organization but is not a functional state. The view that I advocate has this form—we might call it *nonreductive functionalism.* It might be seen as a way of combining functionalism and property dualism.

I will not be especially concerned with the nonreductive aspects of my view below, being mostly concerned to argue for the invariance principle. My arguments might even be embraced by reductive functionalists. While the arguments do not establish the full reductive conclusion, they nevertheless can be seen as supporting that position against other reductive views, such as a view on which consciousness is equated with a biochemical property. Of course I think that all reductive views ultimately fail, but the following discussion will be largely independent of that issue.

I have already argued for a version of the invariance principle, in effect, with the "X-factor" argument of Chapter 6. In this chapter, however, I will use thought experiments to argue for the principle in a much more direct way.

Absent qualia and inverted qualia

The invariance principle is far from universally accepted. Many people of both dualist and materialist persuasions have argued against it. Many have held that for a system to be conscious, it must have the right sort of biochemical makeup; if so, a metallic robot or a silicon-based computer could never have experiences, no matter what their causal organization. Others have conceded that a robot or a computer might be conscious if it were organized appropriately, but have held that it might nevertheless have experiences quite different from ours.

Corresponding to these two views, there have generally been two kinds of argument against the invariance principle. The first kind comprises arguments from *absent qualia*. In these arguments, a particularly bizarre realization of a given functional organization is described, in a system so outlandish that it is natural to suppose that the qualities (qualia) of conscious experience must be *absent*. A popular example from Block (1978) is a case in which our organization is realized in the population of a country (as in Chapter 3). Surely, it is argued, *that* could not give rise to conscious experience. If not, then consciousness cannot arise from functional organization.

The second class of arguments includes those from *inverted qualia,* or the *inverted spectrum*. According to these arguments, if our functional organization were realized in a different physical substrate, a system might still have experience, but it would have a different kind of experience. Where we have red experiences, it might have blue experiences, and so on. Often these arguments are made via complex scenarios that appeal to brain surgery, in which we wake up one morning seeing blue instead of red even though our functional organization is unchanged.

Many of those arguing for the possibility of absent and inverted qualia have been arguing only for logical possibility; this is all that is required to refute a reductive form of functionalism. Indeed, I have used such arguments myself, in Chapter 3. These proponents are not subject to the counterarguments in this chapter. What is at issue here is a weaker form of functionalism, one which does not turn on questions of logical possibility.

The key question in this chapter is whether absent or inverted qualia are *naturally* (or *empirically*) possible. It is logically possible that a plate may fly upward when one lets go of it in a vacuum on a planetary surface, but it is nevertheless naturally impossible. The laws of nature forbid it. In a similar way, establishing the logical possibility of absent qualia and inverted qualia falls far short of establishing their natural possibility. The invariance principle holds that functional organization determines conscious experience by some lawful link in the actual world; here, matters of logical possibility are irrelevant. In this chapter, whenever "possibility" is used alone, it is natural possibility that is intended.

In what follows, I will discuss arguments that have been put forward in favor of the natural possibility of absent and inverted qualia, and will then offer detailed arguments *against* those possibilities. These arguments will crucially involve thought experiments. Against the possibility of absent qualia, I will offer a thought experiment concerning *fading qualia*. Against the possibility of inverted qualia, I will offer a thought experiment concerning *dancing qualia*.

These arguments from thought experiments are only plausibility arguments, as always, but I think they have considerable force. To maintain the natural possibility of absent and inverted qualia in the face of these thought experiments requires accepting some implausible theses about the nature of conscious experience, and in particular about the relationship between consciousness and cognition. Given certain natural assumptions about this relationship, the invariance principle is established as by far the most plausible hypothesis.

Perhaps it is useful to see these thought experiments as playing a role analogous to that played by the "Schrödinger's cat" thought experiment in the interpretation of quantum mechanics. Schrödinger's thought experiment does not deliver a decisive verdict in favor of one interpretation or another, but it brings out various plausibilities and implausibilities in the interpretations, and it is something that every interpretation must ultimately come to grips with. In a similar way, any theory of consciousness must ultimately come to grips with the fading and dancing qualia scenarios, and some will handle them better than others. In this way, the virtues and drawbacks of various theories are clarified.

2. Absent Qualia

Positive arguments for the natural possibility of absent qualia have not been as prevalent as arguments for inverted qualia, but they have been made. The most detailed presentation of these arguments is given by Block (1978).

These arguments almost always have the same form. They consist in the exhibition of a realization of our functional organization in some unusual medium, combined with an appeal to intuition. It is pointed out, for example, that the organization of our brain might be simulated by the people of China or even mirrored in the economy of Bolivia. If we got every person in China to simulate a neuron (we would need to multiply the population by ten or one hundred, but no matter), and equipped them with radio links to simulate synaptic connections, then the functional organization would be there. But surely, says the argument, this baroque system would not be *conscious*!

There is a certain intuitive force to this argument. Many people have a strong feeling that a system like this is simply the wrong sort of thing to have a conscious experience. Such a "group mind" would seem to be the stuff of a science-fiction tale, rather than the kind of thing that could really exist. But there is *only* an intuitive force. This certainly falls far short of a knockdown argument. Many have pointed out[1] that while it may be intuitively implausible that such a system should give rise to experience, it is equally intuitively implausible that a *brain* should give rise to experience! Whoever would have thought that this hunk of gray matter would be the sort of thing that could produce vivid subjective experiences? And yet it does. Of course this does not *show* that a nation's population could produce a mind, but it is a strong counter to the intuitive argument that it would not.

Of course, we would not *see* any conscious experience in such a system. But this is nothing new; we do not see conscious experience in anyone. It might seem that there is no "room" for conscious experience in such a system, but again the same appears to be true of the brain. Thirdly, we might *explain* the functioning of the system without invoking conscious experience, but again this is familiar in the standard case. Once we absorb the true force of the failure of logical supervenience, it begins to seem no more surprising that the population of a country could give rise to conscious experience than that a brain could do so.[2]

Some have objected to the invariance principle on the grounds that the functional organization might arise by chance, in the Bolivian economy or even in a pail (Hinckfuss, quoted in Lycan 1987, p.32). But this could only happen by the most outrageous coincidence.[3] The system would need to have over a billion parts each with a number of states of its own (say, ten each). Between these states there would have to be a vast, intricate system of just the right causal connections, so that given *this* state pattern, then this state pattern will result, given *that* state pattern, then that state pattern will result, and so on. To realize the functional organization in question, these conditionals cannot be mere regularities (where this state pattern happens to be followed by that state pattern on this occasion); they have to be reliable, counterfactual-supporting connections, such that this state pattern will be followed by that state pattern whenever it comes up.[4]

It is not hard to see that about 10^{10^9} such conditionals will be required of a system in order that it realize the appropriate functional organization, if we suppose a division into a billion parts. The chance that these conditionals could be satisfied by an arbitrary system under a given division into parts and states will be on the order of 1 in $(10^{10^9})^{10^{10^9}}$ (actually much less, as the requirement that each conditional be reliable further reduces the chance that it will be satisfied).[5] Even given the freedom we have in dividing a system into parts, it is extraordinarily unlikely that such organization would be realized by an arbitrary system, or indeed by *any* system that was not shaped by the highly nonarbitrary mechanisms of natural selection.

Once we realize how tightly a specification of functional organization constrains the structure of a system, it becomes less implausible that even the population of China could support conscious experience if organized appropriately. If we take our image of the population, speed it up by a factor of a million or so, and shrink it into an area the size of a head, we are left with something that looks a lot like a brain, except that it has homunculi—tiny people—where a brain would have neurons. On the face of it, there is not much reason to suppose that neurons should do any better a job than homunculi in supporting experience.

Of course, as Block points out, we *know* that neurons can do the job, whereas we do not know about homunculi. The issue therefore remains open. The important point is that this sort of argument provides only very weak evidence that absent qualia are naturally impossible. A more compelling argument is required to settle the matter one way or the other. *Perhaps* it is correct to say, as Block does, that our intuitions throw the burden of proof onto one who holds that qualia are organizationally invariant, although this is not clear to me. In any case, I will take up that burden in what follows.

A separate argument that is sometimes put forward for the natural possibility of absent qualia stems from the phenomenon of blindsight. It is argued that blindsight patients are functionally similar to us in relevant ways—they can discriminate, report contents, and so on—but that they lack visual experience. Therefore the functional organization of visual processing does not determine the presence or absence of experience.

We have seen in Chapter 6 that there is a significant *difference* between processing in normal subjects and those with blindsight, however. These subjects lack the usual kind of direct access to visual information. If the information is accessible at all, the access is indirect, and the information is certainly not available for the control of behavior in the usual way. Indeed, it is precisely because of the difference in the organization of their processing, as manifested in their behavior, that we notice anything unusual in the first place and are led to postulate the absence of experience. These cases therefore provide no evidence against the invariance principle.

3. Fading Qualia

My positive argument against the possibility of absent qualia will be based on a thought experiment involving the gradual replacement of parts of a brain, perhaps by silicon chips. Such thought experiments have been a popular response to absent qualia arguments in the folk tradition of artificial intelligence and sometimes in print. The gradual-replacement scenario is canvased by Pylyshyn (1980), although without a systematic accompanying argument. Arguments not unlike the one I am about to give have been put forward by Savitt (1982) and Cuda (1985), although they develop the arguments in different ways and draw slightly different morals from the scenario.[6]

This "fading qualia" argument will not be my strongest and most central argument against the possibility of absent qualia; that role is played by the "dancing qualia" argument, to be outlined in section 5, which also provides an argument against the possibility of inverted qualia. However, the fading qualia argument is strong in itself, and provides good motivation and background for the more powerful second argument.

The argument takes the form of a *reductio ad absurdum*. Assume that absent qualia are naturally possible. Then there could be a system with the same functional organization as a conscious system (say, me), but which lacks conscious experience entirely. Without loss of generality, assume that this is because the system is made of silicon chips instead of neurons. I will show how the argument can be extended to other kinds of isomorphs later. Call this functional isomorph Robot. The causal patterns in Robot's cognitive system are the same as they are in mine, but he has the consciousness of a zombie.

Given this situation, we can construct a series of cases intermediate between me and Robot such that there is only a very small change at each step and such that functional organization is preserved throughout. We can imagine, for instance, replacing a certain number of my neurons by silicon chips. In the first such case, only a single neuron is replaced. Its replacement is a silicon chip that performs precisely the same local function as the neuron. Where the neuron is connected to other neurons, the chip is connected to the same neurons. Where the state of the neuron is sensitive to electrical inputs and chemical signals, the silicon chip is sensitive to the same. We might imagine that it comes equipped with tiny transducers that take in electrical signals and chemical ions, relaying a digital signal to the rest of the chip. Where the neuron produces electrical and chemical outputs, the chip does the same (we can imagine it equipped with tiny effectors that produce electrical and chemical outputs depending on the internal state of the chip). Importantly, the internal states of the chip are such that the input/output function of the chip is precisely the same as that of the neuron. It does not matter how the chip does this—perhaps it uses a look-up table that associates each input with the appropriate output, perhaps it performs a computation that simulates the processes inside a neuron—as long as it gets the input–output dependencies right. If local interactions are correct, then the replacement will make no difference to the overall function of the system.

In the second case, we replace two neurons with silicon chips. It will be easiest to suppose that they are neighboring neurons. In this way, once both are replaced we can dispense with the awkward transducers and effectors that mediate the connection between the two chips. We can replace these by any kind of connection we like, as long as it is sensitive to the internal state of the first chip and affects the internal state of the second chip appropriately (there may be a connection in each direction, of course). Here we ensure that the connection is a copy of the corresponding connection in Robot; perhaps this will be an electronic signal of some kind.

Later cases proceed in the obvious fashion. In each succeeding case a larger group of neighboring neurons has been replaced by silicon chips. Within this group of chips, the biochemical substrate has been dispensed with entirely. Biochemical mechanisms are present only in the rest of the system, and in the connection between chips at the border of the group and neighboring neurons. In the final case, every neuron in the system has been replaced by a chip, and there are no biochemical mechanisms playing an essential role. (I abstract away here from detailed issues concerning whether, for instance, glial cells play a nontrivial role; if they do, they will be components of the appropriate functional organization, and will be replaced also.)

We can imagine that throughout, the internal system is connected to a body, is sensitive to bodily inputs, and produces motor movements in an appropriate way, via transducers and effectors. Each system in the sequence will be functionally isomorphic to me at a fine enough grain to share my behavioral dispositions. But while the system at one end of the spectrum is me, the system at the other end is essentially a copy of Robot.

To fix imagery, imagine that as the first system I am having rich conscious experiences. Perhaps I am at a basketball game, surrounded by shouting fans, with all sorts of brightly colored clothes in my environment, smelling the delicious aroma of junk food, perhaps suffering from a throbbing headache, and so on. Let us focus in particular on the bright red and yellow experiences I am having from watching the players' uniforms. The final system, Robot, is in the same situation, processing the same inputs and producing similar behavior, but by hypothesis is experiencing nothing at all.

Between me and Robot, there will be many intermediate cases. Question: *What is it like to be them?* What, if anything, are they experiencing? As we move along the spectrum, how does conscious experience vary? Presumably the very early cases have experiences much like mine, and the very late cases have little or no experience, but what of the intermediate cases?

Given that the system at the other end of the spectrum (Robot) is not conscious, it seems that one of two things must happen along the way. Either (1) consciousness gradually fades over the series of cases, before eventually disappearing, or (2) somewhere along the way consciousness suddenly blinks out, although the preceding case had rich conscious experiences. Call the first possibility *fading qualia* and the second *suddenly disappearing qualia.*

It is not difficult to rule out suddenly disappearing qualia. On this hypothesis, the replacement of a single neuron (leaving everything else constant) could be responsible for the vanishing of an entire field of conscious experience. This seems extremely implausible, if not entirely bizarre. If this were possible, there would be brute discontinuities in the laws of nature unlike those we find anywhere else. Any specific point for qualia to suddenly disappear (50 percent neural? 25 percent?) would be entirely arbitrary. We can even imagine running the thought experiment at a finer grain within the neuron, so that ultimately the replacement of a few molecules causes a whole field of experience to vanish (if not, we revert to the fading qualia scenario). As always in these matters, the hypothesis cannot be disproved, but its antecedent plausibility is low.

(One might argue that there are situations in nonlinear dynamics in which one magnitude depends sensitively on another, with large changes in the first arising from small changes in the second. But in these cases the dependence is nevertheless continuous, so there will be intermediate cases in which the dependent magnitude takes on intermediate values; the analogy therefore leads to fading qualia. And in any case, the sensitive dependence in these cases generally arises from the compound effects of a number of more basic gradual dependencies. In all fundamental laws known to date, the dependence of one magnitude on another continuous magnitude is continuous in this fashion, and there is no way to compound continuity into discontinuity. Suddenly disappearing qualia, in contrast to nonlinear dynamics, would require brute discontinuities in fundamental laws.)

If suddenly disappearing qualia are ruled out, we are left with fading qualia. To get a fix on this scenario, consider a system halfway along the spectrum between me and Robot, after consciousness has degraded considerably but before it has gone altogether. Call this system Joe. What is it like to be Joe? Joe, of course, is functionally isomorphic to me. He *says* all the same things about his experiences as I do about mine. At the basketball game, he exclaims about the glaring bright red-and-yellow uniforms of the basketball players.

By hypothesis, though, Joe is not having bright red and yellow experiences at all. Instead, perhaps he is experiencing tepid pink and murky brown. Perhaps he is having the faintest of red and yellow experiences. Perhaps his experiences have darkened almost to black. There are various conceivable ways in which red experiences might gradually transmute to no experience at all, and probably even more ways that we cannot conceive. But presumably in each of these the experiences must stop being *bright* before they vanish (otherwise we are left with the problem of the suddenly disappearing qualia). Similarly, there is presumably a point at which subtle distinctions in my experience are no longer present in an intermediate system's experience; if we are to suppose that all the distinctions in my experience are present right up until a moment when they simultaneously vanish, we are left with another version of suddenly disappearing qualia.

For specificity, then, imagine that Joe sees a faded pink where I see bright red, with many distinctions between shades of my experience no longer present in shades of his experience. Where I am having loud noise experiences, perhaps Joe is experiencing only a distant rumble. Not everything is so bad for Joe: where I have a throbbing headache, he only has the mildest twinge.

The crucial feature here is that Joe is systematically *wrong* about everything that he is experiencing. He certainly *says* that he is having bright red and yellow experiences, but he is merely experiencing tepid pink.[7] If you ask him, he will claim to be experiencing all sorts of subtly different shades of red, but in fact many of these are quite homogeneous in his experience. He may even complain about the noise, when his auditory experience is really very mild. Worse, on a functional construal of belief, Joe will even *believe* that he has all these complex experiences that he in fact lacks. In short, Joe is utterly out of touch with his conscious experience, and is incapable of getting in touch.

This seems to be quite implausible. Here we have a being whose rational processes are functioning and who is in fact *conscious,* but who is utterly wrong about his own conscious experiences. Perhaps in the extreme case, when all is dark inside, it might be reasonable to suppose that a system could be so misguided in its claims and judgments—after all, in a sense there is nobody in there to be wrong. But in the intermediate case, this is much less plausible. In every case with which we are familiar, conscious beings are generally capable of forming accurate judgments about their experience, in the absence of distraction and irrationality. For a sentient, rational being that is suffering from no functional pathology to be so systematically out of touch with its experiences would imply a strong dissociation between consciousness and cognition. We have little reason to believe that consciousness is such an ill-behaved phenomenon, and good reason to believe otherwise.

To be sure, fading qualia are *logically* possible. There is no contradiction in the description of a system that is so wrong about its experiences.[8] But logical possibility and natural possibility are different things. We have no reason to believe that this sort of case could happen in practice, and every reason to believe otherwise. One of the most salient empirical facts about consciousness seems to be that when a conscious being with the appropriate conceptual sophistication has experiences, it is capable of forming judgments about those experiences. Perhaps there are unusual cases where the rational processes in a system are strongly impaired, leading to a malfunction in the mechanisms of judgment, but this is not such a case. Joe's processes are *functioning* as well as mine—by hypothesis, he is functionally isomorphic. It is just that he happens to be completely misguided about his experience.

There are various cases of fading qualia in everyday life, of course. Think of what happens when one is dropping off to sleep; or think of moving back along the evolutionary chain from people to trilobites. In each case, as we move along a spectrum of cases, conscious experience gradually fades away. But in each of these cases, the fading is accompanied by a corresponding change in *functioning.* When I become drowsy, I do not believe that I am wide awake and having intense experiences (unless perhaps I start to dream, in which case I very likely *am* having intense experiences). The lack of richness in a dog's experience of color accompanies a corresponding lack of discriminatory power in a dog's visual mechanisms. These cases are quite unlike the case under consideration, in which experience fades while functioning stays constant. Joe's mechanisms can still discriminate subtly different wavelengths of light, and he certainly judges that such discriminations are reflected in his experience, but we are to believe that his experience does not reflect these discriminations at all.

Searle (1992) discusses a thought experiment like this one, and suggests the following possibility:

> [A]s the silicon is progressively implanted into your dwindling brain, you find that the area of your conscious experience is shrinking, but that this shows no effect on your external behavior. You find, to your total amazement, that you are indeed losing control of your external behavior. You find, for example, that when the doctors test your vision, you hear them say, "We are holding up a red object in front of you; please tell us what you see." You want to cry out, "I can't see anything. I'm going totally blind." But you hear your voice saying in a way that is completely out of your control, "I see a red object in front of me." If we carry the thought-experiment out to the limit, we get a much more depressing result than last time. We imagine that your conscious experience slowly shrinks to nothing, while your externally observable behavior remains the same. (pp. 66–67)

Here, Searle embraces the possibility of fading qualia, but suggests that such a system need not be mistaken in its beliefs about its experience. The system might have true beliefs about its experience; it is just that these beliefs are impotent to affect its behavior.

It seems that this possibility can be ruled out, however. There is simply no room in the system for any new beliefs to be formed. Unless one is a dualist of a very strong variety, this sort of difference in belief must be reflected in the functioning of a system—*perhaps* not in behavior, but at least in some process. But this system is identical to the original system (me) at a fine grain. There is simply no room for new beliefs such as "I can't see anything," new desires such as the desire to cry out, and other new cognitive states such as amazement. Nothing in the physical system can correspond to that amazement. There is no room for it in the neurons, which after all are identical to a subset of the neurons supporting the usual beliefs; and Searle is surely not suggesting that the silicon replacement is itself supporting the new beliefs! Failing a remarkable, magical interaction effect between neurons and silicon—and one that does not manifest itself anywhere in processing, as organization is preserved throughout—such new beliefs will not arise.

An organization-preserving change from neurons to silicon simply does not change enough to effect such a remarkable change in the content and structure of one's cognitive states. A twist in experience from red to blue is one thing, but a change in beliefs from "Nice basketball game" to "Oh no! I seem to be stuck in a bad horror movie!" is of a different order of magnitude. If such a major change in cognitive contents were not mirrored in a change in functional organization, cognition would float free of internal functioning like a disembodied Cartesian mind. If the contents of cognitive states supervened on physical states at all, they could do so only by the most arbitrary and capricious of rules (if this organization in neurons, then "Pretty colors!"; if this organization in silicon, then "Alas!").

It follows that the possibility of fading qualia requires either a bizarre relationship between belief contents and physical states, or the possibility of beings that are massively mistaken about their own conscious experiences despite being fully rational. Both of these hypotheses are significantly less plausible than the hypothesis that rational conscious beings are generally correct in their judgments about their experiences. A much more reasonable hypothesis is therefore that when neurons are replaced, qualia do not fade at all. A system like Joe, in practice, will have conscious experiences just as rich as mine. If so, then our original assumption was wrong, and the original isomorph, Robot, has conscious experiences.

The argument can be straightforwardly extended to other functional isomorphs. To deal with the case where the population of a country implements my organization, we can construct a similar spectrum of cases between my silicon isomorph and the population. Perhaps we first gradually expand the silicon system until it is many square miles across. We also slow it down so that the chips are receiving inputs at a manageable rate. After doing this, we get people to step in one at a time for the chips, making sure that they set off outputs appropriately in response to inputs. Eventually, we will be left with a case where the entire population is organized as my neurons were, perhaps even controlling a body by radio links. At every stage, the system will be functionally isomorphic to me, and precisely the same arguments apply. Either conscious experience will be preserved, or it will fade, or it will suddenly disappear. The latter two possibilities are just as implausible as before. We can conclude that the population system will support conscious experiences, just as a brain does.

We can do the same thing for any functionally isomorphic system, including those that differ in shape, size, speed, physical makeup, and so on. In all cases, the conclusion is the same. If such a system is not conscious, then there exists an intermediate isomorphic system that is conscious, has faded experiences, and is completely wrong about its experiences. Unless we are prepared to accept this massive dissociation between consciousness and cognition, the original system must have been conscious after all.

If absent qualia are possible, then fading qualia are possible. But I have argued above that fading qualia are almost certainly impossible. It follows that absent qualia are almost certainly impossible.

I will now deal with various objections to the argument.

Objection 1: Neural replacement would be impossible in practice

Those of a practical bent might not be impressed by this thought-experimental methodology. They might object that replacing neurons by silicon chips is the stuff of science fiction, not the stuff of reality. In particular, they might object that this sort of replacement would be impossible in practice, so that any conclusions that can be drawn do not reflect the realities of the situation.

If this is just supposed to be a *technological* impossibility, it is not much of a problem.What is at issue here is what kind of experience such systems would have *if* they existed, whether or not we can actually construct such a system. Natural impossibility might be relevant, though. Perhaps silicon simply lacks the capacity to perform the functions in the brain that a neuron performs, so that no silicon chip could be up to the task. It is not clear that there is a principled basis for this objection; we already have prosthetic arms and legs, and prosthetic eyes are on the way, so why not prosthetic neurons? In any case, even if a silicon functional isomorph were impossible (perhaps because neural function is uncomputable?), the argument for the invariance principle would not be affected. The invariance principle says only that *if* there is a functional isomorph of a conscious system, *then* it will have the same sort of conscious experiences. If silicon isomorphs are impossible, the assessment of silicon systems is simply irrelevant here.

An opponent might try to focus on problems with the silicon/neuron *interface,* in which case the pure neural system and the pure silicon system might both be quite possible, but intermediate systems would be challenged. Perhaps there just would not be enough room for the transducers and effectors in the tiny space a chip has available? After all, the effectors may have to store a reservoir of chemicals in order that they can be emitted when necessary. But we only need a small reservoir; the argument only requires isomorphism for a few seconds! And we could always run the thought experiment by supposing an expansion of the system. In any case, it is hard to see how this sort of point could support a deep, principled objection to the invariance principle. There will presumably be *some* systems between which gradual replacement is possible; will an objector argue that the invariance principle holds for those systems, but no other? If so, the situation seems quite arbitrary; if not, then there must be a deeper objection available.

Objection 2: Some systems *are* massively mistaken about their experience

This objection notes that there are actual cases in which subjects are seriously mistaken about their experiences. In cases of blindness denial, for example, subjects believe that they are having visual experiences when they likely have none. In these cases, however, we are no longer dealing with fully rational systems. In systems whose belief formation mechanisms are impaired, anything goes. Such systems might believe that they are Napoleon, or that the moon is pink. My "faded" isomorph Joe, by contrast, is a fully rational system, whose cognitive mechanisms are functioning just as well as mine. In conversation, he seems perfectly sensible. We cannot point to any unusually poor inferential connections between his beliefs, or any systematic psychiatric disorder that is leading his thought processes to be biased toward faulty reasoning. Joe is an eminently thoughtful, reasonable person, who exhibits none of the confabulatory symptoms of those with blindness denial. The cases are therefore disanalogous. The plausible claim is not that no system can be massively mistaken about its experiences, but that no rational system whose cognitive mechanisms are unimpaired can be so mistaken. Joe is certainly a rational system whose mechanisms are working as well as mine, so the argument is unaffected.

Objection 3: Sorites arguments are suspect

Some object that this argument has the form of a Sorites or "slippery-slope" argument, and observe that such arguments are usually suspect. Using a Sorites argument, we can "show" that even a grain of sand is a heap; after all, a million grains of sand form a heap, and if we take a single grain away from a heap we still have a heap. This reaction is based on a superficial reading of the argument, however. Sorites arguments generally gain their leverage by ignoring the fact that some apparent dichotomy is in fact a continuum: there are all sorts of vague cases between heaps and nonheaps, for example. My argument, by contrast, explicitly accepts the possibility of a continuum, but argues that the intermediate cases are impossible for independent reasons.

The argument would be a Sorites if it had the form: I am conscious; if you replace one neuron in a conscious system by a silicon chip it will still be conscious; therefore an all-silicon system will be conscious. But this is not its form. It is true that the argument against suddenly disappearing qualia relies on the impossibility of a sudden transition, but importantly it argues against sudden *large* transitions, from rich conscious experiences to none at all. This is implausible for reasons quite independent of Sorites considerations.[9]

Objection 4: Similar arguments could establish behavioral invariance

A fourth objection suggests that the argument proves too much. If it establishes the principle of organizational invariance, a similar argument would establish a principle of *behavioral* invariance. To do this, we would construct a continuum of cases from me to any behaviorally equivalent system. It would follow by similar reasoning that such a system must be conscious. But it is plausible that some systems, such as Block's (1981) giant look-up table that stores outputs for every pattern of inputs, are not conscious. Therefore there must be a flaw in the argument.

This objection fails in two ways. First, my argument relied partly on the fact that a functionally isomorphic system will have the same cognitive structure as me, and in particular the same judgments. This is what led us to the conclusion that the faded system Joe must be massively wrong in its judgments. The corresponding point does not hold for behaviorally equivalent systems. A perfect actor need not have the same judgments as me. Nor will the look-up table; nor will intermediate systems. These will work by quite different mechanisms.

Second, it is not at all obvious how one could get from me to an arbitrary behavioral isomorph by taking small steps and preserving behavioral equivalence throughout. How would one do this for the look-up table, for instance? Perhaps there are ways of doing it by taking large steps at once, but this will not be enough for the argument: if there are large steps between neighboring systems, then suddenly disappearing qualia are no longer so implausible. With functional isomorphs, there was a natural way to take very small steps, but there is no such natural method for behavioral isomorphs. It therefore seems unlikely that such an argument could get off the ground.

Ultimately, I think the only tenable way for an opponent of organizational invariance to respond to this argument is to bite the bullet and accept the possibility of fading qualia with the consequent possibility that a rational conscious system might be massively mistaken about its experience, or perhaps to bite another bullet and accept suddenly disappearing qualia and the associated brute discontinuities. This position is unattractive in its implication of a dissociation between consciousness and cognition, and the alternative seems much more plausible; but unlike the other objections it is not *obviously* wrong. The dancing qualia argument in section 5 will provide even more evidence against the possibility of absent qualia, however, so opponents of the invariance principle cannot rest easily.

I note briefly that a similar argument might establish that systems whose functional organization is *similar* (as opposed to identical) to that of a conscious system will have conscious experiences. The invariance principle taken alone is compatible with the solipsistic thesis that my organization and only my organization gives rise to experience. But one can imagine a gradual change to my organization, just as we imagined a gradual change to my physical makeup, under which my beliefs about my experience would be mostly preserved throughout, I would remain a rational system, and so on. For similar reasons to the above, it seems very likely that conscious experience would be preserved in such a transition.

4. Inverted Qualia

The fading qualia argument suggests that my functional isomorphs will have conscious experience, but it does not establish that isomorphs will have the *same* sort of conscious experience. That is, functional organization determines the existence or absence of conscious experience, but it might not determine the nature of that experience. To establish that functional organization determines the nature of experience, we will have to establish that functional isomorphs with *inverted* qualia are impossible.

The idea of inverted qualia is familiar to most of us. Few people have not wondered at some point whether what looks red to one person looks blue to another, and vice versa. It is one of those philosophical puzzles where one is at first uncertain whether the idea even makes sense, and that can be baffling even on reflection.

The possibility of inverted qualia was apparently first put forward by John Locke, in his *Essay Concerning Human Understanding*:

> *Though one Man's Idea of Blue should be different from another's.* Neither would it carry any imputation of falsehood to our simple ideas, if by the different structure of our organs it were so ordered that *the same object should produce in several men's minds different ideas* at the same time; v.g. if the idea that a violet produced in one man's mind by his eyes were the same that a marigold produced in another man's, and *vice versa.* For, since this could never be known, because one man's mind could not pass into another man's body, to perceive what appearances were produced by those organs, neither the idea hereby, nor the names, would be at all confounded, or any falsehood be in either. For all things that had the texture of a violet producing constantly the idea which he called blue, and those which had the texture of a marigold producing constantly the idea which he called yellow, whatever those appearances were in his mind, he would be able as regularly to distinguish things for his use by those appearances, and understand and signify those distinctions marked by the names "blue" and "yellow," as if the appearances or idea in his mind received from those two flowers were exactly the same with the ideas in other men's minds. (bk. 2, chap. 32, sec. 15)

Here, Locke is concerned with inverted qualia between systems with similar behavior, rather than between precise functional isomorphs. It certainly seems that a conceptual possibility is being expressed. The question for us is whether an *empirical* possibility is being expressed.

Even those who consider themselves materialists have often supposed that functional isomorphs might have different conscious experiences. For example, it is often thought naturally possible that a functional isomorph of me with different physical makeup might have blue experiences where I have red experiences, or something similar. This is the hypothesis of inverted qualia. If it is true, then while the presence of conscious experience might depend only on functional organization, the nature of experiences would depend on physiological makeup, or some other nonfunctional factor.[10]

We have seen earlier that it is difficult to hold this position consistently with materialism. If it is naturally possible that a functional isomorph could have inverted qualia, then it is logically possible. It is therefore equally logically possible that a *physical* isomorph would have inverted qualia, as there is no more of a *conceptual* connection from neurons to a specific kind of qualia than from silicon. It follows that the nature of specific experiences is a further fact over and above the physical facts, and that materialism must be false (unless one embraces the "strong metaphysical necessity" line). I will leave this point aside in what follows, however. The discussion will be independent of the truth of materialism or dualism.

The possibility of inverted qualia, or of the "inverted spectrum" as it is sometimes known, is sometimes objected to on the verificationist grounds that we could never know that anything different was going on, so that there could be no could be no real difference (e.g., Schlick 1932). Obviously I do not accept these arguments: the mere fact that we cannot tell what qualia a system is experiencing is not sufficient to conclude that there is no fact of the matter, as the nature of qualia is not conceptually tied to behavior; so I will leave this sort of objection aside here. As I discussed in Chapter 3, the hypothesis is also sometimes objected to on the grounds that our color space is asymmetrical, so that no inversion could map things appropriately (e.g., Hardin 1987; Harrison 1967, 1973). Some of the responses I made earlier are still appropriate here, even though the question is now one of natural possibility; in particular, we can still appeal to the possibility of a creature with asymmetrical color space and ask whether it could have an inverted functional isomorph. In any case I will ignore this worry, granting for the sake of argument that we have a symmetrical color space, and arguing that inverted qualia are impossible all the same.

Discussion of inverted qualia can be confusing. When I say "blue experience," do I mean (1) what a *subject* calls a "blue" experience, (2) an experience caused by a blue object, or (3) what *I* call a "blue" experience? I choose the latter usage. Throughout my discussion, by "blue experience" I will mean the kind of experience that *I* call "blue," that I usually have when I see blue things like the sky and the sea, and so on. In this usage, it is conceivable that others (or even a future version of me) might have blue experiences caused by yellow objects, or by objects they call "red," and so on.

Arguments for inverted qualia often consist simply in a conceivability claim, as with absent qualia, but such claims clearly leave the issue of natural possibility open. A couple of arguments have been given for the natural possibility of versions of inverted qualia, but neither threatens the principle of organizational invariance.

The first such argument establishes the possibility of qualia that are inverted while *behavior* is held constant (see Gert 1965; Lycan 1973; and Wittgenstein 1968). We first note that qualia could be inverted *within* a subject, perhaps by rewiring the connection from retina to central areas in my brain while I am asleep. Upon waking, I will assert that the sky suddenly seems red, grass seems yellow, and so on, and there will be every reason to believe that my qualia have been inverted. Next, we raise the possibility of someone whose brain had been rewired this way since birth. Such a person might have qualia that are systematically inverted with respect to the norm, but of course they will have learned to call the sky blue, to call grass green, and so on, so this inversion might never show up in their behavior.[11]

This does not, however, establish the possibility of inverted qualia with fixed functional organization. To see this, we need only note that in crossing my wires, the demon has *changed* my functional organization in a significant way. Similarly, the functional organization of the subject who is rewired from birth has been changed, so he will not be a functional duplicate of me. He may share some of my functional properties at a coarse grain, but he certainly will not share my fine-grained functional organization. The principle of organizational invariance is therefore unthreatened by such cases.[12]

A related argument, put forward by Block (1990), concerns "Inverted Earth," where the sky is yellow, grass is red, and so on.[13] We are to suppose that I am kidnapped and taken to Inverted Earth, but at the same time I am given color-inverting contact lenses so that everything looks normal to me. Block uses this scenario to argue against a representationalist view of qualia, where for example a blue experience is equated with a perceptual state that is about blue things (after some time on Inverted Earth, one's blue experiences will be about *yellow* things). He also uses it against a functionalist view of the sort on which blue experiences are equated with states caused by blue objects.

Again, this case does nothing to refute the organizational invariance principle. After all, when I see the yellow sky through my inverting lenses on Inverted Earth, my internal functional organization will be just as it is when I see blue sky on earth, and my experience will be the same too, just as the principle predicts. At most, the thought experiment dissociates experiences from properties of one's *environment,* and from "wide" functional properties that involve one's environment; but the functional organization I am concerned with is entirely internal. The thought experiment provides no cases where two internally isomorphic systems have different experiences, so the invariance principle is unaffected.[14]

5. Dancing Qualia

One might think that the fading qualia argument could be directly adapted to provide an argument against the possibility of inverted qualia. Unfortunately this will not work. Imagine how an analogous argument would go. We start with me, having a red experience, and an inverted system having a blue experience. By gradual replacement, we construct a series of cases, each having some intermediate color. But there is nothing wrong with this! The intermediate systems are simply cases of mild qualia inversion and are no more problematic than the extreme case.

To be sure, it may not be obvious just what the intermediate systems are experiencing. Perhaps no color from our usual color space can do the job, consistently with the systems' patterns of categorization and differences. But perhaps they are experiencing entirely new colors, ones that I cannot experience but that nevertheless form a continuum from red to blue. This would be odd, but it is not vastly implausible. Importantly, the problem with the fading qualia case will be entirely absent. These systems will *not* be systematically wrong about the features of their experience. Where they claim to experience distinctions, they may still experience distinctions; where they claim intense experiences, they have intense experiences; and so on. To be sure, the colors they call "red" will be different from what I call red, but this is nothing problematic; it happens already in the usual inversion case. What counts is that unlike the fading qualia case, the *structural* features of these systems' experiences are preserved throughout.

Nevertheless, a good argument against the possibility of inverted qualia can be found in the vicinity.[15] Once again, for the purposes of *reductio,* assume that inverted qualia are empirically possible. Then there can be two functionally isomorphic systems, in the same functional state but having different experiences. Suppose for the sake of illustration that these systems are me, having a red experience, and my silicon isomorph, having a blue experience (there is a small caveat about generality, which I discuss later).

As before, we construct a series of cases intermediate between me and my isomorph. Here, the argument takes a different turn. We need not worry about the *way* in which experiences change as we move along the series. Perhaps they change suddenly, perhaps they jump all over the map, although surely it is most plausible that they change gradually. All that matters is that there must be two points *A* and *B* in this series, such that (1) no more than one-tenth of the brain is replaced between *A* and *B,* and (2) *A* and *B* have significantly different experiences. To see that this must be the case, we need only consider the points at which 10 percent, 20 percent, and so on up to 90 percent of the brain have been replaced. Red and blue are sufficiently different experiences that some neighboring pairs here *must* be significantly different (that is, different enough that the difference would be noticeable if they were experienced by the same person); there is no way to get from red to blue by ten unnoticeable jumps.

It is true that there can be unnoticeable differences between different experiences. If one changes a shade of red little enough, I will not be able to tell the difference. One might suppose that this is because there is no difference in experience, only a difference in the world; but if this were all that was going on one could iterate such a change a thousand times, eventually showing that red and blue produce the same experiences, which is ridiculous. So there can be *some* difference in experience that is not noticeable. One can observe this phenomenon by looking at a wide expanse of paint of subtly varying shade; sometimes it is extremely difficult to tell whether one's experiences of different parts is the same or different. But importantly, unnoticeable differences are very *small.* At best, ten such jumps could take us from a shade of red to a subtly different shade of the same color. (This opens up a small loophole in the generality of the argument; I return to this point later.)

Between the red and blue systems, there must therefore be two systems that differ in at most 10 percent of their internal makeup, but that have significantly different experiences. For the purposes of illustration, let these systems be me and Bill. Where I have a red experience, Bill has a slightly different experience. We may as well suppose that Bill sees blue; perhaps his experience will be more similar to mine than that, but it makes no difference to the argument. The two systems also differ in that where there are neurons in some small region of my brain, there are silicon chips in Bill's brain. This substitution of a silicon circuit for a neural circuit is the only physical difference between Bill and me.

The crucial step in the thought experiment is to take a silicon circuit just like Bill's and install it in my own head as a *backup circuit.* This circuit will be functionally isomorphic to a circuit already present in my head. We equip the circuit with transducers and effectors so that it can interact with the rest of my brain, but we do not hook it up directly. Instead, we install a *switch* that can switch directly between the neural and silicon circuits. Upon flipping the switch, the neural circuit becomes irrelevant and the silicon circuit takes over. We can imagine that the switch controls the points of interface where the relevant circuits affect the rest of the brain. When it is switched, the connections from the neural circuit are pushed out of the way, and the silicon circuit's effectors are attached. (We can imagine that the transducers for both circuits are attached the entire time, so that the state of both circuits evolves appropriately, but so that only one circuit at a time is involved in processing. We could also run a similar experiment where both transducers and effectors are disconnected, to ensure that the backup circuit is entirely isolated from the rest of the system. This would change a few details, but the moral would be the same.)

Immediately after flipping the switch, processing that was once performed by the neural circuit is now performed by the silicon circuit. The flow of control within the system has been redirected. However, my functional organization is exactly the same as it would have been if we had not flipped the switch. The only relevant difference between the two cases is the physical makeup of one circuit within the system. There is also a difference in the physical makeup of another "dangling" circuit, but this is irrelevant to functional organization, as it plays no role in affecting other components of the system and directing behavior.

What happens to my experience when we flip the switch? Before installing the circuit, I was experiencing red. After we install it but before we flip the switch, I will presumably still be experiencing red, as the only difference is the addition of a circuit that is not involved in processing in any way; for all the relevance it has to my processing, I might as well have eaten it. *After* flipping the switch, however, I am more or less the same system as Bill. The only difference between Bill and me now is that I have a causally irrelevant neural circuit dangling from the system (we might even imagine that the circuit is destroyed when the switch is flipped). Bill, by hypothesis, was enjoying a blue experience. After the switch, then, I will have a blue experience too.

What will happen, then, is that my experience will change "before my eyes." Where I was once experiencing red, I will now experience blue. All of a sudden, I will have a *blue* experience of the apple on my desk. We can even imagine flipping the switch back and forth a number of times, so that the red and blue experiences "dance" before my eyes.

This might seem reasonable at first—it is a strangely appealing image—but something very odd is going on here. My experiences are switching from red to blue, but *I do not notice any change.* Even as we flip the switch a number of times and my qualia dance back and forth, I will simply go about my business, noticing nothing unusual. By hypothesis, my functional organization remains normal throughout. In particular, my functional organization after flipping the switch evolves just as it would have if the switch had not been flipped. There is no special difference in my behavioral dispositions. I am not suddenly disposed to say "Hmm! Something strange is going on!" There is no room for a sudden start, for an exclamation, or even for a distraction of attention. Any unusual reaction would imply a functional difference between the two circuits, contrary to their stipulated isomorphism. By design, my cognitive organization is just as it usually is, and in particular is precisely as it would have been had the switch not been flipped.

Certainly, on any functional construal of belief, it is clear that I cannot acquire any new beliefs as the flip takes place. Even if one disputes a functional account, it is extremely implausible that a simple replacement of a neural circuit by a silicon circuit while overall organization is preserved could be responsible for the addition of significant new beliefs such as "My qualia just flipped." As in the case of fading qualia, there is simply no room for such a change to take place, unless it is in an accompanying Cartesian disembodied mind.

We are therefore led once more into a *reductio ad absurdum*. It seems entirely implausible to suppose that my experiences could change in such a significant way, with my paying full attention to them, without my being able to notice the change. It would suggest once again a radical dissociation between consciousness and cognition. If this kind of thing could happen, then psychology and phenomenology would be radically out of step; much further out of step than even the fading qualia scenario would imply.

This "dancing qualia" scenario may be logically possible (although the case is so extreme that it seems *only just* logically possible), but that does not mean that it is plausible as an empirical possibility, any more than it is plausible that the world was created five minutes ago. As an empirical hypothesis, it seems far more plausible that when one's experiences change significantly, then as long as one is rational and paying attention, one should be able to notice the change. If not, then consciousness and cognition are tied together only by the most slender of threads.

Indeed, if we are to suppose that dancing qualia are naturally possible, we are led to a worrying thought: they might be *actual* and happening to us all the time. The physiological properties of our functional mechanisms are constantly changing. The functional properties of the mechanisms are reasonably robust; one would expect that this robustness would be ensured by evolution. But there is no adaptive reason for the nonfunctional properties to stay constant. From moment to moment there will certainly be changes in low-level molecular properties. Properties such as position, atomic makeup, and so on can change while functional role is preserved, and such change is almost certainly going on constantly.

If we allow that qualia are dependent not just on functional organization but on implementational details, it may well be that *our* qualia are in fact dancing before our eyes all the time. There seems to be no principled reason why a change from neurons to silicon should make a difference while a change in neural realization should not;[16] the only place to draw a *principled* line is at the functional level.[17] The reason why we doubt that such dancing is taking place in our own cases is that we accept the following principle: When one's experiences change significantly, one can notice the change. If we were to accept the possibility of dancing qualia in the original case, we would be discarding this principle, and it would no longer be available as a defense against skepticism even in the more usual cases.

It is not out of the question that we could actually perform such an experiment. Of course the practical difficulties would be immense, but at least in principle, one could install such a circuit in me and *I* could see what happened, and report it to the world. But of course there is no point performing the experiment: we know what the result will be. I will report that my experience stayed the same throughout, a constant shade of red, and that I noticed nothing untoward. I will become even more convinced than I was before that qualia are determined by functional organization. Of course this will not be a *proof,* but the evidence will be hard to seriously dispute.

I conclude that by far the most plausible hypothesis is that replacement of neurons while preserving functional organization will preserve qualia. The problems with the dancing qualia scenario can be blamed on the initial assumption that a functionally isomorphic silicon system might experience blue where I experience red. The most reasonable reaction is to withdraw this assumption, thus concluding that experience is wholly determined by functional organization.

It should be noted that this thought experiment works just as well against the possibility of absent qualia as against that of inverted qualia. We simply take two points on the way to absent qualia between which experience differs significantly and install a backup circuit in the same way. As before, if absent qualia are possible, then switching will cause my qualia to oscillate before my eyes, from vivid to tepid and back, without my ever noticing. Again, it is far more plausible that such dancing without noticing is impossible, so that absent qualia are impossible.

Personally, I find this an even more convincing argument against absent qualia than the argument in section 3, although both have a role to play. An opponent might just bite the bullet and accept the possibility of fading qualia, but dancing qualia seem an order of magnitude more difficult to accept. The very immediacy of the switch seems to make a significant difference, as does the fact that the phenomenon the subject cannot notice is so dynamic and striking. Fading qualia would mean that some systems are out of touch with their conscious experience, but dancing qualia would establish an even stranger gap.

Because of the structure of the dancing qualia argument, it leaves open a few more loopholes than the fading qualia argument. It does not seem that any of these loopholes can be exploited to lead to an attractive position for an opponent, however. I will discuss these loopholes in what follows, alongside another objection to the argument. The objections to the fading qualia case can all be made again, and the replies are more or less the same; I will not bother to repeat them.

Objection 1: Loopholes concerning speed and history

The argument I have given here can naturally be extended from the neural/silicon case to many other examples of functional isomorphs, but there are a couple of exceptions involving speed and history. If an isomorph is much faster or slower than the original system, we cannot simply substitute a circuit from one system into the other and expect everything to function normally. So the argument as I have given it does not rule out the possibility that a change in speed that leaves functional organization constant might be responsible for an inversion in qualia. A similar loophole is left open for physical isomorphs that differ merely in their *history*: perhaps if I was born in the Southern Hemisphere I will experience green, whereas a physical twin born in the North will experience red. History cannot be varied in a dancing qualia scenario (although it can be varied in a fading qualia scenario), so the argument does not bear on the hypothesis that qualia supervene on the past.

But neither of these hypotheses were very plausible in the first place. It is reasonable that history should affect our qualia by affecting our physical structure, but the history dependence required above would be much stronger: there would in effect be a "nonlocal" effect of distal history on present qualia, unmediated by anything in physical structure or nearby in space and time. As for speed, it would seem quite arbitrary that a change in speed would invert qualia when nothing else could. The hypotheses here are coherent, so an opponent *could* embrace them, but there is little reason to. Once we have established that all other organization-preserving changes preserve qualia, there is little attraction in the idea that speed or history might be the only things that make a difference.

Objection 2: What about mild inversions?

Another small loophole is that the argument does not refute the possibility of very mild spectrum inversions. Between dark red and a slightly darker red, for instance, there may be nine intermediate shades such that no two neighboring shades are distinguishable. In such a case the dancing qualia scenario is not a problem; if the system notices no difference on flipping the switch, that is just what we would expect.

Of course, there is nothing special about the figure of one-tenth as the amount of difference between two neighboring systems. But we cannot make the figure too high. If we made it as high as one half, we would run into problems with personal identity: it might reasonably be suggested that upon flipping the switch, we are creating a new person, and it would not be a problem that the new person noticed no change. Perhaps we might go as high as 20 percent or 25 percent without such problems; but that would still allow the possibility of very mild inversions, the kind that could be composed of four or five unnoticeable changes. We can reduce the impact of this worry, however, by noting that it is very unlikely that experience depends equally on all areas of the brain. If color experience depends largely on a small area of the visual cortex, say, then we could perform any qualia inversion in one fell swoop while only replacing a small portion of the system, and the argument would succeed against even the mildest noticeable qualia inversion.

In any case, any loophole here is an unthreatening one. At best, we have left open the possibility that an extremely mild underdetermination of experience by organization is possible. This sort of underdetermination might seem so slight as to be uninteresting, but in any case, we can note that it leads to an unattractive position. It would seem reasonable that experiences should be invertible across the board, or not invertible at all, but why should the world be such that a small inversion is possible but nothing more? This would seem quite arbitrary. We cannot rule it out, but it is not a hypothesis with much antecedent plausibility.

Objection 3: Unattended qualia

In a similar way, the argument leaves open the loophole that *unattended* qualia might be invertible. If we are not attending to the fringes of our visual field, for example, a qualia inversion might take place there without our noticing. Indeed, recent experiments (Rensink, O'Regan, and Clark 1995) show that one can change quite significant features of an image that a subject is looking at without the subject noticing, if they are not concentrating on those features (these experiments typically involve a short time interval between the display of two images, so it is not quite like the dancing qualia scenario, but it is close). So these arguments leave open the possibility that *unattended* qualia might be invertible.

Nothing in this sort of consideration suggests that *attended* qualia could be invertible, however. So to exploit this loophole would leave one in the unattractive position that qualia are organizationally invariant when they are central enough in one's attention, but dependent on other features when they are not. (Presumably an inverted green experience on the fringe will flip back to red when one attends to it?) It seems most unlikely that such a position could be made theoretically satisfying. As with the other loopholes, this loophole opens the way only to positions that lack any significant antecedent plausibility.

Objection 4: Double switching

Another objection is the following.[18] We can imagine a related experiment in which we rewire the connections from red and blue inputs to central areas of the brain so that blue inputs play the role that red inputs once played, and in which we also systematically rewire connections *downstream* from the central area to compensate. When a blue input causes the central area to go into a state previously associated with red, connections from the central area to the rest of the brain are rewired so that the rest of the brain functions just as it would function had there been no rewiring at all. This way, my experience will almost certainly switch from red to blue, but my behavioral dispositions will stay constant throughout. In this case, a repeated switch would surely lead to dancing qualia. So aren't dancing qualia reasonable after all?

First, I should note that this rewiring would be a much vaster task than any other cases I have described. The central area will affect the rest of the brain at all sorts of different places. Each of these connections will have to be rewired, and crucially, no simple rewiring could do the job at any of them. We cannot simply switch "red outputs" to "blue outputs," as we could with inputs; the outputs from the central system may represent such diverse things as retrieved memories, motor instructions, and so on, with no simple difference in "polarity" between an output for red and an output for blue. To determine an appropriate "blue output," one would probably need to simulate the entire processing of the central area, given its initial state and input, to see what it produces. If so, it will be this simulation that is doing the causal work, not the central area itself, and the force of the scenario will be lost.

Second, even if there somehow turned out to be a simple way in which outputs could be rewired, note that *only* behavioral dispositions are preserved, and not functional organization. What might this feel like? In this case, I imagine that I would *notice* the switch and try to act accordingly, but would feel as if some jarring puppeteer was interfering with my actions. Unlike the previous case, there will be *room* for these extra beliefs and other cognitive states; they will be supported by the different states of the central area. And we can imagine that once feedback takes place, and input to the central areas indicates that its motor movements have been entirely different from what was planned, we can imagine that the central area state will be severely shaken up. In fact, this leads us back to the first objection, as it would seem almost impossible to systematically compensate for these feedback effects. In any case, the significant difference in functional organization means that the cases are not analogous.

6. Nonreductive Functionalism

To summarize: We have established that if absent qualia are possible, then fading qualia are possible; if inverted qualia are possible, then dancing qualia are possible; and if absent qualia are possible, then dancing qualia are possible. But it is implausible that fading qualia are possible, and it is extremely implausible that dancing qualia are possible. It is therefore extremely implausible that absent qualia and inverted qualia are possible. It follows that we have good reason to believe that the principle of organizational invariance is true, and that functional organization fully determines conscious experience.

It should be noted these arguments do not establish functionalism in the strongest sense, as they establish at best that absent and inverted qualia are empirically (or naturally) impossible. There are two reasons why the arguments cannot be extended into arguments for the *logical* impossibility of absent and inverted qualia, as some functionalists might like. First, both fading qualia and dancing qualia seem to be coherent hypotheses, even if they are not plausible. Some might dispute the logical possibility of these hypotheses, perhaps holding that it is constitutive of qualia that we can notice differences in them. This conceptual intuition is disputable, but in any case there is a second reason why these arguments fail to establish the logical determination of experience by functional organization.

To see this second reason, note that the arguments take as an *empirical* premise certain facts about the distribution of functional organization in physical systems: that I have conscious experiences of a certain kind, or that some biological systems do. If we established the logical impossibility of fading and dancing qualia, this might establish the logical necessity of the *conditional*: if one system with fine-grained functional organization F has a certain sort of conscious experience, then any system with organization F has those experiences. But we cannot establish the logical necessity of the conclusion of this conditional without establishing the logical necessity of the premise, and the premise is itself empirical. To establish the logical determination of experience by functional organization, we would first have to establish the logical supervenience of experience on the physical, which I have argued cannot be done. Even if we *could* establish logical supervenience on the physical, it would probably be through a functional definition, but with such a definition the logical impossibility of absent and inverted qualia would follow without any need for any fancy arguments. So either way, the fading and dancing qualia arguments are of little use in arguing for the logical or metaphysical impossibility of absent or inverted qualia.

The arguments therefore fail to establish a strong form of functionalism upon which functional organization is *constitutive* of conscious experience; but they succeed in establishing the weaker form that I have called *nonreductive functionalism,* on which functional organization suffices for conscious experience with natural necessity. On this view, conscious experience is determined by functional organization, but it need not be reducible to functional organization.

In any case, the conclusion is still a strong one. The invariance principle tells us that in principle, cognitive systems realized in all sorts of media can be conscious. In particular, the conclusion gives strong support to the ambitions of researchers in artificial intelligence, as I discuss further in Chapter 9. If nonreductive functionalism is correct, the irreducibility of consciousness poses no barrier to the eventual construction of a conscious computational device.

Most importantly, we have advanced in our quest to constrain the principles in virtue of which consciousness naturally supervenes on the physical. We have narrowed down the relevant properties in the supervenience base to *organizational* properties. In a certain sense, we can say that not only does consciousness supervene on the physical, but it supervenes on the organizational. This needs to be spelled out carefully, due to the fact that every system realizes numerous kinds of functional organization, but we can say the following: for every physical system that gives rise to conscious experience, there is some functional organization F realized by the system, such that it is naturally necessary that any system that realizes F will have identical conscious experiences. To pick out the relevant F, we need to go to a fine enough grain to fix cognitive states such as judgments. This in turn can be achieved by requiring that F is fine-grained enough to fix the mechanisms responsible for the production of behavior, and to fix behavioral dispositions. This is all that the fading and dancing qualia arguments required, so it is all we need for organizational invariance.

It is therefore a law, for certain functional organizations F, that realization of F will be accompanied by a specific kind of conscious experience. This is not to say that it will be a *fundamental* law. It would be odd if the universe had fundamental laws connecting complex functional organizations to conscious experiences. Rather, one would expect it to be a consequence of simpler, more fundamental psychophysical laws. In the meantime, the principle of organizational invariance acts as a strong constraint on an ultimate theory.

8

Consciousness and Information: Some Speculation

1. Toward a Fundamental Theory

So far, we have isolated a few connections between consciousness and physical processes that deserve to be called psychophysical laws. One of these is the coherence principle connecting consciousness to awareness, or global availability. Another is the more specific principle of structural coherence, connecting the structure of consciousness to the structure of awareness. The principle of organizational invariance is a third. These principles may be *components* of a final theory of consciousness. They enable us to use physical facts to predict and even to explain certain facts about conscious experience. And they certainly *constrain* the form of a final theory of consciousness: if such a theory is not compatible with these laws, it is unlikely to be correct. But there must be more to the story than this. These principles do not themselves add up to a final theory, or anything close to it.

The trouble is that none of these principles are plausible candidates to be *fundamental* laws in a theory of consciousness. All of them express regularities at a fairly high level. The concept of awareness (or global availability) is a high-level concept, for example, and its boundaries are somewhat vague; it is very unlikely that this concept would be involved in a fundamental law. The principle of organizational invariance may be less vague, but it still expresses a regularity at a level that is far from fundamental. Another problem: these principles grossly underdetermine the nature of the psychophysical connection. All sorts of questions about the connection remain unanswered. For example, just what *kind* of organization gives rise to conscious experience? How simple can an organization be before experience vanishes? And how can we predict the specific character of an experience (not just its structure) from its physical basis? We would like a complete theory of consciousness to answer these questions, but the principles covered so far do not help.

For a final theory, we need a set of psychophysical laws analogous to fundamental laws in physics. These fundamental (or *basic*) laws will be cast at a level connecting basic properties of experience with simple features of the physical world. The laws should be precise, and should together leave no room for underdetermination. When combined with the physical facts about a system, they should enable us to perfectly predict the phenomenal facts about the system. Further, just as the basic laws of physics entail all higher-level physical laws and regularities (at least when combined with boundary conditions), the basic laws about consciousness should entail and explain the various nonbasic laws, such as the coherence principles and the principle of organizational invariance. Once we have a set of fundamental physical *and* psychophysical laws, we may in a certain sense understand the basic structure of the universe.

This is a tall order, and we will not achieve it anytime soon. But we can at least move in this direction. The principles of organizational invariance and structural coherence already put a strong constraint on the form of a fundamental theory, and there are not a vast number of candidates for the basic constructs that might be the theory's fundamental ingredients. In this chapter, I present some ideas toward a fundamental theory. I do not present a full-fledged theory with a comprehensive set of basic laws, but I put forward suggestions about the constructs involved in these laws, and about what the broad shape of the laws might be. This could be considered a *prototheory*: a skeleton around which a theory might be built.

The ideas in this chapter are much sketchier and more speculative than those elsewhere in the book, and they raise as many questions as they answer. They are also the most likely to be entirely wrong. In putting forward these loose ideas, the goal is not to set out a framework that will withstand close philosophical scrutiny; instead, they are put forward in the spirit of getting ideas onto the table. We have to *start* thinking about fundamental theories of consciousness, and perhaps there will be something useful here that might be carried forward.

2. Aspects of Information

The basic notion I will deal with in this chapter is that of *information*. There are many different concepts of information afloat in the space of contemporary ideas, so the first thing one has to do when talking about information is to clarify what one is talking about. The concept of information I am concerned with has much in common with that discussed by Shannon (1948). Here, I present an adaptation and development of this idea.

I leave the development relatively informal, providing just enough formalism to capture the most central aspects of the concept that will be relevant. There are a few technicalities in this section, but later sections are more straightforward.

Shannon was not concerned with a semantic notion of information, on which information is always information *about* something. Rather, he focused on a formal or syntactic notion of information, where the key is the concept of a state selected from an ensemble of possibilities. The most basic sort of information is the *bit*, which represents a choice between two possibilities: a single bit (0 or 1) selected from a two-state space is said to carry information. In a more complex case, a "message" such as "0110010101" chosen from a space of possible binary messages carries information in a similar way. What is important, on Shannon's account, is not any *interpretation* of these states; what matters is the *specificity* of a state within a space of different possibilities.

We can formalize this idea by appealing to the concept of an *information space*. An information space is an abstract space consisting of a number of states, which I will call *information states,* and a basic structure of *difference relations* between those states. The simplest nontrivial information space is the space consisting of two states with a primitive difference between them. We can think of these states as the two "bits," 0 and 1. The fact that these two states are different from each other exhausts their nature. That is, this information space is fully characterized by its difference structure.

Other information spaces are more complex. This can happen in two ways: by allowing a more complex difference structure between states, or by allowing the states themselves to have internal structure. To illustrate the first way, we might move to a four-state space involving states 0, 1, 2, and 3. To illustrate the second way, we might move to a structured space involving states such as "110010101." Of course the two ways might be combined, yielding doubly complex states as in the space of messages such as "233102032." I discuss these two sorts of complexity in more detail in what follows.

Starting with the first sort of complexity: most obviously, there is a three-state space, a four-state space, and so on, whose difference structure is a natural extension of that of the two-state space. For example, an element A, B, C, or D chosen from a four-element space carries information in the same sort of way that a bit carries information. Of course, the nature of the labels "A," "B," and so on is irrelevant here; once again, all that is essential to the space is its structure.

More importantly, there are *continuous* information spaces, whose states lie on a continuum analogous to the continuum of real numbers between 0 and 1. Such a space has an infinite number of states. This space has a much more complex difference structure than the previous cases: the structure corresponds directly to the topology of the continuum, with certain states lying between other states, some states closer to each other than other states, and so on. But as before, we can see a single point chosen from the continuum as carrying information.

One can also have an information space whose structure is that of a two-dimensional continuum, or a multidimensional continuum, analogous to the structure of a region of n-dimensional space. A single point selected from a region of three-dimensional space will carry information, for example. In the most general case, the structure can be given by that of an arbitrary topological space, which in effect supplies a set with "proximity" or "neighborhood" relations. The details of this will not matter too much in what follows, however, where I will deal with intuitively familiar structures such as that of the continuum.

The second sort of complexity involves states with *internal structure*. These states are made up from a number of more basic states that I will call *elements*. An example is the space of ten-bit states, analogous to "messages" such as "1001101000." Each state here consists of ten elements, and each element can be seen to fall into its own two-state *subspace* corresponding to the original two-state space. We can see this information space as a kind of product of ten subspaces, each of which is an information space in its own right.

There can also be more interesting internal structures. For example, an information state might have continuous internal structure, so that it is a sort of continuous analog of the ten-element structure discussed earlier. Such a state would have an infinite number of elements, each of which falls into a subspace of its own. We might think of the corresponding information space here as akin to the space of functions over a continuum (with each value falling into a subspace), or over a more complex continuous space.

It can also happen that the *subspaces* are complex in the first way mentioned above: for example, the elements in each subspace might fall along a continuum. So there is room for two simultaneous levels of complexity here. For example, each state might consist in a continuous structure of elements, each of which can take on values within a continuous subspace. An information state in this space might be seen as a waveform, or some other function with continuous domain and range: it is a continuous analog of the discrete "messages" described previously.

In the most general case, an information space will have two sorts of structure: each complex state might have an internal structure, and each element in this state will belong to a subspace with a topological difference structure of its own. We might call the first of these the *combinatorial* structure of the space, and the second of these the *relational* structure of the subspaces. Much of the time, each subspace will have the same relational structure, so we can just speak of the relational structure of the space itself.

The *overall* structure of the space is given by these combinatorial and relational structures together. I will often restrict attention to information spaces with only relational structure and not combinatorial structure—the case in which there is only one element in an information state—as the discussion is much simpler in that case.

This framework does not incorporate anything like a notion of semantic content, so the sort of information discussed here is at best indirectly related to the semantic variety of information discussed by philosophers such as Dretske (1981) and Barwise and Perry (1983). It might be possible to extend the current framework so it has a semantic element, by associating some sort of semantic content with each information state, but as it stands the framework is independent of semantic considerations.

This formalization captures Shannon's idea that information essentially involves a state selected from a number of possibilities (in the relational structure of a space), and also captures the idea that complex information can be built up from simple information (in the combinatorial structure of a space). A single bit can constitute information for Shannon, as can a long "message" such as "10011010." Shannon also considers the case where information falls into a continuous space, or into a space of functions over a continuous domain. In each case, it is the selection of a single element from a space of contrasting possibilities that is crucial.

Shannon's own account is often concerned with the *amount of information* in an information state, which measures how *specific* a state is within an information space. A state within a two-state information space carries one bit of information; a state within a four-state space carries two bits; a state within an n-element space carries $\log_2 n$ bits. When a space is a combination of subspaces, a state carries an amount of information equal to the sum of the amounts carried by its elements: so a ten-digit binary "message" carries ten bits of information. This treatment applies to discrete spaces; within continuous spaces, amount of information must be defined more subtly. Here, I will not be very concerned with amounts of information. Rather, I will be concerned with information states themselves, which we might think of as standing to amount of information as matter stands to mass.

Physically realized information

As I have defined them, information spaces are *abstract* spaces, and information states are abstract states. They are not part of the concrete physical or phenomenal world. But we can find information in both the physical and the phenomenal world, if we look at things the right way. To do this, we need to discuss the various ways in which information spaces and states can be *realized* in the world. I will discuss physical realization and phenomenal realization in turn.

It seems intuitively clear that information spaces and states are realized throughout the physical world. We can see my light switch as realizing a two-state information space, for example, with its states "up" and "down" realizing the two states. Or we can see a compact disk as realizing a combinatorial information state, consisting in a complex structure of bits. One can see information realized in a thermostat, a book, or a telephone line in similar ways. How can we make sense of these intuitions?

The natural way to make the connection between physical systems and information states is to see physically realized information in terms of a slogan due to Bateson (1972): information is a *difference that makes a difference*. While my light switch can take on an infinite number of positions in a continuous range, most of this variation makes no difference at all to my light. Whether the switch is all the way up, or one-quarter of the way down, the light will be on. When it is in positions more than about one-third of the way down, on the other hand, the light will be off. As far as the light is concerned, there are only two relevant states of the switch, which we can call "up" and "down." The difference between these two states is the only difference that makes a difference to the light. So we can see the switch as realizing a two-state information space, with some physical states of the switch corresponding to one information state and with some corresponding to the other.

In general, an information space associated with a physical object will always be defined with respect to a *causal pathway* (in this case, the pathway from the light switch to the light) and a space of possible *effects* at the end of the pathway (in this case, the on/off state of the light). Physical states will correspond to information states according to their effects on the causal pathway. When two physical states have the same effect on the pathway—as with two positions of the light switch both of which lead to the light being on—they will correspond to the same information state. If we carve up physical states in this way, we will arrive at a basic set of physical differences that make a difference, making up the physical realization of an information space.

The structure of the information space will correspond directly to the structure of the space of effects, which will itself be either a discrete or continuous space. In the case of the light, for example, there are two relevant effects on the causal pathway: the light can be on or off. So the switch can be seen to realize a two-state information space.

We can treat continuous information spaces in a similar way. If my light has a dimmer switch, then rotating the knob to different positions produces different intensities of light in a continuous range. (In practice the range may be discrete, but I idealize.) The effects on light intensity define a continuous information space realized in my light switch. Physical states of the switch that produce the same light intensity (states in areas where the knob is insensitive, perhaps, or states that vary in irrelevant parameters such as color of the switch) will be associated with the same information state. The space of information states has the topological structure of a continuum, with the structure of differences between the states corresponding to the structure of differences in the effect on light intensity.

The information realized in a compact disk can also be analyzed this way. A disk has an infinite number of possible physical states, but when its effects on a compact-disk player are considered, it realizes only a finite number of possible information states. Many changes in the disk—a microscopic alteration below the level of resolution of the optical reading device, or a small scratch on the disk, or a large mark on the reverse side—make no difference to the functioning of the system. The only differences relevant to the disk's information state are those that are reflected in the output of the optical reading device. These are the differences in the presence of pits and lands on the disk, which correspond to what we think of as "bits." Any given state of the disk will have an associated information state within a large information space. The physical states of different pressings of the same recording will be associated with the same information state, if all goes well. Pressings of different recordings, or indeed imperfect pressings of the same recording, will be associated with different information states, due to their different effects.

This is a case in which a physically realized information space has combinatorial structure. Each "bit" on the compact disk has an independent effect on the compact disk player, so that each location on the disk can be seen to realize a two-state subspace of its own. Putting all these independent effects together, we find a combinatorial structure in the space of total effects of a compact disk, and so we can find the same combinatorial structure in the information space that the compact disk realizes. This information space can be seen to be the product of a large collection of two-state subspaces, one for every pit or land on the disk.

Note that on this account, physically realized information is only information insofar as it can be *processed*. As Mackay (1969) puts it, "[I]nformation is as information does." This squares with Shannon's own treatment of information. Shannon's "amount of information" measures how specific a state is within the space of states that can be *transmitted*—that is, that can play distinct roles on a different causal pathway (what Shannon calls a communication channel). For Shannon, information is always a transmittable state, and indeed the extent of an information space is implicitly defined by the function of a transmitter. Information is a difference that can make a difference in transmission.

This is made clear by Shannon's standard diagram (Figure 8.1) and his associated discussion. An information source is a set of "messages" (information states), where it is assumed that distinct messages are coded into distinct

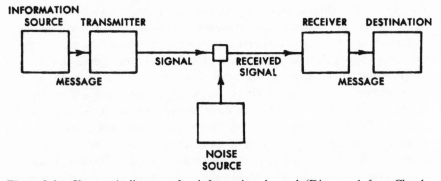

Figure 8.1. Shannon's diagram of an information channel. (Diagram 1, from Claude E. Shannon and Warren Weaver, *The Mathematical Theory of Communication*, 1963. Copyright 1949 by the Board of Trustees of the University of Illinois Press. Used with permission of the University of Illinois Press.)

signals by a transmitter, and that distinct transmitted signals correspond to distinct messages. Indeed, this property *defines* what it is for states to count as distinct messages. If two different physical states of the system are converted into the same signal, then they realize the same message. Corruption and loss of information may be introduced later in the process, as the right-hand side of the diagram indicates, but it is constitutive of an information channel that distinct information states produce different effects through a transmitter. All this is implicit rather than explicit in Shannon's account, where there is no direct treatment of the relationship between physical states and information states. But on a close look it is clear that when information states are individuated, the transmittability principle is doing the work.

I will not try to give precise criteria for the realization of an information space in a physical system. Instead, I will leave things at the informal level of the "difference that makes a difference" principle. There are a number of different ways in which this informal idea might be fleshed out into a formal account, some of which put stronger constraints on realization than others. It would be premature to settle on one of these in particular at this point. By leaving things informal, we allow some room for maneuver in the details, which can be clarified as we get a better idea of what is appropriate for a specific application. For the purpose of a theory of consciousness, fleshing out these details in the right way will be part of the process of fleshing out the theory.

Phenomenally realized information

Physical realization is the most common way to think about information embedded in the world, but it is not the only way information can be found.

We can also find information realized in our *phenomenology*. States of experience fall directly into information spaces in a natural way. There are natural patterns of similarity and difference between phenomenal states, and these patterns yield the difference structure of an information space. Thus we can see phenomenal states as realizing information states within those spaces.

For example, the space of simple color experiences has a three-dimensional relational structure that we have already discussed. Abstracting the patterns of similarity and difference among these experiences, we obtain an abstract information space with a three-dimensional relational structure which the phenomenal space realizes. Any given simple color experience corresponds to a specific location within this space. A specific red experience is one phenomenally realized information state; a specific green experience is another.

More complex experiences, such as experiences of an entire visual field, fall into information spaces with a complex combinatorial structure. When I look at a picture, for example, my experience falls into a space with (at least) the combinatorial structure of a two-dimensional continuum, with each element in that continuum having (at least) the three-dimensional relational structure of simple color space. The structure of color patches in a visual field is not *so* different in kind from the structure of binary digits in a ten-digit message, although both the combinatorial and the relational structure are much more complex.

To find information spaces realized phenomenally, we do not rely on the causal "difference that makes a difference" principle that we used to find information spaces realized physically. Rather, we rely on the intrinsic qualities of experiences and the structure among them—the similarity and difference relations that they bear to each other, and their intrinsic combinatorial structure. Any experience will bear natural relations of similarity and difference with other experiences, so we will always be able to find information spaces into which experiences fall.

The double-aspect principle

This treatment of information brings out a crucial link between the physical and the phenomenal: whenever we find an information space realized phenomenally, we find the same information space realized physically. And when an experience realizes an information state, the same information state is realized in the experience's physical substrate.

Take a simple color experience, realizing an information state within a three-dimensional information space. We can find the same space realized in the brain processes underlying the experience: this is the three-dimensional space of neurally coded representations in the visual cortex. Elements of this three-dimensional space correspond directly to elements of the phenomenal information space.

We do not know exactly how these states are coded, and thus we do not know exactly how the information space is physically realized. But we know that it must be realized, as later processes show all the systematic effects of informational realization. Our reports can vary systematically with the location in color space, for example, as when we assess colors as relatively "darker" and "lighter"; and we can match objects with other objects according to their similarities and differences in color. So we know that there must be relevant differences in the visual cortex that are *transmittable* to other areas of the brain yielding a three-dimensional space of possible effects. The states underlying any two indistinguishable experiences will have the same relevant effects, even if there are slightly different physical details associated—think of the analogy with small differences in the state of the light switch—and states underlying any two *similar* experiences will have similar effects. So we can see the visual cortex as realizing information states in a three-dimensional space.

The same goes for more complex experiences, such as experiences of a whole visual field. These are realized in a combinatorial information space, and the same space must be physically realized in the underlying brain processes. We know that for each location in the field, different simple experiences correspond to differences in various later effects, where these later differences are separable according to the location in the field. For example, we can respond separately to specific queries about the color at a given location; this separate space of effects for each location yields a separate subspace for each location. So somewhere in the visual cortex, there must be an encoding of a combinatorial information state, in order that all the relevant differences can be transmitted to later processes. The space of relevant possible states here is isomorphic to the space of possible experiences; so we can see the same information state realized both physically and phenomenally.

It need not be the case that information is encoded *locally,* in a small structure of neighboring neurons, for example. It is quite possible for information to be physically realized in a holistic fashion, as one finds for example with certain holographic forms of information storage. The relevant differences in states of the visual cortex might correspond to differences spread across the cortex. But as long as these are the differences that are transmitted and that have the relevant effects, the information will be realized all the same.

It is natural to suppose that this double life of information spaces corresponds to a duality at a deep level. We might even suggest that this double realization is the key to the fundamental connection between physical processes and conscious experience. We need *some* sort of construct to make the link, and information seems as good a construct as any. It may be that principles concerning the double realization of information could be fleshed out into a system of basic laws connecting the physical and phenomenal domains.

We might put this by suggesting as a basic principle that information (in the actual world) has two aspects, a physical and a phenomenal aspect. Wherever there is a phenomenal state, it realizes an information state, an information state that is also realized in the cognitive system of the brain. Conversely, for at least some physically realized information spaces, whenever an information state in that space is realized physically, it is also realized phenomenally.[1]

This principle does not on its own come close to constituting a full psychophysical theory. Rather, it forms a sort of template for a psychophysical theory by providing a basic framework in which detailed laws can be cast. In fleshing out the principle into a theory, all sorts of questions need to be answered. For example, to just *which* physically realized information spaces does the basic principle apply? I will discuss this question further in section 4, but in the meantime I leave it open. Another sort of underspecificity stems from the looseness of the definition of physically realized information: for a fully specific psychophysical theory, we will need to know precisely what it is for an information space to be physically realized. But all this is part of the process of developing a theory.

Some other important questions concern the *ontology* of the view. How seriously should we take the "double aspect" talk? To what extent will this framework *reify* information, or treat it as real? Does it claim that the physical, the phenomenal, or both, are ontologically dependent on the informational? I will leave all these questions open for now. Later in the chapter I will consider various possible interpretations of the ontology. Some of these interpretations take information simply as a useful construct in characterizing the psychophysical laws; others give it a more fundamental role in the ontology. Similarly, some interpretations take the idea of a "double aspect" more seriously than others.

In the meantime, I abstract away from these metaphysical issues. The principle should simply be considered as a law connecting the physical and phenomenal domains, with ontological implications that are not especially different from those of the laws already considered. We already know that experience arises from the physical in virtue of certain laws, which apply to certain physical features of the world. The key suggestion here is that the basic level at which the laws apply to the physical world is that of physically realized information.

Of course, information may not be a *primitive* feature of the physical world in the way that mass and charge are primitive, but it need not be primitive to play a role in fundamental psychophysical laws. We already have all the fundamental properties we need, in basic physical and phenomenal properties. What we need now is a construct to connect the domains. Information seems to be a simple and straightforward construct that is well suited for this sort of connection, and which may hold the promise of yielding a set of laws that are simple and comprehensive. If such a set of laws could be achieved, then we might truly have a fundamental theory of consciousness.

It may just be, however, that there is a way of seeing information itself as fundamental. The idea that physics ultimately deals in information has already been canvased by some physicists, for example. If this idea could be made to pan out, it could be that in some way the physical is derivative on the informational, and the ontology of this view could be worked out very neatly. I discuss some ideas along these lines later in the chapter.

3. Some Supporting Arguments

I do not have any knockdown arguments to prove that information is the key to the link between physical processes and conscious experience, but there are some indirect ways of giving support to the idea. I have already discussed the first sort of supporting consideration: the observation that the same information spaces are realized physically and phenomenally. I will mention another major source of support and two minor sources in what follows.

The two minor sources of support lie with the fact that the double-aspect view of information is compatible with the psychophysical principles developed earlier: in particular, the principle of structural coherence and the principle of organizational invariance. These principles are strong constraints, and it is not obvious how a fundamental theory could meet them, so it is a mark in favor of the informational view that it is compatible with both.

The compatibility with structural coherence is particularly easy to see: in some ways the informational view is tailor-made to satisfy this constraint. The structure of experience is just the structure of a phenomenally realized information space, and the structure of awareness is just the structure of a physically realized information space. To see the first point, note that what I have called the implicit structure of an experience corresponds to the relational structure of an information space, and what I have called the explicit structure of an experience corresponds to the combinatorial structure of the space. To see the second, note that the various details in the structure of awareness are by definition differences that make a difference in later processing, as they are directly available for global control, and so are the physical realization of an information space. Given that these two are in fact realizations of the same information space, the principle of structural coherence follows.

I should note that the double-aspect principle does not on its own ensure that the structure of awareness will be projected into experience. To make sure of that, we must show that the physical information space here is one of those to which the double-aspect principle applies. For this, we would need a more detailed version of the principle that narrows down the information spaces involved in an appropriate way, so that it at least includes information that is made available for global control in familiar cases. As it stands, the double-aspect principle does not yet *predict* the full principle of structural coherence, but at least it is *compatible* with it.

It is also not hard to see that the double-aspect principle is compatible with the principle of organizational invariance. To see this, note that when a system realizes an information space, it does so in virtue of its functional organization. Any other system that is functionally isomorphic at a fine enough grain will have the same pattern of differences that make a difference, and therefore will realize the same information space. So if my experiences arise in virtue of information spaces realized in my brain, then the same information spaces will be realized in a functional isomorph, and the same experiences will arise, as the invariance principle predicts.

A fundamental theory of consciousness will have to invoke physical features that are both organizationally invariant and simple enough to play a role in fundamental laws. Most organizationally invariant features are not very simple, and most simple features are not organizationally invariant. Physically realized information may be the most natural feature that meets both criteria. The fact that it meets both is a mark in favor of an informational approach to psychophysical laws.

Explaining phenomenal judgments

Earlier, we saw that although consciousness cannot be reductively explained, phenomenal *judgments*—judgments of the form "I am conscious," "Isn't consciousness strange," and so on—can be so explained, at least in principle. This put some strain on a nonreductive theory of consciousness, although it did not appear to be fatal. It is counterintuitive that these judgments might be explained without invoking consciousness itself, but it is something that we can learn to live with. We can still hope, though, that the explanation of phenomenal judgments will be tied in some deep way to the explanation of consciousness itself. It would seem unreasonable and coincidental for these two explanations to be entirely independent.

We can put this as a kind of *explanatory coherence* requirement on a theory of consciousness. A completed theory of mind must provide both a (nonreductive) account of consciousness and a (reductive) account of why we judge that we are conscious, and it is reasonable to expect that these two accounts will *cohere* with each other. In particular, we might expect that those features of processing that are centrally responsible for bringing about phenomenal judgments will also be those that are centrally responsible for consciousness itself. In this way, even if consciousness itself is not part of the explanation of phenomenal judgments, the roots of consciousness will be.

Of course one cannot *prove* that a theory of consciousness must satisfy this requirement, but any theory of consciousness that satisfies it will have an element of force to it that other theories will lack. If a theory shows how the explanation of phenomenal judgments centrally involves the explanatory basis of consciousness, then we will have woven the two together into a more unified picture of the mind, and some of the feeling of outrageous coincidence will be removed.

I have often thought that this might be the key to finding a theory of consciousness.[2] First, we need to do our best to understand why judgments about consciousness are produced. This might be a difficult question, but it should not involve deep metaphysical mysteries; in principle, it is a question in the domain of cognitive science. Then, we need to abstract out the key features in that explanation, and consider how they might play a role in a theory of consciousness itself. There is no guarantee that this will lead to a satisfying theory of consciousness, but it is a promising strategy.

The search for a reductive explanation of our judgments about consciousness is likely to be enlightening in any event, and among the most worthwhile uses for reductive methods in working toward a theory of consciousness. We might focus on why a processing system should produce judgments that consciousness is present, and in particular, on why it should judge that consciousness is such a strange phenomenon. I have already said a few words in this direction in Chapter 5; here, I will go into more detail. The "explanation" that I will give is merely a plausible-sounding just-so story, but one can hope that it might be fleshed out, with the aid of empirical research, into a detailed theory. There are likely to be rich rewards for cognitive science and neuroscience in coming to grips with these phenomena.

So, let us leave consciousness itself aside for the moment, and concentrate on the cognitive processing system from a third-person point of view. Think of this explanation as applying to a zombie, if you like. Why might we *expect* that a processing system should produce this sort of judgment? What sort of process might subserve the judgment that a color sensation is present, for example? To think about this, consider what might be going on when we perceive colors.

Without going into low-level details, the story is roughly as follows. A particular spectral envelope of light impinges on our eyes, activating different sorts of retinal cells. Three varieties of cones abstract out information according to the amount of light present in various overlapping wavelength ranges. Immediately, many distinctions present in the original light wave are lost. This information is transmitted down the optic nerve to the visual cortex, where it is further transformed by neural processing into information corresponding to values on three axes: perhaps the red–green, yellow–blue, and achromatic axes. What happens after this is poorly understood, but it seems that information corresponding to a given color's position in this three-dimensional space is preserved, before eventually being categorized into the familiar category of "red," "green," "brown," and so on. Verbal categories are attached to these labels, and eventually a report such as "I see red now" is issued.

Now, let us take the system's "point of view" toward what is going on. What sort of judgments will it form? Certainly it will form a judgment such as "red object there," but if it is a rational, reflective system, we might also expect it to be able to reflect on the process of perception itself. How does perception "strike" the system, we might ask?

The crucial feature here is that when the system perceives a red object, central processes do not have direct access to the object itself, and they do not have direct access to the physical processes underlying perception. *All* that these processes have access to is the color information itself, which is merely a location in a three-dimensional information space. When it comes to linguistically reporting on the situation, the system cannot report, "This patch is saturated with 500- to 600-nanometer reflections," as all access to the original wavelengths is gone. Similarly, it cannot report about the neural structure, "There's a 50-hertz spiking frequency now," as it has no direct access to neural structures. The system has access only to the location in information space.

Indeed, as far as central processing is concerned, it simply *finds itself* in a location in this space. The system is able to make distinctions, and it *knows* it is able to make distinctions, but it has no idea how it does it. We would expect after a while that it could come to *label* the various locations it is thrown into—"red," "green," and the like—and that it would be able to know just which state it is in at a given time. But when asked just *how* it knows, there is nothing it can say, over and above "I just know, directly." If one asks it, "What is the difference between these states?" it has no answer to give beyond "They're just different," or "This is one of *those,*" or "This one is *red,* and that one is *green.*" When pressed as to what that means, the system has nothing left to say but "They're just different, qualitatively." What else could it say?

It is natural to suppose that a system that can know directly the location it occupies in an information space, without having access to any further knowledge, will simply label the states as brutely and primitively different, differing in their "quality." Certainly, we should expect these differences to strike the system in an "immediate" way: it is thrown into these states which in turn are immediately available for the direction of later processing; there is nothing inferential, for example, about its knowledge of which state it is in. And we should expect these states to be quite "ineffable": the system lacks access to any further relevant information, so there is nothing it can say about the states beyond pointing to their similarities and differences with each other, and to the various associations they might have. Certainly, one would not expect the "quality" to be something it could explicate in more basic terms.

It might be objected that the system could be set up so that it accesses the information as "hunches," in much the same way as a subject with blindsight might. Perhaps it might say, "The judgment 'red' just popped into my head," without any claims about "quality." But this would likely be an inefficient setup, with the system required to wait on a hunch. And what of the times—when one is playing tennis, say—when one needs to react to visual information without forming judgments? Presumably the system would say, "I just found myself knowing where the ball was and doing the right thing, without *experiencing* it"? Perhaps this is a coherent scenario, but it does not seem to be a natural design for a cognitive system. If one were designing such a system, it would be much more natural to design it so that it just "sees" the difference between red and green for itself, bases its behavior immediately on the perceived difference, and responds confidently and directly when queried. In any case, the latter is at least *one* reasonable way that one might design a system, which is all that is needed here.

Given this kind of direct access to information states, then, it is natural to expect the system to use the language of "experience" and "quality" to describe its own cognitive point of view on perception. And it is unsurprising that all this will seem quite strange to the system: these immediately known, ineffable states, which seem so central to its access to the world but which are so hard to pin down. Indeed, it is natural to suppose that this would seem odd to the system in the same sort of way in which consciousness seems odd to us.

So this is the beginning of a potential reductive explanation of our judgments about consciousness: these judgments arise because our processing system is thrust into locations in information space, with direct access to those locations but to nothing else. This direct knowledge will strike the system as a brute "quality": it knows that the states are different, but cannot articulate this beyond saying, in effect, "one of *those*." This immediate access to brute differences leads to judgments about the mysterious primitive nature of these qualities, about the impossibility of explicating them in more basic terms, and to many of the other judgments that we often make about conscious experience.

In all this, it is information that plays the key role. It is because the system has access only to information states that the various judgments of brute "qualities" are formed. The system is simply thrust into different states, and later processes have access only to the difference structure of these earlier states, and not to anything concrete. What is doing the work here is a system of differences that make a difference. It is information, and our access to it, that reductively explains the judgments that we make about consciousness.

Some might end things here, declaring that the mystery of consciousness has been removed and that an explanation has been given. Of course, I do not think this is correct: we have only explained certain judgments, which is a much more straightforward matter. But we can now use the principle of explanatory coherence to gain some leverage in a theory of consciousness. If the information states that are realized in this processing carry the main responsibility for our judgments about consciousness, perhaps these information states carry responsibility for consciousness itself.

In fact, this is how I was led to the informational view of consciousness in the first place. If the explanatory basis for our phenomenal judgments lies in a structure of differences that make a difference, it is natural to suppose that the explanatory basis for consciousness might lie in the same place. This would explain why our judgments are so well tuned to actual states of consciousness. A conscious experience is a realization of an information state; a phenomenal judgment is explained by another realization of the same information state. And in a sense, postulating a phenomenal aspect of information is all we need to do to make sure those judgments are truly correct: there really *is* a qualitative aspect to this information, showing up directly in phenomenology and not just in a system of judgments. So this allows consciousness to cohere very nicely with cognitive structure, leading to a more tightly knit view of the mind.

We can also note that there is a nice fit between the cognitive role of information states and the epistemology of experience. Corresponding to experiences with which we are directly acquainted are physically realized information states to which the system has direct (cognitive) access. The system forms its phenomenal judgments based on its direct access to the information states; this causal connection maps nicely onto the claim that the experience—the phenomenal realization of the same information state—is what *justifies* the phenomenal beliefs that are formed. On both sides, it is the same information state that is playing the crucial role; it is just the physical realization in one case, and the phenomenal realization in the other.

None of this is a knockdown proof that the information-based approach to consciousness must be correct. But it does provide the approach with further support.

4. Is Experience Ubiquitous?

By now, readers are probably lining up to object that information is *ubiquitous*. We find information everywhere, not just in systems that we standardly take to be conscious. My compact-disk player realizes information; my car's engine realizes information; even a thermostat realizes information. In fact, as I have spelled out the notion, we find information everywhere we find causation. We find causation everywhere, so we find information everywhere. But surely we do not find experience everywhere?

There are two ways that a supporter of the information-based approach might react to this situation. The first and most obvious is to look for further constraints on the *kind* of information that is relevant to experience. Not just any physically realized information space is associated with experience, but only those with certain properties. This would require careful consideration of what the further constraints might be, and of how they might fit into fundamental laws. I will consider strategies along these lines later, but for now I wish to consider the alternative. This is to bite the bullet and accept that all information is associated with experience. If so, then it is not just information that is ubiquitous. Experience is ubiquitous too.

If this is correct, then experience is associated even with very simple systems. This idea is often regarded as outrageous, or even crazy. But I think it deserves a close examination. It is not *obvious* to me that the idea is misguided, and in some ways it has a certain appeal. So here, I will examine the reasons one might reject the view, to see if they are compelling, while simultaneously considering various positive reasons to take the view seriously.

What is it like to be a thermostat?

To focus the picture, let us consider an information-processing system that is almost maximally simple: a thermostat. Considered as an information-processing device, a thermostat has just three information states (one state leads to cooling, another to heating, and another to no action). So the claim is that to each of these information states, there corresponds a phenomenal state. These three phenomenal states will all be different, and changing the information state will change the phenomenal state. We might ask: What is the character of these phenomenal states? That is, what is it like to be a thermostat?

Certainly it will not be very interesting to be a thermostat. The information processing is so simple that we should expect the corresponding phenomenal states to be equally simple. There will be three primitively different phenomenal states, with no further structure. Perhaps we can think of these states by analogy to our experiences of black, white, and gray: a thermostat can have an all-black phenomenal field, an all-white field, or an all-gray field. But even this is to impute far too much structure to the thermostat's experiences, by suggesting the dimensionality of a visual field, and the relatively rich natures of black, white, and gray. We should really expect something much simpler, for which there is no analog in our experience. We will likely be unable to sympathetically imagine these experiences any better than a blind person can imagine sight, or than a human can imagine what it is like to be a bat; but we can at least intellectually know something about their basic structure.

To make the view seem less crazy, we can think about what might happen to experience as we move down the scale of complexity. We start with the familiar cases of humans, in which very complex information-processing gives rise to our familiar complex experiences. Moving to less complex systems, there does not seem much reason to doubt that dogs are conscious, or even that mice are. Some people have questioned this, but I think this is often due to a conflation of phenomenal consciousness and self-consciousness. Mice may not have much of a sense of self, and may not be given to introspection, but it seems entirely plausible that there is *something* it is like to be a mouse. Mice perceive their environment via patterns of information flow not unlike those in our own brains, though considerably less complex. The natural hypothesis is that corresponding to the mouse's "perceptual manifold," which we know they have, there is a "phenomenal manifold." The mouse's perceptual manifold is quite rich—a mouse can make many perceptual distinctions—so its phenomenal manifold might also be quite rich. For example, it is plausible that for each distinction that the mouse's visual system can make and use in perceiving the environment, there corresponds a phenomenal distinction. One cannot *prove* that this is the case, but it seems to be the most natural way to think about the phenomenology of a mouse.

Moving down the scale through lizards and fish to slugs, similar considerations apply. There does not seem to be much reason to suppose that phenomenology should wink out while a reasonably complex perceptual psychology persists. If it does, then either there is a radical discontinuity from complex experiences to none at all, or somewhere along the line phenomenology begins to fall out of synchrony with perception, so that for a while, there is a relatively rich perceptual manifold accompanied by a much more impoverished phenomenal manifold. The first hypothesis seems unlikely, and the second suggests that the intermediate systems would have inner lives strangely dissociated from their cognitive capacities. The alternative is surely at least as plausible. Presumably it is much less interesting to be a fish than to be a human, with a simpler phenomenology corresponding to its simpler psychology, but it seems reasonable enough that there is *something* there.

As we move along the scale from fish and slugs through simple neural networks all the way to thermostats, where should consciousness wink out? The phenomenology of fish and slugs will likely not be primitive but relatively complex, reflecting the various distinctions they can make. Before phenomenology winks out altogether, we presumably will get to some sort of maximally simple phenomenology. It seems to me that the most natural place for this to occur is in a system with a corresponding simple "perceptual psychology," such as a thermostat. The thermostat seems to realize the sort of information processing in a fish or a slug stripped down to its simplest form, so perhaps it might also have the corresponding sort of phenomenology in its most stripped-down form. It makes one or two relevant distinctions on which action depends; to me, at least, it does not seem unreasonable that there might be associated distinctions in experience.

Of course, there are other ways that things *might* go as we move down the scale of complexity, and this is not any sort of demonstration that thermostats *must* have experiences. But this seems one reasonable way for things to go, and on reflection perhaps as natural a way as any. It is arguable that the reasoning involved here is just an extension of the reasoning whereby we attribute experience to dogs or mice. At least, once we start to think about what might be going on in the experience of a mouse, and the grounding in its perceptual psychology, the extension to simpler systems begins to seem much more natural than it might have at first.

Someone who finds it "crazy" to suppose that a thermostat might have experiences at least owes us an account of just *why* it is crazy. Presumably this is because there is a property that the thermostat lacks that is obviously required for experience; but for my part no such property reveals itself as obvious. Perhaps there is a crucial ingredient in processing that the thermostat lacks and a mouse possesses, or that a mouse lacks and a human possesses, but I can see no such ingredient that is *obviously* required for experience, and indeed it is not obvious that such an ingredient must exist.

Of course, to say that thermostats have experience is not to say that they have much in the way of a mental life. A thermostat will not be *self*-conscious; it will not be in the least intelligent; and I would not claim that a thermostat can *think*.[3] Some of the resistance to the idea of a conscious thermostat may arise from running together experience with these other mental features, all of which almost certainly require much more complexity. These features all have a large psychological component, and it is likely that a complex system would be needed to support the relevant causal roles. But once we have distinguished phenomenal properties from psychological properties, the idea of a conscious thermostat seems less threatening. We need imagine only something like an unarticulated "flash" of experience, without any concepts, any thought, or any complex processing in the vicinity.

Another reason why some may reject the idea of a conscious thermostat is that one cannot find any *room* for consciousness in the system. It seems too simple, and there seems no role for consciousness to play. But to have this reaction is to fail to learn the lesson of the nonreductive view: one will never find consciousness within a system on a close examination, and we will always be able to understand processing without invoking consciousness. If consciousness is not logically supervenient, we should not expect to have to find "room" for consciousness in a system's organization; consciousness is quite distinct from the processing properties of the system.

It may be that some are unwilling to accept the possibility of conscious thermostats simply because we *understand* thermostats too well. We know everything about their processing, and there seems no reason to invoke consciousness. But thermostats are really no different from brains here. Even once we understand brain processing perfectly, there will still seem to be no reason to invoke consciousness. The only difference is that right now, what is going on inside a brain is enough of a mystery that one may be tempted to suppose that consciousness is somehow "located" in those brain processes that we do not yet understand. But as I have argued, even coming to understand those processes will not alone bring consciousness into the picture; so here, once again, brains and thermostats are on a par.

One might be bothered by the fact that one could *build* a thermostat oneself, without putting any consciousness in. But of course the same applies to a brain, at least in principle. When we build a brain (in reproduction and development, say), consciousness comes along for free; the same will go for a thermostat. We should not expect to locate consciousness as a physical component of the system! Some may worry about the fact that a thermostat is not *alive*; but it is hard to see why that should make a principled difference. A disembodied silicon brain of the sort discussed in the last chapter would arguably fail to qualify as alive, but we have seen that it might be conscious. And if the arguments in the last chapter are right, then the fact that a thermostat is not made up of *biological* components makes no difference, in principle.

Some intuitive resistance may come from the fact that there does not seem to be room in a thermostat for someone or something to *have* the experiences: where in the thermostat can a *subject* fit? But we should not be looking for a homunculus in physical systems to serve as a subject. The subject is the whole system, or better, is associated with the system in the way that a subject is associated with a brain. The right way to speak about this is tricky. We would not say that my *brain* has experiences, strictly speaking, but that *I* have experiences. However we make sense of this relation, the same will apply to thermostats: strictly speaking it is probably best not to say that the thermostat has the experiences (although I will continue to say this when talking loosely), but that the experiences are associated with the thermostat. We will not find a subject "inside" the thermostat any more than we will find a subject inside a brain.

To return to positive points in favor of simple systems having experiences: this way, we avoid the need for consciousness to "wink in" at a certain level of complexity. There is something odd about the idea that a system with n elements could not be conscious but a system with $n + 1$ elements could be. And we cannot avoid making a decision in the way that we might avoid making a decision about just when someone becomes "bald": in the latter case, there is plausibly a degree of semantic indeterminacy, but it is much less plausible that it can be indeterminate whether a system is conscious. (This holds especially if we take a nonreductive view, on which we cannot explicate facts about experience in terms of more basic facts, as we explicate indeterminate issues about baldness in terms of determinate facts about the number of hairs on a head.) While it *could* be the case that experience winks in at a particular point, any specific point seems arbitrary, so a theory that avoids having to make this decision gains a certain simplicity.

A final consideration in favor of simple systems having experience: if experience is truly a fundamental property, it seems natural for it to be widespread. Certainly all the other fundamental properties that we know about occur even in simple systems, and throughout the universe. It would be odd for a fundamental property to be instantiated for the first time only relatively late in the history of the universe, and even then only in occasional complex systems. There is no *contradiction* in the idea that a fundamental property should be instantiated only occasionally; but the alternative seems more plausible, if other things are equal.

Whither panpsychism?

If there is experience associated with thermostats, there is probably experience *everywhere*: wherever there is a causal interaction, there is information, and wherever there is information, there is experience. One can find information states in a rock—when it expands and contracts, for example—or even in the different states of an electron. So if the unrestricted double-aspect principle is correct, there will be experience associated with a rock or an electron.

(I would not quite say that a rock *has experiences,* or that a rock *is conscious,* in the way that I might loosely say that a thermostat has experiences or is conscious. A rock, unlike a thermostat, is not picked out as an information-processing system. It is simply picked out as an object, so the connection to experience is less direct. It may be better to say that a rock *contains* systems that are conscious: presumably there are many such subsystems, none of whose experiences count canonically as the rock's (any more than my experiences count as my office's). For the thermostat, by contrast, there is a canonical associated information space, so it seems more reasonable to talk of the thermostat's canonical experiences. Of course even this usage is somewhat loose, as noted above.)

The view that there is experience wherever there is causal interaction is counterintuitive. But it is a view that can grow surprisingly satisfying with reflection, making consciousness better integrated into the natural order. If the view is correct, consciousness does not come in sudden jagged spikes, with isolated complex systems arbitrarily producing rich conscious experiences. Rather, it is a more uniform property of the universe, with very simple systems having very simple phenomenology, and complex systems having complex phenomenology. This makes consciousness less "special" in some ways, and so more reasonable.

An interesting question is whether *active* causation is required for experience. Could a thermostat have experience when it is sitting in a constant state (in a sense "causing" an output, but without really *doing* anything)? Or does it have experience only when in a state of flux? Most of the causation underlying experience in the brain seems to be active, in that relevant information is being processed constantly, neurons are firing, and so on. On the other hand, it may be that the distinction between active and passive causation cannot be drawn at a fundamental level, in which case the two might be treated equally. I do not know the answer to this question, but there is an intuition that some sort of activity is required for experience.

One possibility that I have not considered so far but that cannot be ruled out is that simple systems do not have phenomenal properties, but have *protophenomenal* properties. I mentioned in Chapter 4 the possibility that there might be properties more fundamental than phenomenal properties from which the latter are constituted. If there are indeed such properties then it would seem natural for them to be instantiated in simple systems. If so, then thermostats might not have experiences as we usually think of them, but instead instantiate a related sort of property that we do not fully understand (a sort of protoexperience, perhaps). This would retain the unified view of the natural order mentioned above, and might also help with the "winking out" problem (if protophenomenal properties are fundamental, then experiences constituted out of these properties might gradually "wink in" after all). By not claiming that thermostats have full-fledged experiences, this view may also seem a little less "crazy" than the alternative. Of course, the cost is the postulation of a class of unfamiliar properties that we do not understand; but the possibility has to be left open.

Either way, this view has a lot in common with what is often known as *panpsychism*—the view that everything has a mind. There are a few reasons I do not generally use the term myself: (1) because I think that having experiences may fall well short of what we usually think of as having a mind, although it may qualify as mind in its simplest form; (2) because protophenomenal properties may be even further away from the usual concept of "mind"; (3) because I do not think it is strictly accurate to say that rocks (for example) have experiences, for the reasons mentioned above, although rocks may have experiences associated with them. Perhaps the central reason why the term is misleading, though, is that it suggests a view in which the experiences in simple systems such as atoms are fundamental, and in which complex experiences are somehow the sum of such simpler experiences. While this is one way things could go, there is no reason that things have to go this way: complex experiences may be more autonomous than this suggests. In particular, the informational view suggests a picture on which complex experiences are determined more holistically than this.

With these caveats noted, it is probably fair to say that the view is a variety of panpsychism. I should note, however, that panpsychism is not at the metaphysical foundation of my view: what is rather at the foundation is naturalistic dualism with psychophysical laws. Panpsychism is simply one way that the natural supervenience of experience on the physical might work. In a sense, natural supervenience provides the *framework*; panpsychism is just one way of working out the *details*.

Personally, I am much more confident of naturalistic dualism than I am of panpsychism.The latter issue seems to be very much open. But I hope to have said enough to show that we ought to take the possibility of some sort of panpsychism seriously: there seem to be no knockdown arguments against the view, and there are various positive reasons why one might embrace it.

Constraining the double-aspect principle

Even if one is prepared to accept that very simple systems have experiences, the idea that all information is associated with experience might still make one uncomfortable. For example: only a small amount of the information in human cognitive processing seems to correspond to the information in conscious experience. Is it not simply a fact that most of our information processing is unconscious?

If the unrestricted double-aspect principle is correct, then presumably the answer is that all that "unconscious" information *is* realized in experience— it is just not realized in *my* experience. For example, if there is experience associated with one of my neurons in the way that there is experience associated with a thermostat, we would not expect it to be part of *my* experience, any more than we would expect my experience to be radically transformed if the neuron were replaced by a small conscious homunculus. Similarly, there might be experience associated with various "unconscious" information-processing subsystems in the brain—it is just that those experiences belong to a different subject. There are many different information-processing systems in the brain, and the one that corresponds to *me*—perhaps the system that makes some information available for a certain sort of global control and report—is just one of them. I would not expect myself to have direct access to the experiences of the other systems, any more than I would expect myself to have direct access to the experiences of other humans.

One might also worry about all the relatively complex information-processing systems in the world, found anywhere from my compact-disk player to my stomach. Do all these qualify as conscious individuals with complex experiences? In reply, it is worth noting that these systems do not have anything like the coherent cognitive structure of our own system, so that any associated experiences are likely to be nothing like our own. If a compact-disk player has associated experiences, for example, it is likely to be nothing more than a "flat" structure of bits; and if the information in my stomach is associated with experience, then there is no reason to think this experience would correspond to the sort of thing we think of as a mind. The sorts of experience that we have will only arise when information-processing systems have been shaped by evolution to have complex, coherent cognitive structures reflecting a rich representation of the outside world. It is likely that only a very restricted group of subjects of experience would have the psychological structure required to truly qualify as *agents* or as *persons*.

Still, this great proliferation of experiences, especially the proliferation within a single brain, might be cause for discomfort. This is exacerbated by noting that when given an information space, it is usually easy to find many slightly different information spaces simply by individuating a relevant causal pathway differently, or by carving up the relevant effects (the "differences" that the information makes) in a slightly different way. Are we to suppose that there are different sets of experiences floating around for all these information spaces? If so, then I might have a number of very close but slightly different phenomenal relatives arising from the processes in my own head!

The alternative is to *constrain* the double-aspect principle so that it narrows down the class of physically realized information spaces that have phenomenal counterparts. The most natural strategy may be to constrain the *way* that the information is processed. After all, I have already said that the information in my system that corresponds most directly to my experience is the information that is directly available for global control. As it stands, this "criterion" is most unlikely to play a role in a fundamental law, as it is too vague and high-level a notion; indeed, we can use the principle only if we have already individuated a high-level system such as a person or a brain. But perhaps there is a more precise, simpler criterion that could do the work.

One possibility is that *amplification* of information is crucial. Physically realized information is also realized in experience only if the information is *amplified* in certain ways, becoming available to make a large difference along certain causal pathways. Perhaps one could even say that the intensity of an experience corresponds to the degree of amplification, or some such. This could fit nicely with the global availability criterion, although it might have other problems: there is plenty of amplified information that is not intuitively conscious, for example; and it is not obvious just how the notion of amplification is to be made precise.

Another possibility is that we could restrict the kind of *causation* involved in a system. We have seen that wherever there is causation, there is information; but perhaps only a certain sort of causation counts in individuating the information spaces underlying experience. Perhaps only certain sorts of "active" causal relations are relevant, for example, or perhaps certain sorts of "natural" causal relations are required. There is an intuition that many of the information spaces that can be found according to the criteria given so far are in a sense unnatural; perhaps there is a way to clarify the relevant restriction. This would probably still let in a very wide class of information states, but it might prevent an astronomical proliferation.

I am not certain of what the relevant constraining criterion should be, but this is not to say that there might not be one. It might even be that a constraining criterion could restrict the relevant information spaces so that information in simple systems such as thermostats does not qualify. My own intuition is that there may well be a constraint on the double-aspect principle but information in simple systems such as thermostats might qualify all the same. For my part, the proliferation of many related experiences in the brain seems more counterintuitive than the presence of experiences in simple systems, though neither matter is cut and dried. In any case, there are many different ways things might go, as the prototheory is elaborated into a theory.

5. The Metaphysics of Information

The issue remains: How do we understand the ontology of the double-aspect view of information? How seriously do we take this talk of information spaces and information states: are these just useful constructs, or are they in some way ontologically fundamental? Is information primary, or is it really the physical and the phenomenal that are primary, with information merely providing a useful link?

There are various ways all this might be understood. The most straightforward, and the least adventurous, is to take the physical and phenomenal realizations of information to be wholly separate features, with no ontological link over and above a lawful connection and a sort of structural isomorphism. On this view, the ontology remains the straightforward ontology of property dualism, with physical properties, separate phenomenal properties, and a lawful connection between the two. Here, talk of a "double aspect" must be taken in a deflationary way: it is merely a colorful way of talking about two different sorts of correlated properties with a similar structure. And information is simply a useful tool in characterizing this common structure; it does not correspond to anything ontologically "deep."

This may be a perfectly adequate way to look at things, but there are some more interesting possibilities. Most of these involve taking the role of information more seriously. I will consider one way of doing this in what follows. The reader is warned that the discussion falls well into the realm of speculative metaphysics, but speculative metaphysics is probably unavoidable in coming to terms with the ontology of consciousness.

It from bit

It is sometimes suggested within physics that information is fundamental to the physics of the universe, and even that physical properties and laws may be derivative from informational properties and laws. This "it from bit" view is put forward by Wheeler (1989, 1990) and Fredkin (1990), and is also investigated by papers in Zurek (1990) and Matzke (1992, 1994). If this is so, we may be able to give information a more serious role in our ontology. To get a better grip on this, I will consider one key way in which information can be seen as fundamental to physics. This is not the only way in which the "it from bit" ideas have been put forward (in particular it differs somewhat from Wheeler's view),[4] but it strikes me as perhaps the most natural way of making sense of the notion. This interpretation is closely related to the "Russellian" ideas discussed in Chapter 4 (pp. 153–55), as we will see.

This approach stems from the observation that in physical theories, fundamental physical states are effectively individuated as *information states*. When we look at a feature such as mass or charge, we find simply a brute space of differences that make a difference. Physics tells us nothing about what mass *is,* or what charge *is*: it simply tells us the range of different values that these features can take on, and it tells us their effects on other features. As far as physical theories are concerned, specific states of mass or charge might as well be pure information states: all that matters is their location within an information space.

This is reflected in the fact that physics makes no commitment about the way these states are *realized.* Any realization of these information states will serve as well for the purposes of a physical theory, as long as it maintains the correct structure of causal or dynamic relations between states. After all, as long as the shape of these relations is the same, physics will *look* the same to our perceptual systems: we do not have access to any further properties of the realization in the external world, over and above the shape of the causal network. (Except, perhaps, insofar as our phenomenal properties are tied directly to realizing properties.)

Sometimes it has even been suggested that the universe could be a giant computer. Fredkin (1990) has suggested that the universe could be a huge cellular automaton, realized at bottom in a vast structure of bits.[5] Leckey (1993) has suggested that all of space-time could be grounded in a computational process, with separate registers for each instantiated fundamental feature of the world. As long as these registers have the appropriate causal relations among them, none of the creatures in that world would be any the wiser. The computer example illustrates the great range of possible ways that the physical entities that we "know" can be realized, just as long as there are entities that play the appropriate causal roles. This qualifies as part of the "metaphysics of physics": speculation about the ontology underlying the causal structure of space-time itself.

This sort of metaphysics is clearly not something that physics itself deals in. Physics can remain quite neutral on these questions of how its features are realized, and indeed about whether the features are "realized" in some such way at all. As far as physics is concerned, the state of the world might as well be *exhausted* by an informational characterization. If there are any further underlying "realizing" properties, they play no direct role in physical theories. So one might be tempted to dispense with them altogether.

This would lead to a picture of the world as a world of *pure* information. To each fundamental feature of the world there corresponds an information space, and wherever physics takes those features to be instantiated, an information state from the relevant space is instantiated. As long as these information states have the right relations among them, then everything will be as it needs to be. On this picture of the world, there is nothing more to say. Information is all there is.

This is how I understand the "it from bit" conception of the world. It is a strangely beautiful conception: a picture of the world as pure informational flux, without any further substance to it. (Some versions of the view may also allow *space-time* as a primitive framework within which the information spaces are embedded; other versions see space-time itself as constituted by the relations among information spaces.) The world is simply a world of primitive differences, and of causal and dynamic relations among those differences. On this view, to try to say anything further about the world is a mistake.

Grounding information in phenomenology

There seem to be two main problems with this picture of the world. The first is posed by consciousness itself. It seems that here, we have something over and above a *pure* information space. Phenomenal properties have an intrinsic nature, one that is not exhausted by their location in an information space, and it seems that a purely informational view of the world leaves no room for these intrinsic qualities.

The second problem is that it is not obvious that the notion of pure informational flux is coherent. One may feel that on this view the world is too lacking in substance to *be* a world. Could there be differences that are *primitive* differences, not grounded in differences in any underlying quality? One might find it plausible that every concrete difference in the world must be grounded: that is, that it must be a difference *in* something.

This problem is closely related to the problems of the "pure causal flux" view discussed in Chapter 4 (p. 153), of which this view is a variant. That view subtracted the world of all intrinsic qualities, leaving a world of causal relations, with nothing, it seemed, to do the causing. The current view may do slightly better by allowing information states as what the causal relations relate, but these states are remarkably insubstantial, being merely *different* from each other and having no nature of their own. One might find this picture of a world without intrinsic nature not to be a picture of a world at all.

Indeed, one might argue that information spaces *must* have something of a further nature. It may be that two fundamental properties will have the same sort of informational structure, both involving real quantities on a continuum, for example. If physics is pure information, there will be nothing to distinguish instantiations of the two information spaces. But there must be *some* difference between them, as the two properties enter into quite different laws, and have different effects on other features of the world. So there must be something further to distinguish these instantiations; something that goes beyond pure information. It would seem that some sort of intrinsic quality is needed to make the distinction.

There are a number of ways one might try to deal with these problems. One could decide that the second problem is not in the end a fatal problem and be happy with a physics of pure information; and then one could try to incorporate phenomenal properties as lawfully tied to that information in some fashion. Alternatively, one might answer the second problem by postulating intrinsic properties in which physical information spaces are grounded, and deal with the first problem by introducing phenomenal properties separately.

The most intriguing strategy, however, is to try to answer both problems together. The first problem suggests that we have direct knowledge of some intrinsic nature in the world, over and above pure information, in phenomenal properties; and the second suggests that we may *need* some intrinsic nature in the world, to ground information states. Perhaps, then, the intrinsic nature required to ground the information states is closely related to the intrinsic nature present in phenomenology. Perhaps one is even constitutive of the other. That way, we get away with a cheap and elegant ontology, and solve two problems in a single blow.

Once again, this is closely related to the Russellian suggestion described in Chapter 4, on which the unknown intrinsic properties of the world are themselves taken to be phenomenal (or protophenomenal) properties. Russell needed these properties to underlie the causal relations given by physics, and we need them here to ground the information states (the differences that make a difference) postulated by physics. These are essentially the same problem. In both cases, we have the feeling of two solutions for the price of one. We need some intrinsic properties to make sense of the physical world, and we need to find a place for the intrinsic properties revealed in phenomenology. The two problems seem to be well-matched.

So the suggestion is that the information spaces required by physics are themselves grounded in phenomenal or protophenomenal properties. Each instantiation of such an information space is in fact a *phenomenal* (or protophenomenal) realization. Every time a feature such as mass and charge is realized, there is an intrinsic property behind it: a phenomenal or protophenomenal property, or a *microphenomenal* property for short. We will have a set of basic microphenomenal spaces, one for each fundamental physical property, and it is these spaces that will ground the information spaces that physics requires. The ultimate differences are these microphenomenal differences.

Of course, this view again requires a variety of "outrageous" panpsychism, but I have already argued that such a panpsychism is not as unreasonable as commonly supposed. Given that I have already suggested that there may be phenomenal properties wherever there is information, we might as well press these properties into service in a useful role.

The ontology that this leads us to might truly be called a double-aspect ontology. Physics requires information states but cares only about their relations, not their intrinsic nature; phenomenology requires information states, but cares only about the intrinsic nature. This view postulates a single basic set of information states unifying the two. We might say that internal aspects of these states are phenomenal, and the external aspects are physical. Or as a slogan: Experience is information from the inside; physics is information from the outside.

What about macroscopic phenomenology?

All this works very nicely as ontology, although it is certainly on the wild side. But before we get too carried away, an enormous question remains: How can this ontology be made compatible with the details of a psychophysical *theory*? In particular, how can it be made compatible with psychophysical regularities at the macroscopic level? The trouble is that the double-aspect principle here applies at the fundamental physical level, with *microscopic,* physically realized information having a phenomenal realization. But for the purposes of a theory of consciousness, we need *macroscopic,* physically realized information to have a phenomenal realization also. And it is not at all obvious that this sort of "macroscopic phenomenology" can be derived from the microscopic phenomenology.

On the face of it, our conscious experience does not seem to be any sort of sum of microphenomenal properties corresponding to the fundamental physical features in our brain, for example. Our experience seems much more holistic than that, and much more homogeneous than any simple sum would be. This is a version of the "grain problem," raised by Sellars (1965) as a problem for materialism: How could an experience be identical to a vast collection of physiological events, given the homogeneity of the former and the fine-grainedness of the latter? The analogous problem is particularly pressing for Russellian views of the sort I am discussing.[6] If the roots of phenomenology are exhausted by microphenomenology, then it is hard to see how smooth, structured macroscopic phenomenology could be derived: we might expect some sort of "jagged," unstructured phenomenal collection instead.

There are various ways one might try to handle this. First, one might try to set things up so that the double-aspect ontology holds at all levels, not just at the microscopic level. That is, even physical information spaces at the macroscopic level are grounded in a phenomenal realization. It can be argued that there is nothing privileged about the microscopic level: things are simpler there, but it need not be ontologically special. The arguments we have given for seeing the physical world in informational terms also apply at the macroscopic level. One could argue that even at this level, there is just a space of macroscopic differences that make a difference, each of which could be realized in corresponding phenomenology.

The trouble is that there may not be room for all these separate phenomenal realizations. Once we have fundamental physical features realized in phenomenal information spaces, then macroscopic information seems to be grounded already: the differences that make a difference here are now grounded in configurations of microscopic physical features, which are themselves grounded in microphenomenology. One could try to introduce a separate phenomenal grounding all the same, but this would seem to be redundant, and less theoretically elegant than the corresponding move in the microscopic case. One could try to remove the redundancy by making macroscopic grounding *primary,* but it would then be hard to deal with cases of isolated microscopic systems and the like. So it is not clear that the "grounding" approach to the double-aspect ontology can work directly at the macroscopic level.

Second, one could try to understand a way in which macroscopic phenomenology might be *constituted* by these microphenomenal properties. On the face of it, it does not seem to be any simple sum or collection of these properties; that would lead directly to "jaggedness" problems. But perhaps the problem is just that we do not understand the mental part–whole relation, as Nagel (1986) has put it. That is, we lack an accurate conception of the way in which low-level microphenomenal properties "add up" to yield high-level phenomenology. We tend to think about this in terms of a physical analogy, based on the way in which microphysics adds up to macrophysics, but this may be the wrong way to think about it. Perhaps phenomenology is constituted in a different way entirely.

For example, it might be that microphenomenal properties add up to macrophenomenology in a way that reflects their joint *informational* structure, rather than their joint spatiotemporal structure. If a collection of these properties jointly realize a complex information state by virtue of the causal relations between them, perhaps we could expect any derived macrophenomenology to have the shape of that information state. After all, the central role of the microphenomenal properties is to realize information states, so it would not be entirely surprising for informational structure to play a role in the constitutional relations between the properties. If this were so, then any derived macrophenomenal states would have the "smooth" informational structure that the original double-aspect principle predicts. This is not *easy* to understand, but after all we cannot expect our everyday understanding of the physical domain to apply to the phenomenal domain. So it may just be that a better understanding of the nature of phenomenology itself would be compatible with this view of its constitution.

If it turned out that no constitution relation could work this way, we might try the third option, which is to link macrophenomenology to microphenomenology by *laws*.[7] For example, it could simply be a law that when microphenomenal states realize an information state of a certain sort by virtue of the causal relations between them (by the "difference that makes a difference" principle), then a direct phenomenal realization of the same state will arise. This would solve the theoretical problems, at the cost of complicating the ontology. No longer would we have the simple ontology with phenomenology being the intrinsic aspect of physically realized information: some phenomenology would be "dangling" from this information by laws in the fashion of a more standard property dualism. So some of the attraction of a Russellian view would be lost, although the view would still be quite coherent.

In any case, I will leave this question open. It is certainly the hardest problem for any sort of Russellian view; but it is not obvious that it cannot be solved. If it could be made to work, the second strategy seems a particularly promising way to go; or it might be that some entirely new idea is needed to solve this problem. Looking at things optimistically, we can see the problem—how to make a psychophysical theory compatible with both the macro-level facts about our phenomenology and its physical basis and the micro-level ontology of the Russellian view—as one of the crucial constraints that might eventually lead us to a detailed theory of consciousness. One of the difficulties in constructing such a theory is that there are not many constraints around. It might just be that this problem could provide some much-needed focus.

If none of these strategies turns out to be satisfactory, we will have to retreat from the Russellian view to some other view of the metaphysics. One might try to work with the metaphysics of pure information, for example, as a way of understanding the physical world; and then somehow hook phenomenology up, perhaps by way of a lawful connection to pure information. Or one could simply retreat to the "tame" ontology with separate physical and phenomenal realms, each with their own intrinsic nature, tied together by lawful connections along the lines of the information principle. This would mean that talk of a "double aspect" would have to be taken less seriously, and the ontology would be somewhat less elegant, but it could still lead to a perfectly satisfactory theory.

6. Open Questions

The sketch I have given of the informational framework for psychophysical laws leaves an enormous number of questions open. For the picture to be turned into a final theory, all of these questions would have to be answered. I have mentioned a few problems about the ontology of the view in the previous section. But there are also numerous questions about the shape of the *laws,* and about just how our phenomenology is to be explained. Some of these questions include:

1. When an information space is phenomenally realized, why is it realized one way rather than another? For example, given that our phenomenal color space might have been inverted, it seems somewhat arbitrary that it is the way it is. Do we need to add further laws, or postulate contingent "constants," to settle this matter?
2. Is the character of a phenomenal information space settled by the structure of the space (or at least settled up to the possibility of inversions)? It might seem, for example, that color space and taste space are both simple three- or four-dimensional spaces, but they have very different characters despite their similar shape. It is arguable that the similarity in the structures is an illusion, and that when we embed both of these in a wider structure—seeing color experiences as part

of the full, deep structure of visual experiences, for example—the similarity will disappear. But the question remains: Is something with the approximate character of our color experiences the *only* way that visual color information might have been projected into phenomenology, or is there a different way entirely? I suspect that the answer may be closer to the former than to the latter, but it is not at all obvious how one would go about arguing for this.

3. I have used this framework mostly to discuss simple perceptual experiences, such as color experiences. It is not obvious how one would extend it to deal with more subtle experiences, such as complex emotional experiences, for example, and the experience of occurrent thought. Can this extension be made?

4. What sort of formal structure is best suited for capturing the structure of phenomenal information? What sort of topological spaces are needed to capture the relational structure of experience? Should we move to a more specific sort of structure, such as a metric space or a differential manifold? The combinatorial structure of an experience is even more interesting: a simple multidimensional continuum is probably a great simplification of the structure of a visual field, for example. How can we best capture the full structure? Should the definition of an information space be modified for this purpose?

5. How, within this framework, can one account for the *unity* of consciousness? That is, what makes my visual experiences, auditory experiences, and so on, all experiences of the same subject? I suspect that the answer involves the way that the relevant information is processed, so that the unity of consciousness corresponds to the fact that the relevant information is available to be integrated in a certain way. But just how to cash this out is unclear.

6. What, exactly, are the criteria that determine which information in the brain corresponds to *my* experiences? Is there a particular causal pathway, or a particular sort of causal flux, that is relevant? Presumably something like direct availability for global control plays a central role here, in individuating the information and the relevant pathways.

The existence of all these questions shows just how far these sketchy ideas are from being a true theory. Another way of seeing this is to note how far these ideas are from allowing us to *predict* exactly what the phenomenal properties associated with a physical system will be from the physical properties of the system. As it stands, the idea lacks a strong explanatory and predictive *power*: it needs to be beefed up considerably in order to be truly useful.

A number of new insights would be required to turn this idea into a satisfying theory. Perhaps a breakthrough could come from considering the problem of the previous section: how to square phenomenal information on the macroscopic scale with the "intrinsic property" view of information at the microscopic scale. Another might come from trying to find a constraint that yields the class of physically realized information spaces that are realized in experience. Others may come from sources I have not considered at all.

The idea may prove to be entirely misguided. That would not surprise me; in fact, I think it is more likely than not that the key to a fundamental theory will lie elsewhere. But I have put these ideas forward because we need to start thinking about these matters, and because seeing even an inadequate example in the genre may be instructive. I also hope that some of the ideas raised along the way—about how to explain phenomenal judgments, about the ubiquity of experience, and about the connection between experience, information, and intrinsic properties of the physical—may turn out to be useful even when translated into a different framework. Perhaps a more adequate theory of consciousness could share something of the feel of the ideas put forward here, even if its details are very different.

It is often said that the problem with theories of consciousness of this sort is that they are too speculative and untestable. But I think the real problem with the "theory" I have put forward is different: it is too unspecific in its predictions. *If* we had a theory of a comparable level of simplicity that could *predict* all the specific facts about our experiences—even only those facts familiar from the first-person case—when given the physical facts about our processing system, that would be a remarkable achievement, and would give us very good reason to accept the theory as true. Right now we have no such theory, but there is no reason to believe that such a theory is impossible.

PART IV

Applications

9

Strong Artificial Intelligence

1. Machine Consciousness

Could a machine be conscious? Could an appropriately programmed computer truly possess a mind? These questions have been the subject of an enormous amount of debate over the last few decades. The field of *artificial intelligence* (or *AI*) is devoted in large part to the goal of reproducing mentality in computational machines.So far progress has been limited, but supporters argue that we have every reason to believe that eventually computers will truly have minds. At the same time, opponents argue that computers are limited in a way that human beings are not, so that it is out of the question for a conscious mind to arise merely in virtue of computation.

Objections to artificial intelligence typically take one of two forms. First, there are *external* objections, which try to establish that computational systems could never even *behave* like cognitive systems. According to these objections, there are certain functional capacities that humans have that no computer could ever have. For example, sometimes it is argued that because these systems follow rules, they could not exhibit the creative or flexible behavior that humans exhibit (e.g., Dreyfus 1972). Others have argued that computers could never duplicate human mathematical insight, as computational systems are limited by Gödel's theorem in a way that humans are not (Lucas 1961; Penrose 1989).

External objections have been difficult to carry through, given the success of computational simulation of physical processes in general. In particular, it seems that we have good reason to believe that the laws of physics are computable, so that we at least ought to be able to *simulate* human behavior computationally. Sometimes this is disputed, by arguing for a noncomputable element in physical laws (as Penrose does), or by arguing for nonphysical causation (as Lucas does), but it is clear that those putting forward these objections are fighting an uphill battle.

More prevalent have been what I call *internal* objections. These objections concede at least for the sake of argument that computers might simulate human behavior, but argue that they would lack minds all the same. In particular, it is suggested that they would have no inner life: no conscious experience, no true understanding. At best, a computer might provide a *simulation* of mentality, not a replication. The best known objection in this class is John Searle's "Chinese room" argument (Searle 1980). According to these objections, computational systems would at best have the hollow she█ a mind: they would be silicon versions of a zombie.

T█ who take a nonreductive view of conscious experience have often be██ attracted to internal objections to artificial intelligence, with many arguing that no mere computer could be conscious. Indeed, those who have been impressed by the problem of consciousness have sometimes characterized the problem by pointing to consciousness as the feature that we have but that any computer would lack! Many have found it hard to believe that an artificial, nonbiological system could be the sort of thing that could give rise to conscious experience.

A nonreductive view of consciousness does not automatically lead to a pessimistic view of AI, however. The two issues are quite separate. The first concerns the *strength* of the connection between physical systems and consciousness: Is consciousness constituted by physical processes, or does it merely arise from physical processes? The second concerns the *shape* of the connection: Just *which* physical systems give rise to consciousness? Certainly it is not *obvious* that executing the right sort of computation should give rise to consciousness; but it is not obvious that neural processes in a brain should give rise to consciousness, either. On the face of it, there is no clear reason why computers should be any worse off than brains in this regard. Given that we have accepted the surprising fact that brains give rise to consciousness, it would not be a *further* sort of surprise to find that computation might give rise to consciousness. So the mere embrace of a nonreductive view of consciousness ought to leave the matter open.

In this chapter, I will take things further and argue that the ambitions of artificial intelligence are reasonable (Figure 9.1). In particular, I will argue for the view that Searle calls *strong artificial intelligence*: that there is a nonempty class of computations such that the implementation of any computation in that class is sufficient for a mind, and in particular, is sufficient for the existence of conscious experience. This sufficiency holds only with natural necessity, of course: it is *logically* possible that any computation might take place in the absence of consciousness. But the same goes for brains, as we

Figure 9.1. Bloom County on strong AI. (© 1985, Washington Post Writers Group. Reprinted with permission)

have seen. In evaluating the prospects of machine consciousness in the actual world, it is natural possibility and necessity we are concerned with.

(Lest this conclusion be thought a triviality, given the panpsychist suggestions in the last chapter, I note that nothing in this chapter rests on those considerations. Indeed, I will argue not just that implementing the right computation suffices for consciousness, but that implementing the right computation suffices for rich conscious experience like our own.)

I have already done most of the work required for this defense of strong AI, in arguing for the principle of organizational invariance in Chapter 7. If that argument is correct, it establishes that any system with the right sort of functional organization is conscious, no matter what it is made out of. So we already know that being made of silicon, say, is no bar to the possession of consciousness. What remains to be done is to clarify the link between computation and functional organization, in order to establish that implementing an appropriate computation is sufficient to ensure the presence of the relevant functional organization. Once this is done, strong AI falls out as a consequence. I will also answer a number of objections that have been put forward against the strong AI enterprise.

2. On Implementing a Computation

In its standard form, the theory of computation deals wholly with *abstract* objects: Turing machines, Pascal programs, finite-state automata, and so on. These are mathematical entities inhabiting mathematical space. Cognitive systems in the real world, on the other hand, are *concrete* objects, physically embodied and interacting causally with other objects in the physical world. But often we want to use the theory of computation to draw conclusions about concrete objects in the real world. To do this, we need a bridge between the abstract and concrete domains.[1]

This bridge is the notion of *implementation*: the relation between abstract computational objects—"computations" for short—and physical systems that holds when a physical system "realizes" a computation, or when a computation "describes" a physical system. Computations are often implemented on synthetic, silicon-based computers, but they can be implemented in other ways. Natural systems such as the human brain are often said to implement computations, for example. Computational descriptions are used to make sense of physical systems in all sorts of domains. Whenever this happens, a notion of implementation is implicitly or explicitly doing the work.

The notion of implementation is rarely analyzed in detail; it is usually simply taken for granted. But to defend strong AI, we need a detailed account of it. The strong AI thesis is cast in terms of computation, telling us that implementation of the appropriate computation suffices for consciousness. To evaluate this claim, we need to know just what it is for a physical system to implement a computation. Once we know this, we can combine it with our earlier analysis of psychophysical laws to determine whether the conclusion might follow.

Some have argued that no useful account of implementation can be given. In particular, Searle (1990b) has argued that implementation is not an objective matter, but instead is "observer-relative": any system can be seen to implement any computation if interpreted appropriately. Searle holds, for example, that his wall can be seen to implement the Wordstar word processing program. If this were so, it would be hard to see how computational notions could play any foundational role in a theory that ultimately deals with concrete systems. As for strong AI, it would either be emptied of content or would imply a strong form of panpsychism. But I think this sort of pessimism is misplaced: an objective account of implementation can straightforwardly be given. In this section I will outline such an account. (The account is a little technical, but the rest of the chapter should make sense even if the details here are skimmed.)

Any account of what it is for a computation to be implemented will depend on the class of computations in question. There are many different computational formalisms, with correspondingly different classes of computations: Turing machines, finite-state automata, Pascal programs, connectionist networks, cellular automata, and so on. In principle, we need an account of implementation for each of these formalisms. I will give an account of implementation for a single formalism, that of *combinatorial-state automata*. This class of computations is sufficiently general that the associated account of implementation can be easily extended to apply to other classes.

A combinatorial-state automaton is a more sophisticated cousin of a *finite-state* automaton. A finite-state automaton (FSA) is specified by giving a finite set of inputs, a finite set of internal states, and a finite set of outputs, and by giving an associated set of *state transition* relations. An internal state of an FSA is a simple element S_i without any internal structure; the same goes for inputs and outputs. The state transition relations specify, for every possible pair of inputs and internal states, a new internal state and an output. If the initial state of an FSA is given, these state transition relations specify how it will evolve over time and what outputs it will produce, depending on what inputs are received. The computational structure of an FSA consists in this relatively simple set of state transition relations among a set of unstructured states.

Finite-state automata are inadequate to represent the structure of most computations that are relevant in practice, as the states and state transition relations in these computations generally have complex internal structure. No FSA description can capture all the structure present in a Pascal program, for example, or a Turing machine, or a cellular automaton. It is therefore more useful to concentrate on a class of automata that have structured internal states.

Combinatorial-state automata (CSAs) are just like FSAs, except that their internal states are structured. A state of a CSA is a *vector* $[S^1, S^2, \ldots, S^n]$. This vector can be either finite or infinite, but I will focus on the finite case. The elements of this vector can be thought of as the *components* of the internal state; they correspond to the cells in a cellular automaton or the tape-squares and head-state in a Turing machine. Each element S^i, can take on a finite number of values S^i_j, where S^i_j is the jth possible value of the ith element. These values can be thought of as "substates" of the overall state. Inputs and outputs have a similar sort of complex structure: an input is a vector $[I^1, \ldots, I^k]$, and an output is a vector $[O^1, \ldots, O^m]$.

A CSA is determined by specifying the set of internal state vectors and input and output vectors, and by specifying a set of *state transition rules* that determine how the state of the CSA evolves with time. For each element of the internal-state vector, a state transition rule determines how its new value depends on old values of the input and internal state vectors. For each element of the output vector, a state transition rule determines how its new value depends on old values of the internal state vector. Every finite CSA can be represented as an FSA with equal computational power, but the FSA description will sacrifice most of the structure that is crucial to a CSA. That structure is central in using CSAs to capture the organization that underlies a mind.

We are now in a position to give an account of implementation. Computations such as CSAs are abstract objects, with a *formal structure* determined by their states and state transition relations. Physical systems are concrete objects, with a *causal structure* determined by their internal states and the causal relations between the states. Informally, we say that a physical system *implements* a computation when the causal structure of the system mirrors the formal structure of the computation. That is, the system implements the computation if there is a way of mapping states of the system onto states of the computation so that physical states that are causally related map onto formal states that are correspondingly formally related.

This intuitive idea can be straightforwardly applied to yield an account of implementation for CSAs. A physical system implements a CSA if there is a decomposition of internal states of the system into substates, a decomposition of the system's inputs and outputs into input and output substates, and a mapping from substates of the system onto substates of the CSA, such that the causal state transition relations between physical states, inputs, and outputs reflect the formal state transition relations between the corresponding formal states, inputs, and outputs.

The formal criterion for implementing a CSA is as follows:

A physical system P implements a CSA M if there is a decomposition of internal states of P into components $[s^1, \ldots, s^n]$, and a mapping f from the substates s^j into corresponding substates S^j of M, along with similar decompositions and mappings for inputs and outputs, such that for every state transition rule $([I^1, \ldots, I^k], [S^1, \ldots, S^n]) \rightarrow ([S'^1, \ldots, S'^n], [O^1, \ldots, O^l])$ of M: if P is in internal state $[s^1, \ldots, s^n]$ and receives input $[i^1, \ldots, i^n]$, which map to formal state and input $[S^1, \ldots, S^n]$ and $[I^1, \ldots, I^k]$ respectively, this reliably causes it to enter an internal state and produce an output that map to $[S'^1, \ldots, S'^n]$ and $[O^1, \ldots, O^l]$ respectively.

We may stipulate that in a decomposition of the state of a physical system into a vector of substates, the value of each element of the vector must supervene on a separate region of the physical system, to ensure that the causal organization relates distinct components of the system. Otherwise, it is not clear that the detailed causal structure is really present within the physical system. There is room to tinker with this and with other details in the definition above. The notion of implementation is not written in stone, and it might be tightened or loosened for various purposes. But this gives the basic shape that will be shared by any account of implementation.

It may seem that CSAs are not much of an advance on FSAs. After all, for any finite CSA, we can find a corresponding FSA with the same input–output behavior. But there are some crucial differences. First and foremost, the *implementation* conditions on a CSA are much more constrained than those of the corresponding FSA. An implementation of a CSA is required to consist in a complex causal interaction among a number of separate parts; a CSA description can therefore capture the causal organization of a system to a much finer grain. Second, CSAs provide a unified account of the implementation conditions for both finite and infinite machines. And third, a CSA can directly reflect the complex formal organization of computational objects such as Turing machines and cellular automata. In the corresponding FSA, much of this structure would be lost.

Indeed, we can use this definition of implementation to straightforwardly provide implementation criteria for other sorts of computations. To specify what it takes to implement a Turing machine, for example, we need merely redescribe a Turing machine as a CSA and apply the definition above. To do this, we describe the state of the Turing machine as a giant vector. One element of the vector represents the state of the machine head, and there is an element for each square of the tape, representing the symbol in the square and also indicating whether or not the machine head occupies that square. The state transition rules between the vectors are those derived naturally from the mechanisms specifying the behavior of the machine head and the tape. Of course, the vectors here are infinite, but the implementation conditions in the infinite case are a straightforward extension of those in the finite case. Given this translation from the Turing machine formalism to the CSA formalism, we can say that a Turing machine is implemented whenever the corresponding CSA is implemented. We can give similar translations of computations in other formalisms, such as cellular automata or Pascal programs, yielding implementation conditions for computations in each of these classes.

This yields a perfectly objective criterion for implementing a computation. Implementation of a computation does not collapse into vacuity in the way that Searle suggests. It is true that *some* computations will be implemented by every system. For example, the single-element, single-state CSA will be implemented by every system, and a two-state CSA will be implemented almost as widely. It is also true that most systems will implement more than one computation, depending on how we carve up that system's states. There is nothing surprising about this: it is only to be expected that my workstation implements a number of computations, as does my brain.

What is crucial is that there is no reason to believe that *every* CSA will be implemented by *every* system. For any given complex CSA, very few physical systems will have the causal organization required to implement it. If we take a CSA whose state vectors have one thousand elements, with ten possibilities for each element, then arguments along the lines of those presented in Chapter 7 suggest that the chance of an arbitrary set of physical states having the requisite causal relations is something less than one in $(10^{1000})^{10^{1000}}$ (actually much less than this, because of the requirement that the transition relations be reliable).[2]

What of Searle's claim that computational descriptions are "observer-relative," then? It is true that there is a limited degree of observer relativity: any given physical system will implement a number of computations, and which one of these an observer chooses to focus on will depend on her purposes. But this is not threatening to AI or computational cognitive science. It remains the case that for any given computation, there is a fact of the matter about whether or not a given system implements it, and there will be only a limited class of systems that qualify as implementations. For computational accounts to have metaphysical and explanatory bite, this is all that the fields require.

To say that a physical system implements a given complex computation P is to say something very substantial about the causal structure of that system, something that may be quite useful in providing cognitive explanations and perhaps in understanding the basis of consciousness. Only systems with a very specific sort of causal organization will have a hope of satisfying the strong constraints of implementation. So there is no danger of vacuity, and there is room to hope that the notion of computation can provide a substantial foundation for the analysis of cognitive systems.

3. In Defense of Strong AI

What it takes to implement a CSA is strikingly similar to what it takes to realize a functional organization. Recall that a functional organization is determined by specifying a number of abstract components, a number of states for each component, and a system of dependency relations indicating how the states of each component depend on previous states and on inputs, and how outputs depend on previous states. The notion of a CSA is effectively a direct formalization of this notion.

Indeed, given any functional organization of the sort described in Chapter 7, it can be straightforwardly abstracted into a CSA. We need only stipulate that the CSA's state vectors have an element for each component of the organization, and that the formal state transitions between the CSA states correspond to the causal dependency relations between components. To realize the functional organization comes to almost exactly the same thing as implementing the corresponding CSA. There are a few small differences, such as different treatments of inputs and outputs, but these are not significant.

The account of implementation that I have given thus makes clear the link between causal and computational organization. This way, we can see that when computational descriptions are applied to physical systems, they effectively provide a formal description of the systems' causal organization. The language of computation provides a perfect language in which this sort of abstract causal organization can be specified. Indeed, it can be argued that this is precisely why computational notions have had such wide application throughout cognitive science. What is most relevant to the explanation of the behavior of a complex cognitive system is the abstract causal organization of the system, and computational formalisms provide an ideal framework within which this sort of organization can be described and analyzed.[3]

This link makes the defense of strong artificial intelligence straightforward. I have already argued for the principle of organizational invariance, which tells us that for any system with conscious experiences, a system with the same fine-grained functional organization will have qualitatively identical conscious experiences. But we know that any given functional organization can be abstracted into a CSA that is implemented whenever the organization is realized. It follows that for a given conscious system M, its fine-grained functional organization can be abstracted into a CSA M, such that any system that implements M will realize the same functional organization, and will therefore have conscious experiences qualitatively indistinguishable from those of the original system. This establishes the thesis of strong artificial intelligence.

For example, we might abstract a neural description of the brain into a CSA, with an element of the state vector for each neuron and with substates for each element reflecting the relevant range of each neuron's states. The state transition rules of the CSA reflect the way in which the state of each neuron depends on the state of other neurons, and the way in which neural states are related to inputs and output. If nonneural components of the brain are relevant, we can include components for those, too. Any physical system that implements this CSA will have a fine-grained functional organization that duplicates the neuron-level functional organization of the brain. By the invariance principle, this system will have experiences indistinguishable from those associated with the brain.

It is easy to think of a computer as simply an input–output device, with nothing in between except for some formal mathematical manipulations. This way of looking at things, however, leaves out the key fact that there are rich causal dynamics inside a computer, just as there are in the brain. Indeed, in an ordinary computer that implements a neuron-by-neuron simulation of my brain, there will be real causation going on between voltages in various circuits, precisely mirroring patterns of causation between the neurons. For each neuron, there will be a memory location that represents the neuron, and each of these locations will be physically realized in a voltage at some physical location. It is the causal patterns among these circuits, just as it is the causal patterns among the neurons in the brain, that are responsible for any conscious experience that arises.

We can also defend the strong AI thesis directly, using the fading qualia and dancing qualia arguments. Given any two implementations of a CSA, there will be a spectrum of cases between them, in which physical components of the implementations are replaced one at a time while the pattern of their causal interaction with the rest of the system is preserved. If one of the systems is conscious, and if the CSA abstracts its fine-grained functional organization, then the arguments in question imply that the other system must be conscious and that it must have indistinguishable conscious experiences. If the other system were not conscious, there would be an intermediate system with fading qualia. If the other system were not conscious or had different conscious experiences, then we could construct an intermediate system with dancing qualia. These consequences are implausible, for the reasons outlined in Chapter 7. Given that qualia cannot fade or dance in this way, it follows that the second of the original systems has experiences indistinguishable from the first, and that the strong AI thesis holds.

There is a small caveat. The argument assumes that the brain's organization can be abstracted into a CSA description. This requires only that the relevant organization can be described in terms of a finite number of parts each having a finite number of relevant states. Nevertheless, some might dispute this. For example, perhaps an infinite number of states are needed for each neuron, to capture the vital role of continuous processing. And some might claim that the transitions between these infinite states might be uncomputable. I will discuss this sort of objection later; for now, I am happy to embrace the conclusion that *if* cognitive dynamics are computable, then the right sort of computational organization will give rise to consciousness. That is, I am more concerned with internal than external objections here. All the same, I will address some external objections later in the chapter.

4. The Chinese Room and Other Objections

Of course, opponents of strong AI have sometimes put forward concrete arguments against the position. The best known of these are due to John Searle, in his 1980 paper, "Minds, Brains, and Programs," and elsewhere. Here I will use the framework I have outlined to answer these arguments.

The Chinese room

In a celebrated argument against strong AI, Searle (1980) argues that any program can be implemented without giving rise to a mind. He does this by exhibiting what he takes to be a *counterexample* to the strong AI claim: the Chinese room, inside which a person manipulating symbols simulates someone who understands Chinese. The Chinese room is intended to provide an example, for any given program, of a system that implements that program but that lacks the relevant conscious experience.

In the original version, Searle directs the argument against machine *intentionality* rather than machine consciousness, arguing that it is "understanding" that the Chinese room lacks. All the same, it is fairly clear that consciousness is at the root of the matter. What the core of the argument establishes directly, if it succeeds, is that the Chinese room system lacks conscious states, such as the conscious experience of understanding Chinese. On Searle's view, intentionality requires consciousness, so this is enough to see that the room lacks intentionality also. Others deny this, however. In any case we can factor out the issue about the connection between consciousness and intentionality, and cast the issue solely in terms of consciousness. The issues may be somewhat clearer this way.

(That is, we can separate Searle's conclusions into two parts: (1) no program suffices for consciousness; and (2) no program suffices for intentionality. Searle believes that (1) implies (2), but others deny this. Things are clearest if the argument about strong AI is taken to focus on (1): all parties will accept that if (1) is true, then the most interesting form of strong AI is doomed, and even Searle would accept that refuting (1) would show that the Chinese room argument fails. The link between consciousness and intentionality can then be set aside as a separate issue, not crucial to the argument against AI.

This way one avoids the situation in which opponents argue against (2) without bothering to argue against (1). For example, replies that focus on the connection between the Chinese room and its environment [Fodor 1980; Rey 1986] and replies that give procedural or functional accounts of intentionality [Boden 1988; Thagard 1986] may or may not shed light on the issue of intentionality, but they do nothing to make it more plausible that the Chinese room is conscious. Consequently, they leave one with the feeling that the problem the scenario poses for AI has not been addressed. At best, what has been disputed is the auxiliary premise that intentionality requires consciousness.)[4]

The Chinese room argument runs as follows. Take any program t supposed to capture some aspect of consciousness, such as understa Chinese or having a sensation of red. Then this program can be impleme by a monolingual English speaker—who we will call the *demon*—in a bl and-white room. The demon follows all the rules specified by the program manually, keeping a record of all the relevant internal states and variables on slips of paper, erasing and updating them as necessary. We can imagine that the demon is also connected to a robotic body, receiving digital inputs from perceptual transducers, manipulating them according to the program's specifications, and sending digital outputs to motor effectors. In this way, the program is implemented perfectly. Nevertheless, it seems clear that the demon does not consciously understand Chinese, and that the demon is not having a sensation of red. Therefore implementing a program is not sufficient for these conscious experiences. Consciousness must require something more than the implementation of a relevant program.

Proponents of strong AI have typically replied by conceding that the *demon* does not understand Chinese, and arguing that understanding and consciousness should instead be attributed to the *system* consisting of the demon and the pieces of paper. Searle has declared this reply manifestly implausible. Certainly, there is something counterintuitive about the claim that a system of an agent and associated pieces of paper has a collective consciousness. At this point, the argument reaches an impasse. Proponents of AI argue that the system is conscious, opponents find the conclusion ridiculous, and it seems difficult to proceed any further. I think that the arguments already given provide grounds for breaking the impasse in favor of strong AI, however.

Let us assume that the relevant program is in fact a combinatorial-state automaton that reflects the neuron-level organization of a Chinese speaker who is looking at a juicy red apple. The demon in the room is implementing the CSA by maintaining a slip of paper for each element of the state vector, and updating the slips of paper at every time-step according to the state transition rules. We may run the fading and dancing qualia arguments by constructing a spectrum of cases between the original Chinese speaker and the Chinese room.[5] This is not difficult to do. First, we can imagine that the neurons in the Chinese speaker's head are replaced one at a time by tiny demons, each of whom duplicates the input–output function of a neuron.[6] Upon receiving stimulation from neighboring neurons, a demon makes the appropriate calculations and stimulates neighboring neurons in turn. As more and more neurons are replaced, demons take over, until the skull is filled with billions of demons reacting to each others' signals and to sensory inputs, making calculations, and signaling other demons and stimulating motor outputs in turn. (If someone objects that all those demons could never fit in a skull, we can imagine a scenario with radio transmission equipment le the skull instead.)

xt, we gradually cut down on the number of demons by allowing them uble up on their work. At first, we replace two neighboring demons a single demon doing the job of both of them. The new demon will keep a record of the internal state of both neurons he is simulating—we can imagine that this record is kept on a piece of paper at each location. Each piece of paper will be updated depending on signals from neighboring demons and also on the state of the other piece of paper. The demons are consolidated further, until eventually there is just a single demon, and billions of tiny slips of paper. We may imagine that each of these slips is at the original location of its corresponding neuron, and that the demon dashes around the brain, updating each slip of paper as a function of the states of neighboring slips, and of sensory inputs where necessary.

Despite all these changes, the resulting system shares the functional organization of the original brain. The causal relations between neurons in the original case are mirrored by the causal relations between demons in the intermediate case, and by the causal relations between slips of paper in the final case. In the final case, the causal relations are mediated by the actions of a demon—a piece of paper affects the state of the demon, which affects a neighboring piece of paper—but they are causal relations nevertheless. If we watch the system function at a speeded-up rate, we will see a whir of causal interaction that corresponds precisely to the whir among the neurons.

We can therefore apply the fading and dancing qualia arguments. If the final system lacks conscious experience, then there must be an intermediate system with faded conscious experiences. This is implausible for just the same reasons as before. We can also imagine switching between a neural circuit and a corresponding backup circuit implemented with demons, or with a single demon and pieces of paper. As before, this would lead to dancing qualia with constant functional organization, so that the system could never notice the difference. Once again, it is much more plausible to suppose that qualia stay constant throughout.

It is therefore reasonable to conclude that the final system has precisely the conscious experiences of the original system. If the neural system gave rise to experiences of bright red, so will the system of demons, and so will the network of pieces of paper mediated by a demon. But of course, this final case is just a copy of the system in the Chinese room. We have therefore given a positive reason to believe that that system really has conscious experiences, such as that of understanding Chinese or of experiencing red.

This way of looking at things makes clear two things that may be obscured by Searle's description of the Chinese room. First, the "slips of paper" in the room are not a mere pile of formal symbols. They constitute a concrete dynamical system with a causal organization that corresponds directly to the organization of the original brain. The slow pace that we associate with symbol manipulation obscures this, as does the presence of the demon manipulating the symbols, but nevertheless it is the concrete dynamics among the pieces of paper that gives rise to conscious experience. Second, the role of the demon is entirely secondary. The interesting causal dynamics are those that take place among the pieces of paper, which correspond to the ne in the original case. The demon simply acts as a kind of causal facil The image of a demon scurrying around in the skull makes it clear that attribute the experiences of the system to the *demon* would be a serious confusion of levels. The fact that the demon is a conscious agent may tempt one to suppose that if the system's experiences are anywhere, they are in the demon; but in fact the consciousness of the demon is entirely irrelevant to the functioning of the system. The demon's job could be performed by a simple look-up table. The crucial aspect of the system is the dynamics among the symbols.

Searle's argument gains its purchase on our intuitions by implementing the program in a bizarre way that obscures the realization of the relevant causal dynamics. Once we look past the images brought to mind by the presence of the irrelevant demon and by the slow speed of symbol shuffling, however, we see that the causal dynamics in the room precisely reflect the causal dynamics in the skull. This way, it no longer seems so implausible to suppose that the system gives rise to experience.

Searle also gives a version of the argument in which the demon *memorizes* the rules of the computation, and implements the program internally. Of course, in practice people cannot memorize even one hundred rules and symbols, let alone many billions, but we can imagine that a demon with a supermemory module might be able to memorize all the rules and the states of all the symbols. In this case, we can again expect the system to give rise to conscious experiences that are not the demon's experiences. Searle argues that the demon must have the experiences if anyone does, as all the processing is internal to the demon, but this should instead be regarded as an example of two mental systems realized within the same physical space. The organization that gives rise to the Chinese experiences is quite distinct from the organization that gives rise to the demon's experiences. The Chinese-understanding organization lies in the causal relations between billions of locations in the supermemory module; once again, the demon only acts as a kind of causal facilitator. This is made clear if we consider a spectrum of cases in which the demon scurrying around the skull gradually memorizes the rules and symbols, until everything is internalized. The relevant structure is gradually moved from the skull to the demon's supermemory, but experience remains constant throughout, and entirely separate from the experiences of the demon.

Some may suppose that because my argument relies on duplicating the neuron-level organization of the brain, it establishes only a weak form of strong AI, one that is closely tied to biology. (In discussing what he calls the "Brain Simulator" reply, Searle expresses surprise that a supporter of AI would give a reply that depends on the detailed simulation of human biology.) This would be to miss the force of the argument, however. The brain simulation program merely serves as the thin end of the wedge. Once we know that *one* program can give rise to a mind even when implemented Chinese-room style, the force of Searle's in-principle argument is entirely removed: we know that the demon and the paper in a Chinese room can indeed support an independent mind. The floodgates are then opened to a whole range of programs that might be candidates to generate conscious experience. The extent of this range is an open question, but the Chinese room is not an obstacle.

Syntax and semantics

A second argument, put forward by Searle (1984), runs as follows:

1. A computer program is syntactic.
2. Syntax is not sufficient for semantics.
3. Minds have semantics.
4. Therefore, implementing a program is insufficient for a mind.

Once again, this is put forward as an argument about intentionality, but it can also be taken as an argument about consciousness. For Searle, the central sort of intentionality is phenomenological intentionality, the kind that is inherent in consciousness.

There are various ways in which this argument can be interpreted and criticized, but the main problem is that the argument does not respect the crucial role of implementation. *Programs* are abstract computational objects and are purely syntactic. Certainly, no mere program is a candidate for possession of a mind. *Implementations of programs,* on the other hand, are concrete systems with causal dynamics, and are not purely syntactic. An implementation has causal heft in the real world, and it is in virtue of this causal heft that consciousness and intentionality arise. It is the program that is syntactic; it is the implementation that has semantic content.

Searle might argue that there is a sense in which even implementations are syntactic, perhaps because the dynamics of implementations are determined by formal properties. Any sense of "syntax" in which implementations are syntactic, however, loses touch with the sense in which it is plausible that syntax is not sufficient for semantics. While it may be plausible that static sets of abstract symbols do not have intrinsic semantic properties, it is much less clear that formally specified causal processes cannot support a mind.

We can parody the argument as follows:

1. Recipes are syntactic.
2. Syntax is not sufficient for crumbliness.
3. Cakes are crumbly.
4. Therefore, implementing a recipe is insufficient for a cake.

In this form the flaw is immediately apparent. The argument does not distinguish between recipes, which are syntactic objects, and implementations of recipes, which are full-bodied physical systems in the real world. Again, all the work is done by the implementation relation, which relates the abstract and concrete domains. A recipe implicitly specifies a class of physical systems that qualify as *implementations* of the recipe, and it is these systems that have such features as crumbliness. Similarly, a program implicitly specifies a class of physical systems that qualify as implementations of the program, and it is these systems that give rise to such features as minds.

A simulation is just a simulation

A popular objection to artificial intelligence (e.g., Searle 1980, Harnad 1989) is that a simulation of a phenomenon is not the same as a replication. For example, when we simulate digestion computationally, no food is actually digested. A simulated hurricane is not a real hurricane; when a hurricane is simulated on a computer, no one gets wet. When heat is simulated, no real heat is generated. So when a mind is simulated, why should we expect a real mind to result? Why should we expect that in this case but not others, a computational process is not just a simulation but the real thing?

It is certainly true that for many properties, simulation is not replication. Simulated heat is not real heat. On the other hand, for some properties, simulation *is* replication. For example, a simulation of a system with a causal loop *is* a system with a causal loop. So the real question here is, how do we distinguish those types X such that a simulation of an X really is an X from those such that it is not?

I suggest that the answer is as follows: A simulation of X is an X precisely when the property of being an X is an *organizational invariant*. The definition of an organizational invariant is as before: a property is an organizational invariant when it depends only on the functional organization of the underlying system, and not on any other details. A computational simulation of a physical system can capture its abstract causal organization, and ensure that that causal organization is replicated in any implementation, no matter what the implementation is made out of. Such an implementation will then *replicate* any organizational invariants of the original system, but other properties will be lost.

The property of being a hurricane is not an organizational invariant, as it depends partly on nonorganizational properties such as the velocity, shape, and physical composition of the underlying system (a system with the same causal interactions implemented very slowly among a large set of billiard balls would not be a hurricane). Similarly, digestion and heat depend on aspects of underlying physical makeup that are not wholly organizational. We could gradually replace the biological components in a digestive system so that acid-base reactions are replaced by causally isomorphic interactions among pieces of metal, and it would no longer count as an instance of digestion. So we should not expect a simulation of systems with these properties to itself have these properties.

But phenomenal properties are different. As I have argued in Chapter 7, these properties are organizational invariants. If so, it follows that the right sort of simulation of a system with phenomenal properties will itself have phenomenal properties, by virtue of replicating the original system's fine-grained functional organization. Organizational invariance makes consciousness different in principle from the other properties mentioned, and opens the way to strong AI.

5. External Objections

I have been most concerned with internal objections to strong artificial intelligence, as these are most relevant to the topic of this book, but I will also at least mention some external objections. As I said earlier, the *prima facie* case against external objections to artificial intelligence is strong: there is every reason to believe that the laws of physics, at least as currently understood, are computable, and that human behavior is a consequence of physical laws. If so, then it follows that a computational system can simulate human behavior. Objections are occasionally mounted all the same, however, so I will discuss these briefly.

Objections from rule following

Perhaps the oldest external objection to AI is that computational systems always follow rules, so they will always lack certain human capacities, such as creativity or flexibility. This is in many ways the weakest of the external objections, partly as it is so vague and underspecified. Indeed, it can easily be replied in turn that at the neural level, the human brain may be quite mechanical and reflexive, but this is no bar to creativity and flexibility at the macroscopic level. Of course, an opponent could always choose to deny the thesis about mechanism at the neural level, but in any case there seems to be no good argument for the thesis that computational dynamics at a basic causal level is incompatible with creativity and flexibility at the macroscopic level.

This sort of objection may gain some leverage from the implicit identification of computational systems with *symbolic* computational systems: systems that perform symbolic manipulations of high-level conceptual representations—in the extreme case, systems that inflexibly draw conclusions from premises in first-order logic. Perhaps the objection has some force in these cases, although even that is disputable. But in any case, the class of computational systems is much broader than this. A low-level simulation of the brain is a computation, for example, but is not a symbolic computation of this sort. At an intermediate level, connectionist models in cognitive science have appealed to a sort of computation that does not consist in symbolic manipulation. In these cases, there may be a level at which the system follows rules, but this is not directly reflected at the level of behavior; indeed, connectionists often claim that theirs is a method of yielding high-level flexibility from low-level mechanicality. As Hofstadter (1979) has put it, the level at which I think is not necessarily the level at which I sum.[7]

Objections from Gödel's theorem

It is sometimes held that Gödel's theorem shows that computational systems are limited in a way that humans are not. Gödel's theorem tells us that for any consistent formal system powerful enough to do a certain sort of arithmetic, there will be a true sentence—the system's *Gödel sentence*—that the system cannot prove. But we can see that the Gödel sentence is true, it is argued, so we have a capacity that the formal system lacks. It follows that no formal system can precisely capture human capacities. (Arguments of this sort are made by Lucas [1961] and Penrose [1989, 1994], among others.)

The short answer to these arguments is that there is no reason to believe that humans can see the truth of the relevant Gödel sentences, either. At best, we can see that *if* a system is consistent, then its Gödel sentence is true, but there is no reason to believe that we can determine the consistency of arbitrary formal systems.[8] This holds particularly in the case of complex formal systems, such as a system that simulates the output of a human brain: the task of determining whether such a system is consistent might well be beyond us. So it may well be that each of us can be simulated by a complex formal system F, such that we cannot determine whether F is consistent. If so, we will not be able to see the truth of our own Gödel sentences.

There are many variants on the Gödelian argument, with replies that an opponent might make to this suggestion and further byways that come up in turn. I will not discuss these here (although I discuss them at length in Chalmers 1995c). These issues lead to many stimulating points of interest, but I think it is fair to say that the case that Gödelian limitations do not apply to humans has never been convincingly made.

Objections from uncomputability and continuity

The objections above are "high-level" arguments that cognitive functioning is uncomputable. One might also try to attack the AI position at the low level, by arguing that physical functioning is not computable. Penrose (1994) argues that there may be a noncomputable element in a correct theory of quantum gravity, for example. His only evidence for this conclusion, however, lies in the Gödelian argument above. There is nothing in physical theory itself to support the conclusion; so if the Gödelian argument is overturned, any reason for believing in uncomputable physical laws disappears. Indeed, one might argue that given that every element of the brain, such as a neuron, has only a finite number of relevant states, and given that there are only a finite number of relevant elements, then the relevant causal structure of the brain *must* be capturable in a computational description.

This leads to the final objection, which is that brain processes may be essentially *continuous* where computational processes are discrete, and that this continuity may be essential to our cognitive competence, so that no discrete simulation could duplicate that competence. Perhaps in approximating a neuron by an element with only a finite number of states, one loses something vital to its functioning. An opponent might appeal, for example, to the presence of "sensitive dependence on initial conditions" in certain nonlinear systems, which implies that even a small round-off error at one stage of processing can lead to major macroscopic differences at a later stage. If brain processing is like this, then any discrete simulation of the brain will yield results that differ from the continuous reality.

There is good reason to believe that absolute continuity cannot be essential to our cognitive competence, however. The presence of background noise in biological systems implies that no process can depend on requiring more than a certain amount of precision. Beyond a certain point (say, the 10^{-10} level on an appropriate scale), uncontrollable fluctuations in background noise will wash out any further precision. This means that if we approximate the state of the system to this level of precision (perhaps a little further to be on the safe side—to the 10^{-20} level, for example), then we will be doing as well as the system itself can reliably do. It is true that due to nonlinear effects, this approximation may lead to behavior different from the behavior produced by the system on a given occasion—but it will lead to behavior that the system *might* have produced, had biological noise been a little different. We can even approximate the noise process itself, if we want to.[9] The result will be that the simulating system will have the same behavioral *capacities* as the original system, even if it produces different specific behavior on specific occasions. The moral is that when it comes to duplicating our cognitive capacities, a close approximation is as good as the real thing.

It is true that a system with unlimited precision might have cognitive capacities that no discrete system could ever have. For example, one might encode an analog quantity corresponding to the real number whose nth binary digit is 1 if and only if the nth Turing machine halts on all inputs. Using this quantity, a perfect continuous system could solve the halting problem, something no discrete system can do. But the presence of noise implies that no biological process could reliably implement this system. Biological systems can rely on only a finite amount of precision, so human and animal brains must be limited to capacities that discrete systems can share.

6. Conclusion

The conclusion is that there do not appear to be any in-principle barriers to the ambitions of artificial intelligence. The external objections do not appear to carry much force. The internal objections may be more worrying, but none of the arguments for these objections seem to be compelling on analysis; and indeed if the arguments I have given in previous chapters are correct, then we have good positive reason to believe that implementation of an appropriate computation will bring conscious experience along with it. So the outlook for machine consciousness is good in principle, if not yet in practice.

I have said little about just what *sort* of computation is likely to suffice for conscious experience. In most of the arguments I have used a neuron-by-neuron simulation of the brain as an example; but it is likely that many other sorts of computations might also suffice. It might be, for example, that a computation that mirrors the causal organization of the brain at a much coarser level could still capture what is relevant for the emergence of conscious experience. And it is likely that computations of an entirely different form, corresponding to entirely different sorts of causal organization, could also give rise to rich conscious experiences when implemented.

This picture is equally compatible with the symbolic and connectionist approaches to cognition, and with other computational approaches as well. Indeed, one could argue that the centrality of computation in the study of cognition stems from the way that computational accounts can capture almost *any* sort of causal organization. We can see computational formalisms as providing an ideal formalism for the expression of patterns of causal organization, and indeed (in combination with implementational methods) as an ideal tool for their replication. Whatever causal organization turns out to be central to cognition and consciousness, we can expect that a computational account will be able to capture it. One might even argue that it is this flexibility that lies behind the often-cited *universality* of computational systems. Proponents of artificial intelligence are not committed to any one sort of computation as the sort that might suffice for mentality; the AI thesis is so plausible precisely because the class of computational systems is so wide.[10]

So it remains an open question just what class of computations is sufficient to replicate human mentality; but we have good reason to believe that the class is not empty.

10

The Interpretation of Quantum Mechanics

1. Two Mysteries

The problem of quantum mechanics is almost as hard as the problem of consciousness. Quantum mechanics gives us a remarkably successful calculus for predicting the results of empirical observations, but it is extraordinarily difficult to make sense of the picture of the world that it delivers. How could our world be the way it has to be, in order for the predictions of quantum mechanics to succeed? There is nothing even approaching a consensus on the answer to this question. Just as with consciousness, it often seems that *no* solution to the problem of quantum mechanics can be satisfactory.

Many people have thought that these two most puzzling of problems might be intimately linked (e.g., Bohm 1980; Hodgson 1988; Lockwood 1989; Penrose 1989; Squires 1990; Stapp 1993; Wigner 1961). Where there are two mysteries, it is tempting to suppose that they have a common source. This temptation is magnified by the fact that the problems in quantum mechanics seem to be deeply tied to the notion of observership, crucially involving the relation between a subject's experience and the rest of the world.

Most often, it has been suggested that quantum mechanics may hold the key to a physical explanation of consciousness. But as we have seen, this project will always fall short of its goal. At the end of the day quantum "theories" of consciousness suffer from the same sort of explanatory gap as classical theories. Either way experience must be taken as something over and above the physical properties of the world. Perhaps quantum mechanics might play a role in characterizing the psychophysical link, but quantum theory alone cannot tell us why consciousness exists.

But the problems may be linked in a more subtle way. Even if quantum mechanics does not explain consciousness, perhaps a theory of consciousness might shed light on the problems of quantum mechanics. After all, it is widely agreed that these problems have something to do with observership and experience. It is natural to suppose that a theory of experience might help us come to grips with the issues. Some have proposed an active role for consciousness in quantum theory—suggesting that consciousness brings about the "collapse of the wave function," for example—but I will argue for a more indirect role for consciousness in dealing with these questions. In particular, I will argue that we can reconceive the problems of quantum theory as problems about the relationship between the physical structure of the world and our experience of the world, and that consequently an appropriate theory of consciousness can lend support to an unorthodox interpretation of quantum mechanics.

2. The Framework of Quantum Mechanics

The basic framework of quantum mechanics consists in a calculus for predicting the results of experimental measurements. I will describe a version of that calculus here, glossing over a number of technical details in order to provide a simple description that covers the most crucial features. In this section, I present the framework merely as a calculus for empirical predictions, leaving open the question of whether it provides a direct description of physical reality. The deep problems of interpretation are discussed in the next section.

Within a classical framework, the state of a physical system can be expressed in very simple terms. The state of a particle, for example, is expressed by giving determinate values for each of a number of properties, such as position and momentum. We can call this sort of simple value a *basic value.* Within the quantum framework, things are not so simple. In general, the state of a system must be expressed as a *wave function,* or a *state vector.* Here, the relevant properties cannot be expressed in simple values, but instead must be expressed as a kind of combination of basic values. A quantum state can be seen as a *superposition* of simpler states.

The simplest example is a property such as *spin,* which has only two basic values.[1] These basic values can be labeled "up" and "down." In quantum mechanics, the spin of a particle is not always up or down, however. Instead, a particle's spin must in general be expressed as a *combination* of up and down, each with a different complex magnitude. The spin of a particle is therefore best regarded as a vector in a two-dimensional vector space. It is most naturally visualized as a superposition of a spin-up state and a spin-down state, with different magnitudes corresponding to each.

The same goes for position and momentum, except that each of these has an infinite number of basic values. The position and the momentum of a classical particle can each take on any of an infinite number of values in a continuum. The position of a quantum particle, correspondingly, must be expressed as a kind of infinite-dimensional vector with a different magnitude for each of these locations. This vector is best regarded as a *wave,* with different amplitudes at different locations in space; the function that takes a location to the corresponding amplitude is the wave function. Similarly, the momentum of a quantum particle can be regarded as a wave with different amplitudes at different basic values of momentum. Again, we can think of the position or momentum of such a particle as a superposition of basic values of position or momentum.

Because these states are just vectors, they can be decomposed into components in many ways. While it is often useful to see a two-dimensional spin vector as a sum of an "up" component and a "down" component, it can be decomposed in many other ways, depending on the basis chosen for the vector space. All of these bases are equally "natural"; none is preferred by nature. In fact, it turns out a single vector represents both the position and the momentum of a particle. Decomposed according to one basis, we get the "position" amplitudes; decomposed according to a different basis, we get the "momentum" amplitudes. In general, the decomposition that is relevant in a given case depends on which quantity we are interested in, and in particular on which quantity we choose to *measure,* as I discuss shortly.

The states of systems consisting of more than a single particle are somewhat more complex, but the basic idea is the same. Take a system consisting of two particles, *A* and *B.* The state of the system cannot generally be expressed by combining a wave function for *A* and a wave function for *B* in any simple way; the states of the two particles will often be *nonseparable.* Rather, the state of the system must be expressed as a wave function in a more complex space. This wave function can be seen as a kind of superposition of simpler states of the two-particle system, however, so the general picture still applies. The same goes for more complex systems, in which a state is still best represented as a wave function corresponding to a superposition of states.

All this is counterintuitive, but it is not yet paradoxical. If we take this formalism at face value as a description of reality, it is not *too* hard to make sense of. Some have supposed that it is incompatible with an "objective" view of the world, as it implies that entities in the world do not have an objective, determinate state. But this does not follow. On this picture, the state of an entity is best expressed by a wave function rather than by discrete quantities, but it is a perfectly determinate state. The picture simply tells us that on the basic level reality is wavelike. This requires a new way of thinking, but we can get used to it. After all, the basic level of microscopic reality is very far from the macroscopic level we usually deal with, and it is not entirely surprising that it should have some unfamiliar properties. Any problems that arise stem from *further* properties of quantum mechanics.

The core of quantum mechanics consists of two principles that determine the *dynamics* of the wave function: the *Schrödinger equation* and the *measurement postulate*. Between them, these two very different principles determine how the wave function of a system evolves with time.

Most of the substance of quantum mechanics is found in the Schrödinger equation. This is a differential equation that determines how the wave function of a system evolves under *almost* all circumstances. The detailed structure of the equation is not important for our purposes. The most important feature here is that it is a *linear* differential equation: given two states *A* and *B* such that *A* evolves into *A'* and *B* evolves into *B'*, then a state consisting in a superposition of *A* and *B* will evolve into a superposition of *A'* and *B'*. It is also worth noting that under the dynamics of the Schrödinger equation, relatively discrete states usually become more spread out over time. A state that starts as a superposition of values in a limited range will generally evolve into a superposition of values in a much wider range. Finally, the Schrödinger equation is entirely deterministic.

The Schrödinger equation is relatively straightforward and well understood. It is here that the meat and potatoes of quantum theory resides. In applying quantum theory to a practical or experimental problem, the bulk of the work consists in calculating how various states evolve according to the Schrödinger dynamics.

The Schrödinger equation cannot be *all* there is to say, however. According to the equation, the vast majority of physical states will soon evolve into a superposition of a wide range of states. But this does not square with our observations of the world. When we measure the position of a particle, we find a definite value, not the superposition of values that the Schrödinger equation would predict. If the Schrödinger equation were all there is to quantum dynamics, then even at the macroscopic level the world would evolve into a wildly superposed state. But in our experience it does not. Pointers have definite locations, moving objects have a definite measurable momentum, and so on. So there must be more to the story: something that leads us from the equation to the sorts of discrete events that characterize our experience.

The second part of the story in the standard formalism is the *measurement postulate* (also known as the collapse or projection postulate). This asserts that under special circumstances, the Schrödinger dynamics do not apply. Specifically, it says that when a *measurement* is made, the wave function *collapses* into a more definite form. The way that it collapses depends on the property that is being measured. For example, if we measure the spin of a particle, then even if it is in a superposed state beforehand, it will collapse into a state in which the spin is either up or down. If we measure the position of a particle, its wave function will collapse into a state with a definite position.[2] The resulting state still corresponds to a wave function, but it is a wave function in which all the amplitude is concentrated at a definite position; the amplitude everywhere else is zero. To every quantity that we might measure there corresponds an operator, and upon measurement the state will collapse into a state which is an *eigenstate* of that operator. An eigenstate of an operator is always a state in which the corresponding measurable quantity has a definite value. It follows that when we make a measurement of a quantity, a definite value for that quantity always results, which squares precisely with our experience.

The dynamics of collapse are probabilistic rather than deterministic. If a particle is in a state that is a superposition of positions, then when position is measured we know that it will collapse into a state with definite position, but we do not know what that position will be. Rather, for each potential collapsed state, the measurement postulate specifies the *probability* that the system will collapse into that state. This probability[3] is given by the square of the amplitude of the wave function, at the location corresponding to the definite value in question. For example, if the spin of a particle is a superposition of spin up (with amplitude $\frac{1}{2}$) and spin down (with amplitude $\frac{\sqrt{3}}{2}$), then when spin is measured it will collapse into a spin-up state with probability $\frac{1}{4}$, and into a spin-down state with probability $\frac{3}{4}$. The amplitudes in a wave function always have the property that the corresponding probabilities add up to 1.

3. Interpreting Quantum Mechanics

Together, these two principles constitute an extremely powerful calculus for predicting the results of experimental measurements. To predict the results of an experiment, we express the state of a system as a wave function, and calculate how the wave function evolves over time according to the Schrödinger equation, until the point where a measurement is made. Where a measurement is made, we use the amplitudes of the calculated wave function to determine the probability that various collapsed states will result, and to calculate the probability that the measurement will yield any given quantity. Experimental results have been unwavering in their support for the predictions of the theory; few scientific theories have been as successful at a predictive task. As a calculus, the theory is all but watertight.

The problems arise when we ask *how* it could be that the calculus works. What could be happening in the real world to make the predictions of the calculus so accurate? This is the problem of the *interpretation* of quantum mechanics. There are many different options available in grappling with this problem, none of which is wholly satisfactory.

Option 1: Take the calculus literally

The natural first reaction is to take the formalism of quantum mechanics at face value, as we do with most scientific theories. The calculus involves a wave function governed by the dynamics of the Schrödinger equation and the measurement postulate, and the calculus works, so we should suppose that it gives us a direct picture of what is going on in the world. That is to say, the state of a system in reality is precisely the wave state expressed by the wave function, evolving according to the dynamics expressed by the two basic principles. Most of the time, the state evolves according to the Schrödinger equation, but when a measurement is made, the state evolves according to the measurement postulate. On this view, the world consists of waves that usually evolve linearly in a superposition, and that occasionally collapse into a more definite state when a measurement is made.

But it is not easy to make sense of this picture. The problems all stem from the measurement postulate. According to this postulate, a collapse occurs when a measurement is made, but what counts as a measurement? How does *nature* know when a measurement is made? "Measurement" is surely not a basic term in the laws of nature; if the measurement postulate is to be remotely plausible as a fundamental law, the notion of measurement must be replaced by something clearer and more basic. If wave function collapse is an objectively existing process in the world, then we need clear, objective criteria for when it occurs.

One solution that is obviously unsatisfactory is to say that a collapse occurs whenever a quantum system interacts with a *measuring apparatus*. The problem here is that it is just as implausible that the notion of "measuring apparatus" should appear in the basic laws as it is that the notion of "measurement" should. Before, we needed criteria for what counts as a measurement; now, we need criteria for what counts as a measuring apparatus.

A suggestion popular in the early days of quantum mechanics was that a measuring apparatus is a *classical* system, and that a measurement occurs whenever a quantum system interacts with a classical system. But this is clearly unsatisfactory. Quantum theory is meant to be a universal theory, and it should apply to processes within a measuring instrument just as much as it applies to processes elsewhere. Unless we are to suppose that there are two fundamentally different kinds of physical objects in the world—a supposition that would require the development of an entirely new theory—then "classical system" cannot be a term in a fundamental law of nature any more than "measurement" can.

A related suggestion is that a measurement occurs whenever a quantum system interacts with a *macroscopic* system. But it is just as clear that "macroscopic" is not a notion that can figure in a basic law. It must be replaced by something more precise: something like "system with mass one gram or greater." It would be extraordinarily arbitrary for something like this to figure in a basic law, however.

There is no physical criterion for collapse that seems remotely acceptable. A criterion cast at the microscopic level—suggesting that collapse takes place when a system interacts with a proton, for example—is ruled out by experimental results. The alternative is that the criterion must involve a higher-level physical property, so that collapse takes place when systems take on a certain high-level configuration. But any such higher-level property would seem arbitrary, and no plausible candidate has ever been proposed. There is also something very odd about the supposition that the Schrödinger dynamics of microscopic systems should be suddenly overridden when those systems happen to find themselves in the context of certain special configurations.

The only remotely tenable criterion that has been proposed is that a measurement takes place when a quantum system affects some being's *consciousness*. Unlike the previous criteria, this criterion is at least determinate and nonarbitrary.[4] The corresponding interpretation of the calculus is reasonably elegant and simple in its form, and it is the only *literal* interpretation of the calculus that has any wide currency. This interpretation was first suggested by London and Bauer (1939), but it is most closely associated with Wigner (1961).

Note that this interpretation *presupposes* mind–body dualism. If consciousness were just another physical property, then all the previous problems would arise. The view would turn into another "high-level property" view, on which the wave functions of physical systems just happen to collapse in the context of certain complex physical configurations. If dualism holds, on the other hand, then the criterion for collapse can be truly fundamental. Further, the fact that the cause of collapse is external to physical processing allows for a much simpler theory. All purely physical systems are now governed by the Schrödinger dynamics alone, and the very different measurement dynamics have an independent source.

The interpretation has some counterintuitive consequences, though. Take a measuring apparatus such as a pointer that measures the state of an electron, and suppose that the state of the electron is initially superposed. If there is no consciousness in the vicinity, the whole system is governed by the linear Schrödinger dynamics: given that different discrete electron states would produce different discrete pointer states, it follows that a superposed electron state will produce a *superposed* pointer state. That is, the theory predicts that the pointer is pointing to many different locations simultaneously! It is only when I *look* at the pointer that it points to a definite position.

The scenario of Schrödinger's cat brings on even stranger consequences. In this scenario a cat is locked inside a cabinet, an electron's spin is measured by an instrument, and an apparatus is set up so that the cat is killed if and only if the electron's spin is "up." (Assume that the cat is anesthetized, so that its consciousness does not enter the picture.) If the electron is initially in a superposed state, then the cat will move into a state that is a superposition of life and death! Only when a conscious being looks inside the cabinet will it become determinate whether the cat is dead or alive.

In this picture, *any* macroscopic system will usually be in a large-scale superposition if there is no consciousness in the vicinity. Before consciousness evolved, the entire universe was in a giant superposition, until presumably the first speck of consciousness caused its state to suddenly collapse. This may sound crazy, but it is a direct consequence of the only tenable literal interpretation of the principles of quantum mechanics. I hope this helps to bring out just how strange quantum mechanics is, and how serious the problems posed by its interpretation are.

The counterintuitive consequences could perhaps be accepted, but I nevertheless do not advocate this interpretation. For a start, it is incompatible with the view that I have advocated on which consciousness is ubiquitous. If consciousness is associated even with very simple systems, then on this interpretation collapse will happen at a very basic level and very frequently. This is inconsistent with the physical evidence, which requires that low-level superpositions often persist uncollapsed for a significant time. A second problem is that there is nothing approaching a good theory of what *sort* of effect on consciousness brings about collapse, or of what form the resulting collapse will take. There are many different ways this might be spelled out, but no single way of working out the details looks especially compelling.

Other problems stem from the very notion of collapse. For a start, collapse must be *nonlocal*: when two particles have entangled states, measuring the first particle will cause the state of the second to collapse simultaneously. This leads to some tension with relativity theory. For example, it seems that nonlocal collapse requires an appeal to a privileged reference frame. Without such a reference frame, the time of collapse of the second particle will be underdetermined, as simultaneity across locations is not well defined.

More generally, the whole process of collapse sits uneasily with the rest of physics. Taken literally, it is an instantaneous, discontinuous, temporally asymmetric, nonlocal process that is entirely unlike every other process that physical theory gives us reason to believe in. It seems odd that such a strange process should exist alongside the straightforward, continuous, temporally symmetric, local Schrödinger equation. Indeed, compared to the elegance and power of the Schrödinger equation, which is at the heart of quantum theory, collapse seems almost to be an arbitrary, tacked-on element. There is something very awkward about the idea that the world has two such entirely different sorts of dynamics at its basic level.

These are far from knockdown arguments, of course, and the interpretation on which consciousness collapses the wave function deserves to be taken very seriously. Nevertheless, I think there is good reason to look for another interpretation, one that gives us a simpler and more straightforward view of nature's basic processes.

Option 2: Try to get the measurement postulate for free

The problems with the literal interpretation all stem from taking the measurement postulate as a fundamental law. It is tempting to suppose that instead the postulate might be *nonbasic,* a consequence of more fundamental principles. There are two ways this might go. We might try to introduce *further* basic principles, less problematic than the measurement postulate, that have the same effect. This is the strategy of option 4. Or we might try to derive the effects as a consequence of known basic principles, such as the Schrödinger equation. That is, we might try to get the measurement postulate for free.

It is easy to see the intuitive motivation for this strategy. There is an intuition that superposition effects apply primarily at a microscopic level and might somehow "cancel out" at the macroscopic level. Perhaps when there are many microscopic superpositions, they interact in such a way to produce a macroscopic state that is relatively definite. Because of some mathematical properties of complex configurations, we might be able to see how an *effective* collapse could be the consequence of microscopic indefiniteness. A fundamental probabilistic collapse would then be replaced by an emergent statistical process in a complex system.

There have been numerous attempts to work out the mathematics of this, often appealing to the statistical principles of thermodynamics (e.g., Daneri, Loinger, and Prosperi 1962). Unfortunately, all these attempts have failed, and it is now widely accepted that they *must* fail. Because the Schrödinger dynamics are linear, it is always possible to construct situations in which microscopic superpositions lead to macroscopic superpositions. If an "up" electron leads to one macroscopic state, and a "down" electron leads to another, then a superposed electron must lead to a superposed macroscopic state (Albert 1992, p. 75, gives a very straightforward argument for this point). Unless further basic principles are introduced, then, we have to expect superposition on the macroscopic level.

These strategies can offer something. This sort of appeal to statistics, as well as more recent work on "decoherence" by Gell-Mann and Hartle (1990) and others, suggests that a superposed wave function will often resolve into a relatively clearcut superposition of distinct macroscopic states, rather than being a jumbled mess. These macroscopic states "decohere" from each other, with only minimal interference effects between them. This at least helps us find some element of the familiar classical world in the superposed wave function. But the wave function is still a superposition, and nothing in this sort of work tells us why only one element of the macroscopic superposition should be actual. So more work is required in order to solve the basic problem. This sort of work is perhaps most useful when combined with one of the other options, such as option 5.

Option 3: Whereof one cannot speak . . .

Perhaps the dominant view among working physicists is that one simply should not ask what is going on in the real world, behind the quantum mechanical calculus. The calculus works, and that is that. There are two versions of this view. According to the first version, maybe *something* is going on in the world, but we can never know what it is. The calculus gives us all the empirical information that we will ever have, so that anything further is pure speculation. We might as well stop worrying and continue to calculate. This view makes sense for practical purposes, but it is unsatisfying for anyone who wants physics to tell us about the basic level of reality. Given that the calculus works, we want to have at least some idea of *how* it could possibly work. Perhaps we can never know for sure, but it makes sense to ask.

The second version takes a harder line, and says that there is no fact of the matter about what is going on in the world. According to this view, the facts are exhausted by the fact that the calculus works. This view is often not put forward quite as explicitly as this, perhaps because put so straightfor- wardly the view is almost impossible to believe. It offers us a picture of reality that leaves out the world! It leads to a version of idealism, on which all that exists are our perceptions, or to something very close to this. Before we open the cabinet containing Schrödinger's cat, it is not in a dead state, it is not in an alive state, and it is not in a superposed state; it is simply in no state at all. By giving up on a fact of the matter about what lies behind our measurements, this view gives up on an independently existing reality.

The "Copenhagen interpretation" due to Bohr and his colleagues is often taken to be a version of this view, although Bohr's writings are somewhat ambiguous and interpretation is not easy. These writings also sometimes suggest elements of the first option, and of the epistemological version of this option. Bohr put great emphasis on the "classical" nature of a measuring apparatus, and his views can be read as suggesting that only classical (or macroscopic) objects have an objective state. Questions about the real state of an object described by a superposition are simply proscribed. But this relies on a division between classical and quantum systems that is difficult to draw on any objective grounds, and it is hard to imagine that reality simply "fades out" as we descend from the macroscopic to the microscopic level. It has seemed to many that if Bohr's view is taken seriously, it leads to the strong operationalism discussed in the last paragraph. Like that view, it offers a picture of the basic level of reality that is no picture at all.

Option 4: Postulate further basic physical principles

Given that the literal interpretation of the measurement postulate is unacceptable, and that it cannot be derived from existing physical principles, it is natural to suppose that something more must be going on. Perhaps if we postulate *further* basic physical principles, we might be able to explain the effectiveness of the quantum-mechanical calculus in a less problematic way.

The first way to do this is to retain the idea of collapse, but to explain it differently. Such a strategy retains the assumption that basic physical states are wave functions governed by the Schrödinger equation, but introduces new principles to explain how microscopic superpositions turn into macroscopic discreteness.

The best-known example of this strategy is the "GRW" interpretation due to Ghirardi, Rimini, and Weber (1986; see also Bell 1987a).[5] This interpretation postulates a fundamental law according to which the position state vector of any elementary particle may undergo a microscopic "collapse" at any moment, with some very small probability (the chance that a particle will collapse in a given second is about one in 10^{15}). When such a collapse occurs, it will generally lead to a collapse of the state of a macroscopic system in which it is embedded, due to nonseparability effects. There are many such particles in any macroscopic system, so it follows that any given macroscopic system at any given time will usually be in a relatively discrete state. It is possible to show that this comes very close to reproducing the predictions of the measurement postulate.

The alternative is to eliminate the need for collapse by denying that the basic level of reality is represented by a superposed wave function. If properties such as position have determinate values even at the basic level, then collapse never needs to happen. Such a theory postulates "hidden variables" at the basic level, which directly explain the discreteness of reality at the macroscopic level. The cost of this suggestion is that new principles are needed to explain why the principles of wave function evolution and collapse *seem* to work so well.

The most prominent example here is the theory developed by Bohm (1952). On this theory, the position of basic particles is always determinate. The wave function retains a role as a kind of "pilot wave," guiding the evolution of a particle's position, and the wave function itself is governed by the Schrödinger equation. The probabilistic predictions of the measurement postulate are reinterpreted as *statistical laws*. It turns out that on this theory we can never know the exact position of a particle before measuring it, but only its wave function. The measurement postulate tells us the *proportion* of particles with a given wave function that will have a given position. It therefore yields the best statistical predictions we can expect, given our ignorance.

All of the proposals in this class have problems. Both the GRW interpretation and the Bohm interpretation give a special determinacy to *position*, thus breaking the symmetry between position and momentum in the quantum mechanical calculus. This makes sense for predictive purposes, as it is arguable that determinate positions always underlie our judgments of macroscopic determinacy (think of the position of a pointer, for instance), but it makes for a more awkward theory. For related reasons, there are serious difficulties reconciling these approaches with relativity theory.

The GRW theory has some further difficulties, perhaps the most serious of which is that it does not strictly imply that the macroscopic world is discrete at all. A macroscopic state is still represented by a superposed wave function: although most of its amplitude is concentrated in one place, the amplitude is nonzero wherever the amplitude of the uncollapsed wave function is nonzero. So the problems of superposition recur. The pointer is still pointing to many locations, even after a measurement. It is true that the amplitude for most of these locations is very small, but it is hard to see why a low-amplitude superposition is any more acceptable than a high-amplitude one.

Bohm's theory has fewer technical problems than the GRW interpretation, but it has some strange consequences. Most strikingly, it is *nonlocal* to an extraordinary degree. (Any hidden-variables theory satisfying the predictions of the calculus must be nonlocal, for reasons given by Bell 1964.)[6] It is not just that the properties of a particle can instantly affect the properties of a particle some distance away. It turns out that in determining the trajectory of a particle, one may have to take into account the wave functions of particles in other galaxies! All of these things play a role in composing the global wave function, and that wave function simultaneously governs the trajectories of particles all over the universe.

Perhaps the most basic reason to be suspicious of these interpretations, however, is that they postulate *complexity behind simplicity*. Whatever its problems, the quantum-mechanical calculus is extraordinarily simple and elegant. These interpretations, on the other hand, introduce complex and relatively *ad hoc* further principles to replace and explain this simple framework. This applies slightly less to the GRW interpretation, whose further complexity consists only in introducing two new fundamental constants and in breaking the symmetry between position and momentum; but it remains the case that it is extraordinarily "lucky" that the values of the constants just happen to be such as to almost reproduce the predictions of the standard framework. The extra complexity of the Bohm interpretation is worse: it postulates determinate positions *and* a wave function, a complex new fundamental principle by which the wave function determines the position of particles, and it breaks the symmetry of the original framework.

We might say that these interpretations make it look like the world was constructed by Descartes's evil demon, as they lead us to believe that the world is one way when really it is another. As Albert and Loewer (1989) put it, the God of the Bohm view does not play dice, but he has a malicious sense of humor. The scenario in which the complex Bohm interpretation happens to duplicate the predictions of the simple framework differs only in degree from the case in which the inputs to a brain in a vat are manipulated to produce the appearance of a straightforward external world. It is reminiscent of an "interpretation" of evolutionary theory according to which God created the fossil record intact a few thousand years ago and ensured that the predictions of evolutionary theory would be duplicated. The simplicity of an explanatory framework has been sacrificed for a complex hypothesis that happens to reproduce the results of the original theory.

The framework of quantum mechanics is so simple and elegant that a basic theory that does not replicate that simplicity and elegance can never be satisfying or fully plausible. If there were a few anomalies in quantum theory, some experimental results that the framework did not predict perfectly, it might be more plausible to think that this simplicity is the tip of a complex iceberg. As it stands, though, the framework is so robust that it seems extraordinary that we should need to postulate a complex apparatus to explain its simple predictions.

Given the problems with *every* interpretation of quantum mechanics, these interpretations need to be taken seriously. But it is natural to look for a simpler picture of the world.

Option 5: The Schrödinger equation is all

The centerpiece of quantum mechanics is the Schrödinger equation, and it is present in some form in every interpretation of quantum mechanics. The various interpretations we have considered all add something to the Schrödinger equation, in order to explain the macroscopic discreteness of the world. But the simplest interpretation by far is the one that says that the Schrödinger equation holds, and that is all. That is, the physical state of the world is completely described by a wave function, and its evolution is completely described by the Schrödinger equation. This is the interpretation given by Everett (1957, 1973).

A strategy canvased earlier (option 2) also held that the Schrödinger equation is all, but argued that this is compatible with discreteness at the macroscopic level. We have seen that this must fail for straightforward mathematical reasons. The Everett interpretation is much more radical. On this view, the Schrödinger equation is taken at face value, and the state of the world at every level is described by a wave function. It follows that contrary to appearances, the world is in a superposed state even at the macroscopic level.

4. The Everett Interpretation

The motivation for this interpretation is obvious. The heart of quantum mechanics is the Schrödinger equation. The measurement postulate, and all the other principles that have been proposed, feel like add-on extras. So why not get rid of them? The problem with this interpretation is equally obvious. If the Schrödinger equation is all, then the world is superposed at every level. But it does not *look* superposed: we never perceive pointers that are in a superposition of two states. Why not?

At the very least, this interpretation is highly counterintuitive. According to this view, not only is the state of an electron best described by a superposition, but so is the state of a pointer that measures it! Objectively, it is not strictly true to say that the pointer is pointing up, or pointing down. Rather, it is in a superposition of the states of pointing up and down. The same goes for the macroscopic state of almost everything, which is in a state described by a wave function that will almost never correspond to a single "discrete" state. Superposition, on this view, is everywhere. Why then does the world appear discrete?

Everett's answer to this question is to *extend superposition all the way to the mind*. If we take Schrödinger's equation seriously, then if the pointer measuring an electron is in a superposition of states, the brain of a person perceiving the pointer will itself be in a superposition. The state of the brain will be described as a superposition of one state in which it perceives a pointer pointing upward, and another state in which it perceives a pointer pointing downward. Everett's key move is to suppose that each of these two states should be associated with a separate observer. What happens after such a measurement is that two observers are produced. One of them experiences an "up" pointer, and the other perceives a "down" pointer. It follows that *each* observer will experience a discrete state of the world.

Everett goes on to show that according to this framework, these observers will have most of the properties that we expect observers to have, and that most of the predictions of the quantum-mechanical calculus can be derived. For example, it is not hard to see that each of the two superposed states here will have no access to the other superposed state, so that the superposition of the mind will not be betrayed in any single state. It is even possible to show that when an observer making a measurement perceives another observer measuring the same quantity, the perceived results of the measurements will be in accord, so that the world will seem quite coherent. In short, any single observer will experience the world in largely the way that we expect, even though the world itself is in a superposed state.

This interpretation should not be confused with the *splitting-worlds* interpretation, according to which the world literally splits into many separate worlds every time a measurement is made. There is one world in which the pointer is pointing up, and an entirely separate world in which the pointer is pointing down. Taken this way, the view is the furthest thing from simple. For a start, it requires a new and extraordinary basic principle to describe the "splitting" process. It is far from clear just when "splitting" should take place (the "measurement" problem revived in a new form), and it is very unclear what the worlds resulting from a split should be. For a literal split to happen, a wave function has to "divide" into numerous components; but there are many ways to decompose a wave function, and quantum mechanics delivers no preferred basis for the decomposition. This interpretation seems even more complex and *ad hoc* than the various "collapse" interpretations, and there is little reason to accept it.

The splitting view is frequently attributed to Everett (largely due to the expositions of Everett's work by DeWitt (1970, 1971), but it cannot be found in his writing. Everett's own view is not entirely clear, but it is interpreted much more naturally along the lines I have suggested; this interpretation is also recommended by Albert and Loewer (1988) and by Lockwood (1989). On this view, there is no objective "splitting." Rather, the wave function evolves into a superposition of states, where the superposed states are best regarded as components of a single world. Everett's view is sometimes called a *many-worlds* interpretation (thus suggesting the splitting-worlds view), but the view I am discussing is more accurately a *one-big-world* interpretation. There is only one world, but it has more in it than we might have thought.[7]

On this view, if there is any splitting, it is only in the minds of observers. As superpositions come to affect a subject's brain state, a number of separate minds result, corresponding to the components of the superposition. Each of these perceives a separate discrete world, corresponding to the sort of world that we perceive—call this a *miniworld,* as opposed to the *maxiworld* of the superposition. The real world is a maxiworld, and the miniworlds are merely in the minds of the subjects. Everett calls his view a *relative-state* interpretation: the state of a miniworld, in which pointers point to discrete positions, only counts as the state of the world *relative* to the specification of an observer. The objective state of the world is a superposition.

A key element is left unanalyzed in this interpretation, however. Why is it legitimate to identify each component of an associated brain state with a separate observer? Why is there not instead a single observer with a confused, superposed mental state? Why indeed does such an incoherent brain state give rise to any minds at all? Everett's treatment skates over these crucial questions. Indeed, it may seem that in associating the wave function of a brain state with a number of minds each perceiving a discrete state, Everett is making an illegitimate appeal to a *preferred basis,* just as the splitting-worlds interpretation did. A wave function does not come with an objective division into components, but can be decomposed in many ways, depending on the choice of a basis for the corresponding vector space. It is often natural for our purposes to decompose a wave function one way, according to a particular basis, but such a decomposition does not reflect an objective property of the wave function. Where the brain state can be decomposed into a "perceiving up" and a "perceiving down" state, it can equally be decomposed into two states each of which have confused perceptions. In postulating an objective decomposition, Everett seems to go beyond the resources that the Schrödinger equation provides.

The crucial element omitted from Everett's treatment is an analysis of the relationship between mind and body. Everett assumes that a superposed brain state will have a number of distinct subjects of experience associated with it, but he does nothing to justify this assumption. It is clear that this matter depends crucially on a theory of consciousness. A similar suggestion is made by Penrose (1989):

> In particular, I do not see why a conscious being need be aware of only "one" of the alternatives in a linear superposition. What is it about consciousness that demands that one cannot be "aware" of that tantalizing linear combination of a dead and a live cat? It seems to me that a theory of consciousness would be needed before the many-worlds view can be squared with what one actually observes. (p. 296)

Indeed, it is possible to see the central question in quantum mechanics as a question about the relationship between physical processes and experience. The centerpiece of quantum mechanics is the picture in which microscopic reality is described by a superposed wave function evolved according to the Schrödinger equation. But we *experience* the world as discrete. The central question is, how is this so? Different interpretations give different answers. Some (such as Bohm's) deny the first premise, positing that reality is discrete even at the basic level. Some posit basic principles (the measurement postulate, or the GRW collapse law) to mediate a transition from the superposed to the discrete. Some theories (those of option 2) try to explain how superposed microscopic states can statistically produce a discrete macroscopic reality.

These last three strategies are all *indirect* strategies, attempting to explain the discreteness of experience by explaining an underlying discreteness of macroscopic reality.

An alternative strategy is to answer the question about experience *directly*. If we take the primacy of the Schrödinger equation seriously, the central question is why, given that the physical structure of the world is like *this,* do we experience it like *this*? This is precisely a question about the way that certain physical structures give rise to experience. That is, it is the kind of question that I have been discussing throughout this book, and it is the kind of question that a theory of consciousness ought to be able to answer.

If we have to postulate an *ad hoc* theory of consciousness to answer this question, the attractiveness of the Everett interpretation is diminished significantly. Its best feature was always its simplicity, but new and arbitrary psychophysical laws would make it as *ad hoc* as the Bohm interpretation. If on the other hand an *independently motivated* theory of consciousness can answer the question, then the Everett interpretation begins to look attractive indeed.

The theory of consciousness that I have advocated can answer this question, and can give the right sort of answer. It turns out that the theory *predicts* that a superposed brain state should be associated with a number of distinct subjects of discrete experience. To see this, let a *maximal phenomenal state* be a phenomenal state that characterizes the entire experience of a subject at a given time. Let a *maximal physical state* be a physical state that fully characterizes the intrinsic physical state of a system at a given time. To establish the conclusion, it suffices to establish the following *superposition principle*:

> If the theory predicts that a system in maximal physical state P gives rise to an associated maximal phenomenal state E, then the theory predicts that a system in a superposition of P with some orthogonal physical states will also give rise to E.

If this principle holds, then a superposition of orthogonal physical states will give rise to at least the maximal phenomenal states that the physical states would have given rise to separately. This is precisely what the Everett interpretation requires. If a brain is in a superposition of a "perceiving up" state and a "perceiving down" state, then it will give rise to at least two subjects of experience, where one is having an experience of a pointer pointing upward, and the other is experiencing a pointer pointing downward. (Of course, these will be two *distinct* subjects of experience, as the phenomenal states are each maximal phenomenal states of a subject.) The same holds in the general case. A superposition will always give rise to the ensemble of subjects that the Everett interpretation requires.

So we need to establish that the theory I have outlined implies the superposition principle. The easiest way to see this is to appeal to the framework of Chapter 9, and in particular to the claim that consciousness arises from implementation of an appropriate computation. To use this to establish the principle, we need to establish that if a computation is implemented by a system in maximal physical state P, it is also implemented by a system in a superposition of P with orthogonal physical states.

Accordingly, assume that the original system (in maximal physical state P) implements a computation C. That is, there is a mapping between physical substates of the system and formal substates of C such that causal relations between the physical substates correspond to formal relations between the formal substates. Then a version of the same mapping will also support an implementation of C in the superposed system. For a given substate S of the original system, we can find a corresponding substate S' of the superposed system by the obvious projection relation: the superposed system is in S' if the system obtained by projecting it onto the hyperplane of P is in S. Because the superposed system is a superposition of P with orthogonal states, it follows that if the original system is in S, the superposed system is in S'. Because the Schrödinger equation is linear, it also follows that the state-transition relations between the substates S' precisely mirror the relations between the original substates S. We know that these relations in turn precisely mirror the formal relations between the substates of C. It follows that the superposed system also implements C, establishing the required result. By the principle of organizational invariance, if the original system gives rise to a subject of experience, the superposed system will give rise to a qualitatively indistinguishable subject of experience.

It may also be possible to argue for the superposition principle by applying the double-aspect theory of information and arguing that the relevant information embodied in the original physical state is also present in the superposition. Because of the underdetermination of that theory, however, this argument is less clear than the previous one, so I will not go into it here. What matters is that one way or another, the theory of consciousness that I have partially developed *predicts* the result that the Everett interpretation requires. That is, it predicts that even if the world is in a giant superposition, there will still be subjects who experience a discrete world.

If there are no other problems, it follows that a combination of the Schrödinger equation with an independently motivated theory of consciousness can predict our manifest image of the world. That is, the only physical principle needed in quantum mechanics is the Schrödinger equation, and the measurement postulate and other basic principles are unnecessary baggage.

To be sure, we need psychophysical principles as well, but we need those principles in any case, and it turns out that the principles that are plausible on independent grounds can do the requisite work here. This adds up to a powerful argument for taking the Everett interpretation seriously.

5. Objections to the Everett Interpretation

Everett's interpretation has come under frequent attack in the literature, with some objections more powerful than others. I will group these objections into a number of classes.

Objections based on "splitting"

Many objections arise from interpreting or misinterpreting Everett's view as a "splitting-worlds" view. This is understandable, given that it is often called the "many-worlds" interpretation. For example, Bell (1976) objects that it is unclear when a "branching" event should take place, due to unclarity in the notion of measurement, and that there is no preferred basis for the division into worlds. It is clear that these objections do not apply to the present interpretation, which requires no objective "branching" and no preferred basis. Similarly, Hughes (1989) objects to the "ontological cloudburst" in the splitting process, and Healey (1984) notes that the creation of new worlds violates the conservation of mass-energy! It is a pity that the "splitting" interpretation of Everett's view has gained such wide currency, for its obvious difficulties have meant that the more interesting interpretation has not received the attention it deserves.

Objections to a preferred basis

Some of the objections to the splitting-worlds interpretation arise from its need for a preferred basis, but so also do some objections to the single-world version. In particular, the question arises: Why do the only minds associated with a superposed brain state correspond to its decomposition along the preferred basis? Why are there not minds that arise from other decompositions, or indeed from the superposed state as a whole? This is a reasonable objection to Everett's own version, which seems to require such a canonical decomposition. No such objection arises for the version I have outlined, however, which entails that a superposition gives rise to the associated subjects of discrete experience without any need to postulate a preferred basis. And I have had no need for the assumption that these are the *only* minds that the superposed system gives rise to.

What about superposed minds?

The question arises, "Are there other minds associated with a superposition?" To this the answer is "perhaps." If the double-aspect theory of information is accepted, then we already know that there may be experiences associated with lower-level processes in such a system. It may also be that there are subjects of experience associated with the structure of processing in a superposition. Perhaps there are minds associated with other decompositions of the system. Perhaps there is a big superposed mind associated with the whole superposed system. The existence of such minds depends on the details of a theory of consciousness, but it is hard to see how their existence is a problem.

One might try to parlay the possibility of superposed minds into an objection to the theory. Objection: Why is *my* mind not superposed? Answer: Because I am who I am. The theory predicts that nonsuperposed minds exist, and my mind happens to be one of them. To ask why my mind is not one of the superposed minds is like asking why I am not a mouse. It is simply part of the brute indexicality of my existence. Mouse minds exist, and superposed minds may exist, but my mind is not one of them. Objection: Why don't I have any access to superposed minds, such as memories of superposed experiences? Answer: The theory predicts that the discrete minds in question will experience the world as entirely discrete, and they will have no direct access to other parts of the superposition. All their memories will be of discrete observations, for example.

It is arguable, in any case, that the only *interesting* minds associated with a superposed system are the familiar sort of discrete minds. These minds are complex and coherent, with experience reflecting the structure of rational processes. Any further minds that are associated will be relatively incoherent, without much in the way of interesting structure. This conclusion is lent support by the "decoherence" framework of Gell-Mann and Hartle (1990) and others. According to this framework, the interesting structure in a wavelike, complex adaptive system is generally found within the components of a "natural" decomposition; the system "decoheres" naturally along certain lines. In rational systems, then, coherent cognitive structure may be found only in the components of this natural decomposition, and only these will give rise to complex, coherent minds. Any other subjects of experience in the system will not be the sort of subjects that qualify as persons.

Objections based on personal identity

There is a cluster of intuitive worries based on the identity of the observer. Take the mind M_1 that I remember being around this time yesterday. Today, there will be a large number of minds descending from that mind, in different "branches" of the superposition. My mind M_2 is only one of them. I might well ask: Why did I end up *here,* rather than in one of the other branches? As Hofstadter (1985b) puts it:

> Why is my unitary feeling of myself propagating down *this* random branch rather than down some other? What *law* underlies the random choices that pick out the branch I feel myself tracing out? Why doesn't my feeling of myself go along with the other me's as they split off, following other routes? What attaches *me-ness* to the viewpoint of this body evolving down this branch of the universe at this moment in time?

To this, we must again invoke brute indexicality: my mind is *this* one, and that is that. There is feeling that something deeper must be going on, and that it is somehow a deep fact about the world that yesterday's mind M_1 has evolved into today's mind M_2 and not one of the others. But from an objective point of view, there is nothing especially privileged about this branch. Even from the point of view of M_1, all of today's minds are equally privileged. None of them is the single rightful heir of M_1; all of them carry M_1's "me-ness" to the same degree. It is only from *this* point of view, the point of view of M_2, that M_2 seems privileged (of course, my counterparts elsewhere in the superposition have the same feeling about themselves). This privileged role of M_2 is just another indexical phenomenon, like the fact that I am David Chalmers rather than Rolf Harris. *This* mind is here rather than there. It is as puzzling as indexical facts usually are, but there is no further asymmetry in the world.

There is a strong intuition that there must always be a fact of the matter about personal identity: if there are numerous minds descending from my current state, there must be a fact about which one of them will be *me.* But this idea has been subjected to a powerful critique by Parfit (1984), who argues persuasively that there is no more to the fact of personal identity than facts such as psychological continuity, memory, and the like. If we accept this analysis, then each of tomorrow's minds are equal candidates to count as *me,* and there is no fact to distinguish them. There is something disturbing about this conclusion, which reduces the determinate "flow" of personal identity to an illusion, but Parfit's analysis gives reason to believe that this determinate flow was an illusion all along.

The interpretation of probabilities

The most substantial objection to the Everett interpretation is that it cannot make sense of the *probabilities* that the measurement postulate delivers.[8] In a given case the measurement postulate may tell us that on making a certain measurement, there will be a 0.9 chance of finding an "up" pointer and a 0.1 chance of finding a "down" pointer. According to the Everett interpretation, what really happens is that both the pointer and the brain state of an observer go into a superposition, with (at least) two subjects of experience resulting. One of these has an experience of an "up" pointer, and another experiences a pointer pointing down. Exactly the same would have happened if the probabilities had been 50:50. It is true that in the 90:10 case, most of the *amplitude* of the superposed wave function is concentrated in the area of the "up" brain state, but what does this have to do with probabilities?

Everett deals with this question by placing a *measure* on the space of observers, corresponding to the probabilities delivered by the measurement postulate (i.e., corresponding to the square of the amplitude of the corresponding part of the wave function). Using this measure, he argues that in the limit, *most* observers (that is, a subset of observers with measure one) will have memories of observations that accord with the frequencies predicted by the probabilities in the measurement postulate. For example, among observers who have made a measurement like the one described above many times, most of them will remember finding an "up" pointer 90 percent of the time and a "down" pointer 10 percent of the time. Thus a role is found for the probabilities. The question arises, however: What justifies this measure on the space of observers? If we measured the space differently, then very different frequencies might arise. For example, if we assigned equal measures every time two observers arise from a superposition (regardless of amplitude), then most observers would recall an "up"–"down" ratio of 50:50. Neither the Schrödinger equation nor the psychophysical laws ensures that either of these measures is the "correct" one.

Albert and Loewer (1988) respond to this worry by dispensing with measures. Instead they postulate more radical psychophysical laws, according to which there is an infinity of minds associated with every brain state. For every mind postulated by the previous view, this theory postulates an infinite ensemble of qualitatively identical minds. Further, wherever the Everett theory predicts that a mind will diverge into two minds, this theory says that any given mind will go in one direction or the other, with the probabilities given by the measurement postulate. So, if we take an arbitrary mind associated with the brain state before the measurement above, it will have a 90 percent chance of evolving into a "perceiving up" state and a 10 percent chance of evolving into a "perceiving down" state. This way the probabilistic predictions of the quantum-mechanical calculus are preserved.

There is clearly a loss in simplicity here. The new psychophysical laws have no independent motivation, and the theory also needs extra "intrapsychic" laws governing the *evolution* of minds. By making these *ad hoc* postulates, the theory sacrifices some of the key virtues of the Everett interpretation. It is also arguable that the intrapsychic laws are problematic, in that they postulate deep irreducible facts about personal identity over time. It is hard to know what to make of these facts. Accepting them would require discarding Parfit's analysis of personal identity, for example. They fail to supervene even naturally on physical facts, and so complicate the metaphysical picture. This interpretation should be kept in mind as a possibility, but it comes at a significant cost.

The alternative is to do without the extra apparatus, and to see if the probabilities can be recovered some other way. It is tempting to see this as a problem about indexicality. Why is it that of all the places in the wave function that I could have ended up, I ended up in a region where my memories match the predictions of the calculus? One possibility is simply to take this as a brute indexical fact: *some* minds are in this area, and I happen to be one of them. But this seems unsatisfying, as the remarkable regularity of the calculus turns out then to be a huge fluke. What we need is some way to argue that it is not such a fluke.

Even in noting that it is a fluke that I ended up *here,* the idea is implicit that there is some kind of measure on the space of minds. The suggestion is that it is antecedently more likely that I should end up being a mind of one type rather than another, perhaps because of the relative abundance of those classes. This sort of implicit measure is present in much of our reasoning about the world. When I reason inductively from some evidence to a conclusion, I know that for *some* observers in a similar epistemic position the conclusion will not hold, but I assume that for *most* such observers the conclusion will hold, even if there are an infinite number in each class. That is, I assume that it is antecedently more likely that I will turn out to be in one class rather than another. This sort of reasoning implicitly supposes some kind of measure on the space of minds.

Perhaps we can justify the probabilities, then, by explicitly introducing this sort of measure. Certainly the bulk of the amplitude of the wave function is concentrated in areas where the memories of observers match the predictions of the calculus. Maybe it is more likely that my mind should turn out to be in a high-amplitude area than in a low-amplitude area. In particular, if we assume that the antecedent likelihood that I will turn out to be one mind rather than another is proportional to the squared amplitude of the associated part of the wave function, then it follows that I will almost certainly turn out to have memories in the frequencies predicted by the quantum-mechanical calculus.

But to what does this measure objectively correspond? Does it need to be taken as a basic fact about the distribution of selves? Can it somehow be justified as the canonical measure on this space? These are difficult questions that are closely tied to the mystery of indexicality itself—why did I turn out to be *this* person rather than someone else? This is one of the basic mysteries, and it is very unclear just how it should be answered. Nevertheless, the idea of a measure on the space of minds seems to have some promise, and may even be needed for some other purposes, such as the justification of induction. In the meantime, the interpretation of the probabilities remains the most significant difficulty for the Everett interpretation.

6. Conclusion

It must be admitted that the Everett interpretation is almost impossible to believe. It postulates that there is vastly more in the world than we are ever aware of. On this interpretation, the world is really in a giant superposition of states that have been evolving in different ways since the beginning of time, and we are experiencing only the smallest substate of the world. It also postulates that my future is not determinate: in a minute's time, there will be a large number of minds that have an equal claim to count as *me*. A minute has passed since I wrote the last sentence; who is to know what all those other minds are now doing?

On the other hand, it is clear by now that *all* interpretations of quantum mechanics are to some extent crazy. That is the fundamental paradox of quantum mechanics. The three leading candidates for interpretation are perhaps Wigner's interpretation on which consciousness brings about collapse, Bohm's nonlocal hidden variables interpretation, and the Everett interpretation. Of these, Wigner's interpretation implies that macroscopic objects are often in superpositions, until a casual look from an observer causes them to collapse. Bohm's view implies that the trajectory of every particle in the universe depends on the state of every other. And the Everett view implies that there is much more in the world than we ever would have thought.

Of these, perhaps Bohm's view is the least crazy and Everett's the most, with Wigner's in between. Ranked in order of theoretical virtue, on the other hand, the sequence is reversed. Bohm's view is unsatisfying due to its complex, jury-rigged nature. Wigner's view is quite elegant, with its two basic dynamical laws mirroring the quantum-mechanical calculus, if all the details can be worked out. But Everett's view is by far the simplest. It postulates only the Schrödinger equation, the principle that is accepted by all interpretations of quantum mechanics. It also has the virtues of being an entirely local theory, and of being straightforwardly compatible with relativity theory, virtues that the other interpretations lack.

It is also worth noting that both of the other interpretations contain elements of what is counterintuitive about the Everett interpretation. On the Wigner view, we must accept that the universe evolved in an Everett-style giant superposition—perhaps with superposed stars and superposed rocks, if not with superposed cats—at least until the first conscious entity evolved to collapse the wave function. On the Bohm view, Everett's uncollapsed wave function remains present as the "pilot wave" that guides the position of the various particles. All the structure that is present in other components thus remains present in the state of the world, even though most of it is irrelevant to the evolution of the particles. Given that these views, too, require an uncollapsed wave function in central roles, one might argue that the relative implausibility of the Everett view is diminished.

Of course, it is always possible that a new theory might be developed that surpasses all of these in plausibility and theoretical virtue. But it does not seem especially likely. The complete absence of experimental anomalies suggests that the quantum-mechanical calculus is here to stay as a predictive theory. If so, we cannot expect empirical developments to solve the problem. Perhaps conceptual developments could lead to a new and improved interpretation, but it may be that by now the most promising niches in conceptual space have already been exploited. If so, we may be stuck with something like the current range of options—perhaps with significant refinements, but with advantages and disadvantages of a qualitatively similar kind. Of these options, the Everett interpretation seems in many ways the most attractive, but at the same time it is the hardest to accept.

I have advocated some counterintuitive views in this work. I resisted mind–body dualism for a long time, but I have now come to the point where I accept it, not just as the only tenable view but as a satisfying view in its own right. It is always possible that I am confused, or that there is a new and radical possibility that I have overlooked; but I can comfortably say that I think dualism is very likely true. I have also raised the possibility of a kind of panpsychism. Like mind–body dualism, this is initially counterintuitive, but the counterintuitiveness disappears with time. I am unsure whether the view is true or false, but it is at least intellectually appealing, and on reflection it is not too crazy to be acceptable.

The craziness of the Everett interpretation is of another order of magnitude. I find it easily the most intellectually appealing of the various interpretations of quantum mechanics, but I confess that I cannot wholeheartedly believe it. If God forced me to bet my life on the truth or falsity of the doctrines I have advocated, I would bet fairly confidently that experience is fundamental, and weakly that experience is ubiquitous. But on the Everett interpretation I would be torn, and perhaps I would not be brave enough to bet on it at the end of the day.[9] Maybe it is simply too strange to believe. Still, it is not clear whether much weight should be put on these intuitive doubts in the final analysis. The view is simple and elegant, and it predicts that there will be observers who see the world just as I see it. Is that not enough? We may never be able to accept the view emotionally, but we should at least take seriously the possibility that it is true.

Notes

Chapter 1

1. See Nagel 1974. The first use of this phrase in philosophical contexts is usually attributed to Farrell (1950). See also Sprigge 1971.

2. Different authors use the term "qualia" in different ways. I use the term in what I think is the standard way, to refer to those properties of mental states that type those states by what it is like to have them. In using the term, I do not mean to make any immediate commitment on further issues, such as whether qualia are incorrigibly knowable, whether they are intentional properties, and so on. Qualia can be properties of "internal" mental states as well as of sensations. It is often convenient to speak as if qualia are properties instantiated directly by a subject, rather than by that subject's mental states; this practice is harmless, and justified by the fact that qualia correspond to mental state-types in their own right.

3. I use expressions such as "red sensation," "green experience," and the like throughout this book. Of course by doing this I do not mean to imply that experiences instantiate the same sort of color properties that are instantiated by objects (apples, trees) in the external world. This sort of talk can always be rephrased as "experience of the type that I usually have (in the actual world) when looking at red objects," and so on, but the briefer locution is more natural.

4. Cook 12 cups of dried black-eyed peas in boiling water to which 4 tablespoons of salt have been added. Cook until tender, and immerse in cold water. Combine 2 diced red peppers, 5 diced green peppers, 2 diced large onions, 3 cups of raisins, and a bunch of chopped cilantro in a dressing made of 1.5 cups of corn oil, 0.75 cup of wine vinegar, 4 tablespoons of sugar, 1 tablespoon of salt, 4 tablespoons of black pepper, 5 tablespoons of curry powder, and a half-tablespoon of ground cloves. Serve chilled. Thanks to Lisa Thomas and the Encore Café.

5. For a wealth of reflection on the varieties of specific experiences, see Ackerman's *A Natural History of the Senses* (1990), which provides material for those absorbed by their conscious experience to mull over for days.

6. Interestingly, Descartes often excluded sensations from the category of the mental, instead assimilating them to the bodily, so not every phenomenal state (at least as I am understanding the notion) would count as mental, either.

7. This common interpretation of Ryle does not do justice to the subtlety of his views, but it is at least a useful fiction.

8. There are other forms of functionalism, such as that developed by Putnam (1960). I do not consider these here, as they were put forward as empirical hypotheses rather than as analyses of mental concepts.

9. Nagel (1970) makes a similar point against Armstrong, with reference to the problem of other minds.

10. Searle's argument depends on the claim that without consciousness, there is no way to explain the "aspectual shape" that intentionality exhibits, as when someone believes something about Venus under its "morning star" aspect but not under its "evening star" aspect. It is not clear to me that aspectual shape cannot be accounted for in other ways; one might even argue that present-day computers exhibit something like it, storing information about me under one "aspect" but not another (e.g., under my name but not under my social security number). It might be objected that this is only "as-if" aspectual shape, as the only true aspectual shape is *phenomenal* aspectual shape; but this would seem to trivialize the argument.

11. Such a position is suggested by some remarks of Lockwood (1989) and Nagel (1986), although I am not sure that either is committed to this position.

12. Some might point to arguments such as that of Kripke (1982) to the effect that the content of a belief is not determined by psychological and phenomenal properties. These arguments are controversial, but in any case it is notable that the conclusion of these arguments is not that content is a further irreducible element of the mind, but rather that content itself is indeterminate. In effect, what is going on here is that considerations such as those in the text give us good reason to believe there is no third, independently variable aspect of the mind; so any matters that are not settled by the first two elements are not settled at all.

13. This is a "topic-neutral" analysis of specific phenomenal notions not unlike those advocated by Place (1956) and Smart (1959). To be an orange experience, very roughly, is to be the kind of experience that is generally caused by oranges. Place: "[W]hen we describe the after-image as green . . . we are saying that we are having the sort of experience which we normally have when, and which we have learned to describe as, looking at a green patch of light" (p. 49); Smart: "When a person says 'I see a yellowish-orange after-image', he is saying something like this: '*There is something going on which is like what is going on when* I have my eyes open, am awake, and there is an orange illuminated in good light in front of me'" (p. 150). But because of the occurrence of the unanalyzed notion of "experience," this analysis is not sufficient to immediately establish an identification between phenomenal and physical states, in the way that Place and Smart suggested. Smart's account avoids this problem by leaving "experience" out of the analysis in favor of the equivocal phrase "something going on." If "something going on" is construed broadly enough to cover any sort of state, then the analysis is inadequate; if it is construed narrowly as a sort of experience, the analysis is closer to the mark but it does not suffice for the conclusion.

14. Jackendoff distinguishes the "phenomenological mind" and the "computational mind." This distinction comes to much the same as the phenomenal–psychological distinction outlined here, although I would not like to beg the question about whether psychological processes are computational.

15. Nelkin (1989) distinguishes CN (consciousness in the "Nagel" sense) from C1 (a first-order information-processing state) and C2 (second-order direct noninferential accessing of other conscious states). In another paper (Nelkin 1993), he makes a related distinction between phenomenality, intentionality, and introspectability. Bisiach (1988) distinguishes C1 (phenomenal experience) from C2 (the access of parts or processes of a system to other of its parts or processes). Natsoulas (1978)

distinguishes a large number of senses of the term "consciousness." Dennett (1969) distinguishes two kinds of "awareness," the first associated with verbal reports and the second more generally with the control of behavior, although neither of these is a clearly phenomenal notion.

16. Rosenthal explicitly separates consciousness from "sensory quality," and says he is giving a theory only of the first, which might suggest that phenomenal aspects are not under discussion. But he also says that a state is conscious when there is something it is like to be in that state, which suggests that the subject is phenomenal consciousness after all. However, there is very little in Rosenthal's account to suggest an *explanation* of phenomenal consciousness. Why should the existence of a higher-order thought about a state lead to there being something it is like to be in that state? Aside from arguing that the two phenomena plausibly go together in practice, Rosenthal offers no answer to this question.

17. One exception is the field of psychophysics, which arguably sheds light on various features of conscious experience, even if it does not provide a full explanation. I discuss this further in Chapter 6.

Chapter 2

1. The idea of supervenience was introduced by Moore (1922). The name was introduced in print by Hare (1952). Davidson (1970) was the first to apply to the notion to the mind–body problem. More recently, a sophisticated theory of supervenience has been developed by Kim (1978, 1984, 1993), Horgan (1982, 1984c, 1993), Hellman and Thompson (1975), and others.

2. I use "A-fact" as shorthand for "instantiation of an A-property." The appeal to facts makes the discussion less awkward, but all talk of facts and their relations can ultimately be cashed out in terms of patterns of co-instantiation of properties; I give the details in notes, where necessary. In particular, it should be noted that the identity of the individual that instantiates an A-property is irrelevant to an A-fact as I am construing it; all that matters is the instantiation of the property. If the identity of an individual were partly constitutive of an A-fact, then any A-fact would entail facts about that individual's essential properties, in which case the definition of supervenience would lead to counterintuitive consequences.

3. I assume, perhaps artificially, that individuals have precise spatiotemporal boundaries, so that their physical properties consist in the properties instantiated in that region of space-time. If we are to count spatially distinct objects as physically identical for the purposes of local supervenience, any properties concerning absolute spatiotemporal position must be omitted from the supervenience base (although one could avoid the need to appeal to spatially distinct objects by considering only merely *possible* objects with the same position). Also, I always talk as if the same sort of individual instantiates low-level and high-level properties, so that a table, for example, instantiates microphysical properties by virtue of being characterized by a distribution of such properties. Perhaps it would be more strictly correct to talk of microphysical properties as being instantiated only by microphysical entities, but my way of speaking simplifies things. In any case, the truly central issues will all involve global rather than local supervenience.

4. There are various ways to specify precisely what it is for two worlds to be identical with respect to a set of properties; this will not matter much to the discus-

sion. Perhaps the best is to say that two worlds are identical with respect to their A-properties if there is a one-to-one mapping between the classes of individuals instantiating A-properties in both worlds, such that any two corresponding individuals instantiate the same A-properties. For the purposes of global supervenience we then need to stipulate that the mappings by which two worlds are seen to be both A- and B-indiscernible are compatible with each other; that is, no individual is mapped to one counterpart under the A-mapping but to another under the B-mapping. The definition of global supervenience takes this form: Any two worlds that are A-identical (under a mapping) are B-identical (under an extension of that mapping).

A more common way to do this is to stipulate that A-identical worlds must contain exactly the same individuals, instantiating the same properties, but as McLaughlin (1995) points out, this is unreasonably strong: it ensures that such things as the cardinality of the world and essential properties of individuals supervene on any properties whatsoever. The definition I propose gets around this problem, by ensuring that *only* patterns of A-properties and nothing further enter into the determination relation.

5. With one exception: God could not have created a world that was not created by God, even though a world not created by God is presumably logically possible! I will ignore this sort of complication.

6. The relationship of this sort of possibility to deducibility in formal systems is a subtle one. It is arguable that the axioms and inference rules of specific formal systems are justified precisely in terms of a prior notion of logical possibility and necessity.

7. The intuitive notion of natural possibility is conceptually prior to the definition in terms of laws of nature: a regularity qualifies as a law just in case it holds in all situations that could come up in nature; that is, in all situations that are naturally possible in the intuitive sense. As it is sometimes put, for something to count as a law it must hold not just in actual but in counterfactual situations, and the more basic notion of natural possibility is required to determine which counterfactual situations are relevant.

8. The terms "physical necessity" and "causal necessity" are also often used to pick out roughly this brand of necessity, but I do not wish to beg the question of whether all the laws of nature are physical or causal.

9. The important distinction between logical and natural supervenience is frequently glossed over or ignored in the literature, where the modality of supervenience relations is often left unspecified. Natural (or nomological) supervenience without logical supervenience is discussed by van Cleve (1990), who uses it to explicate a variety of emergence. Seager (1991) spells out a related distinction between what he calls *constitutive* and *correlative* supervenience. These correspond in a straightforward way to logical and natural supervenience, although Seager does not analyze the notions in quite the same way.

10. Weak supervenience requires only that "no B-difference without an A-difference" holds within a world, rather than across worlds (see Kim 1984 for details). The lack of modal strength in this relation makes it too weak for most purposes. At best, it may have a role in expressing conceptual constraints on nonfactual discourse (as in Hare 1984), although as Horgan (1993) points out, even these constraints seem to involve cross-world dependence. Seager (1988) appeals to weak supervenience to express a kind of systematic within-world correlation that is not strictly necessary, but natural supervenience serves this purpose much better.

11. Global natural supervenience without localized regularity is a coherent notion on a non-Humean account of laws, although perhaps not on a Humean (regularity-based) account. Even on a non-Humean account, though, it is hard to see what the evidence for such a relation could consist in.

12. Horgan (1982), Jackson (1994), and Lewis (1983b) address a related problem in the context of defining materialism.

13. The revised definition can be spelled out more precisely along the lines of note 4. Let $B(W)$ be the class of individuals with B-properties in a world W. We can say that W' is *B-superior* to W if there is an injection $f: B(W) \rightarrow B(W')$ (i.e., a one-to-one mapping from $B(W)$ onto a subset of $B(W')$) such that for all $a \in B(W)$, $f(a)$ instantiates every B-property that a does. Then B-properties supervene logically on A-properties in W if every world that is A-indiscernible from W is B-superior to W, where the relevant B-mappings are again constrained to be extensions of the A-mappings.

To see that the constraint is necessary, imagine that our world has a countably infinite number of psychologically identical minds, of which one is realized in ectoplasm and the rest are physically realized. Intuitively, the psychological does not supervene on the physical in this world, but every physically indiscernible world is psychologically superior. Although we expect the ectoplasm-free world to count against supervenience, there is a one-to-one mapping between the psychologies in that world and in our world. The problem is that this mapping does not respect physical correspondence, as it maps a physical entity to an ectoplasmic entity; so we need the further constraint.

14. For the purposes of this definition, the containment relation between worlds can be taken as primitive. Lewis (1983a) and Jackson (1993) have noted that it is fruitless to analyze this sort of notion forever. Something needs to be taken as primitive, and the containment relation seems to be as clear as any. Some might prefer to speak, not of worlds that contain W as a proper part, but of worlds that contain a qualitative duplicate of W as a proper part; this works equally well.

15. Note that by this definition, there are positive facts that are not instantiations of positive properties. Think of instantiations of the property of being childless-or-a-kangaroo, for example. Perhaps positive facts should be defined more strictly as instantiations of positive properties, but as far as I can tell the weaker definition has no ill effects.

16. Arguably, the logical supervenience of properties in our world should be a *lawful* thesis. If it were the case that there *would* have been nonphysical living angels if things had gone a little differently in our world (perhaps a few different random fluctuations), even though the laws of nature were being obeyed, then it would be a mere accident of history that biological properties are logically supervenient on physical properties. One gets a stronger and more interesting metaphysical thesis by replacing the references to our world and actual individuals in the definitions of logical supervenience by a reference to naturally possible worlds and individuals. This rules out scenarios like the one above. As a bonus, it allows us to determine whether or not uninstantiated properties, such as that of being a mile-high skyscraper, are logically supervenient. On the previous definition, all such properties supervene vacuously.

This yields the following definition: B-properties are logically supervenient on A-properties iff for any naturally possible situation X and any logically possible situation Y, if X and Y are A-indiscernible then Y is B-superior to X (with the usual constraint). Or more briefly: for any naturally possible situation, the B-facts about that situation are entailed by the A-facts. This modification makes no significant difference to the discussion in the text, so I omit it for simplicity's sake. The discussion can easily be recast in terms of the stricter definition simply by replacing relevant references to "our world" by references to "all naturally possible worlds" throughout the text, usually without any loss in the plausibility of the associated claims.

The result resembles the standard definition of "strong" local supervenience (Kim 1984), in which there are two modal operators. According to that definition, B-properties supervene on A-properties if necessarily, for each x and each B-property F, if x has F, then there is an A-property G such that x has G, and necessarily if any y has G, it has F. (The A-properties G may be thought of as complexes of simpler A-properties, if necessary.) The angel issue makes it clear that the first modal operator should always be understood as natural necessity, even when the second is logical necessity. The standard definition of global supervenience (that A-indiscernible worlds are B-indiscernible) is less well off, and needs to be modified along the lines I have suggested. A parallel definition of "metaphysical" supervenience can be given if necessary. Of course, the angel problems do not arise for natural supervenience, as there is no reason to believe that ectoplasm is naturally possible, so the straightforward definition of natural supervenience is satisfactory.

17. Arguably, we should use the stronger definition of logical supervenience, so that materialism is true if all the positive facts about all *naturally possible* worlds are entailed by the physical facts about those worlds. Take an ectoplasm-free world in which nonphysical ectoplasm is nevertheless a natural possibility—perhaps it would have evolved if a few random fluctuations had gone differently. It seems reasonable to say that materialism is false in such a world, or at least that it is true only in a weak sense.

18. To gain the equivalence, we need the plausible principle that if world A is a proper part of world B, then some positive fact holds in B that does not hold in A; that is, there is some fact that holds in B and in all larger worlds that does not hold in A.

19. It also comes to much the same thing as definitions by Horgan (1982) and Lewis (1983b), but unlike these it does not rely on the somewhat obscure notion of "alien property" to rule out ectoplasmic worlds from the range of relevant possible worlds.

20. In the philosophical literature multiple realizability is often pointed to as the main obstacle to "reduction," but as Brooks (1994) argues, it seems largely irrelevant to the way that reductive explanations are used in the sciences. Biological phenomena such as wings can be realized in many different ways, for example, but biologists give reductive explanations all the same. Indeed, as has been pointed out by Wilson (1985) and Churchland (1986), many physical phenomena that are often taken to be paradigms of reducibility (e.g., temperature) are in fact multiply realizable.

21. Some would say that one should not speak of what "water" would refer to if the XYZ-world turned out to be actual, because in that case the word that sounds like "water" would be a different word altogether! If one is worried about this, we can simply talk about what the homophonous word would refer to; or better, one can think of these scenarios as *epistemic* possibilities (in a broad sense) and the conditionals as epistemic conditionals, so that worries about essential properties of words are bypassed. In any case the general point that actual-world reference depends

on how the world turns out is clear no matter how we describe the scenario. In the text I will generally ignore this nicety.

22. Not everyone is convinced that Kripke and Putnam are correct in their claim that water is necessarily H_2O, and that XYZ is not water; for some doubts, see Lewis 1994. Certainly, it would seem that *most* of our linguistic practices would be just as they are even if we used the term "water" to pick out watery stuff in counterfactual worlds. The fact that it is easy to sway both ways on this matter suggests that not too much that is really central to the explanation of a phenomenon such as water can turn on the nature of the secondary intension. Indeed, the fact that one is always free to use terms such as "watery stuff" instead of "water" in these matters is a clue that *a posteriori* necessity is unlikely to change anything really central to questions about explanation, physicalism, and the like. Siewert (1994) bypasses questions about *a posteriori* necessity in this fashion. I was tempted to do so myself, but in the end I think the two-dimensional framework is independently interesting.

23. There may of course be borderline cases in which it is indeterminate whether a concept would refer to a certain object if a given world turned out to be actual. This is no problem: we can allow indeterminacies in a primary intension, as we sometimes allow indeterminacies in reference in our own world. There may also be cases in which there is more than one equally good candidate for the referent of a concept in a world (as, perhaps, with "mass" in a relativistic world, which might refer to rest mass or relativistic mass); just as we tolerated divided reference in such actual cases, we should occasionally expect divided reference in the value of a primary intension.

With some borderline cases, it may even be that whether we count an object as falling under the extension of a concept will depend on various accidental historical factors. A stimulating paper by Wilson (1982) discusses such cases, including for example a hypothetical case in which druids might end up classifying airplanes as "birds" if they first saw a plane flying overhead, but not if they first found one crashed in the jungle. One might try to classify these two different scenarios as different ways for the actual world to turn out, and therefore retain a fixed, detailed primary intension; or one might regard such cases as indeterminate with respect to a core primary intension. In any case, a little looseness around the edges of a primary intension is entirely compatible with my applications of the framework.

24. See Field 1973. I think an analysis in terms of primary intensions can provide a way of regarding "meaning change" as being much less frequent than is often supposed. The case of relativity provides no reason to believe that the primary intension of "mass" has changed from the last century to this one, for example, although our beliefs about the actual world have certainly changed. (For related reasons, one might try to use an analysis in terms of primary intensions to resist "meaning holism" about thought.) Any "development" in primary intensions is at best likely to be of the more subtle kind suggested by the examples in Wilson 1982, where the core stays fixed but accidents of history can make a difference to classification practices around the edges. But all this deserves a much more extensive development.

25. Some differences: (1) Kaplan's content corresponds very closely to a secondary intension, but he presents character as a function from context to content, whereas a primary intension is a function from context to extension. Given rigidification, however, a primary intension is straightforwardly derivable from a character and

vice versa. I use the former for reasons of symmetry and simplicity. (2) Kaplan uses his account to deal with indexical and demonstrative terms like "I" and "that," but does not extend it to deal with natural-kind terms such as "water," as he takes "water" to pick out H_2O in all contexts (the sound-alike word on Twin Earth is simply a different word), and he takes the process of reference fixation here to be part of "metasemantics" rather than semantics. As before, whether it is part of metasemantics or semantics makes little difference for my purposes; all that matters is that reference fixation depends in some way on how the actual world turns out.

26. It might seem that the primary intension is only well defined over possible worlds centered on individuals thinking an appropriate thought, or making an appropriate utterance. I think the primary intension is naturally extendible to a wider class of worlds: we can retain the concept from our own world, and consider how it applies to other worlds considered as actual (see Chalmers 1994c), though it may have indeterminate reference in some worlds. But this will not make much difference in what follows.

27. Note that strictly speaking the primary intension picks out the liquid in our *historical* environment: if I travel to Twin Earth and say "water," I still refer to H_2O.

28. The relation between the second and third considerations in this section—that is, between Quine's empirical revisability and Kripke's *a posteriori* necessity—is complex and interesting. As Kripke observes, the framework he develops accounts for some but not all of the problems raised by Quine. Kripke's analysis accounts for *a posteriori* revisions in intensions, and therefore for changes in a certain sense of "meaning." However, the two-dimensional analysis agrees with the single-intension account on the truth-values it assigns at the actual world, so it does not account for the Quinean possibility of certain purported *a priori* conceptual truths turning out to be false in the actual world, in the face of sufficient empirical evidence. It seems to me that such purported conceptual truths are simply not conceptual truths at all, although they may be close approximations.

29. A subtle point that comes up in using the two-dimensional framework to capture the contents of thought is that sometimes a thought can endorse a centered world as a potential environment even if it does not contain a copy of the thought itself. For example, if I think "I am in a coma," I endorse those centered worlds in which the individual at the center is in a coma, whether or not they are having thoughts. So one has to tread carefully in defining primary intensions and primary propositions for thoughts; more carefully than I have trodden here in the case of language.

30. Worlds should be seen prelinguistically, perhaps as distributions of basic qualities. Worlds are probably best not seen as collections of statements, as statements *describe* a world, and we have seen that they can do so in more than one way. To regard a world as a collection of statements would be to lose this distinction. Perhaps worlds can be regarded as collections of propositions (Adams 1974), if propositions are understood appropriately, or as maximal properties (Stalnaker 1976), or as states of affairs (Plantinga 1976), or as structural universals (Forrest 1986), or as concrete objects analogous to our own world (Lewis 1986a). Perhaps the notion can simply be taken as primitive. In any case, talk of possible worlds is as well or poorly grounded as talk of possibility and necessity in general. As with mathematical notions, these modal notions can be usefully deployed even preceding a satisfying ontological analysis.

I will always be considering worlds "qualitatively," and abstracting away from questions of "haecceity." That is, I will count two worlds that are qualitatively identical as identical, and will not be concerned with questions about whether individuals in those worlds might have different "identities" (some have argued that they might). These issues of transworld identity raise many interesting issues, but are largely irrelevant to my uses of the possible-worlds framework.

31. In particular, some might deny the equation of meaning and intension for mathematical terms. It is often held that statements such as "There are an infinite number of primes" are not true in virtue of meaning despite being true in all possible worlds; those who make this claim would presumably resist an equation of meaning with intension.

Others might resist the claim that the primary intension of a term such as "water" is part of its meaning; perhaps they think that the meaning of the term is exhausted by its reference, and that the primary intension is part of pragmatics rather than semantics. Still others might resist the claim that the *secondary* intension is part of its meaning. In any case, nothing rests on the use of the word "meaning." It is truth in virtue of intension that I am interested in, whether or not intensions are meanings.

32. This definition of conceivability is related to that given by Yablo (1993), according to which P is conceivable if one can imagine a world that one takes to verify P. The difference is that Yablo's "that one takes to verify" clause allows room for misdescription of conceived situations, so that this variety of conceivability is at best a defeasible guide to possibility. On my definition this source of defeasibility is removed. Of course, it reappears in the form of a larger gap between what one finds conceivable at first glance and what is really conceivable; so one has to be more reflective in making judgments of conceivability.

33. One can arguably apply this critique to Descartes's argument that he can conceive of being disembodied, so it is possible that he is disembodied, so he is nonphysical (as any physical entity is necessarily embodied). "I am disembodied" may be 1-conceivable and therefore 1-possible, but it does not follow that it is 2-conceivable or 2-possible. By contrast, the sense in which "I am embodied" would be necessary if he were a physical object is 2-necessity, not 1-necessity. (The primary intension of his concept "I" picks out the individual at the center of any world; the secondary intension picks out Descartes in every world.)

34. One might say that there is nothing especially "metaphysical" about metaphysical necessity. Seen this way, it is merely a brand of conceptual necessity with an *a posteriori* semantic twist, stemming from the two-dimensional nature of our concepts. For more on the theme that *a posteriori* necessity reflects convention as much as metaphysics, see Putnam 1983 and Sidelle 1989, 1992.

35. Horgan (1984c) sets out and argues for the position that all high-level facts supervene logically on microphysical facts. As he puts it, those facts are tied to the microphysical by "semantic constraints," so that all there is in the world is microphysics and "cosmic hermeneutics." He conspicuously avoids the problem of conscious experience, however. Others who advocate versions of the logical supervenience thesis include Jackson (1993), Kirk (1974), and Lewis (1994).

36. For arguments that facts about abstract entities are logically supervenient on the physical, see Armstrong 1982.

37. Conscious experience arguably contributes to the primary intension, if water is individuated partly by the kind of experience it gives rise to. Indexicality certainly

contributes, as seen by the "our" in the "the clear, drinkable liquid in our environment." These facts do not undermine logical supervenience modulo conscious experience and indexicality.

38. As is familiar from the Ramsey-sentence method for the application of theoretical terms; see Lewis 1972.

39. An example suggested as a puzzle case by Ned Block.

40. A similar point about the requirement of analyzability for supervenience is made by Jackson (1993) and Lewis (1994).

41. An alternative plausible account holds that for something to be red, it must be the kind of thing that tends to cause red-*judgments*. This would eliminate the problems discussed here, as judgments are plausibly logically supervenient on the physical.

42. Except, arguably, in that where I have a belief about Bill Clinton, my duplicate has a belief about Clinton's duplicate. As usual, these issues concerning transworld identity can be left aside.

43. The closest thing to such an argument is that given by Kripke's (1982) version of Wittgenstein, who argues in effect that there can be no entailment from physical and phenomenal facts to intentional facts, as the entailment cannot be mediated by a physical, functional, or phenomenal analysis of intentional concepts. The arguments (particularly those against a functional analysis) are controversial, but in any case, as noted earlier, the conclusion of the argument is not that intentional facts are further facts, but that they are not strictly facts at all.

If the Kripke–Wittgenstein argument against entailment is accepted, intentionality stands in a position similar to that in which morality stands below. In both cases, (1) there is arguably no conceptual entailment from A-facts to B-facts, but (2) if there are B-facts in our world, then they hold in every conceivable A-indiscernible world. The only reasonable conclusion is that strictly speaking there are no B-facts, and B-attributions must be treated in some deflationary way. The possibility that B-facts are fundamental further facts is ruled out by conceivability considerations, which show that there must be an *a priori* link from A-facts to B-facts if B-facts are instantiated at all.

44. If there are subjective moral facts, then moral attributions have determinate truth conditions, but these are dependent on the ascriber. If so, moral concepts have an indexical primary intension, and there is logical supervenience modulo indexicality. This analysis is endorsed by proponents of "subjectivist moral realism" (Sayre-McCord 1989), who interpret "good" as something like "good-for-me" or "good-according-to-my-community." The subjectivity involved makes this a very weak kind of realism, however. For example, on this view it turns out that two people arguing over what is "good" might not be disagreeing at all.

45. The arguments of Kripke (1972), such as those concerning the reference of "Gödel" in various situations, suggest that the primary intension associated with the use of a name cannot in general be summarized by a short description. They may also suggest that the primary intension cannot be summarized by any finite description, although I am less sure of this (certainly, they establish that any such description must include a metalinguistic element and a condition requiring an appropriate causal connection to the agent). But nothing in these arguments suggests that a name (as used on any given occasion) lacks a primary intension altogether. Indeed, Kripke's very arguments proceed by considering how the reference of a name depends on

the way the actual world turns out; that is, by evaluating the name's primary intension at various centered worlds.

46. For a lucid discussion of this matter, see Nagel 1986.

47. How do negative facts evade the arguments for logical supervenience above? The argument from conceivability fails, as the angel example shows. The argument from epistemology fails as there clearly *is* an epistemological problem about how we can know universal claims of unrestricted scope (we cannot be *certain* that there are no angels). The argument from analyzability fails, as there is no analysis of these negative facts wholly in terms of positive facts (unless we bring in the second-order "that's all" fact).

48. How do laws evade the arguments for logical supervenience above? The argument from conceivability fails, as the example above shows. The argument from epistemology fails, as there clearly are problems with the epistemology of laws and causation, as witnessed by Hume's skeptical challenge. The argument from analysis fails, as lawhood requires a counterfactual-supporting universal regularity, and the relevant counterfactuals cannot be analyzed in terms of particular facts about a world history (*pace* Lewis 1973). The particular facts about the world's spatiotemporal history are compatible with the truth of all sorts of different counterfactuals.

49. Humean views of laws and causation can be found in Lewis 1986b, Mackie 1974, and Skyrms 1980. For arguments against such views, see Armstrong 1982, Carroll 1994, Dretske 1977, Molnar 1969, and Tooley 1977.

50. By contrast, those who appear to hold that logical supervenience is the rule rather than the exception include Armstrong (1982), Horgan (1984c), Jackson (1993), Lewis (1994), and Nagel (1974).

51. For more on this, see Horgan and Timmons 1992b.

Chapter 3

1. Kirk (1974) provides a vivid description of a zombie, and even outlines a situation that might lead us to believe that someone in the actual world had turned into a zombie, by specifying appropriate intermediate cases. Campbell (1970) similarly discusses an "imitation man" that is physically identical to a normal person, but that lacks experience entirely.

2. Kirk (1974) argues for the logical possibility of zombies in this indirect fashion.

3. Jacoby (1990) makes the excellent point that conceivability arguments pose no more of a problem for functionalist accounts of consciousness than they do for materialist accounts in general. He takes this to be an argument for functionalist accounts, whereas I take it to be an argument against materialist accounts.

4. Actually, this will end up swapping red with yellow rather than blue, as both of these are at the positive ends of their axes. The details are inessential, however. For a lucid discussion of the intricacies of human color-space, see Hardin 1988.

5. Indeed, Hardin (1987, p. 138) concedes this point. He says that this sort of inversion is merely "outlandish" and not "conceptually incoherent."

6. Gunderson (1970) speaks similarly of an "investigational asymmetry" between first-person and third-person claims.

7. Thompson (1992) points out that in a black-and-white room Mary may still have color experiences—when she rubs her eyes, for example. To get around this, perhaps we should stipulate instead that Mary is colorblind since birth.

8. Churchland (1995, p. 193) and Dennett (1991, p. 281) invoke vitalism in this context.

9. At the end of the second part of his book, Dennett promises that in the third part he will show why his functional account can explain everything about consciousness that needs to be explained, but the arguments are hard to locate. Much of the discussion consists in observations about cognitive processing with which someone like me might happily agree. The question is not about whether his account of processing is correct, but about whether it explains experience. The crucial argument seems to be in the dialogue on pp. 362–68, where he claims (in effect) that what needs to be explained is how things *seem,* and that his theory explains how things seem. But as I argue in Chapter 5, this equivocates between a psychological and a phenomenal sense of "seem." What the theory might explain is our disposition to make certain *judgments* about stimuli, but those judgments were never the puzzling explananda.

There are also some arguments in Chapter 12: (1) an argument against the empirical possibility of inverted qualia (while leaving behavior constant); but empirical impossibility here is compatible with the nonreductive position; (2) an argument against Jackson's knowledge argument; I discuss this in Chapter 4; (3) a claim that epiphenomenalism about qualia is ridiculous; I discuss this issue in Chapters 4 and 5. Matters of natural possibility and logical possibility are often run together in Dennett's discussion. For example, Dennett assumes that the "qualophile" will hold that a computational machine will not have experiences, and so devotes a lot of space to arguing that such machines could be conscious in the way that we are. But this is entirely compatible with the nonreductive position; I argue for the same claim myself in later chapters.

10. More recently, Crick and Koch have begun to look beyond the 40-hertz oscillations in their search for a neural basis for consciousness, but similar considerations apply. The oscillations have the virtue of providing a straightforward example.

11. Quoted in *Discover,* November 1992, p. 96. Crick (1994, p. 258) also allows the possibility that science may not explain qualia, although he is more circumspect.

12. Edelman (1989, p. 168) is clear about this. "It is sufficient to provide a model that explains their discrimination, variation, and consequences. As scientists, we can have no concern with ontological mysteries concerned with *why* there is something and not nothing, or *why* warm feels warm." He makes an analogy with quantum field theory, which gives us a basis for discriminating energies and material states, but which does not tell us why there is matter in the first place. This analogy is very much compatible with the nonreductive view that I develop in later chapters.

13. Indeed, if consciousness were logically supervenient on the physical, then these "collapse" interpretations could not get off the ground, as any justification for the special treatment of consciousness in the laws would disappear.

Chapter 4

1. Edelman (1992) similarly subtitles his (purportedly materialist) book *How the Mind Originates in the Brain.*

2. On my reading, Searle's view is much more naturally interpreted as property dualism than as materialism, despite Searle's own view of the matter. The claim that brain states cause phenomenal states and the use of zombie arguments support this

reading, as does the claim that "what is going on in the brain is neurophysiological processes and consciousness and nothing more." Searle's argument about intentionality in his Chapter 8 also supports this reading. Searle argues that intentionality is real (p. 156), but that intentional facts cannot be constituted by neurophysiological facts (pp. 157–58). The only solution to the puzzle, he argues, is that consciousness must be partly constitutive of intentionality, as consciousness is the only other thing in the brain's ontology. This argument seems to *presuppose* property dualism about consciousness.

In explaining his ontology in Chapter 5, Searle argues that consciousness is irreducible, but that this has no deep consequences. He says that phenomena such as heat are reducible only because we redefine them to eliminate the phenomenal aspect (in the way I discussed in Chapter 2), but that this sort of redefinition is trivially inapplicable to consciousness, which consists entirely in its subjective aspect. This seems correct. As I put it in Chapter 2, phenomena such as heat are reductively explainable only modulo conscious experience. But he goes on to say that "this shows that the irreducibility of consciousness is a trivial consequence of the pragmatics of our definitional practices" (p. 122). This seems to get things backward. Rather, the practices are consequences of the irreducibility of consciousness: if we did not factor out the experience of heat, we could not reduce heat at all! Thus irreducibility is a *source,* not a consequence, of our practices. It is hard to see how any of this trivializes the irreducibility of consciousness.

3. Closely related arguments for why a materialist cannot appeal to *a posteriori* necessity have been given by Jackson (1980, 1994), Lewis (1994), and White (1986).

4. Jackson (1980) makes a similar point, arguing that even if *a posteriori* considerations can establish the physicality of the property *pain,* a problem for materialism still arises from the property *pain-presents.*

5. Bealer (1994) also suggests pivoting on the physical term as a strategy here, although he does not follow the reasoning through to the natural conclusion.

6. Few have explicitly taken this position in print. Most who appeal to *a posteriori* necessity in defense of materialism appeal to the Kripkean considerations (e.g., Hill 1991; Lycan 1995; Tye 1995), and almost nobody has explicitly defended the stronger brand of metaphysical necessity to this end. On a natural reading, however, Bigelow and Pargetter (1990), Byrne (1993), Levine (1993), and Loar (1990) are implicitly committed to a position like this. Byrne, Levine, and Terry Horgan have advocated the position in personal communication.

7. One sometimes hears that mathematical truths are metaphysically necessary but not conceptually necessary. This depends on subtle issues concerning the analysis of mathematical concepts and conceptual necessity, but it is nevertheless widely agreed that mathematical truths are *a priori* (with the slight caveat mentioned in the next section of the text). Most crucially, there is not even a conceivable world in which mathematical truths are false. So these truths do not make the space of possible worlds any smaller than the set of conceivable worlds.

It might be suggested that moral supervenience is an example of metaphysical supervenience without an *a priori* connection, but the case for strong metaphysical necessity seems even weaker here than in the case of experience. There are options available here (antirealism, *a priori* connection) that are much more palatable than the corresponding alternatives for conscious experience. Further, there does not even seem to be a conceivable world that is physically and mentally identical to ours but morally distinct. So once again, moral supervenience puts no further constraints on the space of possible worlds.

8. Jackson (1995) gives a simple argument pointing out the oddness of physicalist positions that do not involve an *a priori* link from the physical to the psychological (this might apply equally to the "strong metaphysical necessity" position and the "cognitive limitation" position):

> It is implausible that there are facts about very simple organisms that cannot be deduced *a priori* from enough information about their physical nature and how they interact with their environments, physically described. The physical story about amoebae and their interactions with the environment is the whole story about amoebae. . . . But according to materialism we differ from amoebae essentially only in complexity of ingredients and their arrangement. It is hard to see how that kind of difference could generate important facts about us that in principle defy our powers of deduction. . . . Think of the charts in biology classrooms showing the evolutionary progression from single-celled creatures on the far left to the higher apes and humans on the far right: where in that progression can the physicalist plausibly claim that failure of *a priori* deducibility of important facts about us emerges? Or, if it comes to that, where in the development of each and every one of us from a zygote could the materialist plausibly locate the place in which there emerge important facts about us that cannot be deduced from the physical story about us?

9. John O'Leary-Hawthorne and Barry Loewer independently suggested the analogy between psychophysical supervenience and complex mathematical truths in conversation.

10. Note that this reasoning provides a disanalogy with mathematical truths even for someone who takes the strong position that there are certain mathematical truths so deep that they are not knowable by *any* class of beings *a priori*.

11. In an odd way, this position is quite close to that of reductionists such as Dennett. After all, both hold that the relevant intuitions arise from cognitive impairment. The main difference is that the reductionist thinks some of us can overcome this impairment, whereas the current objector holds that none of us can. But for all this objector knows, enlightenment may already have been achieved by others (perhaps even by Dennett). After all, the impaired would not appreciate a solution by the enlightened!

12. The most explicit version of the argument from logical possibility is given in Kirk (1974). It is also present in Campbell (1970), Nagel (1974), Robinson (1976), and elsewhere. My presentation of the argument differs mostly in the use of the notion of supervenience to provide a unifying framework, and in consideration of the role of *a posteriori* necessity. For a related argument from the possibility of inverted spectra, see also Seager 1991.

13. There seems to be a reasonable sense in which "Water is wet" and "H_2O is wet" express different facts, as for that matter do "Water is H_2O" and "H_2O is H_2O". In this sense, we individuate facts by the primary intensions of the terms used to express them, rather than by secondary intensions.

14. Lockwood (1989, pp. 136–37) makes essentially this point. As he puts it, one's not knowing that it is the same fact that corresponds to each mode of presentation must be attributable to one's failure to know some further substantive fact or facts, under any mode of presentation. A related point is made by Conee (1985a).

15. Loar suggests that phenomenal concepts are *recognitional* concepts, and argues that it is reasonable to expect a recognitional concept R to "introduce" the same property as a theoretically specified property P. He gives the example of someone who is able to recognize certain cacti in the California desert without having theoretical knowledge about them. But this seems wrong: if the subject cannot know that R is P *a priori*, then reference to R and P is fixed in different ways and the reference-fixing intensions can come apart in certain conceivable situations. Unless we invoke the additional machinery of strong metaphysical necessity, the difference in primary intensions will correspond to a difference in reference-fixing properties.

At one point Loar suggests that recognitional concepts refer "directly"without the aid of reference-fixing properties (primary intensions), but this also seems wrong. The very fact that a concept *could* refer to something else (a different set of cacti, say) in a different conceivable situation tells us that a substantial primary intension is involved. So reference cannot be truly "direct" in the relevant sense.

16. Someone much taken with the problem of indexicality might hold that the location of the center of a centered world can have ontological significance, or perhaps that there could be a difference in indexical facts between ordinary possible worlds (if there were such a thing as Nagel's "objective self," perhaps?). These issues, as with the ontological status of indexicality in general, are quite unclear to me. The discussion in the text is premised on the opponent's assumption that indexicality does not lead to an ontological gap, in order to note that even so, the analogy with the gap in the phenomenal case does not go through.

17. There is one further way in which thoughts about experience can be truly like indexicals: namely when we pick out an experience as "*this* experience." When one refers to one of two qualitatively identical experiences (as in the "Two Tubes" scenario of Austin 1990), knowing all the "objective" facts might conceivably leave the matter of which experience is referred to undetermined. (Note that the issue here concerns reference to tokens rather than types.) In case a materialist might like to use this case to gain purchase against the knowledge argument, I note that (1) in this case the epistemically further fact is independent of the phenomenal facts (even knowing all the phenomenal facts does not tell one which is *this* experience); (2) it does not provide a situation in which there is a conceivable *uncentered* world that differs from this world, so it cannot be used to build an ontological argument like the one in the text; (3) at most, the further fact serves to *locate* what is going on at the center of a world, telling us which entity is *this* one in the way that indexical facts tell us which entity is *me*.

The real moral here is that in certain cases, one needs to package more information into the center of a world: not just marking an individual and a time (as "me" and "here"), but also marking an experience (as "this"). Something similar arguably applies with orienting demonstratives, such as "left" and "right" (knowing the objective facts about a world might not tell one what which direction is left and which is right). All of these are associated with epistemic gaps of the relatively unthreatening indexical variety: in none of these cases are there *uncentered* worlds in which the basic facts hold but the further fact does not.

18. In a related objection, Churchland (1985) suggests that Jackson's argument equivocates on "knows": Mary has complete *propositional* or *sentential* knowledge of the physical facts, but she lacks knowledge *by acquaintance* with red experiences. The reply is similar. As long as Mary's knowledge of red experience *narrows down*

the way the world is, it is factual knowledge and the argument succeeds (no claim that factual knowledge must be "sentential" is required). So like Lewis and Nemirow, Churchland is committed to the implausible claim that Mary's knowledge of red experience tells her nothing about the way the world is.

19. Lycan (1995) gives nine (!) arguments to the effect that Mary's knowledge involves new information.

20. There are a number of other replies to the knowledge argument that I have not discussed, but my reply to these should be predictable. To mention just one: Dretske (1995) argues that the knowledge Mary lacks is knowledge of her environment. If she knew more about the composition of red things, she would know what red experiences represent, and so (by Dretske's theory) she would know what red experiences are like. Oddly, Dretske does not address the obvious objection: even if Mary knows all about the composition of red objects, she *still* does not know what it is like to see red!

21. Thanks to Frank Jackson for discussion on this point.

22. Kripke himself concedes (1972, f.74) that the mere absence of identity may be a weak conclusion. But he notes that modal arguments may also be mounted against more general forms of materialism.

23. In a similar way, arguments from disembodiment might establish that mental properties are not identical to physical properties, in that physical properties can only be instantiated by physical objects; such an argument is given by Bealer (1994). But again, this sort of nonidentity is a weak conclusion: it is still compatible with logical supervenience and so with materialism. Indeed, a similar sort of nonidentity argument could be mounted for almost any high-level property.

24. In his careful analysis, Boyd (1980, p. 98) notes that the possibility of zombies, unlike the possibility of disembodiment, entails the falsity of materialism. He therefore provides a separate argument against this possibility, but the argument is sketchy and unconvincing. Boyd makes an analogy with a computer computing a particular function, arguing that (1) it may *seem* to us that one could have all the circuits of the computer just as they are without that function being computed, but that this is nevertheless impossible, and (2) the apparent possibility of zombies is analogous to this. However, the analogy fails. The situation with the computer is analogous to the (very tenuous) "apparent possibility" that there might be a physical replica of me that does not learn what I learn, or does not discriminate what I discriminate. Nothing in this analogy can account for the far more compelling nature of the apparent possibility of a replica without conscious experience.

25. Kripke's remark that the materialist must show that "these things that we can imagine are not in fact things that we can imagine" (in the penultimate paragraph of Kripke 1971) also suggests the weak treatment. Kripke leaves open that the apparent possibility might be explained away in some way quite unlike the standard water/H_2O cases, but says that "it would have to be a deeper and subtler argument than I can fathom and subtler than has ever appeared in any materialist literature that I have read."

26. Although the argument is often taken to be an application of Kripke's theory of rigid designation, a version of it could in principle have been run ten years earlier, before the theory was developed. One could have asked the original identity theorists why the physical facts about H_2O necessitate that it be water (or watery), whereas the physical facts about brain states do not seem to necessitate that there is pain.

27. Horgan (1987) speaks of "metaphysical" supervenience in this context, as does Byrne (1993). If I am right that metaphysical possibility and logical possibility (of worlds) coincide, however, then logical supervenience follows.

28. For other versions of this point, see Blackburn 1990, Feigl 1958, Lockwood 1989, Maxwell 1978, and Robinson 1982.

29. A view of the world as pure causal flux is put forward by Shoemaker (1980), who argues that all properties are "powers," with no further properties to underlie these powers. Shoemaker's argument for this view is largely verificationist, and he does not directly confront the problems that the view faces.

Shoemaker further argues that as the powers associated with a property are essential to it, the laws of nature must be necessary *a posteriori*. (Swoyer [1982] argues similarly, and Kripke [1980] flirts with the conclusion.) The two-dimensional analysis of *a posteriori* necessity suggests that there must be something wrong with this suggestion, or at least that it is more limited than it sounds. At best, it might be that worlds with different laws are not correctly described as containing electrons (say); these considerations cannot rule such worlds impossible. Further, it seems implausible to hold that *all* the powers associated with electrons are constitutive of electronhood. More plausibly, for an entity to qualify as an electron only some of these powers are required, and mildly counternomic worlds containing electrons are possible. Shoemaker argues that there is no way to distinguish constitutive powers from non-constitutive powers, but the two-dimensional analysis suggests that this distinction falls out of the concept of electronhood.

A number of issues should be distinguished. (1) Is reference to physical properties fixed relationally? (Shoemaker, Chalmers: Yes.) (2) Are physical properties identical to relational properties (in secondary intension)? (S: Yes; C: Probably, but semantic intuitions may differ.) (3) Are all the nomic relations of a physical property essential to it? (S: Yes; C: No.) (4) Are there intrinsic properties underlying these relational properties? (S: No; C: Yes).

30. This view has been advocated in recent years by Lockwood (1989) and Maxwell (1978), both of whom put the view forward as an unorthodox version of the identity theory. The view has been relentlessly pushed on me by Gregg Rosenberg.

31. Although see Lahav and Shanks 1992 for a contrary view.

32. Lewis (1990) reaches a similar conclusion in a quite different way.

33. This is the issue on which I have occasionally taken polls when giving talks on consciousness, and on other occasions. The results are consistently 2:1 or 3:1 in favor of there being something further that needs explaining. Of course philosophy is not best done by democracy, but when we come to one of these issues that argument cannot resolve, the balance of prior intuition carries a certain weight.

34. *Biological materialism.* A common view (Hill 1991; Searle 1992) is that consciousness is necessarily biological. On this view, materialism is true, but unconscious systems with the same functional organization as conscious systems are logically possible and probably even empirically possible. Once we have admitted the logical possibility of an unconscious functional isomorph of me, however, we must surely admit the logical possibility of an unconscious *biological* isomorph of me, as there is no more of a conceptual link from neurophysiology to conscious experience than there is from silicon. This view is therefore probably best seen as a version of property dualism, with consciousness as a further fact over and above the physical facts. If not, then at best it must be combined with an appeal to strong metaphysical necessity

in supporting the link between biochemistry and consciousness, inheriting all the problems with that view.

(Searle [1992] admits the logical possibility of zombies, and in fact holds that there is merely a causal connection between the microphysical and conscious experience, so he is perhaps best seen as a property dualist. Hill [1991] tries to avoid the possibility of zombies with an appeal to rigid designators, but we have seen that this strategy does not help.)

35. *Physicalist-functionalism*. On this popular view (e.g., Shoemaker 1982), the property of having a conscious experience is a functional property, but that of having a *specific* conscious experience (a red sensation, say) is a neurophysiological property. On this view, inverted spectra between functional isomorphs are logically and perhaps empirically possible, but wholly unconscious functional isomorphs are not. But again, once we have accepted that an inverted functional isomorph is logically possible, we must also accept that an inverted *physical* isomorph is logically possible, as neurophysiology gives no more of a conceptual connection to a particular experience than does silicon. So once again, it seems that the physical facts do not determine all the facts, and some sort of property dualism follows. Again, physicalism can be maintained only by embracing the problematic notion of strong metaphysical necessity.

This view is often put forward as an *a posteriori* identification of phenomenal properties with neurophysiological properties. As such, it is vulnerable to the usual problems with such *a posteriori* identification (what is the primary intension?) as well as to the argument above. As White (1986) notes in a critique along these lines, those who advocate this view would do better to stick with an across-the-board functionalism.

36. *Psychofunctionalism*. On this view, mental properties are identified with functional properties *a posteriori*, on the basis of their roles in a mature empirical psychology (see Block 1980). If this view applied to phenomenal properties, phenomenal notions would have the same secondary intensions as functional notions, despite a difference in primary intension. The problems with this position are best analyzed along the lines suggested in section 2; that is, by focusing on primary intensions. If the primary intension of phenomenal notions is itself functional, then the position is underwritten by some sort of analytic functionalism after all; but if it is not, then focusing on the property introduced by this intension will invariably lead us to a variety of dualism. Either way, this view does no further work in saving materialism.

Advocates of this view have often ignored the role of concepts in fixing reference via primary intensions. Even given a scientific theory with "belief" as a theoretical term, there will be a conceptual story to tell about why *that* sort of state qualifies as a belief, rather than as a desire or something else entirely. Most likely, this reference-fixing intension will itself be functional, picking out something like the state that plays the most belief-like role within the theory, where "belief-like" is cashed out according to our prior concept. Whatever the nature of the primary intensions for phenomenal properties, the problems will arise there. To concentrate on secondary intensions is just to sweep the problems under the rug.

Another problem with psychofunctionalism: It implies a kind of chauvinism, by giving an extra weight to human psychology in deciding what counts as a belief, say. See Shoemaker 1981 for an excellent critique, although see Clark 1986 for a response. It seems more plausible that for most mental notions, the primary and secondary intensions coincide. Otherwise, we get into situations where we and our Twin Earth counterparts mean different things by "belief," despite our prior concepts being identical.

37. *Anomalous monism.* On this view, each mental state is token-identical to a physical state, but there are no strict psychophysical laws. Anomalous monism was put forward by Davidson (1970) as an account of intentional states rather than phenomenal states, but it might still be thought relevant for two reasons: first, it offers an *a priori* argument for physicalism based simply on the causal interaction (even a one-way interaction) between physical and mental states, and second, it denies the psychophysical laws that my view requires.

To see that my position is not threatened by Davidson's arguments, note that nothing in the arguments counts against the existence of *pointwise* laws of the form "If a system is in maximally specific physical state P, it is in (maximally specific) mental state M." Indeed, Davidson endorses the supervenience of the mental on the physical, which seems to have the existence of such laws as a consequence, upon a natural interpretation (see Kim 1985 for discussion). Davidson might be most charitably interpreted not as denying pointwise laws but as denying more interesting *typewise* laws connecting mental states to physical states under broad types such as those of folk psychology. Certainly that is the most that seems to follow from his arguments from the holism of the mental. If so, natural supervenience is not threatened. It also follows that the argument for token identity cannot go through. This argument relied on there being *no* strict laws to support a causal connection between the physical and the mental (so that an identity is required instead). But even a strict pointwise law is sufficient to underwrite the kind of connection I endorse, from physical states to phenomenal states. So dualism is not threatened either.

38. *Representationalism.* A recently popular position (e.g., Dretske 1995; Harman 1990; Lycan 1996; Tye 1995) has been that phenomenal properties are just *representational* properties, so that yellow qualia are just perceptual states that represent yellow things, or something similar. Of course the interpretation of this suggestion depends on just what account is given of representational properties in turn. Most often, the suggestion is combined with a reductive account of representation (usually a functional or teleofunctional account), in which case it becomes a variant of reductive functionalism and meets the usual problems. A nonreductive account of representation might avoid these problems (though it might have others), but would lead to a nonreductive account of experience.

The surface plausibility of some representationalist accounts may well arise from a slide between inflationary and deflationary readings of "representation," where the second is a purely functional (or teleofunctional) notion, but the first is not. The link between phenomenology and representation is made plausible on the first reading, but the reduction of representation is made plausible on the second. Alternatively, strong metaphysical necessity may be invoked to make the connection between representational states and phenomenal states, with the associated problems. (Among contemporary representationalists, Dretske [1995] and Harman [1990] appear to endorse a strongly reductive type-A position, whereas Lycan [1996] and Tye [1995]) appear to endorse a type-B position that leans on *a posteriori* necessity.)

Another way to approach representationalism is to note that almost everyone agrees that not *all* representational states are phenomenal states (those who disagree are almost certainly nonreductivists about both), so one can ask: What is it that makes some representational states *phenomenal* states? It is this further criterion that really does the work in a representationalist theory of consciousness. Often the criterion will be something along the lines of the requirement that the representational state be made available to central processes in an appropriate sort of way, in which case it is made clear that we are dealing with a reductive functionalist account with the usual problems (why should *that* make a representational state phenomenal?). The alternative is to single out the relevant states just as those representational states that are *phenomenal,* but then the road leads straight back to property dualism.

39. *Consciousness as higher-order thought.* The proposal that a conscious state is one that is an object of a higher-order thought (see e.g., Rosenthal 1996, among others) can be treated in a similar way. If this is combined with a reductive view of what it is to have a higher-order thought, this is essentially a reductive functionalist view with the usual problems. If not, then it will lead to a nonreductive view of experience (type B or type C), and so is compatible with the property dualism I suggest, although it may have other problems (as I discuss in Chapter 6).

40. *Reductive teleofunctionalism.* It is worth mentioning the view of Dretske (1995), on which a teleological component is also included in the criteria for having an experience: To have experiences, not only must a system function in a certain way, but the relevant processes must have been selected for appropriately in their history. This position is said to be able to avoid some of the problems of standard functionalism, in that for example it allows for (and explains) the possibility of functionally identical zombies: these are just systems with the wrong history. But it suffers from its own versions of the central problems. For example, it seems no less logically possible that a functionally identical system with the relevant history could lack consciousness; likewise, knowledge of organization plus history fails to give one knowledge of experience. One might say that this view "avoids" the problems with reductive functionalism in the wrong sort of way. Ultimately this view is closer in flavor to a type-A reductive functionalist view than to a view that takes consciousness seriously.

41. *Emergent causation.* Many have wanted to reject a reductive account of consciousness while giving it a central causal role. A popular way to do this has been to argue for emergent causation—the existence of new sorts of causation in physical systems of a certain complexity. For example, Sperry (1969, 1992) has argued that consciousness is an emergent property of complex systems that itself plays a causal role; the British emergentists such as Alexander (1920) held a similar view (see McLaughlin 1992 for discussion). Similarly, Sellars (1981; see also Meehl and Sellars (1956) suggested that new laws of physical causation might come into play in certain systems, such as those made of protoplasm or supporting sentient beings. (He called this view "physicalism$_1$," as opposed to "physicalism$_2$" on which the basic physical principles found in inorganic matter apply across the board.) These views should not be confused with the "innocent" view of emergent causation found in complex systems theory, on which low-level laws yield qualitatively novel behavior through interaction effects. On the more radical view, there are new fundamental principles at play that are not consequences of low-level laws.

There are two problems with the view. First, there is no evidence for such emergent principles of causation. As far as we can tell, all causation is a consequence of low-level physical causation, and "downward causation" never interferes with low-level affairs. Second and perhaps more important: on a close analysis, the view leaves consciousness as superfluous as before. To see this, note that nothing in the story about emergent causation requires us to invoke *phenomenal* properties anywhere. The entire causal story can be told in terms of links between configurations of physical properties. There will still be a possible world that is physically identical but that lacks consciousness entirely. It follows that at best phenomenal properties *correlate* with causally efficacious configurations. If there is a way to see phenomenal properties as efficacious on this view, the same maneuver will apply to my view. In fact, this view is best seen as a version of my view, with consciousness supervening on the physical by a contingent nomic link. It is modified by the addition of new laws of emergent physical causation, but these simply complicate matters rather than changing anything fundamental.

42. *Mysterianism.* Those unsympathetic to reductive accounts of consciousness often hold that consciousness may remain an eternal mystery. Such a view has been canvased by Nagel (1974) and Jackson (1982) and developed by McGinn (1991). On this view, consciousness may be as far beyond our understanding as knowledge of astronomy is beyond sea slugs.

Such a view can be tempting, but it is premature. To say that there is no reductive explanation of consciousness is not to say that there is no explanation at all. In particular, an account of the principles in virtue of which consciousness supervenes naturally on the physical might provide an enlightening theory of consciousness even on a nonreductive view.

McGinn (1989) argues that there is a necessary connection between brain states and conscious states (otherwise the emergence of consciousness would be a miracle), but that we can never know what this connection is. His discussion suggests that he has logical or metaphysical necessity in mind; but the argument establishes at most natural necessity. Certainly a contingent nomic connection between consciousness and the physical is no more miraculous than any contingent law, and indeed such a connection seems far less mysterious than a logically or metaphysically necessary connection that is beyond our understanding. And it is not obvious why we could not use our knowledge of regularities connecting physical processes and experience to infer such laws. In the next few chapters I will go some way toward characterizing the relevant laws. In this way, we can see that a nonreductive view of consciousness need not lead to pessimism.

Chapter 5

1. Elitzur credits his discussion to Penrose (1987).

2. I leave aside religious experiences here. Arguably, what truly needs explaining here is the experience of deep spirituality and awe.

3. I am not sure whether this line is found explicitly in the literature, but there are related arguments. For example, Foss (1989) responds to Jackson's (1982) knowledge argument by noting that Mary could know everything that a subject with color vision would *say* about various colors, and even everything that a subject *might* say. But of course this falls far short of knowing all there is to know.

4. Of course, this would not really help.

5. Dretske (1995) makes a similar sort of argument, arguing that his theory explains the way things seem and so explains what needs to be explained. Once again, there is an equivocation between psychological and phenomenal senses of

"seem." In general, "seeming" is a poor term to use in characterizing the explananda of a theory of consciousness, precisely because of this ambiguity. It is interesting that it is usually used only by proponents of reductive accounts.

6. There have, of course, been various attacks on the idea of the "Given" and on the idea of "sense-data" in the literature. But I do not think that any of these succeed in overturning the idea that to have an experience provides a source of justification for a belief about experience. They provide good reasons to reject various stronger claims, such as the claim that all knowledge is derivative on knowledge of experience, and the claim that we perceive the world by perceiving sense-data, and the claim that to have an experience is automatically to bring the experience under a concept. But I am not making any of these claims.

Sellars (1956) plausibly criticizes the idea that "sensing a sense content s" entails noninferential knowledge of s. He notes that knowledge is a *conceptual* state, so this sort of knowledge is unlikely to be primitive; but experience seems to be more primitive. Having an experience is arguably a *nonconceptual* state, and our acquaintance with experience is a nonconceptual relation (although this matter depends on how one defines what it is to be "conceptual"). The residual question is therefore that of how a nonconceptual state can provide evidence for a conceptual state. This is a difficult question, but it is not a question unique to the nonreductionist about consciousness. It arises even in the case of standard perceptual knowledge of the world, where even a reductionist must accept that justification for a belief is partly grounded in a nonconceptual source, unless one is willing to accept alternatives that seem to face even greater difficulties. I think that an account of such justification might be given, but that is a lengthy separate project. Here, I simply note that nonreductionism about consciousness does not raise a *special* worry in this area.

7. This general line is taken by Hill (1991) in his detailed response to skeptical arguments concerning experience based on the possibility of "ersatz pain," in particular to the argument of Shoemaker (1975a). Hill makes a number of points that are congenial to the treatment I give of these issues, although he advocates type-B biological materialism rather than property dualism. These include a comparison between skeptical arguments concerning experience and skeptical arguments concerning the external world, and arguments against a "discernibility condition" holding that one is not justified in believing that P unless in every situation in which one lacks evidence for P, one would be able to recognize that one lacks evidence for P.

8. This suggestion was made by John O'Leary-Hawthorne in discussion.

9. It might be thought that the opposing line—in which a zombie's belief "I am conscious" comes out true because his concept picks out a functional property—could be helpful in handling the property dualist's epistemological problems, as it would no longer follow that I have beliefs that are justified where a zombie's belief is not. But whatever line we take here, the zombie will still have *some* false beliefs, such as the belief that he has properties over and above his physical and functional properties, and the problem of justifying my corresponding beliefs would recur in this form.

10. E.g., by Bill Lycan in personal communication. One can also retreat to a concept such as "Experience of the sort typically caused (in most of us) by red things"—although here one escapes relativism at the cost of the possibility of being systematically wrong about the category of one's own experiences.

11. This sort of relativism does not occur with *external* color concepts, such as

redness as a property of *objects* rather than experiences. To a first approximation, reference is fixed to red things as things that typically give rise (in most of us) to the same sort of color experiences as some paradigm examples. This is more "public" in two ways: because of the reference to public paradigm examples, and because of the reference to experiences across a community. Thus someone with an inverted spectrum would use "red things" to refer to the same things as I do, even if his term "red experiences" picks out something different.

One might wonder about individuals with different boundaries in their color space, e.g., someone who thinks that carrots look the same color as roses and tomatoes. It seems most natural to say that her utterance of "Carrots are red" is false, because of the communal element in the concept "red," but perhaps there is also a less communal sense in which it can be taken as true (where "red" comes to "red-for-me"). Even here, though, there is not *much* room for relativism, because for any individual the term will still be tied to external paradigms. Even using this relativistic sense, anyone's term "red" must pick out a good many red things, and similarly for other concepts.

One might also remove all dependence on experience from the characterizations of external color concepts, by characterizing them in terms of *judgments* instead: so red things are those that are typically judged as the same color as paradigm examples. This has the advantage of allowing zombies to speak truly of green objects, as may be reasonable. After all, it seems that intersubjective similarity in judgments, rather than similarity in experience, is all that is required to get the reference of color terms going.

12. The distinction between the qualitative concept and the relational concept of "red experience" is closely related to Nida-Rümelin's (1995) distinction between the "phenomenal" and "nonphenomenal" reading of belief ascriptions such as "Marianna believes that the sky appears blue to Peter." Nida-Rümelin's "phenomenal" reading ascribes a belief involving the relevant qualitative concept of the ascriber; whereas the nonphenomenal reading ascribes a belief involving a relational concept. (The relevant relational concept in Nida-Rümelin's examples seems to be something like the community-based concept mentioned in note 10.)

13. Of course my use of the symbol "*R*" for the concept is deliberately reminiscent of the "*E*" in Wittgenstein's private language argument. I will not even try to analyze that argument here; that project would be made especially difficult by the fact that there is no widely accepted interpretation of just what the argument is. Suffice to say that every version of the argument that I have seen either rests on very dubious premises, or applies as strongly to everyday concepts as to private experiential concepts, or both.

14. Indeed, if one does a little introspection, it is notable that there is little one can even "say to oneself" that distinguishes red and green experiences, again apart from pointing to relational properties, despite one's awareness of their rich intrinsic difference. This might be seen as further evidence that the qualities inhere in the phenomenal realm and are not directly reflected in the psychological.

15. To a certain extent this line of thought mirrors a line in Shoemaker (1975): that if inverted spectra are possible, neither qualitative states nor qualitative beliefs can be functionally defined, although Shoemaker puts things in terms of rigid designation with relational fixation of reference, so in effect he is focusing on secondary intensions here.

16. This observation parallels Nida-Rümelin's observation (1995) that the distinction between phenomenal and nonphenomenal beliefs is not an ordinary instance of the *de re*/*de dicto* distinction.

17. Note that this is not the simple indexical "this," whose primary intension is the same whether the experience is *R* or *S,* and for which it is an uninformative triviality that this experience is *this* sort of experience. Rather, this is the meaty *"this"* with a primary intension that picks out *S* experiences in every centered world.

18. Conee (1985b) leans on this sort of constitution relation between qualia and qualitative beliefs in his response to Shoemaker's (1975a) epistemological argument.

Chapter 6

1. Note that in order for these principles to provide psychophysical laws, we must read second-order judgments such as "I am having a red experience" by the relational reading discussed in the final section of Chapter 5, along the lines of "I am having the sort of experience usually caused by red objects." The relational elements of the "red experience" concept, unlike the intrinsic qualitative elements, will be reflected in physical processing: the corresponding belief involving the qualitative concept of "red experience" will not logically supervene on the physical, so the correctness of such beliefs will not provide a psychophysical law. I do not make too much of this, as my discussion will focus on first-order judgments, for which these issues do not arise.

2. For a rich analysis of the phenomenology associated with occurrent thought, see Siewert 1994.

3. Compare also the observation by Nagel (1974) that "structural features of perception might be more accessible to objective description, even though something would be left out."

4. This is closely related to Jackendoff's hypothesis of computational sufficiency: "Every phenomenological distinction is caused by/supported by/projected from a corresponding computational distinction" (Jackendoff 1987, p. 24).

5. For related discussions of blindsight, see Tye 1993, Block 1995, and especially Dennett 1991.

6. For a discussion of the dangers of conflating conscious experience and consciousness *of* an experience, and also for an excellent critique of higher-order thought approaches in general, see Siewert 1994. For a parallel sort of critique from a reductive standpoint, see also Dretske 1995.

7. The distinction between first-order and second-order accounts reflects Nelkin's distinction between the two functional concepts of consciousness, C1 and C2 (Nelkin 1989).

8. A proposal like this is canvassed by Carruthers (1992), who argues that *availability for reflexive thinking* is naturally necessary and sufficient for a qualitative feel. (Carruthers seems to have a stronger variety of availability in mind, however, insofar as Armstrong's inattentive truck-driver fails to meet his criterion.) Insofar as he explicitly claims that the connection holds with only natural necessity, the proposal seems nonreductive, although Carruthers also characterizes the view as physicalist. Alvin Goldman has suggested a similar account in conversation, intended as a characterization of those states that are conscious in familiar systems, rather than as a reductive proposal.

9. The distinction between first-order registrations and first-order judgments parallels Dretske's (1995) distinction between the *phenomenal* and *doxastic* varieties of

cognitive states. The latter corresponds to the way the system takes things to be, and the former corresponds to the way things are represented to the system. Of course there is a significant difference between Dretske's framework and mine, in that Dretske is essentially a reductive functionalist (actually a reductive teleofunctionalist), *identifying* experiences with (teleo)functionally defined first-order registrations. I resist the identification for the usual reasons, but it remains plausible that experiences *correspond* to first-order registrations. My framework simply has an extra distinction, recognizing three different sorts of states—judgments, registrations, and phenomenal states, with registrations and phenomenal states correlated but distinct—where Dretske's recognizes two: judgments and phenomenal states, without even a conceptual distinction between phenomenal states and the corresponding registrations.

10. There are an enormous number of interesting questions about the *sort* of representational content possessed by the first-order registrations that constitute awareness, and about the sort of content that is possessed in parallel by the corresponding experiences. Issues about content are not central to my discussion, so I raise them only briefly here, but they are among the deepest and most subtle questions about experience and deserve a much more detailed treatment elsewhere.

A central feature of the contents of awareness and of experience is that the content here is generally *nonconceptual*—it is content that does not require an agent to possess the concepts that might be involved in characterizing that content. For example, it is plausible that a simple system—perhaps a dog or a mouse—might have fine-grained color experiences, with a correspondingly fine-grained representation of color distinctions in the cognitive system, while having only the simplest system of color concepts. In humans, similarly, it is common for states of consciousness and awareness in musical perception to have contents that go far beyond the musical concepts in the subject's repertoire.

(For discussion of nonconceptual content, see Crane 1992, Cussins 1990, Evans 1982, Peacocke 1992. There seems to be a consensus in the literature that the contents of experience are nonconceptual. An exception is McDowell [1994], who argues from our ability to reidentify experiences under concepts such as "that shade" to the conclusion that all experiential content is conceptual. It is not clear that such an ability is a requirement for the possession of experience: it is plausible, for example, that certain subtle aspects of musical experience in some subjects [e.g., subtle changes of key] might resist conceptualization and reidentification altogether. Experiences in animals provide another example. McDowell appears happy to embrace the conclusion that animals do not have experiences, but one might find the *modus tollens* at least as compelling as the *modus ponens*. Even if one were to accept McDowell's point, I think that something like the relevant distinction might be rehabilitated in the guise of two grades of conceptual content.)

Of course, there may be a *causal* relationship between concepts and consciousness; it is not uncommon for conceptual change to significantly affect the character of experience. But such conceptual resources do not seem to be a *requirement* for conscious experience. The same goes for awareness, insofar as it is parallel to consciousness. The contents represented by the first-order registrations that correspond to conscious experiences, in visual perception for example, do not require corresponding rich conceptual resources. In this way, the contents of experience and of awareness are in general more primitive than that of judgments, whose contents are most naturally seen as conceptual.

One of the most interesting questions about content is whether experience has representational content intrinsically, or whether its content somehow derives from that of an underlying cognitive state. The latter position can be tempting, but it does not seem quite right: for example, it seems that my visual experience right now represents the world as having a large square object in front of me, and does so simply by virtue of being the experience it is. Even a hypothetical disembodied mind that was having a similar experience would have a similar sort of representational content. Siewert (1994) makes a compelling case that experience by its nature is informative about the state of the world: a visual experience, for example, is something that is assessable for accuracy (it can represent the world correctly and incorrectly), and indeed is assessable in virtue of its very nature as a visual experience. So it may be reasonable to say that experience is intrinsically laden with representational content.

One might be tempted to take the reverse line, and hold that the only true content is present in experience, and that the content of an underlying first-order registration is itself dependent on the content of the associated experience. There might be something to this, but it is not entirely satisfactory either; there is a sense in which one wants to say that even a zombie's first-order registrations represent the world as being a certain way. We certainly have contentful states that are not associated with experiences, and it is hard to see that all of our contents are somehow dependent on the contents of experience. An intermediate line that one might take is that (1) in a certain sense the *original* sort of content was that found within experience, but (2) we evolved a framework for attributing content to cognitive states based in part on coherence with the content of associated experiences, and (3) once in place, this framework became autonomous so that we can speak of the content of cognitive states even in the absence of experience. This would mean that experiences and associated registrations could both have content autonomously, without there being a strange, coincidental overdetermination whereby the same content is constituted twice over. The issues here are quite subtle and would likely repay a detailed analysis.

Another interesting issue is whether the relevant sort of content is "wide" (dependent on objects in the environment) or "narrow" (dependent only on internal processes). Insofar as experience is intrinsically laden with content, and insofar as experience is supervenient on a subject's organization, then the relevant sort of content here must be narrow. (Experiences might still have wide content, but this could not be content fixed by the experience alone.) Sometimes it has been thought that the only true representational content is wide content, but I think there is a natural way to understand narrow representational content (see Chalmers 1994c). Such an account could be elaborated to give an account of the narrow, nonconceptual content of experience and of awareness, as a kind of content that puts constraints on the centered worlds that are candidates to be a subject's actual world.

A further question is whether *all* experiences have representational content. It is plausible that many or most do; certainly most perceptual experiences seem to be intrinsically informative about the world. There are some tricky cases, however: What about orgasms, or nausea, or certain experiences of emotion (see Block 1995 and Tye 1995)? But even in these cases one might find *some* representational content, as the experiences often carry content concerning location (in here, down there) or quality (good, bad). It is not clear that there could be experiences that are devoid of representational content altogether; on the other hand, it is not obvious that there could not be.

Some philosophers have put forward the proposal that phenomenal properties are just representational properties, so that experiences are *exhausted* by their representational content (e.g., Dretske 1995; Harman 1990; Lycan 1996; Tye 1992). Most often this is put forward alongside a reductive view of representational content, so that this view comes down to a version of reductive functionalism, and is implausible for the usual reasons. Another version of the proposal might set it alongside a nonreductive view of representational content, perhaps one in which the only true representation is in experience. This would be more compatible with taking consciousness seriously, but it would still have difficulties. In particular, it would seem that representational content might stay constant between functional isomorphs with spectrum inversion, in which case phenomenology outstrips representational content. The cases in the previous paragraph also tend to suggest that even if all experiences have representational content, they also have features that outstrip their representational content. So it is not clear that even the nonreductive version of this proposal will be successful.

11. In personal communication and forthcoming work.

12. Occasionally, principles such as those I have mentioned have been formulated explicitly as part of the methodology of empirical work on the mind. Not surprisingly, this has happened most often in the area of mainstream psychology that is most concerned with conscious experience, namely *psychophysics*. This field is often construed as relating the properties of our sensations to properties of associated physical stimuli. Typical results here include the Weber-Fechner law and Stevens's power law (Stevens 1975), which give two ways of relating the intensity of a stimulus to the intensity of a corresponding sensation. Although it is sometimes held that the primary explananda in psychophysics are third-person data such as subjective reports, it seems undeniable that features of first-person experience—such as the experience of certain optical illusions—are among the central phenomena that the field seeks to account for.

(Horst [1995] makes a strong case that the primary data in the field are often first-person experiences of various phenomena such as illusions. At conferences, for example, researchers place a premium on being able to "see" various effects for themselves. One might also argue that the disputes between Fechner's and Stevens's approaches to the measurement of sensation [see Stevens 1975] only make sense if one assumes that there is an aim to measure a common target, phenomenal experience; otherwise we simply have noncompeting measurements of different functional phenomena.)

Within psychophysics, there has been occasional discussion of the means by which empirical observations can help in the explanation of subjective sensations. Some researchers have been led to formalize explicit principles on which this work relies—known variously as "psychophysical linking hypotheses" (Brindley 1960) or "general linking propositions" (Teller 1984). The "Axioms of Psychophysical Correspondence" put forward by Müller (1896; quoted in Boring 1942, p. 89) are a good example:

1. The ground of every state of consciousness is a material process, a psychophysical process so-called, to whose occurrence the presence of the conscious state is joined.

2. To an equality, similarity, or difference in the constitution of sensations . . . there corresponds an equality, similarity, and difference in the constitution of the psychophysical process, and conversely. Moreover, to a greater or lesser

similarity of sensations, there also corresponds respectively a greater or lesser similarity of the psychophysical process, and conversely.

3. If the changes through which a sensation passes have the same direction, or if the differences which exist between series of sensations are of like direction, then the changes through which the psychophysical process passes, or the differences of the given psychophysical process, have like direction. Moreover, if a sensation is variable in n directions, then the psychophysical process lying at the basis of it must also be variable in n directions, and conversely.

It is clear that these principles are closely related to the principle of structural coherence. Allowing for certain differences in language, we can see all the propositions along the lines of those above are straightforward consequences of the coherence principle; and together, they constitute a good deal of its force. So once again, we can see that the principle of structural coherence and its variants are playing a central role in allowing empirical research to yield explanatory accounts of various features of experience.

Not surprisingly, the status of such principles has met with debate within psychophysics that parallels the sorts of debate found in the philosophy of mind (see e.g., Brindley 1960; Marks 1978; D. Teller 1984, 1990). Some have regarded them as empirical hypotheses, but it does not appear that they are derived or falsified through empirical test, at least of the third-person variety. Others, especially those of an operationalist bent, have regarded them as definitional claims; this corresponds to a reductive functionalist position in philosophy. Often they have been taken simply as background assumptions, or premises, concerning the nature of the psychophysical connection. In any case, the science has managed to proceed quite nicely without any real resolution of these questions. For explanatory purposes, the shape of the bridge is more important than its metaphysical status.

In general, "philosophical" issues concerning the relationship between physical processes and experience are bubbling just beneath the surface in many theoretical discussions in psychophysics. As far as I can tell, this has not met with much discussion in the philosophical literature (although see Savage 1970 for a philosophical critique of methodology in the measurement of sensation). It would likely make a worthwhile object of extended study.

Chapter 7

1. Lycan 1987, for example.

2. Churchland and Churchland (1981) have objected to the "Chinese nation" arguments on the grounds that such a system would need to handle around $10^{30,000,000}$ inputs to the retina, and an even vaster number of internal states of the brain. The population simulation, requiring one person per input and one person per state, would therefore require vastly more people than a population could provide. This objection overlooks the fact that both inputs and internal states are combinatorially structured. Instead of representing each input pattern (over 10^8 cells) with a single person, thus requiring 2^{10^8} people, we only need 10^8 people to represent the input as a structured pattern. The same goes for internal states. We therefore need no more people than there are cells in the brain.

3. Bogen (1981) and Lycan (1987) make the suggestion that such "accidental" situations would not have qualia, as qualia require teleology. This would have the

odd consequence of making the presence or absence of qualia dependent on the history of a system. Better, I think, to concede that such a system would have qualia while pointing out just how unlikely it is that such a system could arise by chance.

4. I discuss this further in Chalmers 1994a.

5. This figure comes from noting that there are 10^{10^9} possible choices for the consequent of each conditional, representing the global state into which the system transits. The chance that a given global state will transit into the correct following state is therefore 1 in 10^{10^9}. In fact it will be lower, as any given global state will be realizable by many different "maximal" states of the physical system, each of which is required to transit appropriately. There are 10^{10^9} such conditionals to be satisfied, so the figure above falls out.

6. For some related fables, see also Harrison 1981a, 1981b.

7. Perhaps some element of this situation could be explained away via the constitution of belief by experience of the sort discussed in section 7 of Chapter 5: perhaps Joe's concept "red experience" now refers to pink experiences, for example, so he is not entirely wrong. This strategy would certainly not help with the errors in his judgments about distinctions, however.

8. Cuda (1985) claims that a description of systems with such mistaken beliefs is *senseless*. He offers no argument for this apart from the claim that if the description made sense, it would make sense to think that *we* are mistaken in such a way, which (he says) it clearly does not. But this seems fallacious. It makes *sense* to suppose that I could be mistaken in this way, in that the hypothesis is coherent; it is just that my epistemic situation shows me that the hypothesis is not *true* in my own case, because I have direct experience of bright red qualia and the like.

9. This is not to say that there are no Sorites arguments to be found in the ballpark; for an example, see Tienson 1987.

10. This position is mostly closely associated with Shoemaker (1982), but has also been advocated by Horgan (1984a), Putnam (1981), and various others.

11. It may even be that such cases exist in the actual world. In a stimulating paper, Nida-Rümelin (1996) notes that research in color vision leads us to expect that there should be cases of "pseudonormal" color vision, in which (1) R-cones in the retina have the response pattern usually associated with G-cones, and (2) G-cones have the response pattern usually associated with R-cones. Taken separately, (1) and (2) are the standard causes of red–green color blindness. In theory, the genetic abnormalities responsible for (1) and (2) can occur together, giving a subject who will be behaviorally very similar to a normal subject, but who may well have color experiences that are inverted with respect to the rest of the population.

12. Putnam (1981) and Shoemaker (1982) use this example to argue against functionalist accounts of qualia, but at best their arguments count against a "coarse-grained" invariance principle, on which for example the same sort of experience is held to always arise from states that are triggered by blue things and lead to "blue" reports. The fine-grained principle is unthreatened. (Levine [1988] makes a related point.)

There is a variant of this scenario in which the rewired subjects undergo a process of adaptation, learning, and finally amnesia (forgetting that things ever looked different), ending up behaviorally identical to their original state. There is little reason to believe that they will be organizationally identical, however, especially given that the rewiring is still reflected in the state of their brain. If by some special process the organization ended up just as it started, it would not seem implausible that the experiences should also revert to their original state. (Cole [1990] and Rey [1992] advocate versions of a reversion hypothesis here.)

13. A related argument is given by Seager (1991, pp. 39–41), who describes a case in which retinal cells are "tuned" to a higher range on the optical spectrum. This argument can be treated in the same way as Block's.

14. Block responds to a related objection by noting that we can move the "lenses" inward in the system, rewiring things at the optic nerve or in the visual cortex, for instance. As before, however, this does not provide any cases of organizational isomorphs with different experiences. Indeed, Block's description of such cases appears straightforwardly compatible with the view that qualia are dependent on the organization of "central" systems. We are asked to believe that experiences are the same in certain cases precisely because central processing is unaffected; we are supposed to believe that experiences differ in cases where central processing differs. Such arguments cannot refute the invariance principle.

15. The argument in this section is distantly inspired by Dennett's story "Where Am I?" (1978d). A situation bearing a certain resemblance to the one I describe below is considered by Shoemaker (1982). A more closely related discussion can be found in Seager (1991, p. 43), although Seager does not advocate the invariance principle. As this book was going to press, I discovered a stimulating recent article by Arnold Zuboff (1994) that makes what is essentially the dancing qualia argument to support a version of reductive functionalism, by arguing that dancing qualia are impossible *a priori*.

16. White (1986) makes this sort of point, suggesting that if nonfunctional physical differences are relevant to qualia, then even tiny differences in DNA might affect qualia.

17. Shoemaker (1982) gives a complex criterion for how specific a physiological property needs to be to fix qualia, or to "realize a quale," as he puts it. However, it seems to me that if my discussion here has been correct, his criterion will in fact pick out a fine-grained functional property.

18. This suggestion was made by Terry Horgan in conversation.

Chapter 8

1. Others who have suggested links between consciousness and information include Bohm (1980), Sayre (1976), and Velmans (1991), though the details of their proposals are quite different from mine. Sayre's idea of a "neutral monism" of information is quite suggestive, however (thanks to Steve Horst for pointing this out to me). Something quite like the double-aspect principle is discussed in Lockwood 1989, chap. 11, although he does not put it in terms of information.

2. An unpublished paper of mine (Chalmers 1990) focuses on this strategy in understanding the relation between consciousness and judgments about consciousness, and uses it to come up with a basic "theory" of consciousness (involving pattern and information) that is a predecessor of some of the ideas in this chapter. In this paper I call the requirement of explanatory coherence the "Coherence Test" that any theory of consciousness must pass.

3. But for the claim that thermostats have beliefs and desires, see McCarthy 1979.

4. Wheeler's approach focuses on measurement outcomes, or "answers to yes–no questions," as the basis for everything, and as such may be closer to a form of idealism than the view I am putting forward here.

5. See also the interesting account of Fredkin's ideas in Wright (1988) for more on the underlying metaphysics.

6. There are stimulating discussions of these problems for the Russellian view in Foster (1991, pp. 119–30) and Lockwood (1992).

7. Lockwood (1992) suggests that a Russellian view can invoke brute laws for this sort of purpose. He does not address the objection that introducing further laws in this capacity seems to compromise the original attractions of the Russellian view. They raise the problems of epiphenomenalism that the Russellian view held promise of avoiding, for example, and they also require a considerable expansion in the ontology over and above the intrinsic properties that are required to ground physics. (I should note that Lockwood does not rely on these laws to solve the grain problem; his main idea about solving the problem is an intriguing separate suggestion involving quantum mechanics).

Chapter 9

1. The material in this section is largely drawn from Chalmers (1994a).

2. Putnam (1988, pp. 120–25) gives a separate argument for the conclusion that every ordinary open system implements every finite-state automaton. I analyze this argument in detail in Chalmers 1995a. Upon analysis, the argument appears to gain its force by allowing the physical state transition conditionals in the definition of implementation to lack any strong modal force.

3. I pursue this way of understanding the explanatory role of computation in cognitive science in Chalmers (1994b).

4. Related points are made by Korb (1991) and Newton (1989), both of whom suggest that the Chinese room may provide a good argument against machine consciousness if not against machine intentionality.

5. Hofstadter (1981) outlines a similar spectrum of cases intermediate between a brain and the Chinese room.

6. The idea that the homunculus in the Chinese room is analogous to a demon running around inside the skull is suggested by Haugeland (1980).

7. It is notable that although Dreyfus (1972) entitled his book making this sort of objection *What Computers Can't Do,* he later conceded that the right *sort* of computational system (such as a connectionist system) would escape these objections. In effect, "what computers can do" is identified with what a very narrow class of computational systems can do.

8. This straightforward counter to Gödelian arguments was first made in print by Putnam (1960), I believe, and as far as I can tell it has never been overturned, despite the best efforts of Lucas and Penrose. Penrose (1994, sec. 3.3) argues that he must be able to determine the consistency of the formal system that captures his own reasoning, as he could surely determine the truth of the axioms and the validity of the inference rules. This seems to depend on the assumption that the computational system is an axiom-plus-rules system in the first place, which it need not be in the general case (witness the neural simulation of the brain). Even in the axiom-plus-rules case, it is not clear to me that we would be able to determine the validity of *every* rule that our system might use, especially those applying to the outer limits of ordinal counting in iterated Gödelization, which is where the Gödelian arguments in the human case will really have their force.

9. Probably it is a good idea to do this, just in case a specific pattern of round-offs at the 10^{-10} level produces a biased distribution of behavior. To be safe, given that there is noise at the 10^{-10} level, we might approximate the system to the 10^{-20} level, approximating the distribution of noise to the 10^{-20} level, too.

10. Sometimes—usually only in the philosophy of mind—terms such as "computation" are used to refer only to the class of symbolic computations, or computations over representations (that is, systems in which the basic syntactic objects are also the basic semantic objects). Of course little rests on this terminological issue: what counts from the point of view of artificial intelligence is that there be some sort of formal system such that implementation suffices for mentality, whether or not it counts as a "computation" by this criterion. But it should be noted in any case that to use the term in this way is to lose touch with its origins in the theory of computation. Even most Turing machines will not count as "computational" in this sense, as only a few of these can be interpreted as performing computations over conceptual representations. For similar reasons, to limit the class of "computations" in this way is to lose hold of the (Church–Turing) *universality* of computation, which provides perhaps the best reason for believing in the (functional) AI thesis to begin with.

Chapter 10

1. At least for a spin $\frac{1}{2}$ particle such as an electron. I leave aside cases in which spin has further basic values.

2. I simplify here, as elsewhere. No measurement is perfectly precise, so a state with a truly definite position never emerges. Instead, the wave function will collapse into a state in which all the amplitude is concentrated in a very narrow range of locations. It is easier to speak as if collapsed positions are truly definite, however.

3. A probability density, in the continuous case.

4. Albert (1992) suggests that "consciousness" is as vague as "measurement" and "macroscopic"; but it seems to me that this criterion is attractive partly because there *is* plausibly a fact of the matter about whether a system is conscious.

5. I am indebted to Albert and Loewer (1990) and Albert (1992) in my discussion of the GRW interpretation.

6. Note that this is the only point at which Bell's theorem and the Einstein-Podolsky-Rosen (EPR) results come up in this chapter. Sometimes these results are taken to be the main source of the philosophical problems with quantum mechanics, but I think the problems arise prior to EPR considerations. Even without EPR, the difficult choice between collapse, hidden variables, and Everett would come up. EPR simply adds to the difficulties of hidden-variables theories, by showing that they (like collapse) must be nonlocal; and arguably, it increases the attractiveness of the Everett interpretation, which is the only local interpretation compatible with the result.

7. The one-big-world view appears to be the most common understanding of the Everett interpretation among physicists (especially among quantum cosmologists, who use this framework all the time). The "splitting-worlds" understanding is largely an artifact of popularizations. Sometimes even proponents of the one-big-world view talk of "splitting," but this is just a vivid way of talking about the fact that a wave function evolves into a superposition. There is no special process of splitting of worlds; at most, there is a sort of local split of the wave function. In any case I think that talk of "splitting" is best avoided, as it inevitably promotes confusion.

8. This objection has been made by Bell (1981), Bohm and Hiley (1993), and Hodgson (1988), among many others.

9. The most sensible strategy might be to make my bet according to a quantum device that produces a "no" answer with probability 0.999, and "yes" with probability 0.001. That way, if the Everett view is false I will almost certainly be right, and if it is true, at least *one* of my descendant minds will survive.

Bibliography

Ackerman, D. 1990. *A Natural History of the Senses.* New York: Random House.

Adams, R. M. 1974. Theories of actuality. *Nous* 8:211–31.

Akins, K. 1993. What is it like to be boring and myopic? In B. Dahlbom, ed., *Dennett and His Critics.* Oxford: Blackwell.

Albert, D. 1992. *Quantum Mechanics and Experience.* Cambridge, Mass: Harvard University Press.

Albert, D., and B. Loewer. 1988. Interpreting the many-worlds interpretation. *Synthese* 77:195–213.

———. 1989. Two no-collapse interpretations of quantum mechanics. *Nous* 23: 169–86.

———. 1990. Wanted dead or alive: Two attempts to solve Schrödinger's paradox. *PSA 1990*, vol. 1, pp. 277–85.

Alexander, S. 1920. *Space, Time, and Deity.* London: Macmillan.

Armstrong, D. M. 1968. *A Materialist Theory of the Mind.* London: Routledge and Kegan Paul.

———. 1973. *Belief, Truth, and Knowledge.* Cambridge: Cambridge University Press.

———. 1981.What is consciousness? In *The Nature of Mind.* Ithaca, N.Y.: Cornell University Press.

———. 1982. Metaphysics and supervenience. *Critica* 42:3–17.

———. 1983. *What Is a Law of Nature?* Cambridge: Cambridge University Press.

———. 1990. *A Combinatorial Theory of Possibility.* Cambridge: Cambridge University Press.

Austin, D. F. 1990. *What's the Meaning of "This"?* Ithaca, N.Y.: Cornell University Press.

Baars, B. J. 1988. *A Cognitive Theory of Consciousness.* Cambridge: Cambridge University Press.

Bacon, J. 1986. Supervenience, necessary coextension, and reducibility. *Philosophical Studies* 49:163–76.

Barwise, J., and J. Perry. 1983. *Situations and Attitudes.* Cambridge, Mass.: MIT Press.

Bateson, G. 1972. *Steps to an Ecology of Mind.* San Francisco: Chandler.

Bealer, G. 1994. Mental properties. *Journal of Philosophy* 91:185–208.

Bell, J. S. 1964. On the Einstein-Podolsky-Rosen paradox. *Physics* 1:195–200. [Reprinted in Bell 1987b]

———. 1976. The measurement theory of Everett and de Broglie's pilot wave. In M. Flato, ed., *Quantum Mechanics, Determinism, Causality, and Particles.* Dordrecht: Reidel. [Reprinted in Bell 1987b]

——. 1981. Quantum mechanics for cosmologists. In C. Isham, R. Penrose, and D. Sciama, eds., *Quantum Gravity.* Vol. 2. Oxford: Oxford University Press. [Reprinted in Bell 1987b]

——. 1987a. Are there quantum jumps? In *Schrödinger: Centenary of a Polymath.* Cambridge: Cambridge University Press.

——. 1987b. *Speakable and Unspeakable in Quantum Mechanics.* Cambridge: Cambridge University Press.

Bigelow, J., and R. Pargetter. 1990. Acquaintance with qualia. *Theoria* 56:129–47.

Bisiach, E. 1988. The (haunted) brain and consciousness. In A. Marcel and E. Bisiach, eds., *Consciousness in Contemporary Science.* Oxford: Oxford University Press.

Blackburn, S. 1971. Moral realism. In J. Casey, ed., *Morality and Moral Reasoning.* London: Methuen.

——. 1985. Supervenience revisited. In I. Hacking, ed., *Exercises in Analysis: Essays by Students of Casimir Lewy.* Cambridge: Cambridge University Press.

——. 1990. Filling in space. *Analysis* 50:62–65.

Block, N. 1978. Troubles with functionalism. In C. W. Savage, ed., *Perception and Cognition: Issues in the Foundation of Psychology.* Minneapolis: University of Minnesota Press. [Reprinted in N. Block, ed., *Readings in the Philosophy of Psychology.* Vol. 1. Cambridge, Mass.: Harvard University Press, 1980]

——. 1980. What is functionalism? In N. Block, ed., *Readings in the Philosophy of Psychology.* Vol. 1. Cambridge, Mass.: Harvard University Press.

——. 1981. Psychologism and behaviorism. *Philosophical Review* 90:5–43.

——. 1990. Inverted earth. *Philosophical Perspectives* 4:53–79.

——. 1995. On a confusion about a function of consciousness. *Behavioral and Brain Sciences* 18:227–47.

Boden, M. 1988. Escaping from the Chinese Room. In *Computer Models of Mind.* Cambridge: Cambridge University Press.

Bogen, J. 1981. Agony in the schools. *Canadian Journal of Philosophy* 11:1–21.

Bohm, D. 1952. A suggested interpretation of quantum mechanics in terms of "hidden variables," pts. 1 and 2. *Physical Review* 85:166–93.

——. 1980. *Wholeness and the Implicate Order.* London: Routledge.

Bohm, D., and B. Hiley. 1993. *The Undivided Universe: An Ontological Interpretation of Quantum Theory.* London: Routledge.

Boring, E. G. 1942. *Sensation and Perception in the History of Experimental Psychology.* New York: Appleton-Century-Crofts.

Boyd, R. N. 1980. Materialism without reductionism: What physicalism does not entail. In N. Block, ed., *Readings in the Philosophy of Psychology.* Vol. 1. Cambridge, Mass.: Harvard University Press.

——. 1988. How to be a moral realist. In G. Sayre-McCord, ed., *Essays on Moral Realism.* Ithaca, N.Y.: Cornell University Press.

Brindley, G. S. 1960. *Physiology of the Retina and Visual Pathway.* London: Edward Arnold.

Brink, D. 1989. *Moral Realism and the Foundations of Ethics.* Cambridge: Cambridge University Press.

Broad, C. D. 1925. *Mind and Its Place in Nature.* London: Routledge and Kegan Paul.

Brooks, D. H. M. 1994. How to perform a reduction. *Philosophy and Phenomenological Research* 54:803–14.

Byrne, A. 1993. The emergent mind. Ph.D. diss., Princeton University.

Campbell, K. K. 1970. *Body and Mind.* New York: Doubleday.

Carroll, J. W. 1990. The Humean tradition. *Philosophical Review* 99:185–219.

———. 1994. *Laws of Nature.* Cambridge: Cambridge University Press.

Carruthers, P. 1992. Consciousness and concepts. *Proceedings of the Aristotelian Society,* suppl., 66:41–59.

Chalmers, D. J. 1990. Consciousness and cognition. Technical Report 38, Center for Research on Concepts and Cognition, Indiana University.

———. 1994a. On implementing a computation. *Minds and Machines* 4:391–402.

———. 1994b. A computational foundation for the study of cognition. PNP Technical Report 94-03, Washington University.

———. 1994c. The components of content. PNP Technical Report 94-04, Washington University. [http://ling.vcsc.edu/~chalmers/papers/content.html]

———. 1995a. Does a rock implement every finite state automation? *Synthese.*

———. 1995b. Facing up to the problem of consciousness. *Journal of Consciousness Studies* 2:200–219. [Also in S. Hameroff, A. Kaszniak, and A. Scott, eds., *Toward a Science of Consciousness.* Cambridge, Mass.: MIT Press, 1996]

———. 1995c. Minds, machines, and mathematics. *PSYCHE* 2:1.

———. 1995d. The puzzle of conscious experience. *Scientific American* 273:80–86.

Cheney, D. L., and R. M. Seyfarth. 1990. *How Monkeys See the World.* Chicago: University of Chicago Press.

Chisholm, R. 1957. *Perceiving.* Ithaca, N.Y.: Cornell University Press.

Churchland, P. M. 1985. Reduction, qualia and the direct introspection of brain states. *Journal of Philosophy* 82:8–28.

———. 1995. *The Engine of Reason, the Seat of the Soul: A Philosophical Journey into the Brain.* Cambridge, Mass.: MIT Press.

Churchland, P. M., and P. S. Churchland. 1981. Functionalism, qualia and intentionality. *Philosophical Topics* 12:121–32.

Churchland, P. S. 1986. *Neurophilosophy: Toward a Unified Science of the Mind-Brain.* Cambridge, Mass.: MIT Press.

———. 1988. The significance of neuroscience for philosophy. *Trends in the Neurosciences* 11:304–7.

Clark, A. 1986. Psychofunctionalism and chauvinism. *Philosophy of Science* 53: 535–59.

———. 1993. *Sensory Qualities.* Oxford: Oxford University Press.

Cole, D. 1990. Functionalism and inverted spectra. *Synthese* 82:207–22.

Conee, E. 1985a. Physicalism and phenomenal properties. *Philosophical Quarterly* 35:296–302.

———. 1985b. The possibility of absent qualia. *Philosophical Review* 94:345–66.

Cowey, A., and P. Stoerig. 1992. Reflections on blindsight. In D. Milner and M. Rugg, eds., *The Neuropsychology of Consciousness.* London: Academic Press.

Crane, T. 1992. The nonconceptual content of experience. In T. Crane, ed., *The Contents of Experience.* Cambridge: Cambridge University Press.

Crick, F. H. C. 1994. *The Astonishing Hypothesis: The Scientific Search for the Soul.* New York: Scribner.

Crick, F. H. C., and C. Koch. 1990. Towards a neurobiological theory of consciousness. *Seminars in the Neurosciences* 2:263–75.

Cuda, T. 1985. Against neural chauvinism. *Philosophical Studies* 48:111–27.

Cussins, A. 1990. The connectionist construction of concepts. In M. Boden, ed., *The Philosophy of Artificial Intelligence.* Oxford: Oxford University Press.

Daneri, A., A. Loinger, and G. M. Prosperi. 1962. Quantum theory of measurement and ergodicity conditions. *Nuclear Physics* 33:297–319. [Reprinted in Wheeler and Zurek 1983]

Davidson, D. 1970. Mental events. In L. Foster and J. Swanson, eds., *Experience and Theory.* London: Duckworth.

Davies, M. K., and I. L. Humberstone. 1980. Two notions of necessity. *Philosophical Studies* 38:1–30.

Dennett, D. C. 1969. *Content and Consciousness.* London: Routledge and Kegan Paul.

———. 1978a. *Brainstorms.* Cambridge, Mass.: MIT Press.

———. 1978b. Are dreams experiences? In Dennett 1978a.

———. 1978c. Toward a cognitive theory of consciousness. In Dennett 1978a.

———. 1978d. Where am I? In Dennett 1978a.

———. 1979. On the absence of phenomenology. In D. Gustafson and B. Tapscott, eds., *Body, Mind, and Method.* Dordrecht: Kluwer.

———. 1987. *The Intentional Stance.* Cambridge, Mass.: MIT Press.

———. 1988. Quining qualia. In A. Marcel and E. Bisiach, eds., *Consciousness in Contemporary Science.* Oxford: Oxford University Press.

———. 1991. *Consciousness Explained.* Boston: Little, Brown.

———. 1993a. Back from the drawing board. In B. Dahlbom, ed., *Dennett and His Critics.* Oxford: Blackwell.

———. 1993b. The message is: There is no medium. *Philosophy and Phenomenological Research* 53:919–31.

Descartes, R. 1984. *The Philosophical Writings of Descartes.* Translated by J. Cottingham, R. Stoothoff, and D. Murdoch. Cambridge: Cambridge University Press.

DeWitt, B. S. 1970. Quantum mechanics and reality. *Physics Today* 23:30–35. [Reprinted in DeWitt and Graham 1973]

———. 1971. The many-universes interpretation of quantum mechanics. In B. d'Espagnat, ed., *Foundations of Quantum Mechanics.* New York: Academic Press. [Reprinted in DeWitt and Graham 1973]

DeWitt, B. S., and N. Graham, eds., 1973. *The Many-Worlds Interpretation of Quantum Mechanics.* Princeton: Princeton University Press.

Dretske, F. I. 1977. Laws of nature. *Philosophy of Science* 44:248–68.

———. 1981. *Knowledge and the Flow of Information.* Cambridge, Mass.: MIT Press.

———. 1995. *Naturalizing the Mind.* Cambridge, Mass.: MIT Press.

Dreyfus, H. 1972. *What Computers Can't Do.* New York: Harper & Row.

Eccles, J. C. 1986. Do mental events cause neural events analogously to the probability fields of quantum mechanics? *Proceedings of the Royal Society of London* B227:411–28.

Edelman, G. 1989. *The Remembered Present: A Biological Theory of Consciousness.* New York: Basic Books.

———. 1992. *Bright Air, Brilliant Fire.* New York: Basic Books.

Elitzur, A. 1989. Consciousness and the incompleteness of the physical explanation of behavior. *Journal of Mind and Behavior* 10:1–20.

Evans, G. 1979. Reference and contingency. *The Monist* 62:161–89.

————. 1982. *The Varieties of Reference*. Oxford: Oxford University Press.

Everett, H. 1957. "Relative-state" formulations of quantum mechanics. *Reviews of Modern Physics* 29:454–62. [Reprinted in Wheeler and Zurek 1983]

————. 1973. The theory of the universal wave function. In B. S. deWitt and N. Graham, eds., *The Many-Worlds Interpretation of Quantum Mechanics*. Princeton: Princeton University Press.

Farah, M. 1994. Visual perception and visual awareness after brain damage: A tutorial overview. In C. Umilta and M. Moscovitch, eds., *Conscious and Nonconscious Information Processing: Attention and Performance* 15. Cambridge, Mass.: MIT Press.

Farrell, B. A. 1950. Experience. *Mind* 59:170–98.

Feigl, H. 1958. The "mental" and the "physical." In H. Feigl, M. Scriven, and G. Maxwell, eds., *Concepts, Theories, and the Mind–Body Problem*. Minnesota Studies in the Philosophy of Science , vol. 2. Minneapolis: University of Minnesota Press.

Feldman, F. 1974. Kripke on the identity theory. *Journal of Philosophy* 71:665–76.

Field, H. 1973. Theory change and the indeterminacy of reference. *Journal of Philosophy* 40:762–81.

Flanagan, O. 1992. *Consciousness Reconsidered*. Cambridge, Mass.: MIT Press.

Fodor, J. A. 1980. Searle on what only brains can do. *Behavioral and Brain Sciences* 3:431–32.

————. 1987. *Psychosemantics: The Problem of Meaning in the Philosophy of Mind*. Cambridge, Mass.: MIT Press.

————. 1992. The big idea: Can there be a science of mind? *Times Literary Supplement,* July 3, pp. 5–7.

Forrest, P. 1986. Ways worlds could be. *Australasian Journal of Philosophy* 64:15–24.

Foss, J. 1989. On the logic of what it is like to be a conscious subject. *Australasian Journal of Philosophy* 67:305–20.

Foster, J. 1991. *The Immaterial Self: A Defence of the Cartesian Dualism Conception of Mind*. London: Routledge.

Fredkin, E. 1990. Digital mechanics. *Physica* D45:254–70.

Geach, P. 1957. *Mental Acts*. London: Routledge and Kegan Paul.

Gell-Mann, M., and J. B. Hartle. 1990. Quantum mechanics in the light of quantum cosmology. In W. Zurek, ed., *Complexity, Entropy, and the Physics of Information*. Redwood City, Calif.: Addison-Wesley.

Gert, B. 1965. Imagination and verifiability. *Philosophical Studies* 16:44–47.

Ghirardi, G. C., A. Rimini, and T. Weber. 1986. Unified dynamics for microscopic and macroscopic systems. *Physical Review* D34:470.

Goldman, A. 1986. *Epistemology and Cognition*. Cambridge, Mass.: Harvard University Press.

————. 1993. The psychology of folk psychology. *Behavioral and Brain Sciences* 16:15–28.

Gunderson, K. 1970. Asymmetries and mind–body perplexities. In M. Radner and S. Winokur, eds., *Analyses of Theories and Methods of Physics and Psychology*. Minnesota Studies in the Philosophy of Science, vol. 4. Minneapolis: University of Minnesota Press.

Hameroff, S. R. 1994. Quantum coherence in microtubules: A neural basis for an emergent consciousness? *Journal of Consciousness Studies* 1:91–118.

Hardin, C. L. 1987. Qualia and materialism: Closing the explanatory gap. *Philosophy and Phenomenological Research* 48:281–98.

———. 1988. *Color for Philosophers: Unweaving the Rainbow.* Indianapolis: Hackett.

Hare, R. M. 1952. *The Language of Morals.* Oxford: Clarendon Press.

———. 1984. Supervenience. *Proceedings of the Aristotelian Society,* suppl., 58:1–16.

Harman, G. 1982. Conceptual role semantics. *Notre Dame Journal of Formal Logic* 28:242–56.

———. 1990. The intrinsic quality of experience. *Philosophical Perspectives* 4:31–52.

Harnad, S. 1989. Minds, machines and Searle. *Journal of Experimental and Theoretical Artificial Intelligence* 1:5–25.

Harrison, B. 1967. On describing colors. *Inquiry* 10:38–52.

———. 1973. *Form and Content.* Oxford: Blackwell.

Harrison, J. 1981a. Three philosophical fairy stories. *Ratio* 23:63–67.

———. 1981b. Gulliver's adventures in Fairyland. *Ratio* 23:158–64.

Haugeland, J. 1980. Programs, causal powers, and intentionality. *Behavioral and Brain Sciences* 4:432–33.

———. 1982. Weak supervenience. *American Philosophical Quarterly* 19:93–103.

Healey, R. A. 1984. How many worlds? *Nous* 18:591–616.

Heil, J. 1992. *The Nature of True Minds.* Cambridge: Cambridge University Press.

Hellman, G., and F. Thompson. 1975. Physicalism: Ontology, determination and reduction. *Journal of Philosophy* 72:551–64.

Hill, C. S. 1991. *Sensations: A Defense of Type Materialism.* Cambridge: Cambridge University Press.

Hodgson, D. 1988. *The Mind Matters: Consciousness and Choice in a Quantum World.* Oxford: Oxford University Press.

Hofstadter, D. R. 1979. *Gödel, Escher, Bach: an Eternal Golden Braid.* New York: Basic Books.

———. 1981. Reflections on Searle. In D. R. Hofstadter and D. C. Dennett, eds., *The Mind's I.* New York: Basic Books.

———. 1985a. Who shoves whom around inside the careenium? In *Metamagical Themas.* New York: Basic Books

———. 1985b. Heisenberg's Uncertainty Principle and the many-worlds interpretation of quantum mechanics. In *Metamagical Themas.* New York: Basic Books.

Honderich, T. 1981. Psychophysical law-like connections and their problems. *Inquiry* 24:277–303.

Horgan, T. 1978. Supervenient bridge laws. *Philosophy of Science* 45:227–49.

———. 1982. Supervenience and microphysics. *Pacific Philosophical Quarterly* 63:29–43.

———. 1984a. Functionalism, qualia, and the inverted spectrum. *Philosophy and Phenomenological Research* 44:453–69.

———. 1984b. Jackson on physical information and qualia. *Philosophical Quarterly* 34:147–83.

———. 1984c. Supervenience and cosmic hermeneutics. *Southern Journal of Philosophy,* suppl., 22:19–38.

———. 1987. Supervenient qualia. *Philosophical Review* 96:491–520.

———. 1993. From supervenience to superdupervenience: Meeting the demands of a material world. *Mind* 102:555–86.

Horgan, T., and M. Timmons. 1992a. Troubles for new wave moral semantics: The "open question argument" revived. *Philosophical Papers.*

————. 1992b. Trouble on moral twin earth: Moral queerness revived. *Synthese* 92:223–60.

Horst, S. 1995. Phenomenology and psychophysics. Manuscript, Wesleyan University.

Hughes, R. I. G. 1989. *The Structure and Interpretation of Quantum Mechanics.* Cambridge, Mass.: Harvard University Press.

Humphrey, N. 1992. *A History of the Mind: Evolution and the Birth of Consciousness.* New York: Simon and Schuster.

Huxley, T. 1874. On the hypothesis that animals are automata. In *Collected Essays.* London, 1893–94.

Jackendoff, R. 1987. *Consciousness and the Computational Mind.* Cambridge, Mass.: MIT Press.

Jackson, F. 1977. *Perception.* Cambridge: Cambridge University Press.

————. 1980. A note on physicalism and heat. *Australasian Journal of Philosophy* 58:26–34.

————. 1982. Epiphenomenal qualia. *Philosophical Quarterly* 32:127–36.

————. 1993. Armchair metaphysics. In J. O'Leary-Hawthorne and M. Michael, eds., *Philosophy in Mind.* Dordrecht: Kluwer.

————. 1994. Finding the mind in the natural world. In R. Casati, B. Smith, and G. White, eds., *Philosophy and the Cognitive Sciences,* Vienna: Holder-Pichler-Tempsky.

————. 1995. Postscript to "What Mary didn't know." In P. K. Moser and J. D. Trout, eds., *Contemporary Materialism.* London: Routledge.

Jacoby, H. 1990. Empirical functionalism and conceivability arguments. *Philosophical Psychology* 2:271–82.

Jaynes, J. 1976. *The Origins of Consciousness in the Breakdown of the Bicameral Mind.* Boston: Houghton Mifflin.

Johnson-Laird, P. 1983. A computational analysis of consciousness. *Cognition and Brain Theory* 6:499–508.

Kaplan, D. 1979. *Dthat.* In P. Cole, ed., *Syntax and Semantics.* New York: Academic Press.

————. 1989. Demonstratives. In J. Almog, J. Perry, and H. Wettstein, ed., *Themes from Kaplan.* New York: Oxford University Press.

Kim, J. 1978. Supervenience and nomological incommensurables. *American Philosophical Quarterly* 15:149–56.

————. 1984. Concepts of supervenience. *Philosophy and Phenomenological Research* 45:153–76.

————. 1985. Psychophysical laws. In B. McLaughlin and E. LePore, eds., *Action and Events.* Oxford: Blackwell.

————. 1989. Mechanism, purpose, and explanatory exclusion. *Philosophical Perspectives* 3:77–108.

————. 1993. *Supervenience and Mind.* Cambridge: Cambridge University Press.

Kirk, R. 1974. Zombies versus materialists. *Aristotelian Society* 48(suppl.):135–52.

————. 1979. From physical explicability to full-blooded materialism. *Philosophical Quarterly* 29:229–37.

————. 1992. Consciousness and concepts. *Proceedings of the Aristotelian Society* 66(suppl.):23–40.

————. 1994. *Raw Feeling: A Philosophical Account of the Essence of Consciousness.* Oxford: Oxford University Press.

Korb, K. 1991. Searle's AI program. *Journal of Experimental and Theoretical Artificial Intelligence* 3:283–96.

Kripke, S. A. 1971. Identity and necessity. In M. Munitz, ed., *Identity and Individuation*. New York: New York University Press.

———. 1972. Naming and necessity. In G. Harman and D. Davidson, eds., *The Semantics of Natural Language*. Dordrecht: Reidel. [Reprinted as Kripke 1980]

———. 1980. *Naming and Necessity*. Cambridge, Mass.: Harvard University Press.

———. 1982. *Wittgenstein on Rule-Following and Private Language*. Cambridge, Mass.: Harvard University Press.

Lahav, R., and N. Shanks. 1992. How to be a scientifically respectable "property dualist." *Journal of Mind and Behavior* 13:211–32.

Langton, C. G. 1989. *Artificial Life: The Proceedings of an Interdisciplinary Workshop on the Synthesis and Simulation of Living Systems*. Redwood City, Calif.: Addison-Wesley.

Leckey, M. 1993. The universe as a computer: A model for prespace metaphysics. Manuscript. Philosophy Department, Monash University.

Levine, J. 1983. Materialism and qualia: The explanatory gap. *Pacific Philosophical Quarterly* 64:354–61.

———. 1988. Absent and inverted qualia revisited. *Mind and Language* 3:271–87.

———. 1991. Cool red. *Philosophical Psychology* 4:27–40.

———. 1993. On leaving out what it's like. In M. Davies and G. Humphreys, eds., *Consciousness: Psychological and Philosophical Essays*. Oxford: Blackwell.

Lewis, D. 1966. An argument for the identity theory. *Journal of Philosophy* 63:17–25.

———. 1972. Psychophysical and theoretical identifications. *Australasian Journal of Philosophy* 50:249–58.

———. 1973. *Counterfactuals*. Cambridge, Mass.: Harvard University Press.

———. 1974. Radical interpretation. *Synthese* 23:331–44.

———. 1979. Attitudes *de dicto* and *de se*. *Philosophical Review* 88:513–45.

———. 1983a. Extrinsic properties. *Philosophical Studies* 44:197–200.

———. 1983b. New work for a theory of universals. *Australasian Journal of Philosophy* 61:343–77.

———. 1986a. *On the Plurality of Worlds*. Oxford: Blackwell.

———. 1986b. *Philosophical Papers*. Vol. 2. New York: Oxford University Press.

———. 1990. What experience teaches. In W. Lycan, ed., *Mind and Cognition*. Oxford: Blackwell.

———. 1994. Reduction of mind. In S. Guttenplan, ed., *A Companion to the Philosophy of Mind*. Oxford: Blackwell.

Libet, B. 1993. The neural time factor in conscious and unconscious events. In *Experimental and Theoretical Studies of Consciousness*. Ciba Foundation Symposium 174. New York: Wiley.

Loar, B. 1990. Phenomenal states. *Philosophical Perspectives* 4:81–108.

Lockwood, M. 1989. *Mind, Brain, and the Quantum*. Oxford: Blackwell.

———. 1992. The grain problem. In H. Robinson, ed., *Objections to Physicalism*. Oxford: Oxford University Press.

Logothetis, N., and J. D. Schall. 1989. Neuronal correlates of subjective visual perception. *Science* 245:761–63.

London, F., and E. Bauer. 1939. The theory of observation in quantum mechanics (in French). *Actualités scientifiques et industrielles*, no. 775. [English translation in Wheeler and Zurek 1983]

Lucas, J. R. 1961. Minds, machines and Gödel. *Philosophy* 36:112–27.

Lycan, W. G. 1973. Inverted spectrum. *Ratio* 15:315–19.

———. 1987. *Consciousness.* Cambridge, Mass.: MIT Press.

———. 1995. A limited defense of phenomenal information. In T. Metzinger, ed., *Conscious Experience.* Paderborn: Schöningh.

———. 1996. *Consciousness and Experience.* Cambridge, Mass.: MIT Press.

Mackay, D. M. 1969. *Information, Mechanism, and Meaning.* Cambridge, Mass.: MIT Press.

Mackie, J. L. 1974. *The Cement of the Universe.* Oxford: Oxford University Press.

———. 1977. *Ethics: Inventing Right and Wrong.* Harmondsworth: Penguin Books.

Marks, L. E. 1978. *The Unity of the Senses: Interrelations among the Modalities.* New York: Academic Press.

Matzke, D., ed. 1993. *Proceedings of the 1992 Workshop on Physics and Computation.* Los Alamitos, Calif.: IEEE Computer Society Press.

———, ed. 1995. *Proceedings of the 1994 Workshop on Physics and Computation.* Los Alamitos, Calif.: IEEE Computer Society Press.

Maxwell, G. 1978. Rigid designators and mind-brain identity. In C. W. Savage, ed., *Perception and Cognition: Issues in the Foundations of Psychology.* Minnesota Studies in the Philosophy of Science, vol. 9. Minneapolis: University of Minnesota Press.

McCarthy, J. 1979. Ascribing mental qualities to machines. In M. Ringle, ed., *Philosophical Perspectives in Artificial Intelligence.* Atlantic Highlands, N.J.: Humanities Press.

McDowell, J. 1994. *Mind and World.* Cambridge, Mass.: Harvard University Press.

McGinn, C. 1977. Anomalous monism and Kripke's Cartesian intuitions. *Analysis* 2:78–80.

———. 1989. Can we solve the mind–body problem? *Mind* 98:349–66.

McLaughlin, B. P. 1992. The rise and fall of the British emergentists. In A. Beckermann, H. Flohr, and J. Kim, eds., *Emergence or Reduction? Prospects for Nonreductive Physicalism.* Berlin: De Gruyter.

———. 1995. Varieties of supervenience. In E. E. Savellos and U. D. Yalcin, eds., *Supervenience: New Essays.* Cambridge: Cambridge University Press.

McMullen, C. 1985. "Knowing what it's like" and the essential indexical. *Philosophical Studies* 48:211–33.

Meehl, P.E., and W. Sellars. 1956. The concept of emergence. In H. Feigl and M. Scriven, eds., *The Foundations of Science and the Concept of Psychology and Psychoanalysis.* Minnesota Studies in the Philosophy of Science, vol. 1. Minneapolis: University of Minnesota Press.

Molnar, G. 1969. Kneale's argument revisited. *Philosophical Review* 78:79–89.

Moore, G. E. 1922. *Philosophical Studies.* London: Routledge and Kegan Paul.

Müller, G. E. 1896. Zur Psychophysik der Gesichtsempfindungen. *Zeitschrift für Psychologie und Physiologie der Sinnesorgane* 10:1–82.

Nagel, T. 1970. Armstrong on the mind. *Philosophical Review* 79:394–403.

———. 1974. What is it like to be a bat? *Philosophical Review* 4:435–50.

———. 1983. The objective self. In C. Ginet and S. Shoemaker, eds., *Knowledge and Mind: Philosophical Essays.* New York: Oxford University Press.

———. 1986. *The View from Nowhere.* New York: Oxford University Press.

Natsoulas, T. 1978. Consciousness. *American Psychologist* 33:906–14.

Nelkin, N. 1989. Unconscious sensations. *Philosophical Psychology* 2:129–41.

———. 1993. What is consciousness? *Philosophy of Science* 60:419–34.

Nemirow, L. 1990. Physicalism and the cognitive role of acquaintance. In W. Lycan, ed., *Mind and Cognition*. Oxford: Blackwell.

Newell, A. 1992. SOAR as a unified theory of cognition: Issues and explanations. *Behavioral and Brain Sciences* 15:464–92.

Newton, N. 1989. Machine understanding and the Chinese Room. *Philosophical Psychology* 2:207–15.

Nida-Rümelin, M. 1995. What Mary couldn't know: Belief about phenomenal states. In T. Metzinger, ed., *Conscious Experience*. Paderborn: Schöningh.

———. 1996. Pseudonormal vision: An actual case of qualia inversion? *Philosophical Studies*.

Papineau, D. 1993. *Philosophical Naturalism*. Oxford: Blackwell.

Parfit, D. 1984. *Reasons and Persons*. Oxford: Oxford University Press.

Peacocke, C. 1992. Scenarios, concepts, and perception. In T. Crane, ed., *The Contents of Experience*. Cambridge: Cambridge University Press.

Penrose, R. 1987. Quantum physics and conscious thought. In B. Hiley and Peat, eds., *Quantum Implications: Essays in Honor of David Bohm*. New York: Methuen.

———. 1989. *The Emperor's New Mind*. Oxford: Oxford University Press.

———. 1994. *Shadows of the Mind*. Oxford: Oxford University Press.

Perry, J. 1979. The problem of the essential indexical. *Nous* 13:3–21.

Petrie, B. 1987. Global supervenience and reduction. *Philosophy and Phenomenological Research* 48:119–30.

Place, U. T. 1956. Is consciousness a brain process? *British Journal of Psychology* 47:44–50.

Plantinga, A. 1976. Actualism and possible worlds. *Theoria* 42:139–60.

Putnam, H. 1960. Minds and machines. In S. Hook, ed., *Dimensions of Mind*. New York: New York University Press.

———. 1975. The meaning of "meaning." In K. Gunderson, ed., *Language, Mind, and Knowledge*. Minneapolis: University of Minnesota Press.

———. 1981. *Reason, Truth, and History*. Cambridge: Cambridge University Press.

———. 1983. Possibility and necessity. In *Philosophical Papers*. Vol. 3. Cambridge: Cambridge University Press.

———. 1988. *Representation and Reality*. Cambridge, Mass.: MIT Press.

Pylyshyn, Z. 1980. The "causal power" of machines. *Behavioral and Brain Sciences* 3:442–44.

Quine, W. V. 1951. Two dogmas of empiricism. *Philosophical Review* 60:20–43.

———. 1969. Propositional objects. In *Ontological Relativity and Other Essays*. New York: Columbia University Press.

Rensink, R. A., J. K. O'Regan, and J. J. Clark. 1995. Image flicker is as good as saccades in making large scene changes invisible. *Perception* 24 (suppl.):26–27.

Rey, G. 1982. A reason for doubting the existence of consciousness. In R. Davidson, S. Schwartz, and D. Shapiro, eds., *Consciousness and Self-Regulation*. Vol 3. New York: Plenum.

———. 1986. What's really going on in Searle's "Chinese Room." *Philosophical Studies* 50:169–85.

———. 1992. Sensational sentences reversed. *Philosophical Studies* 68:289–319.

Reynolds, C. 1987. Flocks, herds, and schools: A distributed behavioral model. *Computer Graphics* 21:25–34.

Robinson, H. 1976. The mind–body problem in contemporary philosophy. *Zygon* 11:346–60.

———. 1982. *Matter and Sense.* Cambridge: Cambridge University Press.

Robinson, W. S. 1988. *Brains and People: An Essay on Mentality and Its Causal Conditions.* Philadelphia: Temple University Press.

Rosenberg, G. H. 1996. Consciousness and causation: Clues toward a double-aspect theory. Manuscript, Indiana University.

Rosenthal, D. M. 1996. A theory of consciousness. In N. Block, O. Flanagan, and G. Güzeldere, eds., *The Nature of Consciousness.* Cambridge, Mass.: MIT Press.

Russell, B. 1927. *The Analysis of Matter.* London: Kegan Paul.

Ryle, G. 1949. *The Concept of Mind.* London: Hutchinson.

Savage, C. W. 1970. *The Measurement of Sensation.* Berkeley: University of California Press.

Savitt, S. 1982. Searle's demon and the brain simulator reply. *Behavioral and Brain Sciences* 5:342–43.

Sayre, K. M. 1976. *Cybernetics and the Philosophy of Mind.* Atlantic Highlands, N.J.: Humanities Press.

Sayre-McCord, G. 1988. Introduction: The many moral realisms. In G. Sayre-McCord, ed., *Essays on Moral Realism.* Ithaca, N.Y.: Cornell University Press.

Schacter, D. L. 1989. On the relation between memory and consciousness: Dissociable interactions and conscious experience. In H. Roediger and F. Craik, eds., *Varieties of Memory and Consciousness: Essays in Honor of Endel Tulving.* Hillsdale, N.J.: Erlbaum.

Schlick, M. 1932. Positivism and Realism. *Erkenntnis* 3.

———. 1938. Form and content: An introduction to philosophical thinking. In *Gesammelte Aufsätze 1926–1936.* Vienna: Gerold [Reprinted in H. L. Mulder and B. van de Velde-Schlick, eds., *Philosophical Papers.* Dordrecht: Reidel, 1979]

Seager, W. E . 1988. Weak supervenience and materialism. *Philosophy and Phenomenological Research* 48:697–709.

———. 1991. *Metaphysics of Consciousness.* London: Routledge.

Searle, J. R. 1980. Minds, brains, and programs. *Behavioral and Brain Sciences* 3: 417–24.

———. 1984. *Minds, Brains and Science.* Cambridge, Mass.: Harvard University Press.

———. 1990a. Consciousness, explanatory inversion and cognitive science. *Behavioral and Brain Sciences* 13:585–642.

———. 1990b. Is the brain a digital computer? *Proceedings and Addresses of the American Philosophical Association* 64:21–37.

———. 1992. *The Rediscovery of the Mind.* Cambridge, Mass.: MIT Press.

Sellars, W. 1956. Empiricism and the philosophy of mind. In H. Feigl and M. Scriven, eds., *The Foundations of Science and the Concepts of Psychology and Psychoanalysis.* Minnesota Studies in the Philosophy of Science, vol. 1. Minneapolis: University of Minnesota Press.

———. 1965. The identity approach to the mind–body problem. *Review of Metaphysics* 18:430–51.

———. 1981. Is consciousness physical? *Monist* 64:66–90.

Shallice, T. 1972. Dual functions of consciousness. *Psychological Review* 79:383–93.

———. 1988a. Information-processing models of consciousness: Possibilities and problems. In A. Marcel and E. Bisiach, eds., *Consciousness in Contemporary Science*. Oxford: Oxford University Press.

———. 1988b. *From Neuropsychology to Mental Structure*. Cambridge: Cambridge University Press.

Shannon, C. E. 1948. A mathematical theory of communication. *Bell Systems Technical Journal* 27:379–423. [Reprinted in C. E. Shannon and W. Weaver, *The Mathematical Theory of Communication*. Urbana: University of Illinois Press, 1949]

Shepard, R. N. 1993. On the physical basis, linguistic representation, and conscious experience of colors. In G. Harman, ed., *Conceptions of the Human Mind: Essays in Honor of George A. Miller*. Hillsdale, N.J.: Erlbaum.

Shoemaker, S. 1975a. Functionalism and qualia. *Philosophical Studies* 27:291–315.

———. 1975b. Phenomenal similarity. *Critica* 7:3–37.

———. 1980. Causality and properties. In P. van Inwagen, ed., *Time and Cause*. Dordecht: Reidel.

———. 1981. Some varieties of functionalism. *Philosophical Topics* 12:93–119.

———. 1982. The inverted spectrum. *Journal of Philosophy* 79:357–81.

Sidelle, A. 1989. *Necessity, essence, and individuation*. Ithaca, N.Y.: Cornell University Press.

———. 1992. Rigidity, ontology, and semantic structure. *Journal of Philosophy* 8:410–30.

Siewert, C. 1993. What Dennett can't imagine and why. *Inquiry* 36:93–112.

———. 1994. Understanding consciousness. Ph.D. diss. University of California, Berkeley. [Forthcoming as a book from Princeton University Press]

Skyrms, B. 1980. *Causal Necessity*. New Haven: Yale University Press.

Smart, J. J. C. 1959. Sensations and brain processes. *Philosophical Review* 68:141–56.

Sperling, G. 1960. The information available in brief visual presentations. *Psychological Monographs* 74.

Sperry, R. W. 1969. A modified concept of consciousness. *Psychological Review* 76:532–36.

———. 1992. Turnabout on consciousness: A mentalist view. *Journal of Mind and Behavior* 13:259–80.

Sprigge, T. L. S. 1971. Final causes. *Proceedings of the Aristotelian Society* 45 (suppl.):149–70.

———. 1994. Consciousness. *Synthese* 98:73–93.

Squires, E. 1990. *Conscious Mind in the Physical World*. Bristol: Hilger.

Stalnaker, R. 1976. Possible worlds. *Nous* 10:65–75.

———. 1978. Assertion. In P. Cole, ed., *Syntax and Semantics: Pragmatics*. Vol. 9. New York: Academic Press.

Stapp, H. P. 1993. *Mind, Matter, and Quantum Mechanics*. Berlin: Springer-Verlag.

Stevens, S. S. 1975. *Psychophysics: Introduction to Its Perceptual, Neural, and Social Prospects*. New York: Wiley.

Sutherland, N. S., ed. 1989. *The International Dictionary of Psychology*. New York: Continuum.

Swoyer, C. 1982. The nature of natural laws. *Australasian Journal of Philosophy* 60:203–23.

Teller, D. Y. 1984. Linking propositions. *Vision Research* 24:1233–46.

———. 1990. The domain of visual science. In L. Spillman, and J. S. Werner, eds., *Visual Perception: The Neurophysiological Foundations.* New York: Academic Press.

Teller, P. 1984. A poor man's guide to supervenience and determination. *Southern Journal of Philosophy,* suppl., 22:137–62.

———. 1992. A contemporary look at emergence. In A. Beckermann, H. Flohr, and J. Kim, eds., *Emergence or Reduction? Prospects for Nonreductive Physicalism.* Berlin: De Gruyter.

Thagard, P. 1986. The emergence of meaning: An escape from Searle's Chinese Room. *Behaviorism* 14:139–46.

Thompson, E. 1992. Novel colours. *Philosophical Studies* 68:321–49.

Tienson, J. L. 1987. Brains are not conscious. *Philosophical Papers* 16:187–93.

Tooley, M. 1977. The nature of laws. *Canadian Journal of Philosophy* 7:667–98.

———. 1987. *Causation: A Realist Approach.* Oxford: Oxford University Press.

Tye, M. 1986. The subjective qualities of experience. *Mind* 95:1–17.

———. 1992. Visual qualia and visual content. In T. Crane, ed., *The Contents of Experience.* Cambridge: Cambridge University Press.

———. 1993. Blindsight, the absent qualia hypothesis, and the mystery of consciousness. In C. Hookway, ed., *Philosophy and the Cognitive Sciences.* Cambridge: Cambridge University Press.

———. 1995. *Ten Problems of Consciousness.* Cambridge, Mass.: MIT Press.

van Cleve, J. 1990. Mind-dust or magic? Panpsychism versus emergence. *Philosophical Perspectives* 4:215–26.

van Gulick, R. 1988. A functionalist plea for self-consciousness. *Philosophical Review* 97:149–88.

———. 1992. Nonreductive materialism and the nature of intertheoretical constraint. In A. Beckermann, H. Flohr, and J. Kim, eds., *Emergence or Reduction? Prospects for Nonreductive Physicalism.* Berlin: De Gruyter.

———. 1993. Understanding the phenomenal mind: Are we all just armadillos? In M. Davies and G. Humphreys, eds., *Consciousness: A Mind and Language Reader.* Oxford: Blackwell.

Velmans, M. 1991. Is human information processing conscious? *Behavioral and Brain Sciences* 14:651–69.

Weinberg, S. 1992. *Dreams of a Final Theory.* New York: Pantheon Books.

Weiskrantz, L. 1986. *Blindsight: A Case Study and Implications.* Oxford: Oxford University Press.

———. 1992. Introduction: Dissociated issues. In D. Milner and M. Rugg, eds., *The Neuropsychology of Consciousness.* London: Academic Press.

Wheeler, J. A. 1990. Information, physics, quantum: The search for links. In W. H. Zurek, ed., *Complexity, Entropy, and the Physics of Information.* Redwood City, Calif.: Addison-Wesley.

———. 1994. It from bit. In *At Home in the Universe.* Woodbury, N.Y.: American Institute of Physics Press.

Wheeler, J. A., and W. H. Zurek. 1983. *Quantum Theory and Measurement.* Princeton: Princeton University Press.

White, S. L. 1986. Curse of the qualia. *Synthese* 68:333–68.

Wigner, E. P. 1961. Remarks on the mind–body question. In I. J. Good, ed., *The Scientist Speculates.* New York: Basic Books.

Wilkes, K. V. 1984. Is consciousness important? *British Journal for the Philosophy of Science* 35:223–43.

Wilson, M. 1982. Predicate meets property. *Philosophical Review* 91:549–89.

———. 1985. What is this thing called "pain"? The philosophy of science behind the contemporary debate. *Pacific Philosophical Quarterly* 66:227–67.

Winograd, T. 1972. *Understanding Natural Language*. New York: Academic Press.

Wittgenstein, L. 1953. *Philosophical Investigations*. London: Macmillan.

———. 1968. Notes for lectures on "private experience" and "sense data." *Philosophical Review* 77.

Wright, R. 1988. *Three Scientists and Their Gods*. New York: Times Books.

Yablo, S. 1993. Is conceivability a guide to possibility? *Philosophy and Phenomenological Research* 53:1–42.

Zuboff, A. 1994. What is a mind? In P. A. French, T. E. Uehling, and H. K. Wettstein, eds., *Philosophical Naturalism*. Midwest Studies in Philosophy, vol. 19. Notre Dame, Ind.: University of Notre Dame Press.

Zurek, W. H. 1990. *Complexity, Entropy, and the Physics of Information*. Redwood City, Calif.: Addison-Wesley.

Index